Internet Policies and Issues

New York

Internet Policies and Issues

The Digital Divide: Access, Issues, and Policies
Simon L. Bech (Editor)
ISBN: 979-8-89530-238-5
eBook ISBN: 979-8-89530-288-0

A Closer Look at Online Deception and Disinformation
Suzanne M. Williams (Editor)
ISBN: 979-8-88697-310-5
eBook ISBN: 979-8-88697-377-8

More information about this series can be found at
https://novapublishers.com/product-category/series/internet-policies-and-issues/

Simon L. Bech
Editor

The Digital Divide: Access, Issues, and Policies

snova
New York

Library of Congress Cataloging-in-Publication Data

ISBN: 979-8-89530-238-5 (Hardcover)
ISBN: 979-8-89530-288-0 (eBook)

Published by Nova Science Publishers, Inc. † New York

Contents

Preface

Technology can be a powerful tool to help transform learning. It has the potential to empower students to expand their learning beyond the confines of the traditional classroom, support self-directed learning, help educators tailor learning experiences to individual student needs, and support students with disabilities. Chapter 1 examines how technologies can raise the bar for all elementary and secondary students. Chapter 2 explores approaches for using technology in a manner that focuses on the distinct benefits of digital learning.

Access to high-speed internet—known as broadband—has become a topic of increasing significance over the past few decades. Deployment of broadband is not uniform across the United States. Some areas lack broadband entirely—creating a so-called digital divide between those who have access to broadband service and those who do not. Chapter 3 provides an overview of the digital divide in broadband deployment and issues that contribute to it persistence. Chapter 4 discusses providing rural communities with access to high-speed, affordable, and reliable broadband internet connectivity.

Chapter 1

A Call to Action for Closing the Digital Access, Design, and Use Divides*

U.S. Department of Education

Introduction

> In its simplest terms, the instructional core is composed of the teacher and the student in the presence of content. It is the relationship between the teacher, the student, and the content – not the qualities of any one of them by themselves – that determines the nature of instructional practice, and each corner of the instructional core has its own particular role and resources to bring to the instructional process. Simply stated, the instructional task is the actual work that students are asked to do in the process of instruction – not what teachers think they are asking students to do, or what the official curriculum says that the students are asked to do, but what they are actually asked to do.
>
> City, Elizabeth A., Richard Elmore, Sarah Fiarman, and Lee Teitel
> Instructional Rounds in Education, 2009

Technology can be a powerful tool to help transform learning. It has the potential to empower students to expand their learning beyond the confines of the traditional classroom, support self-directed learning, help educators tailor

* This is an edited, reformatted and augmented version of Office of Educational Technology, dated January 2024.

In: The Digital Divide: Access, Issues, and Policies
Editor: Simon L. Bech
ISBN: 979-8-89530-238-5

learning experiences to individual student needs, and support students with disabilities.

Technology also has the potential to allow students and educators to collaborate with peers and experts worldwide, engage with immersive learning simulations, and express their learning creatively. Furthermore, it has the potential to collect student performance and engagement data, providing insight into student progress and allowing educators to deploy targeted support.

Yet, as researcher Justin Reich noted, "Predictions of imminent transformation are among the most reliable refrains in the history of educational technology."[1] And, across that history[2] and present-day classrooms, it has failed to realize this full potential. Where technology has realized its potential, it is often for a small minority of learners and contributes to growing inequities.[3,4,5] Similarly, educational technology (edtech) tools sometimes claim (without independent, research-based evidence) that student assessment results will soar if school systems adopt a given digital resource. Such claims are not only misleading, but they can undermine the true potential of edtech. Reliance on a specific tool to accelerate learning or deliver a comprehensive and rigorous education for every student places all responsibility on the content.[6] It ignores educators and students and the relationships between all three.

Somewhere between the promise of transformation and the barriers to realizing that promise lies the potential for states, districts, and schools to build systems that better ensure that edtech's promise is afforded to all students, no matter their geography, background, or individual context.

---

[1] (2020). *Failure to Disrupt: Why Technology Alone Can't Transform Education* (1st ed.). Harvard University Press. https://www.hup. harvard.edu/catalog.php?isbn=9780674089044.

[2] Cuban, Larry. *Oversold and Underused: Computers in the Classroom*. Cambridge, Mass.: Harvard University Press, 2001.

[3] (2017, October). *From Good Intentions to Real Outcomes: Equity by Design in Learning Technologies*. Connected Learning Alliance. Retrieved September 7, 2023, from https://clalliance.org/publications/good-intentions-real-outcomes-equity-design-learning-technologies/.

[4] Attewell, P. (2001). Comment: The first and second digital divides. *Sociology of Education*, 252-259.

[5] Reinhart, J. M., Thomas, E., & Toriskie, J. M. (2011). K-12 teachers: Technology use and the second level digital divide. *Journal of Instructional Psychology*, 38.

[6] City, Elizabeth A., Elmore, R., Fiarman, S., & Teitel, L. (2009). Instructional rounds in education. Harvard Educational Publishing Group.

This 2024 National Educational Technology Plan (NETP) examines how technologies can raise the bar[7] for all elementary and secondary students. It offers examples of schools, districts, classrooms, and states doing the complex work of establishing systemic solutions to inequities of access, design, and use of technology in support of learning. The identification of specific programs or products in these examples is designed to provide a clearer understanding of innovative ideas and is not meant as an endorsement.

Building on the concept of the instructional core, this plan considers the barriers to equitable support of learning through edtech as three divides:

1) *Digital Use Divide:* Inequitable implementation of instructional tasks supported by technology. On one side of this divide are students who are asked to actively use technology in their learning to analyze, build, produce, and create using digital tools, and, on the other, students encountering instructional tasks where they are asked to use technology for passive assignment completion. While this divide maps to the student corner of the instructional core, it also includes the instructional tasks drawing on content and designed by teachers.
2) *Digital Design Divide:* Inequitable access to time and support of professional learning for all teachers, educators, and practitioners to build their professional capacity to design learning experiences for all

[7] (n.d.). *Raise the Bar: Lead the World*. U.S. Department of Education. Retrieved September 7, 2023, from https://www.ed.gov/ raisethebar/.

students using edtech. This divide maps to the teacher corner of the instructional core.

3) *Digital Access Divide:* Inequitable access to connectivity, devices, and digital content. Mapping to the content corner of the instructional core, the digital access divide also includes equitable accessibility and access to instruction in digital health, safety, and citizenship skills.

As a path to closing these divides, the NETP also provides actionable recommendations to advance the effective use of technology to support teaching and learning. The recommendations in each section are also followed by tags identifying *whether* they are most immediately intended for states, districts, or school buildings. These recommendations are meant as components of solutions that bridge each divide but cannot comprise all of what is necessary within a given geography, culture, or context. Throughout each section, examples are offered of states, school districts, and schools engaged in the work of putting these recommendations into practice.

Many schools in the United States are equipped with greater connectivity and access to devices and digital learning resources than ever before as a result of the need for emergency remote learning brought about by the COVID-19 pandemic. However, this continued bridging of the access divide will only add to the failure of edtech to deliver on its promises if systems do not consider its use in conjunction with all components of the instructional core. This NETP attempts to chart a path for all schools, educators, and students to realize the potential of technology in supporting better "everywhere, all-the-time" learning.

The Digital Use Divide

> The Digital Use Divide stands between those students who are asked to use technology for creation, exploration, and critical analysis and those who are not.

As discussed in the 2017 National Educational Technology Plan, a divide exists between those students who regularly encounter opportunities to leverage technology in active, critical, and creative ways and those whose experiences with technology in their learning are limited to more passive expectations of use. Some students experience a school year full of critical media analysis, video and podcast creation, real-world data collection, connections with remote content area experts, and authentic opportunities to share their learning with global audiences.

Other students—often students from historically marginalized backgrounds—have very different experiences with technology.[8,9,10,11] They are guided towards more limited engagements that frame them as passive technology users. They have school years of digital worksheets, point-and-click assessments, locked-down devices, and penalties for organic collaboration. In some cases, they may have access to more technology than their peers on the other side of the divide but seldom have opportunities to use that technology in formal education beyond digitized versions of practices of classrooms of a century ago.

Closing this digital use divide— ensuring all students have transformative, active, creative, critically thoughtful experiences supported by technology— is the focus of the following section. Beginning with a clear vision of what states and districts want for all graduates, it then offers guidance and recommendations for operationalizing, evaluating, and systematizing the experiences necessary for all students to fulfill that vision.

Recommendations for Closing the Use Divide

1) Develop a "Profile of a Learner/Graduate" outlining cognitive, personal, and interpersonal competencies students should have when transitioning between grade levels and graduation. (States, Districts)
2) Design and sustain systems, including needs assessments, technology plans, and evaluation processes supporting the development of competencies outlined in the "Profile of a Learner/Graduate" through the active use of technology to support learning. (States, Districts, Schools)

---

[8] Fishman, B., Dede, C., & Means, B. Teaching and technology: New tools for new times. In D. Gitomer & C. Bell (Eds.), Handbook of Research on Teaching (5th edition).

[9] Valadez, J. R., & Durán, R. P. (2007). Redefining the digital divide: Beyond access to computers and the Internet. The High School Journal, 90(3), 31–44.

[10] Warschauer, M., & Matuchniak, T. (2010). New technology and digital worlds: Analyzing evidence of equity in access, use, and outcomes. Review of Research in Education, 34(1), 179–225.

[11] Albert D. Ritzhaupt, Feng Liu, Kara Dawson & Ann E. Barron (2013) Differences in Student Information and Communication Technology Literacy Based on Socio-Economic Status, Ethnicity, and Gender, Journal of Research on Technology in Education, 45:4, 291-307, DOI: 10.1080/15391523.2013.10782607.

3) Implement feedback mechanisms that empower students to become co-designers of learning experiences. (Districts, Building-Level Administrators)
4) Develop rubrics for digital resource and technology adoptions to ensure tools are accessible and integrated into the larger educational ecosystem, support Universal Design for Learning (UDL) principles, and can be customized in response to accommodation or modification needs of learners with disabilities. (States, Districts, Building-Level Administrators)
5) Review subject area curricula or program scopes and sequences to ensure that student learning experiences build age-appropriate digital literacy skills through active technology use for learning. (States, Districts)
6) Build public-private partnerships with local businesses, higher education institutions, and nonprofit organizations to help students access edtech-enabled hands-on learning and work-based learning experiences. (States, Districts)
7) Provide professional learning and technical assistance to district leaders, building-level administrators, and educators to support the use of evidence to inform edtech use. (States, Districts)
8) Develop guidelines for emerging technologies which protect student data privacy and ensure alignment with shared educational vision and learning principles. (States, Districts)

Closing the Digital Use Divide

Leveraging Technology to Meet the Needs of All Learners

In 2023, to better meet the needs of their community, the Bartholomew Consolidated School Corporation (BCSC) in Indiana began its journey with UDL, a research-driven framework to improve and optimize teaching and learning by reducing barriers in instruction and addressing individual differences, learning preferences, abilities, and backgrounds (see page 12 for a deeper dive into UDL). The goal of creating more inclusive and accessible learning environments for all learners now serves as the foundation for all the district's work. In recent years, the district expanded its UDL implementation by adopting a district-wide learning management system and a 1:1 student-device ratio in grades K-12.

UDL has helped guide the purposeful and innovative use of edtech in BCSC. UDL practitioners regularly reflect upon the learning environment and consider what additional options could make the environment more accessible, engaging, and meaningful to learners. Rather than integrate technology for its own sake in a one-size-fits-all manner, UDL encourages teachers to implement technology to provide options for engaging learners, present content that supports diverse languages and sensory needs, and demonstrate understanding. When entering a BCSC classroom, it is common to see students using options the teacher has designed to accomplish their learning goals. These options could include reading, working with manipulatives, listening to audiobooks, watching videos, going through modules on their devices, working with other students, or having time with a teacher or assistant. The goal is always the priority, not how students accomplish it.

Additionally, UDL, coupled with technology, has transformed how students demonstrate their understanding by creating an environment where learners have options and act as the architects of their own learning.

In one history class, UDL and tech empowered BCSC multilingual learners showed their understanding of topics by creating multimedia-rich eBooks with text, audio, and video recordings in multiple languages. Other learners created a series of explainer videos, while other students opted to write an essay on the same history topic with speech-to-text tools. The students not only had flexible and engaging options to display content knowledge beyond traditional assessments but also could share their knowledge with a broader, relevant audience by publishing their work for viewing by parents, families, other teachers, and the community.

To ensure the consideration of UDL in the procurement process, the BCSC developed UDL-based evaluation rubrics for all curriculum, textbook, and technology adoptions. The district uses rubrics to evaluate resources for critical accessibility features such as text-to-speech, language and translation options, font adjustments, color contrasts, and additional web accessibility standards. These rubrics have led to the adoption of accessible paper and digital resources for curriculum, devices, and other learning materials, ensuring that stakeholders consistently focus on the diversity of end users.

Collaboration and regular meetings between different technology department subdivisions have helped ensure all staff recognize and value the district's commitment to UDL. The technology department regularly collaborates with key district leadership groups to better support each others' work, such as elementary curriculum, secondary curriculum, multilingual learning, and special education. In addition, diverse stakeholder groups that mirror BCSC's ever-diversifying community populations are critical players in the success of their UDL implementation. When exploring edtech, the district solicits input from teaching staff, classified staff, students, and families in its stakeholder engagement process.

Beginning more than 20 years ago, BCSC began the systemic, intentional work of closing the digital use divide for all learners.

Re-Defining the Digital Use Divide

From the printing press to streaming video tutorials, the history of edtech is littered with claims of imminent, disruptive transformation. These prognostications often imply that the advent of technology is sufficient for realizing this transformational potential. However, technology alone has yet to prove adequate to improve education for all students. Marshaling technology in support of learning can be most effective when that technology is in the service of common visions of student learning. However, not all students can access the same high-quality learning experiences. Technology can be deployed in classrooms almost as an afterthought for many students, with little understanding of how best to use it. What is often identified as "professional learning" regarding technology for educators can often be little more than training on basic functions such as entering rosters, generating reports, or assigning prefabricated tasks. The human, in these instances, is taken out of the loop.[12]

The 2017 NETP defined the digital use divide as the disparity between students who use technology to create, design, build, explore, and collaborate and those who are only invited to consume media passively.[13]

Students use technology for passive assignment completion.
Passive Use includes activities such as filling out digital worksheets or consuming digital content without accompanying reflection, imagination, or participation.

The plan noted, "Without thoughtful intervention and attention to the way technology is used for learning, the digital use divide could grow even as access to technology in schools increases." While the field made strides toward more active use for all in subsequent years, 2020 halted many of these efforts. It also expedited the proliferation of technologies and connectivity on a scale and speed for which many districts and schools were unprepared.

---

[12] May 2023. *Artificial Intelligence and the Future of Teaching and Learning*. U.S. Department of Education, Office of Educational Technology. Retrieved August 24, 2023 from https://tech.ed.gov/ai-future-of-teaching-and-learning/.

[13] January 2017. *Reimagining the Role of Technology in Education: 2017 National Education Technology Plan Update*. U.S. Department of Education, Office of Educational Technology. Retrieved August 15, 2023, from https://tech.ed.gov/files/2017/01/NETP17.pdf.

Although this switch to emergency remote learning necessitated by the COVID-19 pandemic and emergency federal funding undoubtedly helped narrow the digital access divide, it did not close the digital use divide.

Students use technology to think critically, build, produce, communicate, collaborate, and create digital content.
Active Use involves critical thinking and includes activites such as coding, immersive simulations, media production, interaction with experts, making global connections, design, and peer collaboration.

In addition to hardware, recent years marked a swell of digital learning resources. During the 2019–2020 school year, a LearnPlatform survey found that school districts used an average of 895 digital tools,[14] and a U.S.

---

[14] Merod, A. (2023, July 10). *Districts used 2,591 ed tech tools on average in 2022-23. K12 Dive*. Retrieved August 15, 2023, from https://www.k12dive.com/news/school-districts-ed-tech-use/685995/.

Department of Education survey found that 45 percent of schools reported having a computer for each student.[15] By comparison, in 2023, a LearnPlatform survey found that school districts used an average of 2,591 edtech tools in the 2022–23 school year.[16] Ninety percent of educators surveyed by the EdWeek Research Center responded that 90 percent of educators said there was at least one device for every middle and high schooler by March 2021 (84 percent said the same about elementary school students).

Because school systems deployed so much technology on an emergency basis without the benefit of thoughtful planning, change management, or in the service of shared goals, many school systems are struggling to make the most of these new technologies.[17] In a 2021–2022 Project Tomorrow Speak Up Survey of over 41,000 students nationwide, 84 percent of grade 6-12 students reported that the number one way they are using new technology in school is for taking online tests or quizzes.[18] The subsequent most frequent uses of technology, as reported by students, were creating documents to share (63 percent), emailing teachers with questions (55 percent), and watching online videos (52 percent). While all those are valid uses of technology to support instruction, for the most part, they reflect technology as a passive substitution for traditional teaching practices. These examples are far from the vision of technology "as a tool to engage in creative, productive, lifelong learning."

Active use of technology utilizes technology to discover, analyze, and apply learning rather than passively receiving information.[19] It can empower students to take ownership of their learning, collaborate with peers, and use

---

[15] Gray, C., & Lewis, L. (2021, November 26). *Use of Educational Technology for Instruction in Public Schools: 2019–20*. U.S. Department of Education, National Center for Education Statistics. Retrieved August 15, 2023, from https://nces.ed.gov/pubsearch/ pubsinfo.asp?pubid=2021017.

[16] (n.d.). *The EdTech Top 40: A Look at K-12 EdTech Engagement During the 2022-23 School Year*. Instructure. Retrieved August 15, 2023, from https://www.instructure.com/resources/research-reports/edtech-top-40-look-k-12-edtech-engagement-during-2022-23-school-year.

[17] Prothero, A. (2023, March 27). *How Educators Feel About the Impact of Technology, in Charts*. Education Week. Retrieved August 15, 2023, from https://www.edweek.org/technology/how-educators-feel-about-the-impact-of-technology-in-charts/2023/03.

[18] Beyond the Classroom Today: From Increasing Technology Access to Improving Student Learning Experiences. Project Tomorrow, Retrieved August 21, 2023 from https://thejournal.com/whitepapers/2023/07/spectrum-beyond-the-classroom/asset. aspx?tc=assetpg&tc=page0.

[19] University of South Florida (n.d.). *Active Learning*. Florida Center for Instructional Technology. Retrieved August 15, 2023, from https://fcit.usf.edu/matrix/project/active-learning/.

their skills practically and meaningfully. It reveals voice and choice in the learning process while enhancing engagement, critical thinking, creativity, and problem-solving abilities, preparing students for success in a technology-driven world.[20,21,22,23] With active use, students frequently engage in self-directed, interest-driven learning using technology outside of school as well, and these learning experiences are representative of their preferences for how learning should be in the classroom.[24]

Passive technology use occurs when students consume digital content or interact with technology in a primarily observational or non-interactive manner. This technology use is less engaging and may not require active participation or student contribution. It may include activities like test prep applications focusing on rote memorization or completing digitized worksheets online without immediate feedback. During the pandemic, many students used technology for emergency remote learning in passive ways, which did not necessarily result in high-quality learning experiences.[25,26] Because school systems deployed technology on an emergency basis, many teachers did not have the time or capacity to design effective online learning environments; in many cases, teachers transferred over traditional lesson plans and structures to a virtual environment, with varying degrees of success.[27]

---

[20] Taylor, S. (2015). Powering up Technology from Passive Access to Active Integration. Odyssey: New Directions in Deaf Education, 16, 60-63. https://eric.ed.gov/?id=EJ1064238.

[21] Romero, M., Laferriere, T., & Power, T. M. (2016). The Move is On! From the Passive Multimedia Learner to the Engaged Co-creator. ELearn, 2016(3). https://doi.org/10.1145/2904374.2893358.

[22] Cardullo, V. M., Wilson, N. S., & Zygouris-Coe, V. I. (2018). Enhanced Student Engagement Through Active Learning and Emerging Technologies. IGI Global. https://doi.org/10.4018/978-1-5225-2584-4.ch019.

[23] Ntulli, E. (2015). Active Learning Strategies in Technology Integrated K-12 Classrooms. Handbook of Research on Educational Technology Integration and Active Learning. https://doi.org/10.4018/978-1-4666-8363-1.ch007ss.

[24] Evans, J. A. (2023). *Free Agent Learning, Leveraging Students' Self-Directed Learning to Transform K-12 Education* (1st ed.). John Wiley & Sons. https://www.tomorrow.org/publications/free-agent-learning/.

[25] West, M. (2023). An ed-tech tragedy? Educational technologies and school closures in the time of COVID-19. UNESCO. https:// unesdoc.unesco.org/ark:/48223/pf0000386701.

[26] Effects of the COVID-19 Pandemic on K-12 Education: A Systematic Literature Review. Educational Research and Development Journal, 24(1), 53-84.

[27] Kamenetz, Anya. The Stolen Year: How COVID Changed Children's Lives, and Where We Go Now. Hachette UK, 2022.

Post-pandemic, teachers and students still use many new digital tools, but not necessarily in ways that foster active technology use.[28,29]

Decades of research from the learning sciences have shown the importance of considering individual learner variability and encouraging active learning experiences.[30] Technology has the potential to support learner needs and create learning opportunities in ways that we could not have imagined 40 years ago, but only when paired with the understanding of how learning can and should look different in the present. Without thoughtful consideration of the learning goals to be supported by technology use and what that should look like, the digital use divide will continue to grow and exacerbate existing inequities already worsened by the pandemic.[31,32,33]

Sparking Interest in STEAM Education Through Student Choice and Project-Based Learning

Pendergast Elementary School District (PESD) in Glendale, AZ, has pursued the ambitious goal of developing a district-wide, student-centered, project-based learning culture. The district implemented the use of FUSE Studios, a research-based STEAM platform created by and housed within Northwestern University and funded by the Macarthur Foundation and National Science Foundation, among others, to support this goal. FUSE Studios puts student interest and agency at the center of its approach. Instead of moving all students through the same adult-selected tasks at the

---

[28] Holland, Beth (July 2022). From Digital Access to Digital Equity: Critical Barriers That Leaders and Policymakers Must Address to Move Beyond "Boxes & Wires" https://practices.learningaccelerator.org/artifacts/from-digital-access-to-digital-equity-critical-challenges-that-leaders-and-policymakers-must-address-to-move-beyond-boxes-wires Retrieved August 25, 2023.

[29] UNESCO. (2023). Global education monitoring report 2023: Technology in education – A tool on whose terms? https://unesdoc. unesco.org/ark:/48223/pf0000386165ss.

[30] National Academies of Sciences, Engineering, and Medicine. 2018. How People Learn II: Learners, Contexts, and Cultures. Washington, DC: The National Academies Press. https://doi.org/10.17226/24783.

[31] Prothero, A. (2021, July 9). *How COVID taught America about inequity in education*. Harvard Gazette. Retrieved August 15, 2023, from https://news.harvard.edu/gazette/story/2021/07/how-covid-taught-america-about-inequity-in-education/.

[32] (2021, June 8). *Education in a Pandemic: The Disparate Impacts of COVID-19 on America's Students.* U.S. Department of Education Office for Civil Rights. Retrieved August 15, 2023, from https://www2.ed.gov/about/offices/list/ocr/docs/20210608-impacts-of-covid19. pdf.

[33] Toness, B. V., & Lurye, S. (2022, October 28). *How COVID taught America about inequity in education*. The Hechinger Report. Retrieved August 15, 2023, from https://hechinger report.org/massive-learning-setbacks-show-covids-sweeping-toll-on-kids/.

same time in the same sequence, students using FUSE Studios choose instead from among more than 30 leveled challenge sequences in areas such as 3D design and printing, digital animation, robotics, and making-with-electronics projects.

In-depth classroom research has shown that students develop essential 21st-century skills in FUSE; they learn to persist, teach and learn from their peers, and be adaptive problem-solvers.[34,35,36,37] This research has also shown students genuinely enjoy their learning experiences in FUSE, which has implications for their choices about future STEM activities.

Now in its 12th year, FUSE Studios has grown through word-of-mouth from a small demonstration project to a program implemented in more than 250 schools in the United States and abroad, and serving more than 50,000 young people during the 2022–23 school year. The majority of students using FUSE are from historically marginalized student populations.

Resetting Destination: Portrait of a Learner/Graduate

Amid this new connectivity, influx of devices, and swell of digital learning resources lies an opportunity to cast a clearer vision of what communities want for the learning of their young people. Before implementing edtech, states and school systems have the opportunity to set a clear vision of cognitive, personal, and interpersonal competencies students should have when they transition between grade levels and at graduation. BCSC's vision was formed by its clear commitment to UDL as a pedagogical framework supported by the active use of technology for learning. In other states and districts, this vision is often

[34] Ramey, K. & Stevens, R. (2020). Best Practices for Facilitation in a Choice-based, Peer Learning Environment: Lessons from the Field. In Gresalfi, M. and Horn, I. S. (Eds.), The Interdisciplinarity of the Learning Sciences, 14th International Conference of the Learning Sciences (ICLS) 2020, Volume 4 (pp. 1982-1989). Nashville, Tennessee: International Society of the Learning Sciences.

[35] Ramey, K. E., Stevens, R., & Uttal, D. H. (2020). In-FUSE-ing STEAM learning with spatial reasoning: Distributed spatial sensemaking in school-based making activities. Journal of Educational Psychology, 112(3), 466–493. https://doi.org/10.1037/ edu0000422.

[36] DiGiacomo, D.K., Van Horne, K. and Penuel, W.R. (2020), "Choice and interest in designed learning environments: the case of FUSE Studios," Information and Learning Sciences, Vol. 121 No. 3/4, pp. 137-154. https://doi.org/10.1108/ILS-09-2019-0098.

[37] Jaakko Hilppö, Reed Stevens, "Failure is just another try": Re-framing failure in school through the FUSE studio approach. International Journal of Educational Research, Volume 99, 2020, https://doi.org/10.1016/j.ijer.2019.10.004.

called the Portrait of a Learner or Portrait of a Graduate, which serves as a guiding framework that influences curriculum, instruction, assessment, and overall educational design. The NETP will use the term "Portrait of a Learner/ Graduate" to describe the entirety of the K-12 journey, a portrait that changes as students progress through grade levels.

Whether at the state or district level, developing a Portrait of a Learner/ Graduate involves soliciting input from various stakeholders— educators, parents/guardians, local business owners, colleges and universities, workforce development organizations, and community members. This development process can foster a sense of shared responsibility and ownership and ensure the final vision aligns with community needs.

Development of a Portrait of a Learner/ Graduate pushes all involved to articulate the full range of outcomes they want for their graduates. Although the specific skills outlined in a Portrait of a Learner/Graduate can vary based on individual states' or school systems' values and goals, they often include "soft skills" such as critical thinking, problem-solving, communication, collaboration, creativity, and digital literacy. These transferable skills are often highly valued by employers across industries and help prepare students for college or careers, and civic and community engagement.[38,39] By explicitly defining the skills and attributes required for success in college, in the workforce, and in civic life, the Portrait of a Learner/Graduate helps prepare students for post-secondary opportunities and lifelong learning.

Painting a Statewide Portrait of a Graduate in Nevada

Seldom is there the opportunity to read the story of the creation of a portrait. The Nevada Department of Education (NDE) has provided one by making the process by which the state is crafting its "Portrait of a Nevada Learner" public and transparent. Begun in October 2022 and drawing on work in Virginia, South Carolina, Utah, and New Mexico, Nevada's process serves as an example of ensuring input from as diverse and representative a sample of constituents as possible. Released in May 2023, the final portrait represents the input of thousands of Nevadans,

[38] McGunagle, D. and Zizka, L. (2020), "Employability skills for 21st-century STEM students: the employers' perspective," Higher Education, Skills and Work-Based Learning, Vol. 10 No. 3, pp. 591-606. https://doi.org/10.1108/HESWBL-10-2019-0148.

[39] Rios, J. A., Ling, G., Pugh, R., Becker, D., & Bacall, A. (2020). Identifying Critical 21st-Century Skills for Workplace Success: A Content Analysis of Job Advertisements. Educational Researcher, 49(2), 80–89. https://doi.org/10.3102/0013189X19890600.

including educators, students, and business leaders. The NDE undertook the effort in partnership with the Future of Learning Network. They began by asking a collection of 200 Nevadans to "envision the future of learning and identify portrait mindsets and skills." From there, the state sought feedback through surveys, pilot cohorts, and a youth fellowship program to allow for shared state-wide ownership. The state took the process one step further. It published documentation of the history and development of the portrait to inform Nevadans not involved in the process and as a potential template for states and districts looking to undertake similar projects.

The result of this multi-pronged, multi-sector, and multi-generational approach is a vision of the attributes Nevada learners "must possess to succeed both academically and in life, now and into a rapidly evolving future."

After articulating the full range of outcomes desired for their learners and graduates, educators and policymakers can work backward to build a school model and technology plan that maps directly to the identified outcomes. While developing a shared vision is an essential first step, execution may require redefining some critical assumptions regarding learning and how technology can and should support that vision. This process should include the thoughtful, intentional work of change management to help all education community members see what's possible.[40,41] Frameworks for managing this transition to innovative learning include the Innovative Learning Implementation Framework from The Learning Accelerator, Change Management from Digital Promise, and The 4 Shifts Protocol.

Rural District Leverages their Portrait of a Learner through Competency-Based Education

Northern Cass School District 97, which serves 690 PK-12 students from six rural communities north of Fargo, North Dakota, is implementing competency-based education founded on its Portrait of a Learner. In 2017, the district embarked on a transformational journey driven in part by a

[40] (2018). Co-Creating School Innovations: Should Self-Determination be a Component of School Improvement? *Teachers College Record: The Voice of Scholarship in Education*, 120, 1-32. https://api.semanticscholar.org/CorpusID:17477009.0.

[41] Depta, M. (2015). Best Practices in Implementation of Technology Change in the K-12 Context. *American Journal of Educational Research*, 3(12B), 41-56.

specific challenge faced by many school systems: the problem of time. What started as a pilot program catalyzed a complete district redesign.

An essential element of Northern Cass's learning redesign is self-directed, flexible pacing. Within guidelines appropriate to their developmental level, learners can take the time needed to achieve proficiency on priority standards and provide three pieces of evidence to demonstrate that learning. The district learning management system allows educators to collect proof of proficiency and track learner progress toward meeting standards.

After embracing flexible pacing, the district changed its approach to grading, moving to a standards-based grading system that reflects a growth mindset.[42,43] Standards-based grading considers evidence of learning and the data it produces differently from traditional grading scales. It measures students against specific skills and standards rather than on conventional measures, such as a percentage of coursework completed, making it clearer where students are thriving and where they need help. With standards-based grading, failure and making mistakes are part of the learning journey. Students are given multiple opportunities to demonstrate mastery and have input as to how they show what they've learned.[44] Score levels of 1-4 (1: Emerging, 2: Foundational, 3: Proficient, 4: Extending) have replaced traditional letter grades and indicate progress toward achieving proficiency on priority standards. In this model, a score of 1 or 2 conveys not failure or deficiency but that the learner is still working toward mastery.

Cass's Portrait of a Learner emphasizes skills students need to succeed throughout life, regardless of their post-secondary path. The focus has shifted to "choice-ready" instead of "college-ready." Even the youngest learners start developing these skills in age-appropriate ways.

Before graduation, students complete a capstone presentation documenting how they built the skills outlined in the district's Portrait. Students have two options for showcasing evidence: they can focus on one

---

[42] Ng, B. (2018). The neuroscience of growth mindset and intrinsic motivation. Brain sciences, 8(2), 20.

[43] Emily Rhew, Jody S. Piro, Pauline Goolkasian & Patricia Cosentino | Olympia Palikara (Reviewing editor) (2018) The effects of a growth mindset on self-efficacy and motivation, Cogent Education, 5:1, DOI: 10.1080/2331186X.2018.1492337.

[44] (2023, October 11). Traditional Grading Systems vs. Standards-based Grading Systems. KnowledgeWorks. Retrieved October 23, 2023, from https://knowledgeworks.org/resources/traditional-grading-vs-standards-based-grading/.

competency from the Portrait and highlight multiple activities through which they demonstrated it, or choose to focus on one learning experience, such as an internship or a powerful school-based project and explore all the Portrait of a Learner skills they developed and demonstrated in its completion.

Although the transition to competency-based learning has taken several years, it empowers students with voice and choice in their education and provides them with the skills needed for post-graduation success.

Leveraging Technology to Support the Portrait of a Graduate in North Carolina

In October 2022, North Carolina Superintendent of Education Catherine Truitt announced the release of the North Carolina Portrait of a Graduate, developed in collaboration with close to 1,200 K-12 educators, administrators, families, employers, communities, and higher education institutions. The North Carolina Department of Public Instruction (NCDPI), in collaboration with educators and technologists from across the state, has also developed a comprehensible Digital Learning Plan aligned to the Portrait of a Graduate.

The Digital Learning Plan includes goals and rubrics for the state, Public School Units (PSUs), and schools that allow organizations to evaluate their progress and track students' growth. The NCDPI has developed a robust professional learning infrastructure to help educators and administrators leverage technology to develop the Portrait of a Graduate competencies. The state has adopted ISTE standards for students, teachers, administrators, and coaches, providing every educator with an ISTE membership. In addition, they sponsor educator cohorts to pursue ISTE educator certification. The state also pays for CoSN memberships for all PSUs and encourages PSU edtech leaders to pursue CoSN's Certified Education Technology Leader (CETL) certification. The NCDPI pays for interested edtech leaders to take the CoSN CETL course, and the annual NCTIES conference offers the CETL certification exam.

Using Digital Learning Initiative funds, the NCDPI launched a series of summer mini-conferences for educators called NCBOLD. The state provides teachers exemplifying best practices in digital teaching and learning with a stipend and travel funds to visit all eight state regions over two weeks to present free mini edtech conferences for educators. Attendees get CEU credit towards their teacher licensure renewal.

By aligning the Digital Learning Plan to the State Portrait of a Graduate and focusing on capacity building at the classroom, building, and PSU levels, the NCDPI is supporting a shared vision of student learning to help North Carolina students be truly prepared for civic life, careers, or college after graduation.

Universal Design for Learning Framing Active Use for All Learners

Effective and active use of technology incorporates the principles of Universal Design for Learning (UDL), a research-driven framework,[45,46,47] to improve and optimize teaching and learning for all people based on scientific insights into how humans learn.[48] UDL aims to make learning accessible and effective for all students by reducing barriers in instruction and addressing individual differences, learning preferences, abilities, and backgrounds. Developed to address the diversity of students' needs and to provide equal opportunities for learning and success, UDL emphasizes the need to design instructional materials, evidence-based learning activities, and assessments to maximize inclusivity and accommodate a wide range of learners. As such, the UDL framework supports an inclusive and equitable education environment for all learners by providing multiple flexibilities. UDL practice includes flexible presentations of content, flexible response options for students to demonstrate their learning, and flexible options for student engagement. UDL also incorporates appropriate accommodations, supports, and challenges for all students, including students with disabilities and students who are English language learners.

---

[45] Assor, A., Kaplan, H., & Roth, G. (2002). Choice is good, but relevance is excellent: Autonomy-enhancing and suppressing teacher behaviours predicting students' engagement in schoolwork. British Journal of Educational Psychology, 72(2), 261-278.

[46] Kalyuga, S., Chandler, P., & Sweller, J. (2000). Incorporating learner experience into the design of multimedia instruction. *Journal of Educational Psychology*, 92(1), 126-136.

[47] Dalton, B. D., Herbert, M., & Deysher, S. (2003, December). Scaffolding students' response to digital literature with embedded strategy supports: The role of audio-recording vs. writing student response options. Paper presented at the 53rd Annual Meeting of the National Reading Conference, Scottsdale, AZ.

[48] (n.d.). *About Universal Design for Learning*. CAST. Retrieved August 15, 2023, from https://www.cast.org/impact/universal-design-for-learning-udl.

While the following section will include a more detailed examination of how UDL can aid in the use of technology to support learning, the three main principles of UDL are outlined below.

PRINCIPLES OF UDL	
Multiple means of representation	Digital tools can allow educators to present information in multiple ways. Examples can include videos, interactive simulations, infographics, and audio recordings. These tools allow students to access content in formats that suit their preferences. Accessibility features, such as closed captions, screen readers, text-to-speech, and adjustable font sizes, also support diverse learners.
Multiple means of expression	Digital tools can provide different ways for students to demonstrate their understanding of learning concepts. Examples include written assignments; audio or video presentations such as podcasts, screencasts, or movies; e-books; mind maps; and digital drawing tools. In addition, because technology allows students to learn outside of the traditional classroom setting, it can provide increased flexibility for students in alternative learning environments.
Multiple means of engagement	Digital tools can provide interactive learning experiences and multiple ways of engaging with learning material. Learners can be engaged or motivated to learn in a variety of ways. Factors influencing these individual variations include neurology, culture, personal relevance, subjectivity, and background knowledge, along with a variety of other factors.[49] Different types of multimedia content (audio, video, infographics, etc.) and the presentation of different content options can help students actively engage in the learning process. Technology can also facilitate collaborative learning experiences through discussion boards, virtual classrooms, and group projects, allowing students to work together and learn from one another.

With the increasing number of digital learning tools and devices available to teachers post-pandemic, educators have even more options to support their use of UDL. Digital tools can offer more flexibility and learning support than traditional educational material formats. They empower educators to personalize and customize learning experiences to align with individual student needs while recognizing learner agency in charting the learning path that best meets these needs.

Educators can implement UDL without modern digital technology;[50] however, edtech is uniquely suited to support it. Including no-tech and tech-

[49] (n.d.). *Principle: Provide Multiple Means of Engagement*. CAST. Retrieved September 5, 2023, from https://udlguidelines.cast.org/ engagement.

[50] Rose, D. H., Gravel, J. W., & Domings, Y. M. (2012). UDL Unplugged: The Role of Technology in UDL. In T. E. Hall, A. Meyer, & D. H. Rose (Authors), Universal design for

enabled choices for learners may be the best way to meet student needs. This flexibility extends to providing students with the option to use a variety of different digital and analog tools to demonstrate their learning. Rather than teachers feeling like they need to be experts on a specific digital tool before including it in the classroom, they can instead allow students to use the tool or tools of their choice to demonstrate mastery of educational content if the final product demonstrates their understanding of the learning goal.

Universal Design for Learning (UDL) aims to make learning accessible and effective for all students by reducing barriers and supporting learner variability.

learning in the classroom: Practical applications (pp. 120-134). New York, NY: Guilford Press.

Example Lesson Utilizing UDL and Technology: A Goal-Driven Unit

As an example of UDL, consider a fictional elementary school lesson created by Ms. Ramirez, who used UDL to develop a unit titled "EcoExplorers."[51] She started by identifying the unit's goal and considered the barriers that might emerge in the learning process. Ms. Ramirez considered how multiple means of representation, engagement, action, and expression might overcome these barriers.

The unit aimed to support all students in understanding ecological concepts associated with diversity and sustainability. To achieve this goal, Ms. Ramirez introduced the unit's goals and central question: "How can we protect and sustain our planet's diverse ecosystems?" She then reviewed the various tools and pathways students had to explore the topic.

In representing information, Ms. Ramirez leveraged technology to ensure all her students could access and understand the content. Some students chose to engage in an immersive 360-degree virtual tour of rainforests, while others, including a blind student, listened to narrated podcasts about aquatic ecosystems. Finally, some learners, including two students with learning differences, used interactive simulations that allowed them to manipulate ecosystem variables. The variety of provided resources ensured all students overcame the barriers to learning the essential content.

To actively engage students in their learning, Ms. Ramirez related the unit to previous units and encouraged students to take on the role of "EcoExplorers." She then reminded the students how to use the online collaboration tools for group projects, and students then chose different roles within the unit. Some students took on the role of scientist, some took on the role of engineer, while others took on the role of reporter.

Across the different roles, students needed to gather information and develop solutions around critical challenges. The students gathered and organized their information through an online information organizing tool. Some designed infographics using graphic design software, while others created videos using tablets. By offering choice in technology tools, students contributed in ways that aligned with their strengths.

Thinking about how all students could act and express their understanding, Ms. Ramirez embraced diverse assessment methods. She tied all assessment methods back to assessment rubrics aligned to each engagement

---

[51] This example lesson was created by Technical Working Group member James Basham for the NETP based on the principles of UDL.

role and the unit's goal of understanding ecological concepts associated with diversity and sustainability. She walked the students through various options for demonstrating their understanding, including developing multimedia presentations, podcasts, written reports, or clay models. A couple of students then asked if they could develop a digital book with text, video, and visuals. Ms. Ramirez told students they could use any number of ways to demonstrate their understanding, including digital books. She then reminded the students to submit a self-completed rubric on their chosen expression of understanding. Encouraging students to reflect on their work helped students develop their executive functioning skills.[52,53]

Using the UDL framework to design the unit, Ms. Ramirez supported all students in learning the content while helping them develop digital literacy and citizenship skills.

UDL Considerations for Educators

UDL principles, especially when combined with active technology use, can help educators better meet student learning needs. However, many policymakers, administrators, and educators do not understand the UDL framework and learner variability. Furthermore, few districts and schools provide educators the time to build their capacity to design educational experiences with that variability in mind. As a result, teachers' experience and training in classrooms may circumscribe student learning opportunities, even within the same school buildings. This difference in student learning opportunities is at the heart of the digital design divide.

The adults associated with an education system—whether educators, administrators, classified staff, policymakers, or parents/caregivers—tend to view education through their own experiences as students. Despite advances in learning science and the advent of technologies that empower educators to design learning experiences to meet the needs of diverse student populations, this information often does not make its way into schools. Instead, teachers

---

52 Lyons, K. E., & Zelazo, P. D. (2011). Monitoring, metacognition, and executive function: Elucidating the role of self-reflection in the development of self-regulation. Advances in child development and behavior, 40, 379-412.

53 Marcovitch, S., Jacques, S., Boseovski, J. J., & Zelazo, P. D. (2008). Self-reflection and the cognitive control of behavior: Implications for learning. Mind, Brain, and Education, 2(3), 136-141.

often teach based on their own learning experiences.[54] Whether or not their educational experiences met their learning needs, changing practices without explicit training in new instructional models can be difficult. In addition, teachers need to experience these new instructional models as learners through ongoing professional training and teacher preparation programs. Unfortunately, many professional learning opportunities and teacher preparation programs are not designed using UDL principles nor provide teachers with opportunities to experience these new instructional models.

An additional challenge educators and administrators face in many school systems is that teachers are overwhelmed with responsibilities. Teachers may have only one 45-minute planning block per day— barely enough time to complete administrative tasks and answer emails, let alone design lessons that meet the needs of all learners. "Here's just one more thing" is a common refrain among educators with overflowing plates who are asked to take on additional tasks. Initiative fatigue often occurs when teachers, administrators, and educational institutions are subject to frequent changes in curriculum, teaching methods, assessment systems, and more, resulting in exhaustion and decreased effectiveness.[55]

Just as students need time and space to learn, grow, and reflect on their learning, so do educators. In short, school systems need to engage in what Justin Reich calls "the power of doing less"—taking the time to step back, eliminate non-essential activities, and provide teachers with the time to reflect on their professional practice.[56] In the words of author John Maxwell, "Learn to say 'no' to the good so you can say 'yes' to the best."

State and district policymakers and leaders can consider the following steps to develop systems that provide educators with the time, space, and capacity teachers need to become learning designers:

- Gain a working understanding of UDL and how to leverage it in the workplace and classroom.

---

[54] Cox, S. E. (2014). Perceptions and Influences Behind Teaching Practices: Do Teachers Teach as They Were Taught? [Master's Thesis, Brigham Young University]. https://scholarsarchive.byu.edu/cgi/viewcontent.cgi?article=6300&context=etds.

[55] How Collective Teacher Efficacy Develops. Educational Leadership, 76 (July 2019), 31-35. https://lceeq-files.s3.ca-central-1.amazonaws.com/cdn/2021-conference/handouts/C3-multiple+resources.pdf.

[56] Reich, J. (2022, October 1). The Power of Doing Less in Schools. ASCD. Retrieved September 6, 2023, from https://www.ascd.org/el/ articles/the-power-of-doing-less-in-schools.

- Plan for and intentionally model UDL in adult interactions and meetings and provide the necessary time for authentic learning/discussions.
- Engage and advocate for adequate connectivity and device access for educators and students at home and school to support learning and instruction.
- Partner and collaborate across agencies and departments to support UDL implementation.

Starting Small to Make a Difference in Mississippi

Engaging students in active use doesn't require an elaborate technological ecosystem. Pascagoula High School (PHS) is a suburban, Title 1 school on the Gulf Coast of Mississippi with a student population of around 1,120, about 70 percent Black or Hispanic. Educator Jami Sheets teaches a leadership class at PHS, which allows students to learn different leadership skills and put those skills into action on campus and in the community.

The class's mission is to ensure all PHS students feel seen and heard. Sheets and her students identified the need to keep all PHS students "in the know" about school activities. During the 2022-23 school year Sheets' leadership class launched the Pascagoula News Network (PNN), a student-led weekly newscast, using only a tablet computer, a free graphic design platform, and a freely available streaming platform. Students were responsible for the newscast, which included developing a weekly content outline and writing, recording, and editing each segment under the guidance of Sheets.

The goal of the PNN is to highlight the entire student body, and it has quickly grown in popularity, with additional students inquiring as to how they can be involved in the project. As a result of this unintentional pilot of active technology use, Pascagoula included a broadcast journalism class during the district's first week-long intersession of the 2023-24 school year.

The experience demonstrates that educators can start with a small pilot, use existing technology tools, and build upon its success. After a successful start, Sheets, in collaboration with the library staff, applied for and received an Ingalls Shipbuilding STEM grant to get additional technology tools to support the broadcast.

- Support active technology use as a foundational UDL strategy.
- Advocate for equity of access to professional learning that is focused on UDL through sustained funding and policy priorities.
- Encourage teacher preparation and residency programs to implement UDL principles and support teachers as learning designers versus practitioners.
- Build on existing partnerships and relationships to develop and deliver professional learning opportunities leveraging UDL and technology.

Rural Kentucky District Empowers Teachers and Students to Be Active Learners

Shifting to active student use can also mean ensuring active teacher learning. Logan County Schools, a rural, high-poverty school system in Russellville, Kentucky, launched a digital transformation initiative in response to industry and community leaders who indicated that the local workforce needed graduates who were better innovators, communicators, and problem-solvers. The school system, a Digital Promise League of Innovative Schools member, wanted to ensure that teachers, principals, and administrators understood authentic student engagement and the importance of student choice and voice. The district hired digital learning coaches to make sure teachers, principals, and administrators received the resources and training to use technology in ways that supported these learning goals. At the same time, the teacher-leadership team (the LC Innovators) worked with the Learner-Centered Collaborative on embedding high-impact educator professional learning.

This initial investment in educator learning has shifted student experiences and expectations. Today, students in grades 5, 8, and 12 give a Defense of Learning Presentation at the end of the school year to reflect on their learning, share evidence and artifacts, and set new goals. Artifacts don't have to be from the classroom; they can be photos of a student leading an after-school club, captaining a sports team, or using math on the farm. The district also started an accountability system, sharing student growth, readiness, well-being, and performance data every quarter with the community.

Additional Technology Standards and Frameworks

States and districts have used several different technology standards and frameworks in conjunction with UDL to guide technology use in instruction. Examples include the SAMR Model,[57,58,59] the TPACK Framework,[60,61,62] the PICRAT Model[63] and the ISTE Standards[64] (available for students, educators, education leaders, technology coaches, and computational thinking competencies). Standards and frameworks such as these can serve as examples for states and districts developing technology plans to align with their Portrait of a Learner/Graduate, Portrait of an Educator (described in the digital design divide section of this document), and Portrait of a Learning Environment (described in the digital access divide section).

Atlanta Elementary School Designs Problem-Based Learning for Students

Spaces like STEAM labs, maker spaces, and innovation creation labs allow students authentic learning experiences that expose them to career paths, as well as settings where they can acquire essential skills such as

57 Puentedura, R. R. (n.d.). *SAMR: A Brief Introduction*. Hippasus.com. Retrieved August 16, 2023, from http://hippasus.com/ rrpweblog/archives/2015/10/SAMR_ABriefIntro.pdf.

58 Christopher N. Blundell, Michelle Mukherjee, Shaun Nykvist, A scoping review of the application of the SAMR model in research, Computers and Education Open, Volume 3, 2022, 100093, ISSN 2666-5573, https://doi.org/10.1016/j.caeo.2022.100093.

59 Terada, Y. (2020, May 4). *A Powerful Model for Understanding Good Tech Integration*. Edutopia. Retrieved August 16, 2023, from https://www.edutopia.org/article/powerful-model-understanding-good-tech-integration/.

60 Kohler, M. J. (2012, September 24). *TPACK Explained*. TPACK.org. Retrieved August 16, 2023, from http://matt-koehler.com/tpack2/ tpack-explained/.

61 Kendon, T., Ph.D., & Anselmo, L. (n.d.). *Technology, Pedagogy, and Content Knowledge (TPACK) Model*. Taylor Institute for Teaching and Learning. Retrieved August 16, 2023, from https://taylorinstitute.ucalgary.ca/resources/SAMR-TPACK#:~:text=Technology%2C%20Pedagogy%2C%20and%20Content%20Knowledge,to%20support%20how%20they%20teach.

62 Stanford University (n.d.). *Technology Integration Framework*. Stanford Teaching Commons. Retrieved August 16, 2023, from https://teachingcommons.stanford.edu/teaching-guides/foundations-course-design/theory-practice/technology-integration-framework.

63 Kimmons, R., Graham, C. R., & West, R. E. (2020). The PICRAT Model for Technology Integration in Teacher Preparation. *Contemporary Issues in Technology and Teacher Education (CITE Journal)*, 20(1). https://citejournal.org/volume-20/issue-1-20/general/the-picrat-model-for-technology-integration-in-teacher-preparation.

64 (n.d.). *The ISTE Standards*. ISTE. Retrieved August 16, 2023, from https://www.iste.org/iste-standards.

collaboration and problem-solving. These spaces allow students to learn through thought and action when exposed to authentic contexts.[65,66] This thinking drove the transformation of Atlanta Public Schools' M. Agnes Jones Elementary School (M.A. Jones), a Title 1 school serving a majority Black student population. The school was committed to having students develop solutions to local problems. Starting in kindergarten, students learn the Stanford Design School's engineering design process and practice it in science, English language arts, and math.

Students also put the process into practice. When 5th-grade students discovered insects were destroying a community garden near the school, they used the design process to tackle the issue. Through research, they learned bats eat thousands of flying insects every hour. The students also used AR/VR technology and TinkerCAD in the school's Innovation Creation Lab to design and build bat houses to bring more bats to the area. Along the way, students learned relevant and applicable facts about gardening, composting, nutrition, wellness, and sustainability.

At M.A. Jones, teachers, coaches, and even custodians participate in professional learning because school leaders recognize that building capacity is the only way to make this type of learning sustainable. By leveraging the active use of technology for solving real-world problems, M.A. Jones educators are helping close the digital use divide.

Considerations for Emerging Technologies

Educators who remember the advent of laser disk players or interactive whiteboards know that the adage of change as the only constant is true in edtech. Whatever the most cutting-edge technology in classrooms is today, tomorrow promises more improvements and innovations. These emerging technologies often promise increased engagement, transformation of the field, and increased learning outcomes. This can be alluring, but school systems should measure the potential benefits against potential student health, safety, and privacy risks. An important first step for districts is to set clear thresholds and expectations for including emerging technologies in learning spaces. They

[65] Sheridan, K., Halverson, E. R., Litts, B., Brahms, L., Jacobs-Priebe, L., & Owens, T. (2014). Learning in the making: A comparative case study of three makerspaces. *Harvard Educational Review*, 84(4), 505-531.

[66] Ryan, J. O., Clapp, E. P., Ross, J., & Tishman, S. (2016). Making, thinking, and understanding: A dispositional approach to maker-centered learning. In *Makeology* (pp. 29-44). Routledge.

should also ensure all educators understand these guidelines and can measure their practices against them.

A Rural District Finds Ways to Make Computational Thinking Accessible to Everyone

It took three years for Talladega County Schools, a rural Alabama district with a student population of 7,000 that is roughly 67 percent White and 28 percent Black, to develop computing pathways for its 7,000 students. Talladega applied to participate in the National Science Foundation-funded Developing Inclusive K-12 Computing Pathways project to offer computer science and computational thinking (CT) opportunities to all students, particularly female students and students from low socioeconomic households. The district clarified the K-12 computing pathway and identified existing resources and gaps. Next, they defined new learning opportunities across grade levels, courses, and schools and developed a competency map linking CT-specific activities and resources.

To focus on classroom-level change, leaders first gathered teacher, administrative, student, and community feedback. They created professional development resources and determined how to measure pathway implementation progress. They also built a website that defined CT for parents and families. The district plans to revise its Inclusive CT Pathways document and website continually, and students will continue using "exit tickets" to help the district gain a better sense of student learning gains.[67]

Building Pathways to Computer Science Success in Early County, Georgia

Before 2021, the Early County School District in Georgia had no Computer Science program for its students. Three years later, the district's high school will have four students complete its new computer science pathway. Through a partnership with the Kapor Center, the 52 percent Black school district has established a complete 6th through 12th-grade computer science pathway for students in Early County. They leveraged

[67] Digital Promise. (2021). Defining computational thinking for a district: Inclusive computing pathways in Talladega County Schools. Digital Promise. https://doi.org/10.51388/20.500.12265/132.

the Kapor Center's Culturally Responsive-Sustaining Computer (CRSC) Framework, developed in partnership with a national collective of education advocates to create more pathways for Black, Latinx, Native American, and other marginalized students to computer science education, tech careers, and STEM-related fields. The rural district faced challenges found in many similar districts across the country—lack of devices, the need for teachers with computer science certification, and a curriculum that helped students achieve industry-standard skills while considering culturally responsive practices. The goal of the partnership is to ensure that the students of Early County fulfill the Kapor Foundation's mission, "To create a more equitable technology ecosystem that addresses longstanding racial inequality, creates economic opportunity, tackles critical societal issues, and reflects the power and perspectives of communities of color."[68,69]

After addressing privacy and other concerns, one must consider the sometimes-brief lifespan of emerging technologies. Developers can move on from projects, or successful tools can be purchased by other companies and locked behind paywalls. A technology freely available to educators one day can be inaccessible the next. Districts like St. Vrain Valley Schools in Longmont, Colorado, developed a tiered approach to emerging technologies, such as the district's Innovative Tech Framework for evaluating emerging technologies. Such frameworks can help evaluate new technologies while helping educators understand which tools they can expect to be supported. While there is no "one size fits all" solution to address emerging technologies, there are some general principles that education leaders should keep in mind when considering new technologies. The following recommendations have been adapted from the Office of Educational Technology publication, Artificial Intelligence and the Future of Teaching and Learning:

68 (n.d.). Kapor Foundation. Kapor Center. Retrieved September 5, 2023, from https://www.kaporcenter.org/kapor-foundation/.

69 Jean Ryoo, Gail Chapman, Julie Flapan, Joanna Goode, Jane Margolis, Christine Ong, Cynthia Estrada, Max Skorodinsky, Tiera Tanksley, Jamika D. Burge, Ryoko Yamaguchi, Frieda McAlear, Allison Scott, Alexis Martin, Sonia Koshy, Kamau Bobb, and Lien Diaz. 2019. Going Beyond the Platitudes of Equity: Developing a Shared Vision for Equity in Computer Science Education. In Proceedings of the 50th ACM Technical Symposium on Computer Science Education (SIGCSE '19). Association for Computing Machinery, New York, NY, USA, 657–658. https://doi.org/10.1145/3287324.3287331.

Emphasize Humans in the Loop

Regardless of technologists' claims, no emerging technology will in and of itself solve the long-standing challenges faced by educational systems.[70] As new technologies emerge, educators must be involved in designing and developing digital tools for classroom use. Evaluating these technologies for potential classroom use at the state, school system, or school level should be iterative and include educator and student input. Evaluators should ensure tools are accessible and meet the needs of all students including students with disabilities. These evaluations should also consider how best to educate teachers, students, and families about these new technologies' potential benefits and risks. Educators should also keep in mind that technologies come and go - companies go bankrupt, get acquired by larger ones, or change their business focus or priorities, which is especially true of emerging technologies. By keeping this fact in mind, school systems can help prevent teachers from relying on tools that disappear.

1) *Align the Use of Emerging Technologies to Your Shared Vision for Education (State and District).* Every conversation about emerging technologies should start first and foremost with the educational needs and priorities of students, including discussions about educational equity. How might an emerging technology support the development of the skills outlined in your state's or district's Portrait of a Learner/Graduate? It is important not to let the excitement surrounding emerging technologies distract from the north star defined by your state or school system. When deploying emerging technologies in classrooms, evaluate their effectiveness against these priorities.
2) *Learning Principles Should Drive the Use of Emerging Technologies.* Consider how modern learning principles such as UDL can leverage emerging technologies. Pay particular attention to the needs of students from historically marginalized populations, including students who are English learners (ELs) and those with disabilities. Before deploying emerging technologies, consider learner variability and the diversity of settings in which teachers and students will use digital tools. New technologies developed and deployed without such

[70] Reich, J. (2020). *Failure to Disrupt: Why Technology Alone Can't Transform Education.* Harvard University Press.

considerations risk exacerbating the digital use divide instead of narrowing it.

3) *Develop Education-Specific Guidelines and Guardrails.* New data privacy and security risks can accompany the practical and powerful functionality of emerging technologies.[71] As with any edtech tool, evaluate emerging technologies to ensure they allow school systems to meet their federal and state legal obligations for protecting student data privacy and security. In addition, evaluate these tools to guard against the potential for bias, and to make sure they support cultural responsiveness, and educational equity. Creating an incubation framework for new and emergent technologies can help ensure alignment with these considerations.

Ethical AI Research: Automated Scoring Data Challenges for Open-Ended NAEP Items

The Institute of Education Sciences (IES), through its National Center for Education Statistics, administers the National Assessment of Educational Progress (NAEP), the largest national representative that offers continuing assessment of what America's students know and can do. NAEP uses open-ended prompts to measure student understanding more broadly than is possible in fixed-choice questions. However, these responses are time-consuming and expensive to score.

Automated Scoring uses natural language processing to "predict" human scores assigned to student responses. If sufficiently accurate, it can improve reporting timeliness, consistency control, and cost reduction. IES conducted two automated scoring challenges for reading and mathematics promts. These challenges were open to any research team that met data security requirements; winning teams came from assessment service providers and research institutions.

While this challenge achieved the technical goal of accurate scoring, the organizational and ethical requirements of the challenge were just as important. All challengers submitted a technical report that described algorithmic choices used, in order to ensure that solutions were clear and built trust in their validity. Further, a fairness/bias analysis was required to

[71] U.S. Department of Education, Office of Educational Technology, Artificial Intelligence and the Future of Teaching and Learning, Washington, D.C., 2023.

demonstrate that models were usable. For more information about the challenges, see the Challenge websites.

Improving Practice, Progress, and Proficiency

Once education leaders and policymakers have defined their vision for learners and implemented a framework to shift teacher practice (to be discussed further in the next section), building evidence about their efforts' success is important. With the more open-ended practices associated with active technology use, both qualitative measures (such as teacher narratives of adoption barriers) and quantitative measures (such as the frequency with which tools are used and student performance) can help education leaders describe implementation, monitor its progress, and adapt practices to better meet their implementation goals.

These self-evaluation questions are adapted from The Learning Accelerator's Digital Equity Guide Self-Assessment Tool:

1) *Are students engaging with materials that are targeted and relevant?* Can they access differentiated content from several different cultural perspectives, using a variety of modalities, such as audio and video, in an accessible way? Can they choose to access content that they find motivating and relevant and do they have strategies *to support how they interact with different forms of media?*
2) *Are students actively engaged with the available technology, tools, and digital materials?* Can students use various technologies, allowing them to choose the modality that best motivates them, meets their learning needs, and fits the circumstance? Is technology used not only for content acquisition, assignments, and instruction but also to connect to students' personal and professional interests?
3) *Do students have opportunities to engage in peer learning, relationship-building, and connection with the broader community?* Do students learn across multiple contexts and modalities? Are they comfortable using a variety of channels to communicate and collaborate, and possess the digital and media literacy skills and competencies to engage in socially connected learning?
4) *Can students use platforms, tools, and software that adapt to meet their needs, help them reflect and monitor progress, and support their acquisition of new knowledge and skills?* Do students experience

authentic and inclusive opportunities for learning, reflection, feedback, and assessment? Do they have choice and agency in engaging with differentiated, standards-aligned materials, tracking their progress toward learning goals, reflecting on their learning, engaging in individual practice, and demonstrating proficiency or mastery? Do they possess the digital literacy skills and competencies to determine how to leverage different tools or platforms to best to meet their unique learning needs?

Montana Offers Artificial Intelligence Course for High School Students

To ensure all students in the state have an opportunity to face the future of work, the Montana Digital Academy (MTDA), a 14-year-old online school that offers more than 100 courses taught by Montana public school educators to students across the state, began offering Artificial Intelligence in the World in Fall 2023. A semester-long introductory survey of AI concepts, tools, and building blocks, the course will give high school students a broad overview of how people use AI to make decisions and solve problems. Students will study AI's ethical impacts, participate in hands-on AI-focused activities, and develop a grounding foundation for watching the technology as it evolves. The course will also focus on the history and future of AI and explore career fields, helping students understand how to embrace and use AI ethically to improve society. By making this course available to public school students across the state, the MTDA is helping ensure students in rural communities have opportunities to better understand the implications of emerging technologies and how to use them to support learning.

Some potential strategies include:

1) Cognitive walkthroughs are an approach to assessing usability in which one or more evaluators work through a series of tasks and ask a set of questions from the perspective of the user.[72] In education, cognitive walkthroughs systematically analyze the usability of educational materials, environments, and experiences from the

[72] (n.d.). *Usability Walkthrough*. Usability Body Of Knowledge. Retrieved September 5, 2023, from https://www.usabilitybok.org/ cognitive-walkthrough.

learner's perspective. Cognitive walkthroughs can help educators identify obstacles students might encounter in the learning environment, including anything from accessibility challenges to a lack of culturally responsive learning materials. Considering education materials and environments from multiple learner perspectives can help ensure they work for more students.

2) Journey mapping refers to creating a detailed visual breakdown of the smaller events that make up a larger experience.[73] This process includes depicting learners' various touchpoints, interactions, and experiences during the learning process. Journey mapping focuses on understanding the learners' perspectives, emotions, and interactions throughout their educational journey.
3) Educator, student, and parent surveys can provide valuable insight into the perceived benefits associated with technology implementations.

The digital use divide stands between students who have opportunities to engage actively with technology as part of their educational experiences and those who don't. All learners deserve an education designed around the active use of technology rather than the passive technology uses they report being offered most frequently in school.

In this section, we have discussed the updated definition of the digital use divide; discussed the importance of active technology use for learning; introduced UDL as a component of active technology use; explained how developing a Portrait of a Learner/Graduate can serve as a "north star" for edtech use; and discussed how to evaluate the usability, feasibility, and implementation of technology used in developing these competencies. The next section will discuss the digital design divide, focusing on educators and the larger education systems that impact their instructional effectiveness.

In the next section, we'll discuss the four Every Student Succeeds Act (ESSA) tiers of evidence and the role of research studies in the evaluation process.

---

73 [Consortium for Public Education]. (2021, February 24). *Design Thinking for Education, Ep. 10: Journey Mapping* [Video]. YouTube. https://www.youtube.com/watch?v=LsDxDYQnHKU.

Ten Examples of Active Use in Practice

Students at Harrison Middle School in Arkansas created a video about Granny Henderson, one of the last residents of the Buffalo National River area, to learn the history of the region and make cultural connections. The Buffalo National River was the first waterway designated a national river.

Chemistry students at William C. Overfelt High School (East Side Union High School District in San Jose, California) used tech to learn how chemicals affect their lives. Students used a visible light spectrophotometer to investigate how fluorescent red-light exposure affects yeast acceleration, how fast yeast grows in cold water, and how fructose corn syrup impacts yeast growth. They worked in groups to conduct preliminary research and then measured how an independent variable of their choosing affected yeast growth.

Students at Highland Academy Charter School (6-12) in Anchorage, Alaska, conducted student-led conferences in the fall and spring at which they presented and shared electronic portfolios of all of their exemplary classwork, goals, and reflections.

Visually impaired and blind students at Breckinridge-Franklin Elementary in Louisville, Kentucky are learning to code using CodeJumper, a coding language developed by Microsoft in collaboration with American Printing House for the Blind.

The National Technical Institute for the Deaf Regional Stem Center (NRSC) has partnered with VEX Robotics and the REC Foundation to provide schools with training and resources that empower deaf students to learn STEM concepts through robotics and participate in robotics competitions.

Teachers at Del Lago Academy in Escondido, California, a high school focused on Applied Sciences, created a digital badging system for students to show evidence of their learning on the school's website. Students in the Principles of Design course created the graphics for the badges.

Verona Area School District in Wisconsin uses Virtual Field Trips for cross-curricular, cross-grade-level experience. Recently, students from different high school athletic and academic programs designed hands-on learning activities for elementary students using the NFL Play 60 Virtual Field Trip.

Second-graders at Central Dauphin School District in Harrisburg, Pennsylvania, used Minecraft to animate their water cycles into cartoons. Their teacher said that after the activity ended, the students continued to create animations in other lessons and ended up animating a story that they read in a separate lesson.

In their music class at Gorham Middle School in Gorham, Maine, students use Soundtrap to create podcasts and songs. They create compositions in music class to learn about form and genre, and use the program's text chat so their teacher can see their planning process.

Fifth-grade students at Escondido Union School District in Escondido, California, videoconferenced with rangers in four different parks along the state's coast (via the California State Parks PORTS Program) to learn how to become advocates for Marine Protected Areas. Later, the students created public service announcements to encourage people to save Marine Protected Areas.

Grapevine-Colleyville ISD students in Texas program robots to automate tasks, such as cutting the grass and cleaning the floors in schools.

The Digital Design Divide

The Digital Design Divide is between and within those systems that provide every educator the time and support they need to build their capacities to design learning experiences with digital tools, and those that do not.

While the digital use and access divides are well documented by decades of scholarship, we present the digital design divide as a new consideration of the intersection of school culture, professional learning, and edtech. The design divide is between and within those systems that provide every educator the time and support they need to build their capacity with digital tools and those that do not. While socio-economic status has historically been a predictor of where schools and school systems may fall on either side of the use and access divides, the same is not true of design. Absent vision and sustained support, effective learning design using edtech can vary between neighboring classrooms within a school, schools within a district, and districts within a state.[74,75,76] Considering the instructional core defined in the introduction of this report, the design divide can limit equitable, active student use, even when all students can access the necessary technologies and content. Not all teachers have the time, support, and capacities necessary to design instruction that incorporates active technology use.

Closing this divide requires a clear vision, re-imagining systems of support, and bringing teachers to the table as co-designers of their professional learning. The guidance, recommendations, and examples that follow lay out a path to supporting teachers inundated by increasing demands on their time and unclear expectations as to how they utilize technology most effectively.

In systems where the average teacher can access more than 2,000 digital tools in a given moment, training on a tool's basic functionality is insufficient. Closing the design divide moves teachers beyond the formulaic use of digital tools and allows them to actively design learning experiences for all students within a complex ecosystem of resources.

Recommendations for Closing the Design Divide

1) Develop a "Portrait of an Educator" outlining the cognitive, personal, and interpersonal competencies educators should have to design

---

[74] Senge, P. M., Hamilton, H., & Kania, J. (2015). The dawn of system leadership. Stanford Social Innovation Review. Retrieved from http://helpinghumansystems.com/wp-content/uploads/2014/01/The_Dawn_of_System_Leadership.pdf AND Dexter, S., Richardson, J. W., & Nash, J. B. (2016). Leadership for technology use, integration, and innovation. In M. D. Young & G. M. Crow (Eds.), Handbook of Research on the Education of School Leaders (2nd ed.). New York: Routledge.

[75] Cuban, L. (2018). The flight of a butterfly or the path of a bullet?: Using technology to transform teaching and learning. Cambridge, MA: Harvard Education Press.

[76] McLendon, M. K., Cohen-Vogel, L., & Wachen, J. (2015). Understanding education policy making and policy change in the American states. In B. S. Cooper, J. G. Cibulka, & Fusarelli (Eds.), Handbook of Education Politics and Policy (2nd ed., pp. 1–34). New York: Routledge. AND Cline, K. D. (2018). Defining the implementation problem: Organizational management versus cooperation. Journal of Public Administration Research and Theory, 10(3), 551–572. Retrieved from http://www.jstor.org/stable/3525628.

learning experiences that help students develop the skills and attributes outlined in the profile of a graduate. (States, Districts)

2) Design and sustain systems that support ongoing learning for new and veteran teachers and administrators, providing them with the time and space needed to design learning opportunities aligned with the Universal Design for Learning (UDL) Framework. (States, Districts, Building-Level Administrators)
3) Implement feedback mechanisms that empower educators to become leaders and co-designers of professional learning experiences. (Districts, Building-Level Administrators)
4) Provide educators and administrators with professional learning that supports the development of digital literacy skills so that they can model these skills for students and the broader school community. (States, Districts, Building-Level Administrators)
5) Develop processes for evaluating the potential effectiveness of digital tools before purchase, including the use of research and evidence. (State, District, Building-Level Administrators)
6) Foster an inclusive technology ecosystem that solicits input from diverse stakeholders to collaborate on decision-making for technology purchases, learning space design, and curriculum planning. (States, Districts, Building-Level Administrators)
7) Support and facilitate a systemic culture that builds trust and empowers educators to enhance and grow their professional practice to meet the needs of each student. (States, Districts, Building-Level Administrators)
8) Regularly solicit educator feedback and evaluate professional learning efforts to ensure alignment with the Portrait of an Educator. (District, Building-Level Administrators)

Closing the Digital Design Divide

Modeling Student Learning Environments Building Educator Capacity

Recognizing that teacher professional learning environments and opportunities should mirror the learning environments desired for their students, education leaders at Arizona's Mesa Public Schools are committed to changing their approach to professional learning. Having identified synergies between professional learning opportunities and the practices they wanted to see in the classroom environment, the district intentionally began weaving the attitudes and skills in their portrait of a graduate into the professional learning experiences for educators.

Modeling desired classroom practices through professional learning experiences is especially important because changing teaching practices takes time. District leaders realized they needed to do things differently to create the environments they wanted in classrooms. They learned that adults who have gone through an educational system with high levels of accountability don't know they can personalize their learning experiences. They required explicit permission along the way.

Mesa provides educators with voice and choice in professional learning by developing badged specializations, allowing teachers to choose how they learn and demonstrate their learning. Developed with Teacher and School Leader Incentive Program grant funding, educators can earn badges by taking Arizona State University classes or designing their learning path to acquire and demonstrate the knowledge and skills required to earn the badge. Specializations are available in Blended and Online Learning and Deeper and Personalized Learning, with additional specializations under development.

In alignment with UDL principles, professional learning experiences are co-constructed with educators and administrators to better meet their needs. Because helping students understand who they are as learners and what does and doesn't work for them is a component of UDL, the school system takes the same approach with their adult learners. Building educator capacity to personalize learning both in the classroom and as facilitators of professional learning is a key component of Mesa's approach.

The district's belief in and commitment to their students drives their commitment to the principles of UDL in professional learning. By doing so, they are working to ensure that all students have opportunities to learn.

Begin with the End Goal in Mind: Design Portrait of an Educator

The previous section discussed the value of developing a Portrait of a Learner/Graduate to define a clear vision of cognitive, personal, and interpersonal competencies students should have when they transition between grade levels and at graduation. As Mesa Public Schools realized, for students to develop the skills and competencies outlined in their Portrait of a Learner/Graduate, they require educators who embody and exhibit these competencies. Developing a Portrait of an Educator, aligned to the Portrait of a Learner/Graduate, connects educator habits and capacities with expected student learning. Setting a clear vision for educators aligns hiring practices, professional learning opportunities, and educator evaluations with these competencies. Moreover, such educator profiles can set clear expectations for educator needs and abilities regarding edtech. From there, state and district leaders can backward design professional learning systems to ensure all educators have the time, space, and capacity necessary to develop key learning design abilities.

Aligning Educator Evaluation Systems with a Portrait of an Educator

New Hampshire's School Administrative Unit 16 (SAU-16) comprises seven smaller school districts and eight school boards around Exeter, NH. In 2020, SAU-16 brought in teachers, paraeducators, principals, and other stakeholders to begin imagining a companion Portrait of an Educator.

SAU-16 leaders recognized that without the right evaluative tools and support, the Portrait of an Educator would be just another piece of paper, so they decided to move to an asset-based evaluation system. Now, teachers develop their own growth goals—a knowledge goal focusing on pedagogy and a skill or mindset goal based on where they want to grow professionally.

Once a year, an assigned administrator observes educators, and twice per year, they can choose among peers, students, community members, and others to conduct observations. SAU-16 trained administrators in appreciative inquiry and framing their feedback through a positive lens. Teachers were asked, "How can this feedback help you grow?" and then were challenged to create their growth plan. Educators complete growth reflection sheets during the year and submit artifacts to document their progress.

Teachers indicate they appreciate the collaborative nature of the process and that observing, sharing, and having rich conversations improves their practice and sense of connectedness. They also understand the relevance of the growth process to their teaching. Teachers report that having a choice in naming their goals, choosing their collaborators, and creating their vehicles for growth is empowering and helps them tailor their professional development to their needs.

Developing a Portrait of an Educator in Rural Wyoming

Sheridan County School District 3 (SCSD3) in Clearmont, Wyoming, is a rural K-12 district with 96 students. To help the district develop a Portrait of an Educator, they hosted facilitators from the University of Wyoming (UW), who asked teachers a series of questions, including:

1) What do students need to be able to do when they graduate?
2) What do teachers need to be able to know and do to help students develop these skills in the classroom?

After collecting data, teachers were grouped to categorize responses to the questions and to paint a portrait of an educator at SCSD3. Teacher responses focused heavily on tailoring their approach to curriculum to meet individual student needs while providing them with opportunities to grow. They also emphasized the importance of creating trusting, safe, positive relationships with students, maintaining clear communication, and improving their professional skills.

SCSD3 teachers identified the following goals and abilities for their Portrait of an Educator:

- Model and cultivate learner-centered mindsets
- Design and implement learner-centered assessments
- Build learner-centered relationships and cultures
- Design and implement learner-centered instruction
- Sustain and cultivate wellness
- Collaborate, communicate, and create in a learner-centered system

- Champion learner-centered systems and communities

By actively involving teachers in the process of developing their Portrait of an Educator, SCSD3 and the UW facilitators helped ensure buy-in by giving teachers a voice.

In addition to the Portrait of an Educator, school systems may also consider creating a Portrait of an Administrator, outlining the skills and competencies needed by district-level leaders. Principals significantly impact school culture at the building level and create the conditions necessary to support the Portrait of an Educator. As Todd Whitaker has said, "When the principal sneezes, the whole school catches a cold. This is neither good nor bad; it is just the truth. Our impact is significant; our focus becomes the school's focus."[77] Just as developing a Portrait of an Educator can help support the learning environments that help students acquire the skills and dispositions of a Portrait of a Graduate, creating a Portrait of an Administrator can set the stage for a school culture that supports the success of both educators and students in using technology to support learning for all.

Considerations in Closing the Design Divide

Closing the design divide requires context-specific solutions. Still, some universal considerations remain the same across geographies. Once systems have set a vision by developing a profile of an educator, the following considerations can help clear the path to transformation.

Capture Current Culture

Understanding the current culture of an education organization is the first step to closing the design divide, whether a state education department, a school district, or an individual school. Capturing a clear understanding helps reveal the disparities between the current system state and where it wants to be. A needs assessment tool, such as the Title IV-A Needs Assessment from the Office of Safe and Supportive Schools, or asset mapping tools like those developed by Digital Promise, the Tarrant Institute for Innovative Education in Vermont, or You for Youth, may be helpful. In addition, organizations can

[77] Whitaker, T. (2020). *What Great Principals Do Differently: Twenty Things that Matter Most* (3rd ed.). Routledge.

gather climate and culture survey data using tools like the Project Tomorrow Speak Up Survey or other survey instruments.

Calculate Cost

Historically, investments in building professional capacity around the use and design of lessons with edtech have paled compared to the billions of dollars invested annually on the technology itself.[78] Costs should include monetary expenses associated with hardware, software, and also professional learning and potential modifications to educator schedules. For example, suppose education leaders expect a digital tool to be used heavily across classrooms. In that case, systems should budget for the time and money necessary for educators to develop proficiency commensurate with that expectation.

Cultivate Capacity

Using a tool and designing learning experiences that include using that tool are different skill sets. States, school systems, and schools working to close the design divide must cultivate educators' capacities with new tools while increasing their proficiency with key learning frameworks. Neither a template nor a curriculum, UDL provides a common research-based structure and language to help all teachers design learning experiences to impact all learners.

Curate Effective Products

With vision, funding, and support in place, systems closing the design divide include structures for collaborative review of impact, barriers, and measured effectiveness. Effective systems intentionally build time and support for educators to share, analyze, and improve their professional

---

[78] (2021, March 1). OVERVIEW: U.S. K-12 Public Education Technology Spending. Edtech Evidence Exchange. Retrieved October 25, 2023, from https://edtechevidence.org/wp-content/uploads/2021/07/FINAL-K12-EdTech-Funding-Analysis_v.1.pdf.

practices.[79,80,81,82,83] These systems deepen educator capacity to design learning experiences using multiple technological tools.

Build evidence

With finite time and funding, it is incumbent upon education systems to verify the effectiveness of technological tools before purchase and adoption, and during classroom implementation. Inquiring about digital resources' evidence base can serve as a first line of defense for worthwhile use of educator and student time. See page 49 for a description of the ESSA evidence tiers.

Deeper Dive: Capture Current Culture

School culture impacts edtech use and student achievement. Research that reviewed two decades of evidence (including six quantitative, longitudinal studies involving 22,000 principals) found that principals have significant positive effects on student learning and that effective principals orient their practice toward instructionally focused interactions with teachers, building a productive school climate, facilitating collaboration and professional learning communities, and strategic personnel and resource management processes.[84]

Analysis of nearly a decade of data from schools in an urban North Carolina district, one of the largest in the country, showed that teachers achieved more significant increases in their student's standardized test scores in schools with supportive professional environments—especially those with

79 Darling-Hammond, L., Hyler, M. E., Gardner, M. (2017). Effective Teacher Professional Development. Palo Alto, CA: Learning Policy Institute.

80 Killion, J. (2023). Establishing time for professional learning (2nd ed.). Learning Forward.

81 Mourshed, M., Chijioke, C., & Barber, M. (2010). How the world's most improved school systems keep getting better. McKinsey & Company. Retrieved from McKinsey: https://www.mckinsey.com/industries/education/our-insights/how-the-worlds-most-improved-school-systems-keep-getting-better.

82 Walton, N. (2017). Worldwide educating for the future index. (M. Gold, Ed.) The Economist Intelligence Unit (pp. 1–40). Retrieved from The Economist website: http://educatingforthefuture.economist.com.

83 World Economic Forum. (2015). New vision for education. Retrieved from The World Economic Forum web site: http://www3. weforum.org/docs/WEFUSA_NewVisionforEducation_Report2015.pdf.

84 Grissom, J.A., Egalite, A.J., Lindsay, C.A. (2021, February). How principals affect students and schools: A systematic synthesis of two decades of research. The Wallace Foundation. www.wallacefoundation.org/principalsynthesis.

more peer collaboration and positive school culture—than did teachers in schools with less supportive professional environments.[85]

Other research analyzing two years of data on more than 9,000 teachers in 336 Miami-Dade County public schools showed that schools with better-quality collaboration—meaning teachers reported that their cooperation in instructional teams was both "extensive" and "helpful"— had higher student achievement gains in math and reading. These results held, even controlling for other characteristics of those schools' students and teachers, meaning the researchers could be more confident that the difference was related to the quality of collaboration at the school and not to differences in the students and teachers themselves.[86]

Changing school culture begins with senior leadership. First, it requires first understanding what educators need to help all students reach the goals in the Profile of a Learner/Graduate and creating policies and systems that help educators do so. Leaders must model the dispositions and practices they wish to see in classrooms, including using technology to support teacher voice and choice.

Reconsidering Educator Learning Time to Improve Student Learning Time

When Brigantine Public Schools in New Jersey considered how they might improve the active use of technology for all students, they realized they needed to attend to educator needs first. They needed to reconsider teacher schedules to provide them with what was needed to design digital learning experiences that meet the needs of all students. They also realized this meant overcoming logistical and cultural challenges, including scheduling, budgeting, mindsets, and tradition. After a thoughtful design process that included school and district administrators, educators, and instructional coaches, the district arrived at a solution. They developed a new schedule that includes an additional planning period for common teacher planning time, articulation meetings, and sharing/teaching new approaches to technology use for staff and students. The new systemic

[85] Ibid.

[86] Ronfelt, M., Farmer, S. O., McQueen, K., & Grissom, J. A. (2015). Teacher Collaboration in Instructional Teams and Student Achievement. *American Educational Research Journal*, 52(3), 475–514. https://doi.org/10.3102/0002831215585562.

approach closes the design divide in ways that translate to greater active use for all students.

To aid in understanding current strengths and needs, systems can use tools such as:

- Needs assessments such as the Title IV-A Needs Assessment from the Office of Safe and Supportive Schools.
- Asset mapping tools like those developed by Digital Promise, the Tarrant Institute for Innovative Education in Vermont, or You for Youth, may be helpful.
- Or surveys like the Project Tomorrow Speak Up Survey.

Shifting expectations of classroom technology use begins with changing how adults in the system are using technology. Understanding strengths and needs can be an important first step in this shift. These processes can also help to uncover biases in practice such as those documented in Matthew Rafalow's Digital Divisions.[87] Once uncovered, schools and districts can begin the work of ensuring high expectations of use for all students that includes mindfulness of unintended bias.

Deeper Dive: Calculate Costs

As discussed above, the costs of foundational changes in teaching practices go beyond the monetary expenses traditionally associated with technology initiatives: hardware, software, and professional learning. Providing educators with the time and support to become learning designers requires education leaders to reconsider time and monetary budgets for professional learning as well.

Teachers in the United States spend far more time engaged in active instruction than in other high-performing countries. Based on self-reported data, teachers in the United States spend 27 hours teaching out of 45 hours of work per week. Compare this with teachers in Singapore, who teach only 17 hours per week, or teachers in Finland, who teach 21 hours per week. Schools

---

[87] Rafalow, M. H. (2021). Digital divisions: How schools create inequality in the tech era. University of Chicago Press.

in these countries prioritize time for planning and collaboration, recognizing that developing and executing lessons takes time and preparation.[88]

Cost Calculation Resources

The following resources developed by or in partnership with the U.S. Department of Education's Institute of Education Sciences (IES) may be helpful for calculating costs:

- The IES Cost Analysis Starter Kit, version 1.0
- Cost Analysis in Practice (CAP) Project
- American Institutes of Research›s Standards for the Economic Evaluation of Education and Social Programs
- Estimator tool
- The Critical Importance of Costs for Education Decisions

Because school system resources are often tightly constrained, it can be difficult for education leaders to think creatively about scheduling. However, school systems are effectively reimagining the school day within existing budget constraints. Even small changes to existing schedules can help make a difference. Leaders considering how they might reconsider time budgets within school days can find examples from the Center for American Progress's Reimagining the School Day and the Wallace Foundation's Reimagining the School Day: More Time for Learning.

State Program Facilitates the Sharing of Instructional Technology Coaches Among Districts

The Learning Technology Center (LTC), a program of the Illinois State Board of Education, provides edtech services, support, and professional learning for K-12 Illinois schools, educators, and technology leaders.

Recognizing that many small and medium-sized school systems could not afford a full-time instructional technology coach, the LTC developed the LTC Instructional Technology Coach Program. The program leverages an innovative cost-sharing model, allowing multiple districts in a similar

[88] https://www.americanprogress.org/article/reimagining-the-school-day/.

geographic area of the state to "share" the costs of an instructional technology coach for a predetermined number of days throughout the school year. This program allows them to access the benefits of coaching without adding staff or committing to a full-time employee.

In the spring of each year, the LTC works with districts to identify their instructional coaching needs, determine the number of days they would like support from a coach (from 10-170 days), and pairs up neighboring districts. Together, the LTC and the districts interview and select a coach with pedagogical and technological experience. Even though the coach is an LTC employee, it is essential that the districts feel the coach is a fit for their culture. Districts then complete an onboarding document that helps situate the coach regarding the district's goals, daily procedures, and technology. Doing so allows the coach to enter classrooms on day one to build relationships and support educators.

The instructional technology coaches support teachers through coaching cycles. Teachers identify an area of need, and coaches work 1:1 with teachers to set goals, create an action plan, and support them through that action plan. The coaching cycle includes time for reflection, where coaches sit down with teachers, identify the impact that they have had on student learning, and plan how to carry that through in future lessons.

In 2022-2023, the LTC had eight coaches working across 75 school buildings in Illinois. In those buildings, more than 2,000 teachers are impacting more than 26,000 students. The instructional technology coaching program helps even the smallest school systems make the most of their technology investments while providing their teachers with personalized, job-embedded professional development.

Leveraging Online Learning to Support Teacher Competency Development

Like many districts, Cajon Valley Union School District in California has faced challenges providing differentiated professional learning for teachers and staff. With limited opportunities for in-person learning, exacerbated by the increasing difficulty of finding substitutes, they decided to leverage online learning to support district employees. Built on the Alludo platform, they developed Cajon 365, a professional learning platform providing educators with anytime, anywhere access.

Through Cajon 365, which includes customized learning content, employees can demonstrate competencies and earn digital badges, points, and rewards. Educators can choose the areas to focus on to meet their classroom, personal, and professional goals. With Cajon 365, district leadership can add new content any time based on current objectives and goals. The platform is also used for onboarding new employees, ensuring they don't miss out on important content.

Cajon 365 provides visibility on learning progress across schools and the district and is used as a metric in the Cajon Valley Local Control and Accountability Plan. In two years, Cajon 365 supported 1548 learners with more than 10,000 hours of professional learning.

Where monetary investment is needed, several federal funding sources can support educator professional learning. The 2023 Dear Colleague Letter: Leveraging Federal Funds for Teaching and Learning With Technology from the U.S. Department of Education provides some examples of how funds under Titles I through IV of the Elementary and Secondary Education Act of 1965, as amended (ESEA) and the Individuals with Disabilities Education Act (IDEA) may support the use of technology to improve instruction and student outcomes. Importantly, informal supports for students with disabilities are not a substitute or replacement for IDEA compliance and reasonable accommodations.

- *Title II, Part A* authorizes programs to improve the quality and effectiveness of teachers and school leaders through professional development and other allowable activities at the state and district levels. Allowable uses of Title II, Part A funds focuses on job-embedded, evidence-based, and classroom-oriented activities. Title II, Part A funds may be used to provide professional development funds to teachers and school leaders, and in some circumstances paraprofessionals such as teaching assistants, instructional support personnel, interventionists, and other staff.
- *Title I, Part A* provides funds that may be used, in a school implementing a Title I schoolwide program, for professional development for teachers and specialized instructional support personnel if that use is supported by the school's comprehensive needs assessment and schoolwide plan.
- *Title I, Part C* provides for professional development programs, including mentoring, for teachers and other program personnel, specifically in support of migratory children.

- *Title I, Part D* provides appropriate training for teachers and other instructional and administrative personnel to meet the educational needs of neglected, delinquent, and at-risk children and youth.
- *Title III* provides funds that may be used to supplement professional development designed to increase the English language proficiency of ELs and immigrant students, for example by supplementing professional development around providing language instruction educational programs and helping ELs meet academic content standards.
- *Title IV, Part A* provides funds that may be used for professional development for the effective use of data and technology, academic assessments, career and technical education, and family and community engagement.
- *Title IV, Part B* (Nita M. Lowey 21st Century Community Learning Centers (21st CCLCs)) supports the creation of community learning centers that provide academic enrichment opportunities during non-school hours for children. 21st CCLCs may use some funds to provide professional development for their staff. States may also reserve some of their 21st CCLC funds to provide training to applicants and recipients of these funds.
- *Title V, Part B* provides supplemental funds for rural LEAs that are either small or serve high numbers of low-income students. The funds may generally be used for supplemental activities that are allowable under Title I-A, Title II-A, Title III, and Title IV-A and -B.
- *Title VII, Impact Aid* is a highly flexible funding stream for eligible school districts serving federally connected children. Districts may use Impact Aid funds at their discretion, including professional learning.
- The *McKinney-Vento Homeless Act* provides funding for professional learning to facilitate and enhance the identification, enrollment, attendance, and success in school of homeless children and youth.
- *Career and Technical Education (Carl D. Perkins Act)* provides funds to Eligible Recipients (generally, LEAs, area CTE schools, or postsecondary non-baccalaureate granting institutions) for the purposes of career and technical education. Professional development programs related to career and technical education for teachers, counselors, and administrators is an allowable use of funds.

- *The Individuals with Disabilities Education Act (IDEA)* provides for professional learning and collaborative planning related directly to the provision of special education. For example, LEAs may use up to 15 percent of their IDEA Part B funds to develop and implement coordinated early intervening services for students who are not currently identified as needing special education or related services, but who need additional academic and behavioral support to succeed in a general education environment, which can include relevant professional development for teachers and other school staff.

In addition to federal funds, school system leaders should consult their state education departments regarding state-specific funding for educator professional learning. Private foundations and other non-governmental organizations also provide grant funds to support educator professional learning.

Considering UDL in Procurement

It can be helpful to evaluate edtech tools against the UDL framework as part of the procurement process. Some practical steps states and school systems can take include:

1) Becoming familiar with *the three UDL principles and their guidelines*. Understanding how each principle aims to address the needs of diverse learners.
2) Reviewing the evaluation framework for the *CAST UDL Product Certification*. Although geared towards edtech products seeking UDL product certification, it is a helpful resource for states and school systems evaluating edtech tools, even if they are not certified.
3) Exploring the features and functionalities of the edtech tool. Does it prioritize student access and engagement? Does it consider learners' interests and motivations? Does it ensure learners have multiple ways to gain comprehension, and does it provide multiple ways to share their knowledge and ideas? Is the tool user-friendly and easy to navigate?
4) Ensuring the tool includes accessibility features like text-to-speech, closed captioning, and keyboard navigation. The *Quick*

Reference Guide for Web Content Accessibility Guidelines (WCAG) can be helpful.
5) Considering if assessments within the tool accommodate diverse ways of demonstrating knowledge and understanding.

Deeper Dive: Cultivate Capacity

High-quality professional learning opportunities can positively impact student achievement, especially when educators have the time to collaborate and design impactful learning experiences.[89,90] However, not all professional learning opportunities are of equal caliber. Fortunately, research has identified the characteristics of effective professional learning structures.

The definition of *professional development*[91] included in the *Every Student Succeeds Act* includes the critical characteristics that should be present in any high-quality professional learning opportunity: sustained (not stand-alone, one-day, or short-term workshops), intensive, collaborative, job-embedded, data-driven, and classroom-focused.[92] A Learning Policy Institute review of 35 methodologically rigorous studies demonstrated a positive link between teacher professional development, teaching practices, and student outcomes. This study identified critical features of effective models, finding that high-quality professional learning:

- *Is content focused:* focuses on teaching strategies associated with specific curriculum content that supports teacher learning within teachers' classroom contexts. This element includes an intentional focus on discipline-specific curriculum development and pedagogies in areas such as mathematics, science, and literacy.

---

89 Learning Forward. (2019). The path to instructional excellence and equitable outcomes. Oxford, OH: Author.

90 Garrett, R., Zhang, Q., Citkowicz, M., & Burr, L. (2021). How Learning Forward's Professional Learning Standards are associated with teacher instruction and student achievement: A meta-analysis. Washington, DC: Center on Great Teachers and Leaders at the American Institutes for Research.

91 Learning Forward (n.d.). *Definition of Professional Development*. Powered By Title II. Retrieved September 6, 2023, from https://poweredbytitleii.com/resources/definition-of-professional-development/.

92 Page 296, ESSA, Section 8002.

- *Incorporates active learning:* Active learning engages teachers directly in designing and trying out teaching strategies, providing them an opportunity to engage in the same style of learning they are designing for their students, using authentic artifacts, interactive activities, and other strategies to provide deeply embedded, highly contextualized professional learning. This approach moves away from traditional learning models and lecture-based environments that have no direct connection to teachers' classrooms and students.
- *Supports collaboration:* High-quality professional learning creates space for teachers to share ideas and collaborate in their learning, often in job-embedded contexts. By working collaboratively, teachers can create communities that positively change the culture and instruction of their entire grade level, department, school, or district.
- *Uses models of effective practice:* Curricular and instruction modeling provide teachers with a clear vision of what best practices look like. Teachers may view models that include lesson plans, unit plans, sample student work, observations of peer teachers, and video or written cases of teaching.
- *Provides coaching and expert support:* Coaching and expert support involve sharing content and evidence-based expertise focused directly on individual teachers' needs.
- *Offers feedback and reflection:* High-quality professional learning frequently provides built-in time for teachers to think about, receive input on, and make changes to their practice by facilitating reflection and soliciting feedback. Feedback and reflection help teachers thoughtfully move toward the expert visions of practice.
- *Is of sustained duration:* Effective professional learning provides teachers with adequate time to learn, practice, implement, and reflect upon new strategies that facilitate changes in their practice.[93]

Several organizations have developed standards for educators and administrators and/or professional learning, which school system leaders may find helpful. The Learning Forward Standards for Professional Learning, the ISTE Standards, and the National Board for Professional Teaching Standards, along with the UDL Guidelines, can help guide the development of high-quality professional learning experiences for educators and administrators.

---

[93] Darling-Hammond, L., Hyler, M. E., Gardner, M. (2017). Effective Teacher Professional Development. Palo Alto, CA: Learning Policy Institute.

Designing Wrap-Around Teacher Support as a New Normal

When Denver Public Schools (DPS) in Colorado considered the patterns of teacher engagement in professional learning opportunities across the district, they noticed a familiar problem. Teachers attended one-off trainings on thoughtfully integrating technology within their practice and then moved on. The district team, including the Senior Manager of EdTech and Library Services, EdTech Manager, and Digital Coaches, knew that research has shown such one-off efforts have limited impact on meaningful change in practice. District leaders wanted to find a way to incorporate full professional coaching cycles into existing professional development sessions.

DPS shifted expectations. Teachers signing up for one-off sessions were also required to participate in professional coaching cycles related to the topics of each session.

The shift resulted in initial attrition in registration numbers and required team attention to navigate the logistics of such a change in practice. The edtech team worked with the DPS professional learning department and the local union to resolve these logistical considerations. The team reports a shift in the effectiveness of their professional learning offerings, noting teachers are more likely to stay in touch or reach out when they have questions due to the coaching. Evidence is more than anecdotal. The team has seen an increase in teacher registration year over year. Additionally, they have seen increased completion rates from registration to end-of-year completion as educators settle into this new normal of ongoing support.

UDL School Implementation and Certification Criteria

The *UDL School Implementation and Certification Criteria* provides school teams with a blueprint for designing and improving school wide UDL implementation. Four domains are central to building a school's UDL ecosystem: School Culture and Environment; Teaching and Learning; Leadership and Management; and Professional Learning. Each domain has four elements describing the essential characteristics of a school implementing UDL.

The criteria were developed using insights from implementation, improvement, and learning science research and informed by ongoing input and feedback from experienced UDL leaders throughout the field of education. While the full certification process is not yet available, the UDL-SICC criteria and related tools— including a *school self-assessment*—support school system UDL implementation efforts.

The Learner Variability Navigator

Learner variability recognizes that each student has a unique constellation of interconnected strengths and challenges. The *Learner Variability Navigator (LVN)* is a free and open-source web-based tool designed to make the science of learning more accessible. By highlighting connections among factors critical to student success and instructional strategies, the LVN helps educators understand why certain strategies may impact students differently, thus empowering them to support the full diversity of learners. The LVN includes six learner models from grades pre-K through 12 in literacy and math, and an adult learner model—all based on a whole learner framework curated by researchers and practitioners.

Building Educator Capacity for Data Visualization and Use Across Nebraska

In Spring 2023, the Nebraska Department of Education (NDE) kicked off its third cohort within its Data Visualization and Use Education Innovation Network. Educators selected to join the network participate in webinars to increase their capacity to design data visualizations to communicate student learning and engage in continuous improvement. The webinars give teachers experience with topics including:

- Why Use Data?
- Data Analysis Basics & Common Tools
- Data Visualization: Charts, Maps that Make Sense
- Storytelling with Data, Diving Deeper into Data
- Diving Deeper into Data
- Data for Improving Outcomes: Turn Data into Action

Sponsored by the NDE Data Management and Navigation Team, data visualization is one of a handful of networks created by NDE to support its "Commitment to Equity of 'ensuring equity of access by supporting quality instructional materials.'"[94] The cohort model ensures a standard level of competency for participating educators and connects participants from across Nebraska's 19 educational services units and 247 school districts. Members meet monthly for discussion and knowledge sharing.

Procurement Best Practices

Rather than relying on retrofitting for accessibility as the need arises, the district team at *Francis Howell School District* in O'Fallon, Missouri, built accessibility into technology planning and procurement.[95] The district also realized they would not find one device that fit the accessibility needs of all students. When special education case managers need a specific device to meet student needs, they know the district technology department has a variety of devices on hand to meet those varying needs. The district has also realized that what is necessary for some can benefit all. Originally, students needing text-to-speech features activated on their devices had to request that the district activate the services. Now, the feature is under the students' control.

Finally, Francis Howell is working to systematize accessibility as a component of technology procurement. When considering new technology purchases, the district team includes the district assistive technology and Americans with Disabilities Act compliance coordinator to ensure that future technology won't mean students waiting to activate or install the needed features.

Deeper Dive: Curate Effective Products

While having a vision or north star for using technology in instruction is critical, carefully considering a given edtech product's prior evidence of effectiveness before purchase and then evaluating the extent to which it is achieving important student learning and other objectives during and post-implementation is equally important. In the digital use divide section, we

94 https://www.education.ne.gov/pmo/the-innovation-grant/education-innovation-networks-ein/#dvu.

95 CAST (n.d.). Procurement as a Collaborative Process. National Center on Accessible Educational Materials. Retrieved September 6, 2023, from https://aem.cast.org/get-started/resources/accessible-learning-experience/s02-ep04-procurementcollaborative-process.

discussed how education leaders can evaluate tools associated with the more open-ended practices of active technology use. The classroom success of these kinds of tools is likely influenced by how they are deployed and utilized, as well as the features of the tools themselves. In this section, we'll discuss the role of research in edtech evaluation, which often aligns with more closed-ended, subject-specific digital tools such as digital textbooks and curricula, math and language learning apps, or adaptive learning/assessment platforms.[96]

Despite the significant financial investments made in education technologies, school districts often make purchasing decisions without considering available evidence regarding the effectiveness of technologies. According to a 2023 LearnPlatform report, only 26 of the 100 most accessed edtech products in K-12 classrooms during the first half of the 2022-23 school year had published research aligned to one of the four tiers of evidence in ESSA. Research has found that nine in 10 educators admit they rely on general web searches to gather information about edtech,[97] while 59 percent base their procurement decisions on recommendations from peers.[98] A 2017 survey found that 90 percent of teachers and education leaders said they didn't insist on research being in place before adopting or buying a product.[99] Even when research is available, it may not take into account contextual differences across districts.[100]

The Elementary and Secondary Education Act (ESEA)[101] encourages state and local educational agencies to prioritize evidence-based practice,

---

[96] The Edtech Genome Project Report. The Edtech Evidence Exchange. Retrieved October 24, 2023, from https://edtechevidence.org/ AboutUs/TheGenomeProject/.

[97] Krueger, N. (2019, December 25). *The Five Pillars of Edtech Procurement.* ISTE. Retrieved August 16, 2023, from https://www.iste. org/explore/empowered-learner/five-pillars-edtech-procurement.

[98] Morrison, J. R., Ph.D., Ross, S. M., Ph.D. DD, Corcoran, R. P., Ph.D., & Reid, A., Ph.D. (2014, September 22). *Fostering Market Efficiency in K-12 Ed-tech Procurement.* Digital Promise. Retrieved August 16, 2023, from https://digitalpromise.org/wp-content/uploads/2016/02/DP_ImprovingEdTechPurchasing_FullReport.pdf.

[99] Abamu, J. (2017, July 17). *How Much Do Educators Care About Edtech Efficacy? Less Than You Might Think.* Edsurge. Retrieved August 16, 2023, from https://www.edsurge.com/news/2017-07-17-how-much-do-educators-care-about-edtech-efficacy-less-than-you-might-think.

[100] https://www.iste.org/explore/empowered-learner/five-pillars-edtech-procurement.

[101] United States. (1965). Elementary and secondary education act of 1965: H. R. 2362, 89th Cong., 1st sess., Public law 89-10. Reports, bills, debate and act. [Washington]: [U.S. Govt. Print. Off.].

which can include the use of edtech in schools.[102] The U.S Department of Education has defined "evidence-based" and other terms for use in ESEA programs and other programs in its regulations (see 34 CFR 77.1). Under ESEA, there are four tiers of evidence, with the first tier providing the strongest form of evidence: (1) Strong Evidence, (2) Moderate Evidence, (3) Promising Evidence, and (4) Demonstrates a Rationale.[103] Refer to the graphic below for definitions of the four tiers of evidence.

UNDERSTANDING THE ESSA TIERS OF EVIDENCE

	TIER 1 Strong Evidence	TIER 2 Moderate Evidence	TIER 3 Promising Evidence	TIER 4 Demonstrates a Rationale
Study Design	Well-designed and implemented experimental study, meets WWC standards without reservations	Well-designed and implemented quasi-experimental study, meets WWC standards with reservations	Well-designed and implemented correlational study, statistically controls for selection bias[a]	Well-defined logic model based on rigorous research
Results of the Study	Statistically significant positive effect on a relevant outcome	Statistically significant positive effect on a relevant outcome	Statistically significant positive effect on a relevant outcome	An effort to study the effects of the intervention is planned or currently under way
Findings From Related Studies	No strong negative findings from experimental or quasi-experimental studies	No strong negative findings from experimental or quasi-experimental studies	No strong negative findings from experimental or quasi-experimental studies	N/A
Sample Size & Setting	At least 350 participants, conducted in more than one district or school	At least 350 participants, conducted in more than one district or school	N/A	N/A
Match	Similar population and setting to your setting	Similar population or setting to your setting	N/A	N/A

a. Findings from experimental and quasi-experimental studies that either (a) meet the first three criteria for Tiers 1 and 2 but not the sample size, setting, or match requirements, or (b) do not meet WWC standards but statistically control for selection bias between the treatment and comparison groups are also eligible to meet Tier 3 Promising Evidence.

Deeper Dive: Build Evidence

High-quality evidence about a given edtech product's effectiveness isn't always available to support adoption decisions—and educators don't always receive the training and support they need to build evidence of a product's

102 U.S. Department of Education, Office of Educational Technology, Using Evidence to Support EdTech Adoption in Schools, Washington, D.C., 2023. Retrieved November 3, 2023, from https://tech.ed.gov/evidence/.

103 United States. (1965). Elementary and secondary education act of 1965: H. R. 2362, 89th Cong., 1st sess., Public law 89-10. Reports, bills, debate and act. [Washington]: [U.S. Govt. Print. Off.].

effectiveness on their own.[104] As a result, there is a substantial need for accessible professional learning resources specifically designed to support schools in evidence-building activities. To help close this gap, the U.S. Department of Education developed the EdTech Evidence Toolkit, which includes four Evidence One-Pagers and a Blog Series. The toolkit offers educational leaders support in using evidence to inform edtech adoption decisions in schools by providing:

- Introductory evidence-building activities for four tiers of evidence, as outlined in ESEA
- Example case studies for using evidence-building activities to inform edtech adoption
- Suggestions for collaborative activities to encourage the use of evidence in schools

The purpose of the EdTech Evidence Toolkit is threefold:

1) To offer an introductory resource for understanding the four tiers of evidence, as outlined by ESEA, concerning edtech adoption,
2) To present a practical school district case study across the four tiers of evidence that uses evidence-building activities incrementally to inform edtech adoption, and
3) To serve as a resource to inform professional development efforts supporting use of evidence in schools.

State education departments can and should help empower districts and schools to expand current uses of evidence (for example, diagnostic data to inform individual student intervention) by providing professional learning and guidance to build district-level capacity. When educational leaders help school systems adopt the scientific method to inform decision-making, school systems can engage in evidence-building activities that support positive

---

[104] U.S. Department of Education (2023, April 11). Every Student Succeeds Act. Office of Educational Technology Blog. Retrieved August 16, 2023, from https://medium.com/@OfficeofEdTech/ng-using-professional-development-to-support-edtech-evidence-building-in-schools-c5d6ddf6cf52. "UNDERSTANDING THE ESSA TIERS OF EVIDENCE" by Institute of Education Sciences is in the Public Domain.

student outcomes. Including schools as participants in evidence-building supports self-advocacy and lessens the gap between research and practice.[105]

Additional resources available to help education stakeholders successfully choose and implement evidence-based project components designed to improve learner outcomes include the following:

1) U.S. Department of Education's *Non-Regulatory Guidance: Using Evidence to Strengthen Education Investments.* This guidance: (1) reviews steps for effective decision-making about evidence use and evidence building; (2) describes in detail the four evidence levels introduced in Section 8101(21)(A) of the ESEA and how they are used by the Department in its discretionary grant programs through EDGAR (34 CFR 77.1); and (3) clarifies how a variety of evidence can be used to inform decision making.
2) The *What Works Clearinghouse* provides *practice guides* and intervention reports *which provide evidence-based recommendations for* educators and research findings for education interventions and practices.
3) The *Regional Educational Laboratory Program (REL)* consists of 10 regional laboratories which collaborate with school districts, state departments of education, and other education stakeholders to help generate and apply evidence with the goal of improving learner outcomes.

Massachusetts State Resources Help Ensure Equitable and Effective Edtech Use

The Massachusetts Department of Elementary & Secondary Education's Office of Educational Technology (OET) promotes the strategic and equitable usage of edtech in the state. The OET recognized that despite significant progress in access to devices and the internet for students, that access was not necessarily translating into equitable learning experiences.

Toward that end, the office published an EdTech Strategic Planning Guide identifying the foundational conditions for a healthy school

[105] U.S. Department of Education (2023, April 11). *Every Student Succeeds Act.* Office of Educational Technology Blog. Retrieved August 16, 2023, from https://medium.com/@OfficeofEdTech/ng-using-professional-development-to-support-edtech-evidence-building-in-schools-c5d6ddf6cf52

technology system. The office then partnered with The Learning Accelerator to produce the more technical Edtech Systems Guide: Equity-Driven Selection, Implementation, and Evaluation to help school system leaders strengthen their edtech processes. The impetus for the Edtech Systems Guide came from edtech leaders asking for support as they struggled to evaluate the effectiveness and impact of tools purchased during the pandemic. Department leaders also saw the opportunity to reinforce the idea that how edtech tools are selected and implemented is integral to their ultimate impact. The EdTech Systems Guide helps edtech leaders work through that process while keeping equity at the forefront. District technology leaders were essential to the development of the guide, ensuring it would be relevant and practical for practitioners. A companion workbook accompanies the guide so district teams can work collaboratively on the recommended action steps. The guide also includes considerations for students who are English language learners; students with individualized education programs; and large and small school systems.

The state has supported leaders to implement its recommendations to bolster the guide's impact. In continued partnership with The Learning Accelerator, OET launched an EdTech Peer Learning Cohort for district teams composed of edtech, instructional leaders, educators, and, sometimes, students. Cohort participants developed a problem of practice related to improving edtech systems, received individualized coaching, and collaborated with other participants in virtual sessions. Examples of issues that cohort teams worked on include incorporating student voice into edtech evaluation and how to increase student information system usage by families of English language learners. These case stories capture the cohort experiences.

Mendon-Upton Includes Student, Teacher Voice in Edtech Procurement

Mendon-Upton Regional School District (MURSD) is a small suburban district in central Massachusetts which provides their teachers access to more than 200 edtech tools. MURSD participated in the Massachusetts Department of Elementary & Secondary Education's OET 2022-2023 EdTech Peer Learning Cohort. During this cohort, MURSD improved edtech evaluations to align with the district's vision and curricular needs.

MURSD incorporated student voice in the edtech evaluation process by appointing a high school student to the technology committee, which determined the criteria for evaluating each edtech tool in the district. The committee also included a teacher, a media center specialist, a technician, and the technology director, who led the committee. They included the student in every conversation and the student and even built a technology inventory database for the district.

The committee also developed a process for teachers interested in piloting edtech tools. Teachers can nominate tools they want to test using the Digital Tool Pilot Proposal Form. The technology team reviews the submitted proposals and scores them on the MURSD Digital Tool Pilot Evaluation Rubric to help ensure the pilot's success. Finally, pilot teachers participate in an annual Digital Tool Evaluation process each school year in May. Educators and students self-report their experience with the tool using the district's evaluation form. The form differentiates questions by role and asks users about impact, usability, engagement, and whether they would recommend the tool. Based on this input, the technology team can renew the pilot and potentially scale the tool, abandon the tool, or consider redesigning the pilot.

By including teacher voices in the selection process, the MURSD technology team hopes to identify the tools supporting student learning and thoughtfully invest in effective solutions.

While the closing of the digital use divide calls on systems to envision and enact equitable active use for all students as a part of the instructional core, the digital design divide calls on schools and districts to leverage resources necessary for all teachers within the core to execute this vision.

Unlike the use and access divides, the design divide cannot be predicted by student socio-economic status because it can exist between teachers in neighboring classrooms teaching students with the same demographics and access to the same technologies. Closing the divide and bringing equity of capacity to these and all other teachers will include mechanisms like professional learning communities, coaching cycles, and feedback systems that provide teachers with the evidence they need to make informed design decisions. It will require insistence on research-supported tools, re-considering schedules, and providing educators with a framework to design effective student learning experiences for all.

For schools to realize the potential of edtech to help transform learning for all students, they must be willing to imagine how they can transform learning for all educators.

Study Indicates Technology Can Support Reduced Juvenile Justice Recidivism

When researchers from Arizona State University and the Oregon Research Institute set out to determine how to reduce recidivism in juvenile justice offenders, they began with two questions:

1. Were youth receiving technology-enabled support services less likely to recidivate than peers who weren't receiving these services?
2. Were any specific components of these supports significantly associated with recidivism reduction? Youth in the treatment group received services such as:

- Technology-enhanced education and cognitive restructuring
- Individualized and intensive educational and vocational programming
- Access to a transition specialist from prerelease to at least 30 days post release
- Intentionally integrated technology practices

Results of the non-randomized comparison study[106] published in 2023 showed "the comparison group had a significant 201 percent greater odds to recidivate two years post-release from the facility." While technology played an integral part in supporting the youth in the treatment group, the study offers a powerful example of the importance of considering each component of the instructional core. Transition specialists served as teachers, technology delivered individualized content, and the youth were called on to be actively involved in their own education. Such studies show the power of what is possible when the design divide narrows in support of all learners.

---

[106] Mathur, S. R., Griller Clark, H., & Gau, J. M. (2023). Technology integration: a promising way to mitigate recidivism of youth in juvenile justice. Preventing School Failure: Alternative Education for Children and Youth, 1-8.

The Digital Access Divide

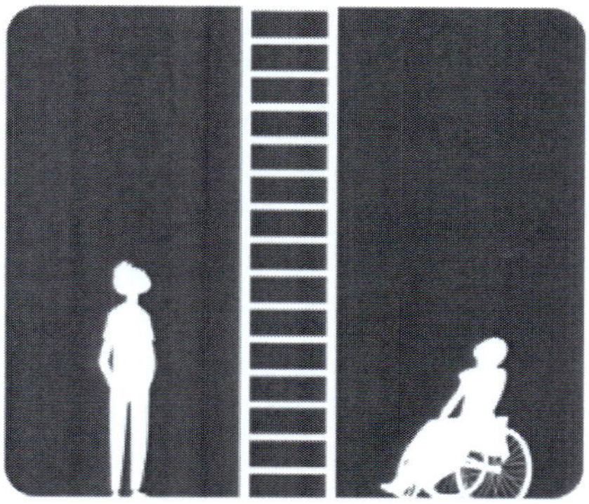

The Digital Access Divide stands between those students and educators who have equitable, sustainable access to connectivity, devices, and digital content and those who do not. This also includes accessibility and digital health, safety, and citizenship.

For all learners to have the deep, complex, active learning experiences described above, states and districts must focus on closing one other key divide - the digital access divide. This divide has historically been defined as providing equitable access to reliable, high-speed connectivity, hardware, and digital resources. Accessibility and digital health, safety, and citizenship are also key to closing the access divide. While school systems have made great strides in closing the digital access divide since the publication of the 2017 NETP, pernicious problems such as geographic barriers and local skill capacity require swift action at all levels to realize the design and use visions laid out above. This section outlines the recommendations and examples of learning environments designed (or re-designed) to close that divide and enable "everywhere all-the-time learning."

Recommendations for Closing the Access Divide

1) Develop a "Portrait of a Learning Environment" to set expectations around habits and abilities no matter what the space. (States, District)
2) Establish and maintain a cabinet-level edtech director to ensure the wise and effective spending of edtech funds. (States, Districts)

3) Conduct regular needs assessments to ensure technology properly supports learning. (States, Districts, Building-Level Administrators)
4) Develop model processes and guidelines for device refresh policies based on local funding structures. (States, Districts)
5) Leverage state purchasing power or regional buying consortia when purchasing edtech hardware, software, and services. (States, Districts)
6) Develop learning technology plans in consultation with a broad group of stakeholders and according to established review cycles. (States, Districts, Building-Level Administrators)
7) Leverage public/private partnerships and community collaboration to bring broadband internet access to previously under-connected areas and ensure student access to "everywhere, all-the-time learning." (States, Districts, Building-Level Administrators)
8) Develop processes and structures that ensure the inclusion of accessibility as a component of procurement processes. (States, Districts, Building-Level Administrators)
9) Plan for and incorporate skills and expectations across all grade levels and subject areas for Digital Health, Safety, and Citizenship, and Media Literacy. (States, Districts, Building-Level Administrators)

Closing the Digital Access Divide

California District Takes Systemic Approach to Equitable Access

In Lindsay Unified School District (LUSD)—a small, rural district located in the Central Valley of California— approximately 93 percent of the students identify as Hispanic/Latino and 42 percent as English Learners; 24 percent receive migrant services; and all students receive free meals. The district has committed to ensuring every learner has the best learning experience daily. Since 2007, this dedication has manifested in system-wide investments in time, resources, and technology to support high-quality, personalized learning in face-to-face and virtual learning environments.

LUSD refers to its students as learners, codifying their active role in their education. The district refers to teachers as learning facilitators who guide learners toward targeted, relevant resources, providing direct support to unique learning needs and designing personalized learning pathways through which learners produce evidence of their learning to demonstrate mastery of relevant standards and skills. The district's approach is inspired by the core belief that preparing learners for their future requires dramatically rethinking educational practices. In 2018, a collaborative project with Transcend Education, Summit Public Schools, and the Center for Public Research and Leadership at Columbia University developed a series of learner actions and experiences, and corresponding educator actions and strategies that exemplify high-quality personalized instruction. LUSD maximizes its use of technology to support this vision and ensure learning is always available everywhere. In 2015, LUSD leaders recognized that providing and encouraging extended learning opportunities would require internet and device access outside of school. Given their rural location, they realized this would require a community solution. As a result, they launched a multi-year project to install nine distribution towers across the district to expand the district's network. They then placed hundreds of hotspots in people's homes to provide free, filtered coverage for all learners. In addition, the district installed cell towers to connect LTE-enabled devices. They collaborated with and engaged critical stakeholders throughout the process, gathering input from students, educators, school leaders, parents, neighbors, business owners, and the local government.

From this experience, LUSD leaders prioritized clarity, transparency, and communication. They developed "SMART" (specific, measurable, attainable, realistic/reasonable, and timely) objectives, shared them publicly, and referred to them regularly to establish a clear and common understanding. The District Director of Technology and 21st Century Learning consistently communicated with stakeholders and iteratively revised messaging to ensure they understood the project's purpose and what would be necessary to ensure success. In addition, the director collaborated with the Chief Business Officer to ensure financial sustainability. The district recognized funding would shift over time and wanted to ensure infrastructure could be installed and maintained. Most importantly, LUSD leadership ensured that every technology decision aligned with the district's vision for learning—all learners can learn, acquire knowledge in different ways and timeframes, and have access to future-focused learning. By the time the COVID-19 pandemic hit in the Spring of 2020, LUSD knew that all their learners had a device, and almost 100 percent had sufficient internet access. Equally important, given the district's embrace of blended learning to personalize instruction, learners had the skills to navigate digital content independently, and educators had the resources and the experience to support them virtually. The district had recognized that providing internet and device access was only the foundation for bridging the digital access divide and had taken steps to address the challenge. As a result, it was well-positioned for the pandemic transition to online learning.

Begin with the End Goal in Mind: Design Portraits of Learning Environments

Just as states and school systems can find value in developing Profiles of a Learner/Graduate and Profiles of an Educator, they can also build a common vision through the development of Portraits of Learning Environments. Setting such expectations for the qualities of all learning spaces—physical and digital—can help ensure equity of access, consistency of experience, and clear expectations of functionality and interoperability when procuring/developing new resources. Designing a Portrait of a Learning Environment can ensure all learning environments have the capacity and resources necessary to shift and meet the needs of all learners and learning goals. In developing such portraits, states, and districts might begin with the questions like those below.

Technology Questions in the Development of Profiles of Learning Environments

1) What aspects of environmental design are necessary to make realizing the system's Profile of an Educator and Profile of a Graduate/Learner possible?
2) How might learning environments be designed to accommodate current and anticipated technological needs, e.g., power supplies, projection capabilities, broadband speeds, and auditory assistance?
3) What standards or certifications of accessibility and interoperability will be required as part of procurement processes to ensure accessibility?
4) How might learning environments be flexibly designed to allow educators and learners to move between the whole group, small group, and individual learning experiences afforded by technology?
5) How can all learning environments be designed with adaptability for varying learner needs and abilities?

For examples of other considerations when setting expectations for learning environments, consider UDL Tips for Designing an Engaging Learning Environment, *The Third Teacher*, or Seven Principles for Classroom Design: The Learning Space Rating System. While these and other resources can assist in thinking through the totality of the learning environment, closing the digital access divide will be a key component in those environments being able to support learners fully.

Three Components of Access: Availability, Affordability, Adoption

Availability: Is there sufficient infrastructure and coverage to deliver reliable, high-speed wired or wireless broadband service and technology tools for learning?

Affordability: Can learners and families/caregivers pay for the total cost of maintaining reliable, high-speed broadband service and technology tools for learning?

Adoption: Do learners and families/caregivers have the information, support, and skills to obtain regular, adequate access to reliable, high-speed broadband service and technology tools for learning?

Readers should refer to the DEER publication's executive summary for a look into what comprises each component.

Defining the Digital Access Divide

The digital access divide refers to the unequal distribution of access to digital technologies, such as computers, the internet, and other digital tools, between historically marginalized learners and their peers. It is closely related to digital equity, which aims to address and overcome this divide to ensure all individuals and communities have the information technology capacity necessary for full participation in the society and economy of the United States.[107] The digital access divide often both mirrors and exacerbates existing educational inequalities. Students without adequate access to digital resources struggle to participate fully in online learning, access educational materials, collaborate with peers, or develop the digital skills and literacies needed for post-graduation success. These disparities can impact a student's ability to participate fully and benefit from digital learning opportunities often taken for granted by their historically better-resourced peers.[108,109,110,111,112]

Digital Access Divide Components

Accessibility

Accessible learning materials include print- and technology-based educational materials— textbooks and related core materials—designed or enhanced in a way that makes them usable across the widest range of learner variability, regardless of format (e.g., print, digital, graphic, audio, video). Accessible

---

[107] U.S. Department of Education, Office of Educational Technology, Advancing Digital Equity for All: Community-Based Recommendations for Developing Effective Digital Equity Plans to Close the Digital Divide and Enable Technology-Empowered Learning, Washington, D.C., 2022.

[108] Attewell, P. (2001). The first and second digital divides. Sociology of education, 74(3), 252-259. http://doi.org/10.2307/2673277.

[109] Cuban, L., Kirkpatrick, H. & Peck, C. (2001). High access and low use of technologies in high school classrooms: Explaining an apparent paradox. American Educational Research Journal, 38(4), 813–834. https://doi.org/10.3102/00028312038004813.

[110] Hohlfeld, T. N., Ritzhaupt, A. D., Dawson, K., & Wilson, M. L. (2017). An examination of seven years of technology integration in Florida schools: Through the lens of the Levels of Digital Divide in Schools. Computers & Education, 113, 135–161. https://doi.org/10.1016/j.compedu.2017.05.017.

[111] Reich, Justin and Mizuko Ito. (2017). From Good Intentions to Real Outcomes: Equity by Design in Learning Technologies. Irvine, CA: Digital Media and Learning Research Hub.

[112] Project Tomorrow. (2022). Beyond the homework gap: Leveraging technology to support equity of learning experiences in school. https://tomorrow.org/speakup/pdfs/Beyond-the-Homework-Gap-2021-Equity-in-Education-Report.pdf.

learning materials can include a wide range of features to support user needs, such as text-to-speech, closed captioning, magnifying screen content, ALT-text, and speech recognition. Many of these features are helpful for all users, not just those with disabilities. For instance, text-to-speech tools are beneficial not only for students with dyslexia but for students who wish to listen to complete readings while in transit.[113] Digital learning technologies can be either the gateway to learning opportunities for individuals with disabilities or a gatekeeper blocking them from accessing the same quality of learning experiences as their peers. Too often, digital learning materials fall into the latter category instead of the former.

Digital Infrastructure (Inside and Outside of School)

Access to reliable internet connectivity and broadband services in different geographical areas varies greatly, especially in economically disadvantaged communities. State and federal government support has made significant progress in providing reliable, high-speed internet access to school buildings. According to Education Superhighway, 99.3 percent of America's schools have a reliable, high-speed broadband connection.[114] However, many students still lack access to reliable, high-speed internet at home, hindering their ability to participate in "everywhere, all-the-time learning," first described in the 2017 NETP. According to the U.S. Census Bureau, 13 percent of American households have no broadband internet subscription.[115] Some students may have limited home internet access (via cellular or satellite), likely inadequate for educational purposes due to data caps, inconsistent or low-quality connectivity, and slow speeds. Other students may only be able to access the internet while at the homes of friends or other family members or in public locations such as restaurants. Still others may share their connection with other members of the household.

---

113 (2023, January 20). *The Importance of Teaching All Students About Tech Accessibility Features.* Edutopia. Retrieved August 14, 2023, from https://www.edutopia.org/article/tech-accessibility-features-k-12-schools/.

114 (2019, October 22). *2019 State of the States Report.* Education SuperHighway. Retrieved August 14, 2023, from https://www. educationsuperhighway.org/wp-content/uploads/2019-State-of-the-States-Full-Report-EducationSuperHighway.pdf.

115 (n.d.). *Why We Ask Questions About...Computer and Internet Use.* United States Census Bureau. Retrieved September 6, 2023, from https://www.census.gov/acs/www/about/why-we-ask-each-question/computer/.

Digital Learning Devices

The availability and quality of digital learning devices available to students varies from district to district and even school to school. Some students and teachers may have access to school system-issued devices at school but not at home. Some students may have personally owned devices they can use for learning, while others may not. Other students may only have access to old or outdated equipment at school or home, limiting their ability to participate in digital learning experiences. In some cases, students may have to share devices with other children or adults in the family, making it difficult to complete homework and continue their learning outside school hours.

Equity Considerations for Student Devices

When configuring devices for students to take home, be aware of potential unintended consequences of device management policies and software. For instance, IT management policies that "lockdown" devices in the name of cybersecurity may also prevent students from configuring their devices to meet their learning needs, such as configuring accessibility features. School systems that use software platforms to monitor student online behavior may create privacy-related equity issues. Students with personally owned devices at home can use the internet without school system monitoring, while students who rely solely on school-issued devices do not have the same opportunity. Consider carefully balancing device security and statutory requirements with device usability and equity considerations.

Digital Health, Safety, & Citizenship

Digital Health, Safety, and Citizenship refers to the ability of individuals to maintain a healthy and empowered relationship with technology and the digital world while using technology appropriately, responsibly, and safely. It encompasses digital literacy, defined as 'the skills associated with using technology to enable users to find, evaluate, organize, create, and communicate information; and developing digital citizenship and the responsible use of technology.'[116] Knowledge and skill inequities in this area can negatively impact student ability to navigate and use digital tools effectively, potentially impacting their readiness for the workforce and post-

[116] Museum and Library Services Act of 2010, Pub. L. 111-340, 22 Dec. 2010.

graduation success. Digital health, safety, and citizenship skills empower students to use technology meaningfully and safely.

Cultural Responsiveness

When selecting and implementing edtech tools, schools and districts can often overlook whether those tools are culturally relevant, responsive,[117]117 and sustaining for all intended users. This can include the design, development, and implementation of educational tools, resources, and platforms that grow from and are tailored to the cultural backgrounds, identities, and experiences of diverse learners. A 2021 report from the National Academies of Science, Engineering, and Medicine, *Cultivating Interest and Competencies in Computing: Authentic Experiences and Design Factors*, made the following set of recommendations for the development of computing programs:

1) Program designers should be intentional in the design and implementation of programs offering authentic learning experiences that build interest and competencies for computing.
2) Practicing teachers in schools and facilitators in out-of-school time settings should seek out opportunities and materials that suggest how to incorporate effective practices for creating authentic learning experiences in computing within an existing program that includes utilizing problem and project-based learning strategies, allowing learner choice among activities, and which takes into consideration learners' contexts outside of school time.
3) Preservice and in-service teacher educators and trainers of out-of-school time facilitators should ensure that educators and facilitators are equipped to engage learners in personally authentic learning experiences in computing. This includes providing ongoing opportunities for educators to learn and practice using inclusive pedagogical approaches, as well as having access to materials and resources that build on learners' interests, identities, and backgrounds.
4) School leaders should consider a variety of ways to provide access to authentic learning experiences for computing. These include (1) addressing challenges (e.g., lack of instructional time and teacher

[117] U.S. Department of Health and Human Services (n.d.). *Cultural Responsiveness*. Child Welfare Information Gateway. Retrieved August 14, 2023, from https://www.childwelfare.gov/topics/systemwide/cultural/.

expertise) associated with integrating authentic computing experiences into instruction in a variety of subjects, (2) increasing access to stand-alone computing courses, and (3) ensuring schools have adequate resources such as equipment, reliable broadband internet, and time.

5) Program providers in out-of-school settings should increase efforts to expand access to authentic learning experiences for computing through growth of opportunities and active program promotion within underserved communities and in rural areas. This includes considering ways to reduce barriers to participation such as time, cost, and transportation. It also includes offering programs multiple times or during the evening and weekends, reducing program costs or offering financial assistance, and subsidizing transportation.
6) Program evaluators should develop and apply robust models of evaluation that take into account the distinctive features of authentic learning experiences in computing. More specifically, this includes attending to personal and professional authenticity, considering connections across settings, and to the extent possible, disaggregating findings and examining differences between and within groups (e.g., gender, race, ethnicity, socio-economic status) for computing outcomes as a central part of model building and evaluation.
7) There should be a broad-based effort to cultivate a network of opportunities, as well as supports for learners to navigate between them both in and out of school to increase access and opportunities for sustained engagement with computing.[118]

The report defines authentic as "close approximations to the work that a...professional would engage in" and "...connected to real-world problems learners' care about and the challenges they face." In addition to this full report, systems working to ensure edtech and teaching practices are culturally responsive, relevant, and sustaining might find resources like the Kapor Center's Culturally Responsive-Sustaining CS Framework helpful as they begin this work. While both examples focus more narrowly on computing and computer science, the principles and frameworks on which they are built are applicable to technology use across disciplines.

---

[118] National Academies of Sciences, Engineering, and Medicine. 2021. Cultivating Interest and Competencies in Computing: Authentic Experiences and Design Factors. Washington, DC: The National Academies Press. https://doi.org/10.17226/25912.

Educator Support & Training

As highlighted in the previous section, the ability of educators to design powerful learning experiences supported by technology varies greatly between school systems, school buildings, and classrooms. Educators need consistent, reliable access to ongoing technical support (to ensure technology is functioning and available) and ongoing, personalized professional learning to help them design effectively with digital tools. This professional learning should meet educators where they are, no matter their current technological skill level. Some systems rely on vendors for technical support and training; however, the availability and quality of technical support and professional development opportunities, which vary greatly between edtech vendors, are factors school systems should consider as part of the procurement process. Such considerations may include asking vendors how they can help educators understand how new products might interact with or support previous purchases or adoptions or how included training may go beyond initial startup and into learning design.

Closing the digital access divide requires careful planning and funding to address infrastructure gaps in order to provide equitable access to internet connectivity both in and outside of school. Sustainability planning is essential as devices purchased with pandemic-related federal and state funding reach end-of-life and need replacement. Without planning for sustainability, the digital access divide – which narrowed due to these one-time funding sources – will again begin to widen. In this section, we'll discuss how districts can address these challenges.

The Role of State and District Edtech Directors

According to a 2021 analysis published by the Exchange, it is estimated that the U.S. federal government, states, and school districts collectively spend between $26 and $41 billion per year on edtech materials (including digital instructional materials, networks and devices, formative and summative assessments, and professional development for educators).[119] Despite this, many states and districts lack a cabinet-level department of education or administrative position—a state or district edtech director—to help ensure digital tools' meaningful and cost-

[119] (2021, March 15). OVERVIEW: U.S. K-12 Public Education Technology Spending. The Exchange. Retrieved August 14, 2023, from https://edtechevidence.org/wp-content/uploads/2021/07/FINAL-K12-EdTech-Funding-Analysis_v.1.pdf.

effective use. According to research from the State Educational Technology Directors Association, 45 percent of states don't have a specific office coordinating edtech. In the 55 percent that do, that office has a variety of names, leadership roles, and placement within the broader organizational structure. Eight states call it the "Office of Educational Technology." This office falls under or adjacent to academics/ learning in other states. In contrast, in others, it falls under or adjacent to information technology.[120]

The responsibilities for State Educational Technology Directors can include:

- Developing and implementing strategic plans for edtech deployment and implementation;
- Providing leadership, advocating for policies and funding that support the effective use of edtech in schools and districts;
- Lending support and guidance in response to rapidly changing technological landscape and cybersecurity needs;
- Proactively identifying challenges and finding innovative solutions to improve educational outcomes through technology;
- Collaborating with cross-agency staff, government officials and stakeholders to develop deeper understanding, guidelines, standards, and regulations governing the use and funding of technology in schools;
- Assessing the effectiveness and impact of technology investments;
- Ensuring the effective implementation of technology and professional learning for educators and IT staff;
- Coordinating with both general and special education leaders;
- Fostering collaboration, networking opportunities and knowledge sharing among educators, universities, businesses, and other organizations; and
- Evaluating the impact of technology initiatives on student outcomes, instructional practices, and administrative processes.

[120] (2022, September 7). 2022 State EdTech Trends Survey and Report. SETDA. Retrieved August 31, 2023, from https://www.setda.org/priorities/state-trends/#:~:text=Download%20Report%20Here.

By leveraging statewide or district purchasing power to negotiate favorable vendor contracts, edtech directors can secure significant savings in procuring edtech hardware, software, and services. The sharing of technology resources and services among school systems and buildings, including infrastructure, software licenses, and digital learning tools, can reduce resource duplication and costs. Edtech directors can help develop model processes and guidelines for device refresh policies based on state and local funding structures. They can also provide context-specific and nuanced guidance in education and technology policy areas, such as student data privacy, to policymakers and school district leaders. By bridging the gap between technology and pedagogy, edtech directors can help break down the silos that can prevent the effective use of edtech while ensuring the wise use of public funds.

A state or district edtech director should be familiar with pedagogy and best practices in IT management. A well-rounded edtech director will have the capacity to actively bridge pK-12 education with IT management by understanding instructional design, assessment/evaluation, professional development, technology integration, instructional design, learning theories, digital content management, Learning Management Systems, and mobile learning solutions while also understanding data security and privacy, infrastructure management, budget and resource allocation, data-driven decision-making, vendor/contract management, stakeholder engagement/communication, and accessibility.

By bridging the gap between policy, practice, and technology implementation, state edtech directors help ensure that edtech initiatives align with state and district needs and goals.

Deeper Dive: Accessibility

Accessibility refers to designing and developing educational materials, resources, and technologies in a way that enables equal access and participation for all students, including students with disabilities. It also involves creating inclusive learning environments that accommodate students with diverse needs and ensuring that all students can effectively participate in educational activities.

- *Accessibility Features:* Features which afford a person with a disability the opportunity to acquire the same information, engage in the same interactions, and enjoy the same services as a person without a disability, in an equally effective and equally integrated manner, with substantially equivalent ease of use.[121]

- *Assistive Technology (AT):* Technology designed to address specific barriers learners with disabilities may face when they interact with their materials. Examples of assistive technology include text-to-speech, screen readers, and speech recognition.[122]
- *Accessible Educational Materials (AEM):* Print- and technology-based educational materials, including printed and electronic textbooks and related core materials that are designed or enhanced in a way that makes them usable across the widest range of learner variability, regardless of format (e.g., print, digital, graphic, audio, video, braille).[123]

Although technology can increase and enhance educational access for learners, it can also create barriers for learners with disabilities. For example, students with visual impairments who cannot modify the font size of a digital tool or who do not have the option to have the text read aloud to them might be unable to engage with the material. A student with a hearing impairment might be unable to access the content in an uncaptioned video or engage with tools that include meaningful sounds. A student who uses a screen reader might be unable to read a pdf document if it lacks proper structure, headings, alternative text for images, or logical reading order. In addition, a student with disabilities may physically need AT to access digital tools (for example, using an external switching device and scanning software instead of a mouse and keyboard.) For learners to meaningfully participate in their education, they must be able to access and engage with their educational materials.

Center on Inclusive Technology & Education Systems

Funded by the Office of Special Education Programs and managed by CAST, the Center on Inclusive Technology & Education Systems (CITES) supports districts in creating and sustaining inclusive technology systems

[121] Joint Letter US Department of Justice and US Department of Education, June 29, 2010, & CAST.

[122] (n.d.). What is Accessibility? CAST. Retrieved August 14, 2023, from https://aem.cast.org/get-started/defining-accessibility.

[123] (n.d.). What is Accessibility? CAST. Retrieved August 14, 2023, from https://aem.cast.org/get-started/defining-accessibility.

that serve all students, including students with disabilities who require assistive technology or accessible educational materials. A framework of evidence-based practices to enhance the successful use of technology to foster learning and life success is in development. Visit https://cites.cast.org/more/district-examples to read stories and vignettes of districts implementing inclusive technology practices.

Key aspects of accessibility in educational tools can include:

1) *Physical accessibility:* Edtech developers should design platforms and materials so students with physical disabilities can navigate them. For example, some students may need to use alternative input devices. These devices allow individuals with mobility impairments to access or control computers or mobile devices without relying on traditional keyboards and mice. Examples can include sip-and-puff switches, eye-gaze tracking systems, and specialized keyboards.
2) *Visual accessibility:* Edtech tools and materials should accommodate students with visual impairments. Examples include compatibility with screen magnification software and screen reader software, high contrast settings that enhance visibility, or descriptions of visual elements within educational materials.
3) *Auditory accessibility:* Several features can make educational tools accessible to students with hearing impairments. Examples include captions, American Sign Language or transcripts for audio or video content, visual aids such as slides, diagrams, or visual illustrations, which can supplement spoken information and enhance understanding, and speech-to-text software. Classroom amplification systems can help students better understand spoken classroom instruction.
4) *Cognitive accessibility:* Cognitive accessibility features help improve the clarity of information for all students, including those with cognitive disabilities or learning differences. Examples include text-to-speech and voice recognition software, text highlighting tools, graphic organizers, language simplification tools that provide alternative versions of complex language or text with reduced vocabulary or simpler syntax, and interactive and multisensory learning opportunities.
5) *Digital accessibility:* Digital accessibility ensures that edtech, digital tools, and educational materials are accessible to students with

disabilities. Educational institutions should adopt user interfaces that are compatible with assistive technologies, adhere to web accessibility standards (such as WCAG 2.2), ensure mobile applications are accessible to individuals with disabilities, and provide customization and personalization options.

6) *Language Accessibility:* Accessible language accommodates people with Limited English Proficiency, defined as individuals who do not speak English as their primary language and who have a limited ability to read, speak, write, or understand English.[124] Examples include providing multilingual versions of digital content, the ability to raise or lower the readability level of content, and creating audio and video content that accommodates users with limited literacy skills.

> To better meet diverse language needs, states like Massachusetts (page 52) and Florida (page 67) have designed their educational technology resources to better reach and serve students who are English Learners and multilingual students and their families.

Achieving the goal of truly inclusive and accessible learning environments requires the participation of and input from a wide range of stakeholders—including the instructional technology, curriculum, special education, and information technology teams. Often, these departments are siloed and do not regularly work together to ensure all students' needs are met. As a result, situations like the following may arise:

- An Individualized Education Program (IEP) Team completes a functional evaluation and determines that a student needs a specific screen reader software. The IEP Team Chair puts in a request for the software, and the district purchases it. When the learner tries to use the software with their district-provided laptop, it does not work because no one ensured that the software was compatible with the operating system installed on student laptops or because the software is internet dependent, and the student doesn't have home internet access.

---

[124] Civil Rights Division of the United States Department of Justice (n.d.). *Commonly Asked Questions and Answers Regarding Limited English Proficient (LEP) Individuals.* LimitedEnglishProficiency.gov. Retrieved August 14, 2023, from https://www.lep.gov/sites/lep/files/media/document/2020-03/042511_QA_LEP_General_0.pdf.

- A general education teacher finds a digital resource purchased by the district that uses videos and games to teach math skills. The teacher assumes the technology is accessible since the district purchased it but quickly finds the videos do not provide closed captioning or transcripts for students. As a result, it doesn't support learners who are deaf and hard of hearing and those with specific learning disabilities. The teacher is frustrated and uncertain about how to support these students.
- A caregiver with a visual disability is trying to access the list of after-school programs on their child's school website. When they reach the website, the after-school programs are listed as images with no additional information or alternative text. The caregiver cannot use their text-to-speech program to review the list and learn what opportunities are available for their child.

School systems must break down these silos when planning, implementing, and evaluating technology purchases. It's also important to include learners with disabilities and their families in these conversations to ensure the technology purchased meets the needs of the students who need it most. This is especially important for learning technologies students use outside of school hours. The more knowledgeable caregivers are about how specific technologies can support their child, the better prepared they will be to support their child's learning at home.

Increasing Statewide Support of Accessible Educational Materials

For New Hampshire, 2024 marks the state's final year as a member of an inaugural cohort of states working to "build a robust and coordinated system for providing AEM and related technologies to all learners with disabilities who need them." Funded by a grant from the US Department of Education Office of Special Education Programs, the cohort connects New Hampshire, Georgia, Missouri, North Carolina, Oklahoma, Oregon, and West Virginia with the National Center on Accessible Educational Materials for Learning (AEM Center). The effort provides cohort members with intensive technical assistance in helping learners with disabilities from early childhood through postsecondary education. The resources developed from the project will be made available nationally through the AEM Center and provide examples of how states can improve accessibility services while providing educators with the capacity to close the digital design divide for all learners.

Another key consideration is to provide educators with the time and training needed to understand the various accessibility features of digital learning tools and how to leverage them. Many accessibility features can benefit all students, not only those with specific disabilities. For example, digital textbooks and e-books can give students flexible access to course materials. Features like searchable text, interactive multimedia, highlighting, digital note-taking capabilities, adjustable font sizes, and captioning can facilitate learning for all students.

Supporting Preschool Children with Assistive Technology

To empower early childhood educators to use evidence-based assistive technology with even the youngest learners, the Miami-Dade County Community Action & Human Services Head Start Program in Florida is partnering with two organizations with external assistive technology specialists. Florida Alliance for Assistive Services & Technology (FAAST) is a nonprofit organization whose mission is to improve the quality of life for Floridians with disabilities by increasing access to assistive technology through empowerment and collaboration. Step Up AT is a customizable professional development program that coaches teachers, teacher assistants, teacher support specialists, school districts, and other agencies to adopt evidence-based AT practices that improve early learning outcomes for young children (ages 3-5) with disabilities.

The program aims to help educators plan for and use AT to support preschool students aged three to five with IEPs or students who otherwise need support. By helping educators match AT with tasks and student strengths, they can more actively engage students in their learning. The Step Up AT team has also created learning modules in English and Spanish describing how to plan for AT, developed teaching practices with guidance from the Council for Exceptional Children's Division of Early Childhood, and videos demonstrating how to use the AT. The learning modules help preschool administrators, such as those with Head Start, get AT where needed and become better advocates for students with disabilities.

Physical Learning Spaces

Another important consideration is the organization of physical learning space. While the guidelines below refer to on-campus learning spaces, it's also important to consider the role of off-campus learning spaces (such as the students' homes). Considerations include:

- Are on-campus learning spaces accessible to students with physical disabilities? For example, are there accessible ramps or elevators and a proposed number of accessible restrooms for student use?
- Are the design and layout of the physical space dynamic and flexible enough to accommodate different learning activities? Can a space where educators deliver whole-class instruction be modified to facilitate individual or small-group activities? For example, flexible furniture, movable partitions, and modular setups can support easy classroom reconfiguration.
- Can physical learning spaces facilitate both individual and collaborative work? Are there areas designed explicitly for group work and collaboration, such as breakout rooms or collaborative workstations? Are there quiet areas or zones for students who need fewer auditory distractions for individual study?
- Are learning spaces equipped with the necessary technology infrastructure to support the desired learning environment(s)? Examples include Wi-Fi access points, A/V equipment, and laptop storage/ charging carts. Does this extend to different classroom contexts, such as providing Wi-Fi access for outdoor classrooms?

For more information and tools for aligning physical spaces, visit the Blended Learning Universe.

Puerto Rico Focuses on STEM Learning for All

Founded in 2004, Puerto Rico's Science, Technology, and Research Trust is on a mission "to continually advance Puerto Rico's economy and its citizen's well-being"[125] through its three main pillars of research & development, entrepreneurship, and public health. The Trust also recognizes the need to support a pipeline of access to STEM learning for all

[125] https://prsciencetrust.org/.

students on the island if it is to succeed in its mission. The Trust's STEM Education Program focuses on STEM education public policy, strategic partnerships, and supporting the local STEM education ecosystem. The program includes activities such as STEM in the Mountain, a weeklong summer program that offers hands- on STEM learning to 5th through 8th grade students. To meet students where they are, the program has also developed STEM Boxed Kits delivered to students' homes. The kits provide everything necessary to provide access to experiential STEM learning and begin to build early pathways to STEM careers.

For digital devices and tools to be effective, usable, and meaningful, they must be accessible to all. The following strategies can help school systems ensure the accessibility of their digital infrastructure:

- Develop a procurement team including IT staff, assistive technology specialists, special and general education staff, curriculum leaders, procurement directors, and EL specialists to create an accessibility rubric the district must use before procurement.
- When possible, hire an AT specialist who can support the evaluation, procurement, training, and implementation of AT, IT, or AEM or work with an organization (such as an Education Service Agency) to do so. If this is not possible, work with the State AT Act program or community partners (e.g., Easter Seals and local groups) to contract the appropriate AT specialist or EL specialist.
- When needed, hire an EL specialist who can support the evaluation, procurement, training, and implementation of technology tools to support students and families/caregivers no matter their home language.
- Ensure all educators have the knowledge, time, and capacity to ensure all educational materials are accessible—including websites, classwork and homework, and communications to staff and families. Accessible materials should be available both internally and externally for all constituents. Consider the accessibility training modules from the U.S. Department of Education's AEM Center and the digital accessibility video series from the U.S. Department of Education Office for Civil Rights.
- Provide opportunities for various experts and specialists (e.g., IT, special educators, EL specialists, general educators, and related

service providers) to discuss and collaborate on evaluating, implementing, and using edtech and AT in the classroom.

- Partner with State AT Act Programs, which provide free AT loans for learners with disabilities before purchasing. For more on AT, see the AT section below.
- Develop an easily findable and searchable directory with all district technology resources and their accessibility features (including language translation services) and all available district assistive technology.
- Ensure all district and school forms, event registrations, and meetings include areas for participants and attendees to indicate accessibility needs before events and meetings. Translate school communications into multiple languages, reflecting the needs of students and families in specific communities.[126]
- When discussing their needs and services, include potentially impacted individuals in all teams, committees, and meetings.
- Form standing groups inclusive of caregivers, students with disabilities, parents, or family members of students with disabilities, and ELs to advise on issues of accessibility and technology procurement and provision. Wherever possible, create specific structured connections between these and all professional groups mentioned above.

State Partnership Brings Assistive Technology Support to Oklahomans

The Oklahoma State Department of Education (OSDE) has partnered with Oklahoma ABLE Tech, the state's Assistive Technology (AT) Act program, to provide AT and information services for children. ABLE Tech provides training, technical assistance, information, and public awareness to help individuals with disabilities, their caregivers/families, service providers, and agencies so they can learn about and improve AT service delivery for students with disabilities. ABLE Tech also provides AT demonstrations, short-term loans, re-utilized devices, and alternative

[126] U.S. Department of Education (2015, January 7). *Information for Limited English Proficient (LEP) Parents and Guardians and for Schools and School Districts that Communicate with Them.* Office for Civil Rights. Retrieved September 6, 2023, from https://www2.ed.gov/about/offices/list/ocr/docs/dcl-factsheet-lep-parents-201501.pdf.

financing options to help Oklahomans make informed decisions about AT devices and acquire needed AT for free or at a reduced cost.

ABLE Tech helps local educational agencies increase skills, knowledge, and competencies related to AT laws, policies, procedures, and practices. They support the quality provision of AT devices and services for students with disabilities, helping them be more independent in the least restrictive environment and progress toward academic standards. ABLE Tech supports districts in implementing the Quality Indicators for AT (QIAT) Service Delivery in the Schools and the Quality Indicators for the Provision of AEM and Technology in the Schools. At the state level, ABLE Tech staff have provided expertise on multiple panels, councils, and committees in areas including assessment, data, MTSS, and procurement, resulting in the extension of AT services.

Due to increased OSDE funding, AT demonstrations and short-term AT loans for educational purposes have increased over the past decade, supporting the AT needs of thousands of Oklahomans, from infants to adults.

Accessibility Resources

By considering accessibility in educational tools, educators and developers can create inclusive learning experiences that address the needs of all students, promoting equal opportunities for participation, engagement, and achievement. For more on accessibility, consider resources such as the following:

- OET Digital Accessibility Webpage: OET launched a new landing page for accessibility resources and funding opportunities available in the U.S. Department of Education.
- Digital Accessibility Video Series: The U.S. Department of Education Office for Civil Rights created 20 brief videos on the importance of accessibility and how to create digitally accessible materials.
- Accessibility Guide for Creating Materials: The National Research and Training Center on Blindness and Low Vision developed simple how-to guides to ensure your documents, QR codes, and surveys are accessible.
- Accessibility Resources for Developers & Document Authors: The Social Security Administration shares resources they use to create

accessible digital content, including a web accessibility testing tool, how to add alternative text, and accessibility checklists.
- The Office of Special Education Programs, part of the Office of Special Education and Rehabilitative Services, is dedicated to improving results for infants, toddlers, children, and youth with disabilities ages birth through 21 by providing leadership and financial support to assist states and local districts. Resources include Tools for Your Toolbox and information about Section 508 Accessibility.
- OCR Digital Accessibility Web Page: The U.S. Department of Education Office for Civil Rights provides a landing page for guidance and technical assistance about educational institutions' legal obligations with respect to digital accessibility.

By considering the accessibility of educational tools, educators and developers can create inclusive learning experiences that address the needs of all students, promoting equal opportunities for participation, engagement, and achievement.

Deeper Dive: Digital Infrastructure

Digital infrastructure refers to the resources that make digital systems possible, as well as how individuals and organizations access and use these resources.[127] It includes various components and networks supporting the transfer, storage, and communication of data and digital resources. In education, digital infrastructure can include:

- *Hardware and devices:* These include computers, laptops, tablets, and other devices that provide access to digital learning materials and platforms.

---

[127] Borrowing from the USAID's definition in their August 2022 Digital Ecosystem Framework: https://www.usaid.gov/sites/default/files/2022-05/Digital_Strategy_Digital_Ecosystem_Final.pdf.

- *Reliable, high-speed internet connectivity:* This is defined by the federal government as 100 megabits per second (Mbps) symmetrical network capacity.[128]
- *Learning Management Systems (LMS):* Learning Management Systems are online platforms for managing and delivering course materials, assignments, assessments, and educational content.
- *Online Content and Resources:* These can include e-books, interactive multimedia resources, educational videos, online tutorials, and virtual simulations.
- *Communication & Collaboration Tools:* These tools, such as video conferencing and shared document editing platforms, support positive relationship building between students and educators.
- *Assessment and Feedback Systems:* These systems are used for online assessments, quizzes, and exams and may include tools for automated grading.
- *Data Management and Analytics Systems:* These systems collect, manage, and analyze data related to student performance, engagement, and learning outcomes.
- *Cybersecurity and Privacy Protections:* These include hardware and software tools such as web filtering, firewalls, encryption, and secure authentication.

Digital infrastructure sets the stage for educational design, which empowers students and educators to leverage technology for effective teaching and learning. On-campus access to these resources and tools is not enough; students and educators also need access when off-campus to fully realize the potential of "everywhere, all-the-time" learning. This vision is shared by the Federal Communications Commission (FCC), which announced its Learn Without Limits initiative in June 2023[129] to support off-campus access. In 2023, the U.S. Department of Education's Office of Educational Technology began releasing a series of technical assistance briefs to provide

[128] (n.d.). *USDA to Make Up to $1.15 Billion Available to Help People Living in Rural Communities Access High-Speed Internet.* U.S. Department of Agriculture. Retrieved August 14, 2023, from https://www.usda.gov/media/press-releases/2021/10/22/usda-make-115-billion-available-help-people-living-rural.

[129] Federal Communications Commission (2023, June 26). *Chairwoman Rosenworcel Announces 'Learn Without Limits' Initiative.* Commission Documents. Retrieved September 6, 2023, from https://www.fcc.gov/document/chairwoman-rosenworcel-announces-learn-without-limits-initiative.

technical assistance to state and district leaders. These briefs, in addition to those resources provided by the Student Privacy Policy Office and the Cybersecurity & Infrastructure Security Agency offer robust assistance to ensure preparedness of educational digital infrastructure.

Digital Infrastructure Beyond Schools

Despite significant growth in school technology use, many learners, families/caregivers, and communities still lack access to reliable, high-speed broadband and technology tools. In the United States, more than 18 million households continue to face challenges gaining access to reliable, high-speed broadband, and households earning less than $30,000 per year are significantly less likely to have a computer than households making more than $100,000.[130] While 40 percent of K-12 learners identify as Black, Hispanic, or Native American, a disproportionately greater percentage of unconnected learners (54 percent) identify as Black, Hispanic, or Native American. Furthermore, Black and Hispanic learners are less likely to have a computer at home compared to white peers.[131] Overall, an estimated 15–16 million K-12 learners do not have sufficient access to reliable, high-speed broadband and technology tools for learning.[132]

Advancing Digital Equity for All

In Spring 2022, the U.S. Department of Education's Office of Educational Technology committed to advancing digital equity through the Digital Equity Education Roundtables (DEER) Initiative. Through DEER, The Office of Educational Technology hosted a series of

[130] DigitalUS Coalition. (2020). Building a digitally resilient workforce: Creating on-ramps to opportunity. https://digitalus.org/wp-content/uploads/2020/06/DigitalUS-Report-pages-20200602.pdf.

[131] Rideout, V.J. & Robb, M.B. (2021). The Common Sense Census presents: Research brief. Remote learning and digital equity during the pandemic. San Francisco, CA: Common Sense. https://www.commonsensemedia.org/sites/default/files/featured-content/files/final_release_digital_equity_research_brief_fact_sheet.pdf.

[132] Ali, T., Chandra, S., Cherukumilli, S., Fazlullah, A., Galicia, E., Hill, H., McAlpine, N., McBride, L., Vaduganathan, N., Weiss, D., & Wu, M. (2021). Looking back, looking forward: What it will take to permanently close the K-12 digital divide. San Francisco, CA: Common Sense Media. https://www.commonsensemedia.org/sites/default/files/featured-content/files/final_-_what_it_will_take_to_permanently_close_the_k-12_digital_divide_vfeb3.pdf.

national conversations with leaders from community-based organizations, families, and learners furthest from digital opportunities. The resource "Advancing Digital Equity for All: Community-Based Recommendations for Developing Effective Digital Equity Plans to Close the Digital Divide and Enable Technology-Empowered Learning" illuminates insights from these conversations to highlight the barriers faced by learner communities and promising solutions for increasing access to technology for learning.

Although the inequity of digital access has been a long-standing problem for United States school systems and communities, the COVID-19 pandemic brought these challenges to the forefront when educators were forced to implement emergency remote learning. Many students did not have access to personal computers, laptops, or tablets at home, making it challenging to participate in online classes and complete assignments. Students with limited or unreliable home internet access had difficulty accessing educational resources and participating in high-bandwidth activities such as videoconferencing. Other factors contributing to inequitable learning experiences included inadequate professional learning and technical support; and home environmental challenges such as insufficient space, noise distractions, or lack of a suitable study/teaching area. Students with disabilities faced additional challenges accessing online content not properly designed for accessibility.[133] The severity of these issues varied based on factors such as socioeconomic status, geographical location, and the resources available in individual school systems. These challenges existed before the pandemic and continue to contribute to educational inequities.

The causes of the digital divide are nuanced and complex but can be categorized into three components of access: availability, affordability, and adoption.

---

133 (n.d.). *Types of Disabilities and Associated Barriers*. Toronto Metropolitan University Pressbooks. Retrieved August 14, 2023, from https://pressbooks.library.torontomu.ca/dabp/chapter/types-of-disabilities-and-associated-barriers/.

Availability

Is There Sufficient Infrastructure and Coverage to Deliver Reliable, High-Speed Wired or Wireless Broadband Service and Technology Tools for Learning?

Availability refers to the level and sufficiency of coverage in delivering reliable, high-speed wired or wireless broadband services and the sufficiency of technology tools for learning. Barriers and strategies related to availability align with typical understandings of "access," focused on whether learners and their families/caregivers can connect to reliable, high-speed broadband through a device, and the necessary physical infrastructure from home and in their communities. Research shows that the quality and type of home broadband access directly impacts learner school participation,[134] performance outcomes, and digital literacy.[135] Learners with insufficient access are also less likely to plan for postsecondary education, affecting their lifetime potential for high earnings.[136]

[134] (2019). Learning at Home While Under-Connected: Lower-Income Families during the COVID-19 Pandemic. *New America*. https:// eric.ed.gov/?id=ED615616.

[135] Hampton, K. N., Fernandez, L., Robertson, C. T., & Bauer, J. M. (2020). Broadband and Student Performance Gaps. James H. and Mary B. Quello Center, Michigan State University. https://doi.org/10.25335/BZGY-3V91.

[136] Hampton, K. N., Fernandez, L., Robertson, C. T., & Bauer, J. M. (2020). Broadband and Student Performance Gaps. James H. and Mary B. Quello Center, Michigan State University. https://doi.org/10.25335/BZGY-3V91.

Access to devices suitable for learning, such as laptops, Chromebooks, and tablets, is another critical consideration for school systems. Lower-income families are less likely to own personal devices appropriate for learning; Pew research found that a quarter of low-income teens lack access to a computer at home.[137] Even if there is a computer in the home, it may have to be shared by multiple family members, including other school-age children. In addition, while many digital tools are web-based, they may not work equally well on all devices—for example, an educational tool might work in a computer web browser but not on a tablet. School systems purchasing digital tools need to ensure they will work on a wide range of devices (including smartphones) and are compatible with devices provided by the school system. If school systems provide students with devices to take home, they must budget for device replacement cycles (generally every 3-5 years),[138] repairs, and technical support.

While there is no single solution to address the internet and device availability challenges many students face, school systems and states are finding creative solutions appropriate for their specific context. Advancing Digital Equity for All highlights some of these solutions in detail. Examples include providing digital devices and wireless hotspots for learners, installing wireless networks on school buses, partnering with internet service providers (ISPs) to provide community internet access, and leveraging community partnerships to provide internet access in public spaces.

In the long term, bringing reliable, high-speed broadband to underserved areas requires infrastructure development, policy initiatives, and cooperative efforts among various stakeholders. Collaboration between governments (local, state, federal, and tribal), ISPs, community agencies, nonprofit organizations, chambers of commerce, industry and trade associations, and other stakeholders is crucial for successful broadband deployment. Public-private partnerships can leverage private-sector investment in broadband infrastructure to benefit larger communities.

---

[137] (2020, March 16). *As schools close due to the coronavirus, some U.S. Students face a digital 'homework gap'*. Pew Research. Retrieved August 14, 2023, from https://www.pewresearch.org/short-reads/2020/03/16/as-schools-close-due-to-the-coronavirus-some-u-s-students-face-a-digital-homework-gap/#:~:text=One%2Din%2Dfour%20teens%20in, according%20to%20the%202018%20survey.

[138] Institute for Education Sciences (n.d.). *Forum Unified Education Technology Suite: Part 6: Maintaining and Supporting Your Technology*. National Center for Education Statistics. Retrieved August 14, 2023, from https://nces.ed.gov/ pubs2005/tech_suite/part_6.asp.

Physical Accessibility

Features allowing individuals with mobility impairments to access or control computers or mobile devices without relying on traditional keyboards and mice

Visual Accessibility

Features that accommodate individuals with visual impairments

Auditory Accessibility

Features that accommodate individuals with hearing impairments

Cognitive Accessibility

Features that help improve the clarity of information for all individuals including those with cognitive disabilities or learning differences

Digital Accessibility

Features ensuring that technologies, digital tools, and educational materials are accessible to students with disabilities

Language Accessibility

Features supporting individuals who do not speak English as their primary language or who have a limited ability to read, speak, write, or understand English

Partnering with Local Government and Community Agencies with HCS EdConnect

When schools transitioned to emergency remote learning in 2020, the Chattanooga, Tennessee community recognized that many students lacked the home internet access necessary to participate. To address the challenge, Hamilton County Schools (HCS), Hamilton County, the City of Chattanooga, the Enterprises Center of Chattanooga, and various local funders partnered to provide free, reliable, high-speed internet access to qualifying Hamilton County families. They named the partnership HCS EdConnect.

Identifying students and families who needed home internet access and encouraging them to participate in the program was the biggest challenge HCS faced. Initially, the school system reached out to students who qualified for Free and Reduced Price Meals. As of Spring 2023, more than 16,000 students were connected to reliable high-speed internet at no charge, representing approximately one-third of the students in the district. The school system continues working to identify families that have not yet opted into this free service.

Anecdotal information from teachers, students, and parents indicates that reliable high-speed internet access at home has made a difference for program participants. Boston University is implementing a qualitative research study to study the program further. Preliminary research findings indicate nearly all the families participating in HCS EdConnect reported positive attitudes toward the use of technology in education.

Affordability

Can Learners and Families/Caregivers Pay for the Total Cost of Maintaining Reliable, High-Speed Broadband Service and Technology Tools for Learning?

Affordability refers to the ability to pay for the cost of installing and maintaining a reliable, high-speed broadband connection and technology tools for learning.[139] High internet service costs disproportionately impact low-income families, who may struggle to allocate funds for internet service while meeting basic needs such as food, gas, shelter, and electricity. This barrier also

---

139 U.S. Department of Education, Office of Educational Technology, Advancing Digital Equity for All: Community-Based Recommendations for Developing Effective Digital Equity Plans to Close the Digital Divide and Enable Technology-Empowered Learning, Washington, D.C., 2022.

exists at the community level, particularly for Tribal communities.[140] In addition, a lack of competition between providers in many areas results in higher prices and lower-quality service.

The cost of devices suitable for learning also challenges families. Lower-cost devices like Chromebooks or refurbished computers can meet the needs of some students but are not suitable for all learners and may need to be shared by multiple family members. Older machines that use operating systems that have reached end-of-life or have limited memory or processor speeds may be unable to run newer applications. Learners with disabilities might have access to assistive technology and devices at school but not at home due to cost. Challenges like these can make it difficult for students to participate in "everywhere, all-the-time" learning.

Collaboration and Research Lay the Foundation for CT State Digital Equity Plan

Prior commitments and policies designed to close the digital divide have helped accelerate the development of Connecticut's Digital Equity Plan, led through its Department of Administrative Services' Commission for Educational Technology..

During the pandemic, the state's governor established the Everybody Learns initiative, which included purchasing and rapidly deploying more than 140,000 student computers and provisioning 50,000 home internet connections. During the same period, the state passed legislation that gave Connecticut advanced insights into the digital divide. Public Act 21-159 established a statewide broadband mapping hub with provider data reflecting nearly universal availability but only a 75 percent adoption rate of high-speed service across the state. These insights enabled Connecticut to focus on the economic, behavioral, and trust barriers to achieving digital equity.

Research into these barriers has come through strong interagency collaboration and partnerships with the University of Connecticut's School of Public Policy and local stakeholder groups. Intensive focus group discussions, statewide resident surveys, and detailed indexing of existing programs point to the need for broader access to training and support for

[140] U.S. Department of Education, Office of Educational Technology, Advancing Digital Equity for All: Community-Based Recommendations for Developing Effective Digital Equity Plans to Close the Digital Divide and Enable Technology-Empowered Learning, Washington, D.C., 2022.

residents, and trusted resources that equip them with affordable connections and devices that meet their needs. While still in development, Connecticut's Digital Equity Plan will aim to put solutions in place that leverage efficiencies at the state and regional level while capitalizing on local partners that have earned the trust of residents to engage fully in today's digital world for learning, work, health, and wellbeing.

Bringing Internet Access to Alaskan Tribal Lands

While the digital access divide may be closing quickly in much of the country, geography and a lack of physical infrastructure present unique challenges in those locations still waiting for reliable broadband. Through a $35M grant from the National Telecommunications and Information Administration's Tribal Broadband Connectivity Program, 73 Alaska Native Tribal governments, Alaska Native Corporations, and tribal organizations will benefit from a Use and Adoption award.

Beginning with a needs assessment and input from target populations, the project will eventually increase access to connectivity and devices. Recognizing that digital health, safety, & citizenship are key components of digital access, the project will also include designing and implementing a training program to build digital skills and familiarity with broadband resources and technology among Alaskan Native populations.

When completed, the project will serve 62 Alaskan Native communities, provide subsidized internet service for an estimated 2,777 Alaskan Native households, provide broadband devices to an estimated 8,877 individuals, and employ and train 10 IT technicians. This is to say nothing of the increased educational opportunities, employment upskilling, and digital cultural possibilities that will be available for generations to come.

Initiatives and partnerships at the federal, state, and local levels can help mitigate the affordability barriers to internet access. In December 2021, Congress authorized the Affordable Connectivity Program (ACP), a $14B program, to ensure all households can afford broadband for education, employment, and more. The ACP allows qualifying households to reduce their internet costs by up to $30/month ($75/month on Tribal lands). Under the White House's Get Internet initiative, several companies further committed to offering ACP-eligible households at least one high-speed plan for $30/month or less, with no additional fees and no data caps. Similarly, state and local initiatives have partnered with ISPs to provide services and devices at a lower cost.[141]

Office of Educational Technology and Federal Communications Commission ACP Outreach Toolkit and Resources for Schools and Districts

As trusted community members, schools and districts are encouraged to engage in outreach to eligible families/caregivers. In doing so, schools and districts can use the FCC's outreach toolkit, with resources translated into multiple languages. In addition, schools and districts can take steps to help learners, families, and caregivers navigate the sign-up process. To access the toolkit and OET's resources for schools and districts, please visit https://getinternet.gov/.

Although programs like those described above can help address affordability issues, more resources and expanded eligibility for affordable broadband programs are still needed. Even with subsidies, devices, and reliable, high-speed internet, plans are still unaffordable for many families. The low-cost broadband plans available may not be robust enough to meet the needs of learners, especially when multiple family members need to use the connection simultaneously. Eligibility restrictions such as immigration and refugee status may also prevent families from participating. Credit checks, deposit requirements, and long-term contract requirements may also pose barriers. In addition, these programs do not address the challenges of homeless or migrant students or students who move frequently. Highly mobile learners need reliable, high-speed broadband connections that do not require them to be in a specific location. Some programs like ACP protect consumers by allowing eligible households to access the benefit regardless of credit status, past due balances, or prior debt.[142]

[141] U.S. Department of Education, Office of Educational Technology, Advancing Digital Equity for All: Community-Based Recommendations for Developing Effective Digital Equity Plans to Close the Digital Divide and Enable Technology-Empowered Learning, Washington, D.C., 2022.

[142] (n.d.). *Frequently Asked Questions*. USAC Affordable Connectivity Program. Retrieved September 6, 2023, from https://www. affordableconnectivity.gov/help/faqs/.

VT Purchasing Consortia Increases Spending Power of Rural Districts

Vermont has a total student population of approximately 83,000—equal to that of a single large urban school district—spread out across several districts within the state. But the smaller size of these often-rural districts doesn't stop them from provisioning access to technology tools at a fair price for all students. Through Vita-Learn, a statewide non-profit dedicated to professional learning, innovative practices, and improved use of edtech, member districts can take advantage of these tools at fractions of the price any of the smaller districts or schools could negotiate on their own. Consortia like Vermont's can also create the secondary benefit of a common set of tools used across districts in a region or state, increasing the chance an educator or student moving from one district to another will have familiarity with these tools and decreasing the costs in time and money in getting new teachers up to speed with a school or district's array of resources.

Washington State Grant Program Builds District Capacity for Edtech Use

Seventy percent of Washington's school districts are categorized as rural/remote and are often less likely than their urban counterparts to adequately raise sufficient local funding to support digital teaching and learning. In 2021, Washington HB 1365 established the "Digital Equity and Inclusion Grant" program to fund districts in three primary areas: attaining a 1:1 student-to-learning device ratio, expanding technical support and training for educators, and developing district-based and school-based capacity to assist families and students. With this recent charge from the state legislature, the Washington Office of Superintendent of Public Instruction (OSPI) actively helps rural/remote districts, which cannot often apply for and manage grants.

Several small, rural, and remote districts have benefitted from the dedicated funds and additional assistance from OSPI. Hoquiam School District, a remote community located on the state's Western edge, received grant funds for professional learning equipment but needed more internal capacity to support the effective integration of technology into instruction. OSPI worked with district leaders and brought in technology directors from peer districts to share resources and solve issues collaboratively.

> OSPI's work on the Digital Equity and Inclusion Grant program demonstrates how dedicated funding and technical assistance for rural/remote and small districts allows them to build the technological and human capacities necessary to meet the specific needs of their communities.

Adoption

Do Learners and Families/Caregivers Have the Information, Support, and Skills to Obtain Regular, Adequate Access to Reliable, High-Speed Broadband Service and Technology Tools for Learning?

Adoption refers to the process by which an individual obtains broadband access at the necessary speed, quality, and capacity; and the digital skills necessary to participate online, on a personal device, and using a secure and convenient network. Barriers and strategies related to adoption tend to focus on human-level challenges and strategies. They go beyond whether reliable, high-speed broadband is available and affordable to focus on whether the necessary information, support, and skill-building opportunities are provided.[143]

Providing students with the devices and high-speed internet needed for learning outside school hours is not enough. Focusing on family/caregiver digital inclusion and skills development is equally important. For example, communication between schools and families often relies heavily on digital tools such as email, online portals, or messaging apps. When families/caregivers lack digital literacy skills, it becomes more challenging for schools and teachers to effectively communicate important information, updates, or individual student progress. This gap in skills can hinder parental engagement, making it difficult for schools to establish strong home-school partnerships and build trust. In addition, families/caregivers without digital literacy skills may not know how to help educate their children about digital health, safety, and citizenship. Without family guidance, students may be at a higher risk of encountering online dangers or engaging in inappropriate online behavior. (See Digital Health, Safety, and Citizenship for more information.)

Digital equity and adoption are intersectional issues. The most successful strategies involve dialogue with various stakeholders, including government agencies, community anchor institutions, community-based organizations,

---

[143] U.S. Department of Education, Office of Educational Technology, Advancing Digital Equity for All: Community-Based Recommendations for Developing Effective Digital Equity Plans to Close the Digital Divide and Enable Technology-Empowered Learning, Washington, D.C., 2022.

tribes, private companies, impacted community members, families/caregivers, and students.

Digital Harbor Foundations Serves as an Example of Long-Term Innovation Investment

Originally "born in Baltimore and dedicated to creating pathways to opportunity through technology,"[144] Maryland's Digital Harbor Foundation has expanded its efforts globally since opening its Tech Center in a defunct recreation center in 2013. Dedicated to digital equity for everyone, diversity in the tech sector, innovative STEM education, and technology for the public good, Digital Harbor's Center of Excellence works "directly with school districts, communities, classroom teachers, and out-of-school educators to scale best-in-class STEM learning opportunities to ensure all students have access to these transformative learning opportunities."[145] These efforts include educator professional development, community workshops, and a digital learning hub launched in 2023 "aimed at reaching more than 100 educators to provide content that empowers them to build youth digital literacy." Digital Harbor also provides fiscal support to national and international efforts such as the Ukraine Math & Science Achievement Fund. "In addition to undergraduate scholarships," the fund provides "flexible funding that responds to students' dynamic circumstances, as well as infrastructure gifts."[146] The Digital Harbor Foundation is an example of what's possible when public-private partnerships focus on closing the digital divides.

Similar to the cultural sensitivity required in selecting edtech tools mentioned above, building trust is a key component of digital adoption and literacy education. Members of historically marginalized communities often do not trust federal and state governments and private companies. Factors such as immigration status and a history of discrimination against LGBTQI+ individuals may cause families/caregivers to be wary of sharing information. Some Indigenous communities distrust government agencies and systems due

---

144 (n.d.). Our History. Digital Harbor Foundation. Retrieved September 6, 2023, from https://digitalharbor.org/our-history/.

145 (n.d.). *Center of Excellence.* Digital Harbor Foundation. Retrieved September 6, 2023, from https://digitalharbor.org/center-of-excellence/.

146 (n.d.). *About Us.* Ukraine Math & Science Achievement Fund. Retrieved September 6, 2023, from https:// ukraineachievementfund.org/about/.

to past and current exclusionary practices.[147] Families/caregivers who had negative experiences with low-cost connectivity programs in the past (such as poor service, unexpected fees, or required credit checks) may also be reluctant to apply for them again. Language and cultural barriers can also pose challenges to adoption.

Accurate data is another important component of digital adoption. At the outset of the COVID-19 pandemic, many school systems did not have accurate information about home internet connectivity and use, making it difficult to know which learners might have trouble participating reliably in emergency remote learning and why. For instance, surveys about home internet access and devices must be carefully worded and administered to ensure the accuracy of the data collected. A household might report access to devices and the internet, but that connectivity might be limited to a single phone.

Providing Multilingual Digital Literacy Support for Learners, Families, and Caregivers

Located just outside of Portland, Oregon, the Beaverton School District serves more than 40,000 students, approximately 24 percent of whom identify as Latino. When the schools first launched their 1-to-1 program in 2014, they discovered not all students had equitable access to reliable, high-speed internet at home. They then implemented several strategies to help bridge the gap. As they began the work, they soon discovered many of their Spanish-speaking parents and guardians could not be contacted via email, creating barriers to communication. Some parents had never created an email address, while others had one but rarely used it and didn't provide it to the school. Realizing they needed to engage their Spanish-speaking parent community with digital literacy and citizenship education, the district began hosting monthly Latino parent technology nights in Spanish in collaboration with their community liaison.

To publicize the event without relying on email or other digital communication tools, district personnel recorded a message about the event in Spanish that was sent to parents by the school autodialer. They also recruited student volunteers from their Latinos Unidos club to spread

[147] U.S. Department of Education, Office of Educational Technology, Advancing Digital Equity for All: Community-Based Recommendations for Developing Effective Digital Equity Plans to Close the Digital Divide and Enable Technology-Empowered Learning, Washington, D.C., 2022

the word about the parent night to the broader community. The district helped remove attendance barriers by providing on-site daycare, refreshments, and interpreters. The goals of the events were to help parents stay abreast of district activities, improve communication with their child's teachers, and help parents support their children with digital citizenship information. The district also provided hands-on computer training at every meeting, teaching such tasks as:

- Establishing email accounts
- Accessing student attendance and academic records
- Navigating the school district web page and accessing it in Spanish
- Practicing locating essential information
- Communicating follow-up information for parent and caregiver support

By cultivating the digital skills of their Spanish-speaking families over several years, Beaverton has been able to improve communications and create a more participatory and inclusive school culture.

Electronically administered surveys requiring an internet connection may actually exclude the people needing the most help. While many school systems use Free and Reduced Lunch eligibility as a proxy indicator for poverty, it may not provide an accurate picture of home internet connectivity and use unless combined with survey data. Through qualitative research, district leaders have reported that some families prioritize internet access despite income level, and vice versa.[148] Inaccurate data can lead to funding and program decisions which widen the digital divide.

Supporting digital adoption among families/caregivers is a complex, multifaceted challenge that requires multi-stakeholder collaboration and iterative processes to address. However, the benefits to learners and their families and the opportunity to build school/home relationships make it worthwhile.

---

[148] Katz, V., & Rideout, V. (2021, June 24). *Learning at home while under-connected*. New America. https://www.newamerica.org/education-policy/reports/learning-at-home-while-underconnected/.

Deeper Dive: Digital Health, Safety, and Citizenship

In the early days of digital connectivity, the internet was called the "information superhighway"— apt metaphor for considering digital health, safety, and citizenship for students and educators. Like a highway, internet access can take users to many places. Some provide tremendous opportunities for learning, community building, socialization, and exploration. Others are potentially harmful or dangerous. In the same way young drivers must learn the rules before getting behind the wheel, districts should plan to build digital health, safety, and citizenship skills before providing access to connectivity and devices.

In addition to in-school concerns about digital health, safety, and citizenship, schools face increased concerns with out-of-school access. Although school and district networks use content filtering per federal requirement, 94 percent of 8-18-year-olds have a smartphone[149] provided by their families, not by a school or district, often with unfiltered, 24/7 internet access. Students often use digital devices long before they set foot on a school campus and from a very young age. The 2023 U.S. Surgeon General's advisory on social media and youth mental health, the American Psychological Association's health advisory on social media use in adolescence, and news headlines discussing the challenges of student phone use in schools have raised key concerns about social use of technology distracting from schooling or contributing to negative peer dynamics. Schools face growing pressure to attend to the larger context of student technology use and concerns surrounding it, even outside of school hours and on commercial digital platforms.

Students and families can benefit from guidance in navigating the safe and healthy use of digital platforms and devices, both in and out of school. According to a 2022 report from Common Sense Media, 43 percent of children ages 8-12 have a smartphone. Nearly 40 percent use social media even though age 13 is generally the required minimum age used by social media platforms in the United States.[150]

---

[149] (2021, August 18). *The Common Sense Census: Media Use by Tweens and Teens*. Common Sense Media. Retrieved August 14, 2023, from https://www.commonsensemedia.org/sites/default/files/research/report/8-18-census-integrated-report-final-web_0.pdf.

[150] The minimum required age set by social media platforms is informed by the Children's Online Protection and Privacy Act that requires social media platforms to collect verifiable parental consent before collecting, storing, and sharing data from children under age 13. Source: Federal Trade Commission. (2023, February 3). Children's Online Privacy Protection

Despite being concerned over their children's social and recreational technology use, many adults admit to not setting the best example. More than 3 out of 5 (62 percent) parents surveyed by MyVision said their tech use influences their children, and 72 percent feel it's a negative influence.[151] A majority of parents report that their phone can get in the way of spending quality time with their children; roughly seven in ten parents (68 percent) say they are at least sometimes distracted by their smartphone, with 17 percent saying this happens often.[152] The MyVision survey found that 65 percent of parents do not monitor their screen time use,[153] and research found a significant association between parental phubbing (the act of snubbing a physically present person in favor of a mobile phone) and student academic performance.[154] Given the challenges adults face managing digital device use,[155] it is essential for schools and parents to work together to help students develop these critical digital health, safety, and citizenship skills.

Students may already be "driving" before they get to school, but without having the necessary knowledge and skills to do so safely and wisely. Just as parents and families play a significant role in student academic achievement, they also play a significant role in the development of student technology habits, making it all the more important that schools and families work together to benefit students.

As community organizations, schools are uniquely positioned to help bridge this gap in understanding and may need guidance in seeking to

---

Rule ("COPPA"). Federal Trade Commission. Retrieved from https://www.ftc.gov/legal-library/browse/rules/childrens-online-privacy-protection-rule-coppa.

[151] (n.d.). *Survey Finds Parents' Screen Use Has Negative Influence on Children*. MyVision.org. Retrieved August 14, 2023, from https:// myvision.org/guides/survey-finds-parents-concerned-over-kids-screen-time/#struggles.

[152] Parenting Children in the Age of Screens: (n.d.). *Parenting in the Age of Screens*. Pew Research. Retrieved August 14, 2023, from https://www.pewresearch.org/internet/2020/07/28/parenting-children-in-the-age-of-screens/#:~:text=Fully%2071%25%20 of%20 parents%20say,same%20about%20developing%20healthy%20friendships.

[153] (n.d.). *Survey Finds Parents' Screen Use Has Negative Influence on Children*. MyVision.org. Retrieved August 14, 2023, from https://myvision.org/guides/survey-finds-parents-concerned-over-kids-screen-time/#struggles.

[154] Jiang, Y., Lin, L., & Hu, R. (2023). Parental phubbing and academic burnout in adolescents: The role of social anxiety and self-control. *Frontiers in Psychology*, 14. https://doi.org/10.3389/fpsyg.2023.1157209.

[155] (2023, July 27). *The Insidious Habit That Can Hurt Your Relationship*. New York Times. Retrieved August 14, 2023, from https:// www.nytimes.com/2023/07/27/well/family/phubbing-phone-snubbing-relationship.html. "The Dual Capacity-Building Framework for Family-School Partnerships" by Dual Capacity is licensed under CC BY-NC-SA 4.0.

communicate about out-of-school activities and habits. The National Center on Safe, Supportive Learning Environments cites the Dual Capacity-Building Framework for Family-School Partnerships to support the development of family engagement strategies, policies, and programs. The framework outlines the challenges, essential conditions, policy and program goals, and capacity outcomes for building family-school partnerships. While the framework was designed for building family-school partnerships more broadly, it is well suited for digital health, safety, and citizenship capacity building among educators, families, and students. Key to the framework is an understanding that both schools and families/caregivers have areas of growth in building their capacities to communicate and collaborate in supporting student learning.

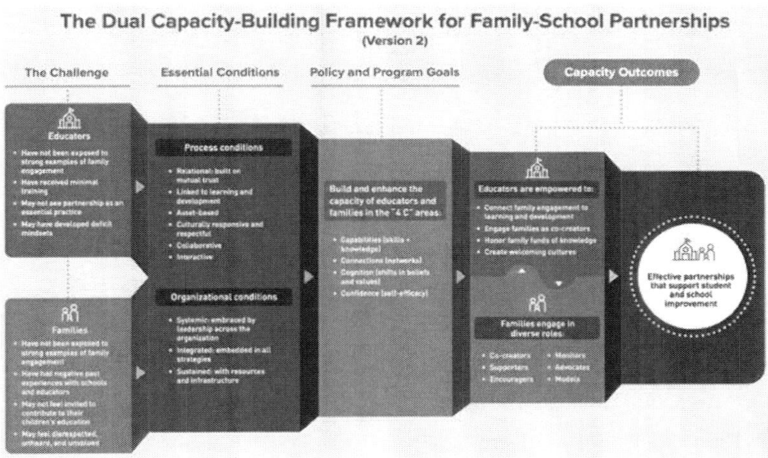

By approaching digital health, safety, and citizenship education holistically and engaging families as partners, school districts can build the capacity of both parents and students to use technology wisely. There has been considerable research on the importance of parent/caregiver involvement and the importance of fostering school-family partnerships to enhance the academic, social, and emotional learning for children and adolescents.[156] Bringing parents/caregivers into the conversation about digital health, safety, and citizenship can support students while building the school-family relationships critical for academic success. Conversely, by helping students

[156] Patrikakou, E. (2015). Relationships Among Parents, Students, and Teachers: The Technology Wild Card. *Procedia - Social and Behavioral Sciences*, 174, 2253-2258. https://doi.org/10.1016/j.sbspro.2015.01.883.

and families differentiate between productive and non-productive online activities and engaging them in more nuanced conversations about digital health, safety, and citizenship, educators can build the capacity of their entire school community to use technology meaningfully and wisely.

Digital Health: The ability of individuals to maintain a healthy and balanced relationship with technology and the digital world.

Digital Safety: Protecting individuals from online risks and ensuring their privacy and security while using digital technologies.

Digital Citizenship: Appropriate, responsible behavior when using technology.

Kansas District Takes Planned Approach to Digital Citizenship

When leaders of Wichita Public Schools considered how they would build digital citizenship into the learning of every student, the 94-site district knew they needed to take a measured approach. The result was a 3-year plan that focused on middle schools the first year, elementary the second, and high schools the third. The district developed common teaching strategies and provided professional learning for teachers to build their capacity. The team leading the charge included the district's Chief Information Officer, Digital Literacy Coordinator, and 12 instructional learning coaches/primary digital citizenship coaches. The core team meets monthly to share new resources, provide professional development, share best practices, address challenges, and offer collaborative support. Keys to Wichita's success include identifying expert teachers to lead professional learning and offering insights and alignment to state standards and initiatives such as computer science, social emotional learning, computer literacy, and media literacy.

Digital Health

Digital Health and well-being refers to the ability of individuals to maintain a healthy and balanced relationship with technology and the digital world. It recognizes the benefits of technology and the potential negative impacts of excessive or unhealthy technology use, including strategies to help promote physical, mental, and emotional well-being in digital usage. Some aspects of digital health include:

- *Mindful Technology Use:* Technology serves many different purposes. It can support formal learning (such as students using synchronous editing software to collaborate with others on a class project) and interest-driven informal learning (such as the student who learns how to knit from YouTube and online forums). It can also be used casually or socially (such as playing video games or scrolling through social media). Mindful technology users are thoughtful and intentional about how they use technology. They know how digital interactions impact mental and emotional well-being and are intentional about the volume and content of their digital media engagement.
- *Setting Digital Boundaries:* Setting boundaries is an important aspect of technology use. Roughly six in ten parents say they spend too much time on their smartphones, while a third say they spend too much time on social media.[157] Similarly, students working on homework assignments can easily get distracted by social media notifications and quickly find themselves off task. Learning to manage and limit these distractions and balancing online and offline activities is a valuable collection of skills and habits. Educating parents about strategies such as creating family media plans, device-free family dinners, and plugging in devices in a centralized location at night can help build the capacity of the entire family to engage appropriately with digital media.

---

[157] (2020, July 28). *Parenting Children in the Age of Screens.* Pew Research. Retrieved August 14, 23, from https://www.pewresearch. org/internet/2020/07/28/parenting-children-in-the-age-of-screens/.

- *Maintaining Healthy Sleep Routines:* Research shows that the light emitted by digital devices can interfere with sleep, especially before bedtime.[158] Digital health emphasizes the importance of maintaining a healthy sleep routine, including avoiding screens for at least an hour before sleep and keeping electronic devices out of the bedroom to improve sleep quality and overall well-being. Healthy sleep routines can play a key role in academic success.[159]

Research in this area is ongoing. The Digital Wellness Lab, the American Academy of Pediatrics (AAP) Center of Excellence on Social Media and Youth Mental Health, and the Harvard Center for Digital Thriving are resources updated regularly with the latest evidence and recommendations.

Incorporating Hawaiian Values and Digital Citizenship into Computer Science Education

Hawai'i is a culturally unique state. To help ensure that its educational system and content are culturally relevant and connected to Hawaiian values, the Hawai'i Department of Educatio (HI DOE) developed the Ha Framework, a state-wide framework to develop the skills, behaviors, and dispositions consistent with of Hawai'i's unique context and honor the qualities and values of its indigenous language and culture. When state legislation mandated that Computer Science (CS) education be offered to all K-12 students, the HI DOE leveraged the Ha Framework and an existing digital citizenship initiative, Akamai Digital Citizenship: Show Aloha in Person and Online, to ensure CS offerings explored ways for individuals and communities to influence computing through their behaviors, culture, and social interactions. By incorporating computer science and digital citizenship into the Ha Framework, the HI DOE and their stakeholder team are helping ensure the new concepts are relevant to students and families.

---

158 Ricketts, E. J., Joyce, D. S., Rissman, A. J., Burgess, H. J., Colwell, C. S., Lack, L. C., & Gradisar, M. (2022). Electric lighting, adolescent sleep and circadian outcomes, and recommendations for improving light health. *Sleep medicine reviews*, 64, 101667. https://doi.org/10.1016/j.smrv.2022.101667.

159 CDC Sleep and Health: https://www.cdc.gov/healthyschools/sleep.htm#:~:text=Children%20and%20adolescents%20who%20do,poor%20mental%20health%2C%20and%20injuries.&text=They%20are%20also%20more%20likely,poor%20academic%20performance%20in%20school.

Digital Safety

Digital safety focuses on protecting individuals from online risks and ensuring their privacy and security while using digital technologies. Following our safe driving metaphor, digital safety is akin to understanding the "rules of the road." It involves adopting measures to safeguard personal information, avoiding cyber threats, and preventing unauthorized access to sensitive data. Digital safety also encompasses educating individuals about online dangers, such as phishing scams, identity theft, cyberbullying and online harassment, and promoting responsible digital citizenship.

Key elements of digital safety include:

- *Privacy:* Students should understand how to protect their personal information online and the importance of doing so. They should understand the risks of sharing sensitive information online, such as their full name, address, phone number, or financial information. Districts should also be transparent with students and families about activity monitoring on school system-owned devices and communicate the context and justification behind monitoring systems. As mentioned previously, emerging artificial intelligence technologies can pose privacy concerns as large language models feed on the information shared with them and should only be utilized in education systems when data privacy and anonymity can be assured and verified.
- *Cybersecurity:* Students should understand the risks of malware, phishing, hacking, and other cyber threats. Examples of good cyber hygiene include:
  - Teaching students how to create secure passphrases for online accounts (and not to share them with others).
  - Knowing how to recognize phishing emails and suspicious links and what to do when encountering them.
  - Being aware of social engineering techniques and thinking critically before sharing information with others.
  - Not downloading files from unknown sources.
  - Keeping personal devices updated with security patches.
- *Cyberbullying:* Cyberbullying is bullying that takes place over digital devices like cell phones, computers, and tablets. It can occur through SMS, text, and apps, or online in social media, forums, or gaming where people can view, participate in, or share content. Cyberbullying

includes sending, posting, or sharing negative, harmful, false, or mean content about someone else. It can include sharing personal or private information about someone else, causing embarrassment or humiliation.[160]

- *Online Harassment:* Online harassment and abuse include various harmful and sometimes illegal behaviors perpetrated through technology. Online harassment and abuse take many forms, including the non-consensual distribution of intimate digital images; cyberstalking; sextortion; doxing; malicious deep fakes; gendered disinformation; rape and death threats; the online recruitment and exploitation of victims of sex trafficking; and various forms of technology-facilitated intimate partner abuse.[161]

Building Media Literacy into State Standards

Media literacy is a key component of both active use and digital citizenship, and states like Delaware are taking steps to ensure all students are engaged, analytical, and informed media consumers. The state passed S.B. 195 in 2022, requiring the inclusion of media literacy standards for K-12 classrooms. The law allows media literacy to "be incorporated into existing curricula standards" and states that "media literacy curricula is needed to guarantee the vitality of American democracy and students' ability to engage in civic life." The draft standards drawon the ISTE student standards and the American Association of School Libraries Student Standards and will be implemented in the 2024-2025 school year. Guiding the work, "The Digital Citizenship Education Act" offers the following definitions:

"Media literacy" means the ability to access, analyze, evaluate, create, and take action with all forms of communication and encompasses the foundational skills of digital citizenship and internet safety, including the norms of appropriate, responsible, ethical, and healthy behavior, and cyberbullying prevention.

---

160 (n.d.). *What is Cyberbullying*. StopBullying.gov. Retrieved August 14, 2023, from https://www.stopbullying.gov/cyberbullying/what-is-it.

161 (2022, June 16). *Memorandum on the Establishment of the White House Task Force to Address Online Harassment and Abuse*. The White House. Retrieved August 14, 2023, from https://www.whitehouse.gov/briefing-room/presidential-actions/2022/06/16/ memorandum-on-the-establishment-of-the-white-house-task-force-to-address-online-harassment-and-abuse/.

> "Digital citizenship" means the diverse set of skills related to participating in digital platforms, including the norms of appropriate, responsible, and healthy behavior.

Digital Citizenship

Digital citizenship is appropriate, responsible behavior when using technology.[162] It encompasses the knowledge, skills, and attitudes required to navigate the digital world respectfully and responsibly. Good digital citizens engage positively and constructively in online communities and possess good digital literacy and critical thinking skills. Key elements of good digital citizenship include:

Responsible Online Behavior: Digital citizenship emphasizes the importance of respectful and responsible online behavior, including treating others with kindness and empathy, being mindful of the impact of one's words and actions in digital spaces, and adhering to ethical standards. Good digital citizens understand the consequences of cyberbullying, harassment, and sharing inappropriate or harmful content.

Managing One's Digital Footprint and Reputation: Good digital citizens realize that everything we do online leaves a digital footprint. They understand the importance of managing and curating one's digital presence and are mindful of the potential impact of online actions on personal and professional reputation. They understand the long-term consequences of sharing and posting personal content online.

Media Literacy: Media literacy includes the skills associated with using technology to enable users to find, evaluate, organize, create, and communicate information; and developing digital citizenship and the responsible use of technology.[163] Good digital citizens can effectively and critically navigate digital spaces. They possess the ability to find, evaluate, and use information from online sources and understand how to communicate, collaborate, and create content using digital tools.

Understanding Copyright and Intellectual Property: Digital citizenship promotes respect for copyright laws and intellectual property rights. It encourages proper citation and attribution when using or sharing the work of

---

[162] (n.d.). *Digital Citizenship Skills Teach Digital Citizenship Skills to Prevent Cyberbullying*. StopBullying.gov. Retrieved August 14, 2023, from https://www.stopbullying.gov/resources/research-resources/digital-citizenship-skills.

[163] Museum and Library Services Act of 2010, Pub. L. 111-340, 22 Dec. 2010, https://www.govinfo.gov/content/pkg/PLAW-111publ340/ pdf/PLAW-111publ340.pdf.

others and discourages plagiarism or copyright infringement. It also teaches students to understand their rights as content creators.

Algorithmic Literacy: AI has exponentially increased the need for students to understand and be able to critically analyze algorithms and how they impact our online and offline lives. Algorithmic literacy includes knowledge of the underlying principles, processes, and biases that shape algorithms[164] and their implications for individuals, society, and decision-making. It also includes understanding how to interact effectively with AI and the ethical implications of using generative AI tools such as ChatGPT.

Teaching children and teens digital citizenship skills can help prevent cyberbullying and its negative effects. When children learn positive online behaviors, they can use social media in productive ways.

Southwestern Pennsylvania Engaged in Decade-long Dedication to Digital Health, Safety, and Citizenship

Allegheny County Intermediate Unit 3 supports the work and implementation of digital citizenship across 42 districts in Southwest Pennsylvania. With generous support from the Grable Foundation and in partnership with Common Sense Media, Unit 3 has worked with districts and other organizations in Greater Pittsburgh to provide innovative resources and support to help educators, families, and students develop the skills they need to harness the power of technology for learning. The partnership aims to help kids and teens in the Greater Pittsburgh area thrive as learners, leaders, and citizens in this digital age. As a result, the area has seen strong public-private partnerships and relationships, positive trends in impact data, customized support across 42 districts, and grants to support innovative learning across southwest Pennsylvania, provided by the local Remake Learning Network. Key to this success has been a strong dissemination plan, role-alike meetings held once a month, a strong professional learning plan, and inviting teachers to present with youth about their experience with the Common Sense digital citizenship resources.

Ten questions schools and districts can ask to help support students' digital health and safety:

[164] Klein, A. (2023, May 10). *Ai Literacy, Explained*. Education Week. Retrieved August 14, 2023, from https://www.edweek.org/ technology/ai-literacy-explained/2023/05.

1) Does your school or district have a clearly articulated vision of digital health and safety for students at all levels and does it account for possible risks related to student demographics?
2) How are you collecting data and evidence to better understand the digital health and safety needs of students, families, and employees within your district or schools (e.g., needs assessments, climate surveys, incident reports)?
3) What measurable goals have you established for the digital health, safety, and mental well-being of students?
4) How might students and families be included in assessing needs, setting district and school goals, and designing learning opportunities?
5) What supports are necessary and do you have in place to ensure key staff (e.g., administrators, school counselors, social workers, educators) have an adequate understanding of and capacity to respond to the unique needs involving support of student digital health and safety?
6) What emergency resources, procedures, and supports are in place to support in moments of crisis regarding digital health and safety?
7) What curricular, extra-, or co-curricular inclusion supports can be or have been established to support student digital health and safety?
8) What external relationships can be or have been established to augment school and district capacity to support student digital health and safety?
9) How do you plan to build community awareness and support of these needs, goals, and efforts?
10) What ongoing funding sources (e.g., Title II, Title IV grants) can or will you leverage to support these efforts?[165]

Planning, implementing, and evaluating the curricular components of question seven above requires planning that answers key questions such as those below:

[165] (2023, May 9). *Has Your School Had Enough?* 10 Questions Schools Can Ask to Build Better Digital Health & Safety. U.S. Department of Education, Office of Educational Technology Blog. Retrieved August 14, 2023, from https://medium.com/@OfficeofEdTech/has-your-school-had-enough-10-questions-schools-can-ask-to-build-better-digital-health-safety-d131c5d4d100.

- What are key expectations for digital health, safety, and citizenship actions and understandings at each grade level?
- Where will instruction in digital health, safety, and citizenship live within curricula as well as the academic day and year?

The ubiquity of social media and digital tools presents the challenge and opportunity for schools and districts to partner with families and caregivers to make sure all students have what they need to maintain their digital health and safety. By integrating digital health tools, fostering digital safety practices, and nurturing digital wellness habits, students can leverage the benefits of technology while safeguarding their physical and mental health.

Protecting Student Data Privacy

In addition to teaching students how to protect their privacy online, school officials, families, and software developers should be mindful of how data privacy, confidentiality, and security practices affect students. Schools and districts should tell students and parents what kind of student data the school or third parties (e.g., online educational service providers) are collecting and how the data can be used, and in which contexts the data can be further disclosed without their consent. In addition to any and all applicable requirements under the Family Educational Rights and Privacy Act (FERPA), education leaders should develop policies that identify who can access student data and communicate to families their rights and responsibilities concerning data collection. These policies should include formal adoption processes for online educational services and click-wrap agreements. Click-wrap agreements appear when users are asked to accept the provider's terms of service before using a website or software application. Click-wrap agreements enter the developer and the user (in this case, the school or district) into a contractual relationship akin to signing a contract. Districts should ensure district employees understand the implications of district policies governing the use of such agreements.

Several federal statutes apply to student privacy in schools. More information on each is below.

Creating a Culture of Student Data Privacy Takes Time

Not long after hiring a new Executive Director of Educational Services, Rocky River School District in Ohio recognized the need to create a system-wide culture focused on protecting student data privacy.

Although the school board had recently reconfirmed its Student Privacy Policy, implementation was inconsistent.

Collaborative stakeholder conversations identified the need to clearly define and educate staff about the difference between personally identifiable information (PII), confidential information, internal information, and directory information. After consultations with teacher leaders identified the need for increased training opportunities and an easier way for teachers to request digital tools, the district simplified the request process for teachers, developed an easily accessible list of pre-approved digital applications, and created a teacher-focused self-help guide.

The district found that pushback often resulted from a lack of understanding or awareness, so they provided staff with a variety of ongoing training opportunities, including in-depth professional learning sessions, faculty meeting pop-ups, monthly bulletins, explanatory videos, and privacy-protecting tips and tricks recommended by other teachers and staff. The district also built an internal website with student data privacy information and resources and designated teacher-leaders as the initial point persons for staff questions. Utilizing multiple communication channels helped get the word out. In addition, the district attorney attended staff meetings to explain the importance of data governance and tied it to their state-required Teacher Code of Ethics training.

The district also updated its textbook adoption procedures to include vetting for data governance requirements. Finally, the district applied for and earned the CoSN Trusted Learning Environment seal, an accomplishment indicating that they have taken strong, measurable steps to protect student data.

Utah Funds Student Data Privacy Office to Support School Systems

Like many states, Utah has recently updated its student data privacy laws. In 2015, Utah passed HB68, which required the Utah State Board of Education (USBE) to make recommendations for updating existing privacy laws and, critically, to develop a funding proposal to implement data privacy changes. This work led to the Student Data Protection Act in 2016, which includes requirements for local educational agencies, state educational agencies, and third-party vendors. Part of Utah's privacy efforts was the decision to create and sustainably fund a Student Data

Privacy Office. In addition to a Chief Privacy Officer, the office includes a student data privacy auditor, a student data privacy project manager, and a student data privacy trainer. This combination of funding, legislation, and dedicated experts has created a sustainable student privacy system that provides local educational agency student privacy training, resources, and reporting. One case study about Utah's student data privacy attributes Utah's success to methodical collaboration between state and local leaders, ongoing dedicated funding for dedicated staff, and continual improvement. "Mandated training at the state (tied to teacher relicensure) and local levels, ongoing reporting requirements, and the development and distribution of high-quality resources by USBE's dedicated staff all serve to keep privacy top of mind."

Federal Privacy Laws and K-12 Education

FERPA (the Family Educational Rights and Privacy Act) affords parents and "eligible students" the right to inspect and review, seek to amend, and exercise some control over the disclosure of student education records maintained by educational agencies (e.g., school districts) and institutions (i.e., schools) to which funds have been made available under any program administered by the Secretary of Education. (Under FERPA, an "eligible student" is a student who has reached 18 years of age or is attending a postsecondary school at any age.) Among other things, for instance, FERPA generally requires educational agencies and institutions to obtain prior written consent from parents and eligible students before disclosing PII from education records. However, one exception to FERPA's general written consent requirement permits an educational agency or institution to disclose, without consent, PII from education records to a third party to whom the educational agency or institution has outsourced institutional services or functions, as long as certain conditions are met. Under this exception, the third party must be determined by the educational agency or institution to constitute a school official who has a legitimate educational interest in the education records under the criteria set forth in its annual notification of FERPA rights; perform an institutional service or function for which the educational agency or institution would otherwise use employees; be under the direct control of the educational agency or institution with respect to the use and maintenance of the education records; and be subject to the FERPA requirements governing the use and redisclosure of PII from education records found in 34 CFR § 99.33. For more guidance on FERPA, visit the U.S. Department of Education's FERPA resources.

COPPA (the Children's Online Privacy Protection Act) governs the online collection of personal information from individuals under 13 years of age. Before a commercial website or online service directed towards individuals under 13 years of age can collect any personal information from such individuals, the operator of such website or service must obtain "verifiable parental consent." Verifiable parental consent is also required if an operator has actual knowledge that it is collecting personal information from an individual under 13 years of age. The Federal Trade Commission (FTC), which enforces COPPA, has said that school officials can, in certain situations, provide consent on behalf of the parents as long as that consent is limited to the educational context—where an operator collects personal information from students for the use and benefit of the school, and no other commercial purpose. For more information on COPPA, please visit the FTC's COPPA FAQ website.

IDEA (the Individuals with Disabilities Education Act) includes confidentiality requirements to protect the privacy interests of children with disabilities from birth until age 21 who are referred for services under the IDEA. IDEA protects PII in the records of children referred to IDEA. IDEA requires that a parent provide prior written consent before PII is disclosed to a third party and that the parental consent is informed. There are some specific exceptions that may apply to the general rule of parental consent.

CIPA (the Children's Internet Protection Act) imposes several requirements on schools or libraries that receive E-Rate discounts for internet access. Schools and libraries must certify that they have technologies in place to block or filter internet access to content that is obscene, pornographic, or harmful to minors, and schools must also monitor the online activities of minors. The FCC's CIPA Guide offers a more in-depth understanding of CIPA requirements.

Consult PTAC Recommendations

The U.S. Department of Education established the Privacy Technical Assistance Center (PTAC) as a one-stop resource to learn about privacy related to student data. PTAC provides information and updated guidance on privacy, confidentiality, and security practices through a variety of means, including training materials and direct assistance. PTAC also provides guidance on FERPA and PPRA. PTAC recently provided additional recommendations on Protecting Student Privacy While Using Online Educational Services and Transparency Best Practices for Schools and Districts.

PTAC Data Breach Scenario is intended to assist schools, districts, and other educational organizations with internal data security training.

The Password Data Breach interactive exercise is aimed at district management and provides a simulated response to a district-level data breach that focuses on the processes, procedures, and skills needed to respond.

PPRA (the Protection of Pupil Rights Amendment) protects the rights of parents and students in a number of ways, some of which are summarized below. (These rights transfer from a parent to a student when the student turns 18 years old or is an emancipated minor under applicable state law.) PPRA requires that a local educational agency (as defined in PPRA) that receives funds under a program administered by the U.S. Department of Education develop and adopt local policies, in consultation with parents, on specifically enumerated privacy issues. A couple of such required local policies are summarized below. PPRA requires that such a local educational agency develop and adopt a policy, in consultation with parents, that affords parents the right to inspect, upon request, among other things, instructional materials, excluding academic tests or academic assessments, used by the local educational agency as part of the educational curriculum for a student. PPRA also requires that such a local educational agency develop and adopt a policy, in consultation with parents, regarding the collection, disclosure, or use of personal information collected from students for the purpose of marketing or for selling that information (or otherwise providing that information to others for that purpose), including arrangements to protect student privacy that are provided by the agency in the event of such collection, disclosure, or use. PPRA also requires that such a local educational agency directly notify parents of students who are scheduled to participate in activities involving the collection, disclosure, or use of personal information collected from the students for the purpose of marketing or sale (or otherwise providing that information to others for that purpose) and give parents the opportunity to opt the students out of these activities. One important exception to the foregoing PPRA requirement is that neither parental notice and the opportunity to opt-out nor the development and adoption of local policies are required for such local educational agencies to use students' personal information for the exclusive purpose of developing, evaluating, or providing educational products or services for, or to, students or schools.

HIPAA (the Health Insurance Portability and Accountability Act) sets national standards and requirements for, among other things, the privacy of protected health information (PHI) and the security of electronic PHI. The HIPAA Privacy Rule does not apply to records that are protected by FERPA. For a better understanding of the intersection between HIPAA and FERPA, see the jointly published guidance from the US Department of Health and Human Services and the U.S. Department of Education.

Of the three digital divides, the United States has made the most progress in closing the digital access divide over the past decade. Millions more students now have access to high-speed internet and devices suitable for learning at school and at home. Educators are faced with digital ecosystems teaming with thousands of digital learning resources. In most spaces, the immediate edtech playing field is leveling. As is ever the case, overcoming these access challenges leads states, districts, and schools to more complex issues. Here, too, progress is being made. New state student data privacy laws have prompted the development of capacity-building resources to support school systems. The importance of supporting student Digital Health, Safety, and Citizenship—in and out of the classroom—is receiving national attention. Accessible and assistive technologies continue to evolve. States and districts have long recognized closing the digital access divide is an essential condition if they hope to improve the design of learning supported by technology to ensure all students are active, analytical learners.

Conclusion

As has ever been true, educational technology holds vast potential to improve teaching and learning for every student and teacher in the United States. In recent years, driven by the emergency of a pandemic, schools have found themselves with more connectivity, devices, and digital resources than at any other moment in history. This current context presents a unique opportunity.

States, districts, and schools across the country can leverage this momentum of a narrowing access divide to focus key efforts in providing all teachers the time, support, and capacity they need to design authentic learning experiences for all learners supported by this proliferation of digital tools. They can set bold new visions of the skills, knowledge, and experiences all students must have as they progress through and graduate from PK-12.

Furthermore, states, districts, and schools can eliminate barriers and uncover biases in practice that have historically limited innovative and promising learning experiences supported by edtech to a predictable minority.

The nation can close the digital access, design, and use divides. The NETP includes examples from every state in the country where schools, districts, and their partners are proving it's possible. For this possibility to reach all students will require an understanding that the kinds of instructional tasks students need to prepare them for the world they will inherit cannot rely on content alone. The instructional core requires attending to both content and people.

Appendix A - Additional Digital Use Divide Examples

The examples below showcase additional states and school districts working to close the Digital Use Divide.

Supporting Teachers and Students in Van Meter, Iowa

Serving more than 1,000 PK-12 students in a single building, the Van Meter Community School District in Iowa has committed to helping educators leverage active technology use to support learning goals. Supported by a team of instructional coaches that focuses on building relationships and meeting teachers where they are, teachers are updating lessons to help students build their digital literacy skills and engage more deeply with content. For example, an annual 5th-grade project on the civil rights movement was transformed after students and teachers watched a speech by late civil rights leader Representative John Lewis and learned about his autobiographical black and white graphic novel trilogy about the civil rights movement, *March*. Inspired by his story, teachers had students use a digital storyboarding tool to create graphic novels about well-known figures in the civil rights movement, which students could share online with their families. By providing teachers with ongoing, job-embedded support, they continue to grow and improve their professional practice.

Developing a Computer Science Immersion Program in South Dakota

In 2017, Sioux Falls School District found ways to bring technology into the district. They started a five-year partnership with Code to the Future to create a computer science immersion program in three Title 1 elementary schools and two high-poverty middle schools. Code to the Future trains the teachers by having them do the assignments and projects their students will do, and then they learn to code and complete hands-on projects. By integrating coding throughout their core classes, students develop critical thinking, collaboration, problem-solving, and other skills that companies need. In addition to this program, the district also created maker spaces in some of its elementary and middle school libraries using a state innovation grant. Teachers encourage students to apply what they learn to create something in the maker space, using items like sewing machines, jewelry-making supplies, Legos, Kinex blocks, 3D drawing pens, and programming kits. Librarians say that one of their favorite outcomes is watching students teach each other how to create things.

Institute of Education Sciences Grant Funds Tool to Support Writing Instruction

Funded through a grant from the Institute of Education Sciences in 2021, Writing Architect[166] is a tool aiming to "assist teachers in connecting evidence-based writing instruction with students' needs as identified in a digital classroom written composition assessment. The goal is to improve late elementary students' written composition in response to text (informational writing) and to use assessment results more effectively for instructional purposes."[167] Led by researchers at Michigan State University and piloted in Michigan elementary schools through 2025, the project aims to create "an integrated tool that combines digital assessment of writing with differentiated instructional recommendations, and the support needed to implement differentiated writing instruction." By "gathering feedback from teacher users, teaching experts, and writing experts," the project highlights the power of keeping "humans in the loop" when designing edtech tools.

[166] https://www.writingresearch.net/.

[167] https://ies.ed.gov/funding/grantsearch/details.asp?ID=4633.

Leveraging Math Badges for Mastery-Based Assessment

The Idaho Math Initiative, led by the State Department of Education (SDE) and funded by Idaho Statute 33-1627, seeks to promote the improvement of mathematical instruction and student achievement in the state while leveraging digital badges to mark student competency. One of four states, along with Illinois, Rhode Island, and Kentucky, Idaho worked with XQ Institute to pilot using Math Badges designed for high school mathematics to implement a mastery-based assessment system. XQ support included the creation of Math Badge assessments and funding a half-time Regional Math Specialist to serve as project lead. The project also provided funding for professional training across eight school districts and planning time for school-level teams. The SDE is also working with the Idaho Division of Career and Technical Education (CTE) to develop a system to track and store student progress and digital badges. The project will allow CTE programs to integrate course content with mathematics assessments and provide an assessment system for awarding mathematics course credit.

Students earn badges by providing evidence demonstrating mastery of the badge content and practicing expectations in a multiple measures system. The badges will align with three standard general education mathematics courses available through Idaho's colleges and universities.

Developing a Graduate Profile and a Graduate Profile Learning Continuum

The Howard-Suamico School District (HSSD) near Green Bay, Wisconsin, has eight schools and serves more than 6,000 students in grades PK-12. The district developed a Graduate Profile to prepare students for a constantly evolving world. The Graduate Profile characteristics include being a self-starter, critical thinker, collaborator, communicator, being adaptable, responsible, and solutionist. Students learn foundational academic skills alongside the graduate profile characteristics to accentuate a whole-student experience in HSSD. Throughout the year, the Board of Education monitors student performance in the seven characteristics of the Graduate Profile.

To help ensure students build these skills at developmentally appropriate levels throughout their PK12 career, the district also developed a Graduate Profile Learning Continuum that explains the progression of learning throughout the Graduate Profile. This continuum guides student learning experiences from PK-12. Edtech is used as needed to help students develop these skills. The goal is to prepare students for success in whatever post-graduation path they choose.

Appendix B - Additional Digital Design Divide Examples

The examples below showcase additional states and school districts working to close the Digital Design Divide.

Maine Project Benefits from Contributions at all Levels

The COVID-19 pandemic highlighted and exacerbated systemic inequities and challenges related to ensuring equitable learning opportunities for all Maine learners and particularly for rural students, students with individualized education plans, and economically underserved students. To address these inequities, the Maine Department of Education (MDOE) Commissioner's Office, through the Rethinking Responsive Education Ventures (RREV) grant,[168] is providing professional development training and funding to support innovative remote learning solutions that have the potential to improve learner outcomes. As a result of this five-year grant, the Institute of Education Sciences Regional Educational Laboratory (REL) Northeast & Islands[169] will collaborate with MDOE and other partners, including students, to build district capacity to use research and data to improve innovations developed through the RREV grant and other sources, assess learner outcomes, and develop promising practices for sustaining and scaling up the innovations.

REL Northeast & Islands will facilitate a training series with district innovation teams to develop and implement a process for examining the implementation fidelity of their remote learning innovations, create a fact sheet summarizing the literature on the innovation areas such as outdoor education and online learning, and produce a co-authored blog series.

---

[168] (n.d.). Rethinking Responsive Education Ventures - RREV. Maine Department of Education. Retrieved September 6, 2023, from https://www.maine.gov/doe/rrev.

[169] U.S. Department of Education (n.d.). Regional Educational Laboratory Northeast and Islands. Institute of Education Sciences. Retrieved September 6, 2023, from https://ies.ed.gov/ncee/rel/region/northeast.

By leveraging federal resources, state-level systems, and local understanding of context and needs, this program aims to better ensure rural Maine educators are able to meet the needs of all learners in innovative ways.

South Carolina Instruction Hub Provides Statewide Access to Digital Learning Resources

Serving more than 780,000 students in 75 Districts, the South Carolina Department of Education (SCDE) needed to address the problem of uneven distribution of learning resources across the state. The SCDE sought to create and provide each school equitable access to up-to-date digital courses and materials, so they partnered with a digital education content provider to develop a Learning Object Repository (LOR). A LOR is a searchable digital library of educational content (learning objects) where teachers, students, and administrators can store, search, access, and share various digital resources from any device and place. The SCDE uses the LOR, called the Instruction Hub, to manage resources and assimilate new content for automated distribution to every school district in the state. Because the LOR utilizes industry-accepted data standards, it integrates with various Learning Management Systems used by South Carolina school systems. In addition to increasing the number of high-quality digital resources available to teachers, the LOR saves teachers valuable planning and preparation time.

The Instruction Hub is implemented across 99 percent of the state's schools. A robust meta-tagging system makes finding content by grade, subject, and keywords easy. Through Instruction Hub, educators can access licensed resources from several content providers and South Carolina Educational Television.

Arkansas Builds Partnership for Equity in Digital Professional Learning Access

Often focused on expanding student opportunities, public-private partnerships hold significant potential for educator learning as well. Tapping into this potential is the aim of ArkansasIDEAS, "a partnership between Arkansas PBS and the Arkansas Department of Education Division of Elementary and Secondary Education.

In a state with a majority-rural population, ArkansasIDEAS provides access to more than 700 online professional development courses free of charge to all Arkansas licensed educators. This equity of access for educators across the state also ensures all districts are able to provide professional learning for their teachers in accordance with state law in areas such as Holocaust education, the science of reading, state history, and others. While the full catalog is available for licensed Arkansas educators, ArkansasIDEAS also provides access to a limited selection of courses for paraprofessionals, pre-licensed educators, and support staff. By including all licensed educators and allowing an on-ramp for pre-licensed teachers, ArkansasIDEAS is ensuring the state's educators and future educators have equitable high-quality digital resources for professional learning.

Sparking Innovation in Response to Teacher Needs

Sometimes, innovation requires a push. A program supporting teachers across West Virginia works to do just that. The West Virginia Public Education Collaborative (WVPEC) housed at West Virginia University, is a "non-partisan collaborative of diverse state and national leaders committed to championing public education at all levels through outreach and innovation while engaging government, education and business leaders to rapidly respond to emerging issues." Among WVPEC's goals is a resolve to elevate and expanding existing initiatives. Its Teacher Innovation Mini-Grant program does just that. From 198 applications requiring teachers to explain how their project would "address post-COVID-19 learning, and how will these classroom enhancements become permanent classroom innovations," WVPEC announced 23 projects for Summer 2023. In partnership with the Claude Worthington Benedum Foundation, WVPEC was able to award $4,000 in funding to each recipient. Projects span pre-k through 12th grade and fall within the categories of career and technical education, ELA, STEAM, Special Education, and Family Engagement. As a result of WVPEC's efforts to listen to and better understand what teachers need in order to innovate, the program is set to spark teacher-led innovation across the state.

Louisiana Teachers Create State-Specific Edtech Integration Guide

When considering how best to support Louisiana educators with edtech integration, the Louisiana Department of Education (LDOE) found that much of the professional learning provided by outside groups was challenging to implement and integrate because it didn't align with the state-approved curriculum. Recognizing the need for state-specific support, they assembled a geographically diverse team of teachers, coaches, leaders, and librarians across the state to develop digital learning guidance to support technology integration within the state curriculum and aligned with the state Educational Technology Plan and Digital Literacy Guidance.

The LDOE created a website with educator-created content for teachers and edtech leaders to communicate this information. Because Louisiana educators develop the content, it is relevant to the specific state context. Additional content integration materials are under development. The LDOE hosts monthly calls for edtech leaders and posts the slide decks online for reference. Department leaders recommend that states facing similar challenges budget for these kinds of projects and tap into and amplify the voices of in-state talent.

Personalizing Student Learning through Tacoma Online

Tacoma Online, an online school founded in 2021 in response to the COVID-19 pandemic, has evolved into an integral part of Tacoma Public Schools' innovative learning landscape. Catering to more than 1,200 students from K-12, it provides a personalized online learning experience and remains committed to bridging educational gaps exacerbated by the digital divide. Tacoma Online provides flexible and accessible learning opportunities that cater to individual student needs anytime and anywhere.

Tangible outcomes of the program's effectiveness include increased credit attainment, improved attendance rates, elevated academic achievements, and prioritized student engagement levels. These successes are quantified through the school's PACE program (Personalized, Accelerated, Connected, Empowered), capturing both quantitative metrics and qualitative feedback. Each student has a PACE Coach, a caring adult staff member committed to supporting each student's social, emotional, and academic growth.

The initiative's success is evident in its enhanced offerings, including optional in-person learning experiences that enrich the educational journey.

These advancements pave the way for expansion beyond the immediate region, reaching students across the wider area. The program is expanding to include Tacoma Flex, the part-time enrollment of secondary learners choosing to engage in in-person and online learning.

According to Adam Kulaas, Director of Innovative Learning & CTE for Tacoma Online, forging robust partnerships with community organizations and technology providers laid a solid foundation for the program's success. In addition, Tacoma Online provides tailored support for students and educators transitioning to online learning. Consistent data collection and analysis of student performance and engagement continue to drive ongoing program refinements and support sustained growth and efficacy.

Appendix C - Additional Digital Access Divide Examples

The examples below showcase additional states and school districts working to close the Digital Access Divide.

Broadband Availability Data Collection and Mapping at Navajo Preparatory School

The Navajo Preparatory School in New Mexico serves learners across the Navajo Nation, which is the size of West Virginia. The school enrolls approximately 270 students from more than 50 majority-rural communities. At the start of the COVID-19 pandemic, the school surveyed learners to understand internet access availability in specific residential locations down to their global positioning system coordinates (latitude and longitude).

Many learners needed access to reliable, high-speed broadband. Based on the survey results, the school created a map identifying which ISPs and cellular services had service available. Their school staff installed the necessary equipment in students' homes, including extending cellular coverage by installing routers and antennas. The school installed HughesNet satellite technology for learners who could not be reached by wired or cellular service. In some cases, the school distributed multiple hotspots to individual households. They are maintaining the home internet options for all learners in case the school needs to transition online again, ensuring that learners have reliable, high-speed broadband for learning at home.

Guam Receives Internet for All Planning Grant

Guam has consistently lagged behind all other United States territories regarding internet speed growth.[170] Approximately 30 percent of the state population lives where high-speed internet is unavailable,[171] including some of the 31,000 students representing diverse ethnic groups who attend Guam's 36 public schools. In areas where high-speed internet is available, Guam residents pay significantly higher rates than on the United States mainland.[172] Speak Up Survey results from Project Tomorrow have indicated that there is a digital divide that exists within Guam's public schools and a gap between Guam's public schools and United States mainland schools in terms of access to and usage of digital technologies.[173] To help address this challenge, Guam received planning grants for deploying high-speed Internet service networks and developing digital skills training programs under the Biden-Harris Administration's "Internet for All" initiative. Guam is receiving $1.4 million in funding from the Bipartisan Infrastructure Law to plan, deploy, and adopt affordable, equitable, and reliable high-speed Internet service throughout the territory. The funding will create new opportunities to expand people's access to high-speed Internet, digital literacy, and IT job training in Guam.[174]

Virginia Implements Statewide Collection of Student Home Broadband Access

During the COVID-19 pandemic, Virginia needed a complete picture of student home access to devices and broadband. The state couldn't apply

---

170 (2023, July 11). The Pulse of Pacific Broadband: Taking a Deeper Dive. Pacific Broadband and Digital Equity. Retrieved September 6, 2023, from https://www.pacificbroadband.org/2023/07/11/the-pulse-of-pacific-broadband-taking-a-deeper-dive/.

171 (n.d.). Guam. Internet For All. Retrieved September 6, 2023, from https://www.internetforall.gov/interactive-map/Guam-GU.

172 U.S. Department of Education (n.d.). Broadband Affordability Tracker. Pacific Broadband and Digital Equity. Retrieved September 6, 2023, from https://www.pacificbroadband.org/resources/#tracker.

173 Velasco, Richard. (2017). Hearing Pacific Island Voices: Digital Divide in Guam's Public Schools. 1. 25-40.

174 (2023, May 16). Biden-Harris Administration Awards $1.4 Million to Guam in 'Internet for All' Planning Grants. National Telecommunications and Information Administration. Retrieved September 6, 2023, from https://www.ntia.gov/press-release/2023/biden-harris-administration-awards-14-million-guam-internet-all-planning-grants.

resources to address the problem without an accurate understanding of student access. In 2022, Virginia passed legislation requiring every school district to submit an annual report to the Virginia Department of Education and the Virginia Department of Housing and Community Development listing the 911 address of all students who do not have home broadband access, defined by speeds at or above 100 megabits per second (Mbps) download and 20 Mbps upload.

Data collection processes can be challenging to establish, and school districts had to devise methods of collecting accurate information from families. In addition, the data includes PII such as student addresses and must be secured. Data collection is more efficient now that systems have been established to gather and protect it. Student information systems must include standardized fields to store the data without requiring districts to make costly custom requests.

By systematically collecting device and access metrics across Virginia, the state has a comprehensive data set for broadband planning. At the local level, districts can understand better how to serve their students and families.

Texas District Partners with SpaceX to Bring Satellite Internet to Underserved Communities

Ector County Independent School District (ECISD) serves about 33,500 students in Western Texas, with approximately 80 percent of students identifying as Hispanic or Latino. When the pandemic interrupted in-person schooling in 2020, surveys indicated that 39 percent of ECISD students either did not have home internet access or had marginal internet access that was inadequate for schoolwork. Looking to find a long-term solution for families in communities where reliable high-speed broadband was unavailable, Ector County ISD became the first school district to partner with SpaceX, the Starlink satellite internet service provider, for broadband.

The district targeted homes in the Pleasant Farms area, a rural community with no high-speed internet options for the initial rollout. Philanthropic partners supporting the initiative included Chiefs for Change, Permian Strategic Partnership (a regional coalition of oil and gas industry leaders), and the Odessa Development Corporation. Challenges included assisting residents with equipment setup and helping some families understand the need for and benefits of home broadband. District personnel made home visits and phone calls to gather feedback about the project.

The work resulted in more than 1,000 families being connected to reliable, affordable internet service. The Ector County partnerships demonstrate how school and government agencies can collaborate to document local broadband needs and identify funding opportunities.

Bringing Broadband to Tribal Lands in Minnesota

The Bois Forte Band of Chippewa Indians, also called Ojibwe, live in northern Minnesota, about 45 miles from the Canadian border. The reservation spans Koochiching, St. Louis, and Itasca Counties. Through the Tribal Broadband Connectivity Program, the tribe received a $19,800,704 Broadband Infrastructure Deployment grant to install fiber directly connecting approximately 2,050 unserved Native American households, plus more than 60 businesses and community anchor institutions, with up to 1 gigabyte per second fiber broadband service. The program's goals include increasing healthcare access, boosting employment and economic development, building telework and entrepreneurship opportunities, providing training and workforce development, and improving the overall quality of life of Tribal residents. Beneficiaries will include Tribal residents, students, educators, adult learners, job seekers, entrepreneurs, employers, and employees, including the employees of Tribal operations.

Massachusetts District Takes a Continuous Improvement Approach to Data Privacy and Security

Protecting student data privacy is an ongoing, ever-evolving challenge. Navigating rapid changes in risk while simultaneously sustaining the appropriate support and continuing to grow a security and privacy-focused district culture is an ongoing challenge. Dedham Public Schools in Massachusetts is tackling these challenges with a growth mindset and continuous improvement approach that began by completing a district-wide self-assessment.

The assessment "provided an excellent opportunity to reflect, prioritize and improve many of our current practices, especially around the need to have a sustained, focused approach to student data privacy and cybersecurity," said District Technology Director Dr. Don Langenhorst. "Not only were we able to adapt and adopt new approaches, but we also discovered a solid network of colleagues around the country who are willing to collaborate and share effective practices for school communities."

At the administrative level, student data privacy topics and ongoing improvement are a component of every bi-monthly meeting. The district established a CyberSecurity Team, which meets monthly to review projects and future needs or goals. They also made data privacy and cybersecurity part of the quarterly professional development plan for all educators and staff. This includes conducting differentiated, AI-based phishing tests quarterly along with quarterly training.

"The biggest indicator of success has been seeing changes in behavior with a significant increase in staff awareness, commitment, and acceptance of practices," Langenhorst said.

Nassau BOCES Supports School System Privacy and Cybersecurity Efforts

The Board of Cooperative Educational Services of Nassau County (Nassau BOCES) is the largest in New York State, serving 56 school systems. Among the many resources available to members is their Data Privacy and Security Service (DPSS), which provides guidance and resources to help districts comply with federal and state student data privacy laws. The service works with districts to improve their cybersecurity posture through the application of the National Institute of Standards and Technology Cybersecurity Framework, working primarily with district-appointed Data Protection Officers (DPOs) and Directors of Technology.

The DPSS mostly focuses on district compliance under New York State Education Law 2-d, a law enacted to protect the PII of students from unauthorized disclosure. The BOCES provides school systems with training and resources to help them avoid accidental data disclosures and cyberattacks, as well as consultation and assistance related to disclosures and other cyber events. Currently, 92 percent of Nassau BOCES members subscribe to the DPSS service and are continuously working to improve their data privacy and security posture.

The BOCES also offers a Data Protection Officer Support Service as an additional member resource. Because the majority of district DPOs have multiple roles and responsibilities, this service provides additional support to comply with state regulations. These services help ensure the security of student data in even the smallest school systems.

Washington, D.C. Provides Access Improving Accessibility

With the announcement of the Community Internet Program, Washington, D.C. granted ISPs "free access to the roofs of DC-owned buildings, operated by the Department of General Services, to install service antennas if they commit to providing resident connectivity with reliable, high-speed connections (200 Mbps up/200 Mbps down or higher) at reduced or no cost to households eligible for the federal Affordable Connectivity Program." While the move provides greater internet connectivity to all DC residents, it has specific implications for DC students requiring internet access to complete school-assigned activities at home.

The move is also likely to aid DC Public School (DCPS) officials as they work to realize the goals set forth by the "DCPS Digital Equity Act of 2022," which calls on district officials to ensure all DCPS students have "sufficient internet access to support in-school and out-of-school learning." The Act also requires DCPS's Comprehensive Student Technology Equity Plan to articulate the digital literacy skills necessary to support their learning - an example of access and digital health, safety, & citizenship planning happening concurrently to close the digital access divide.

Appendix D - NETP24 A Guide for State Leaders

The National Educational Technology Plan (NETP) is the flagship edtech policy document for the United States. It articulates a vision of equity that calls upon all involved in American education to ensure every student has access to transformational learning experiences enabled by technology. State leaders in state departments of education, governors' offices and legislatures play a critical role in achieving this vision. This guide provides these leaders some immediate steps they can take to support the communities and students they serve to advance the goals of the NETP.

As a starting point, every state should have a vision for digital learning. This could take the form of a digital learning plan or a portrait of a learning environment, but most importantly, the vision should address critical questions relating to the three digital divides:

Digital Use (Active Student Creation and Critical Analysis)

- Does the state provide resources, including funding, to enable districts to provide training to teachers on the integration of edtech into effective instruction?
- Is your state collecting information from districts that can help determine if edtech is being used effectively?

Digital Design (Universal Design for Learning; Teacher Time and Capacity)

- Has your state adopted the Universal Design for Learning Framework?
- Does your state have a Profile of a Teacher that incorporates the integration of technology into effective student learning experiences?

Digital Access (Connectivity, Devices, Content, Accessibility, Digital Health, Safety, & Citizenship)

- Has the state communicated expectations around accessibility for students in school and at home?
- Does the state have a plan for supporting student digital health, safety, and citizenship?
- Does the state have a sustainability plan?

The following are some immediate, high impact steps state policymakers can take in their states to advance the equitable and effective use of edtech in their states.

1) Establish a cabinet level edtech director to ensure education technology funds are spent wisely and effectively.
2) Develop a digital equity plan in consultation with a broad group of stakeholders and according to established review cycles.
3) Develop and publish a "Portrait of a Learning Environment" to present a vision for the effective and appropriate use of edtech while setting expectations around habits and abilities no matter what the space.

State leaders are encouraged to read the full report for more recommendations and examples of states, districts and schools that are using technology effectively to drive outcomes for learners.

Appendix E - NETP24 A Guide for District Leaders

The National Educational Technology Plan (NETP) is the flagship edtech policy document for the United States articulating a vision of equity that calls upon all involved in American education to ensure every student has access to transformational learning experiences enabled by technology. This guide provides district leaders— including superintendents and school board members—some immediate steps they can take to support the communities and students they serve to advance the goals of the NETP.

As a starting point, every district should have a vision for student success—such as a profile of a learner or graduate—and a profile of an educator that aligns with that vision. In designing strategies to achieve this vision, district leaders should address critical questions relating to the three digital divides:

Digital Use (Active Student Creation and Critical Analysis)

- Does your district provide professional development and support to district and building-level administrators and educators to support the use of evidence to inform edtech decisions?
- Does your district's subject matter curricula scope and sequence ensure that student learning experiences build age-appropriate digital literacy skills through active technology use for learning?
- Is your district collecting data to determine if teachers and students are using technology effectively?

Digital Design (Universal Design for Learning; Teacher Time and Capacity)

- Has your district adopted the Universal Design for Learning Framework?
- Has your district built in adequate time for teachers to learn about, and practice, the effective incorporation of technology into instruction?

Digital Access (Connectivity, Devices, Content, Accessibility, Digital Health, Safety, & Citizenship)

- Has your district communicated consistent expectations regarding the use of technology in all classrooms and settings?
- Does your district's budget account for long term sustainability of edtech investments?
- Do your district's procurement processes take into account accessibility and inclusivity of edtech tools?

The following are some immediate, high impact steps district leaders can take to advance the equitable and effective use of edtech in their classrooms.

1) Establish a cabinet level edtech director to oversee and support the equitable and effective use of technology across the district.
2) Develop a digital equity plan in consultation with a broad group of stakeholders and according to established review cycles.
3) Develop and publish a "Portrait of a Learning Environment" to present a vision for the effective and appropriate use of edtech while setting expectations around habits and abilities no matter what the space.

District leaders are encouraged to read the full report for more recommendations and examples of states, districts and schools that are using technology effectively to drive outcomes for learners.

Appendix F - NETP24 A Guide for School Leaders

The National Educational Technology Plan (NETP) is the flagship edtech policy document for the United States articulating a vision of equity that calls upon all involved in American education to ensure every student has access to transformational learning experiences enabled by technology. This guide provides district leaders— including superintendents and school board members—some immediate steps they can take to support the communities and students they serve to advance the goals of the NETP.

As a starting point, every school leader needs to communicate a vision for student learning that incorporates the appropriate use of technology in every classroom. That vision should address critical questions relating to the three digital divides:

Digital Use (Active Student Creation and Critical Analysis)

- Does your school provide feedback mechanisms that empower students to become co-designers of their learning experiences?
- Does your school utilize rubrics for effective digital resource and tool adoption that support the Universal Design for Learning (UDL) principles?

Digital Design (Universal Design for Learning; Teacher Time and Capacity)

- Has your school provided time, resources, and support for educators to enhance and grow their professional practice, develop digital literacy skills, and design learning experiences that align with the UDL Framework?
- Does your school solicit feedback from diverse stakeholders to collaborate on decision-making for technology purchases, learning space design, and curriculum planning?

Digital Access (Connectivity, Devices, Content, Accessibility, Digital Health, Safety, & Citizenship)

- Does your school conduct regular needs assessments to ensure technology properly supports learning?
- Does every student in your school have access to "everywhere, all-the-time learning"?

The following are some immediate, high impact steps school leaders can take to advance the equitable and effective use of edtech in their classrooms.

1) Identify an edtech leader in your school who can support educators, conduct needs assessments and develop feedback mechanisms that include a diverse set of stakeholders including students.
2) Develop a digital equity plan in consultation with a broad group of stakeholders and according to established review cycles.
3) Ensure all teachers have the time and support necessary to build capacity as learning designers.

School leaders are encouraged to read the full report for more recommendations and examples of states, districts and schools that are using technology effectively to drive outcomes for learners.

Appendix G - NETP24 A Guide for Educators

Digital Divides

The National Educational Technology Plan (NETP) is the flagship edtech policy document for the United States articulating a vision of equity that calls upon all involved in American education to ensure every student has access to transformational learning experiences enabled by technology. As the individuals entrusted with educating the students in their classrooms, educators play a critical role in achieving this vision, but may not feel empowered to drive system-level change. This guide provides teachers with some practical steps they can take to support their peers and the communities and students they serve to advance the goals of the NETP.

As a starting point, every educator should use the NETP to evaluate their own practice by reflecting on critical questions relating to the three digital divides:

Digital Use (Active Student Creation and Critical Analysis)

- Are all the students I serve having transformative, active, creative, critically thoughtful experiences supported by technology?
- Am I actively empowering students to become co-designers of their learning experiences?

Digital Design (Universal Design for Learning; Teacher Time and Capacity)

- Am I developing my digital literacy skills and am I modeling those skills for the students I serve?
- Am I taking advantage of opportunities to grow and enhance my professional practice?
- Am I designing learning opportunities and experiences that align with the Universal Design for Learning principles?

Digital Access (Connectivity, Devices, Content, Accessibility, Digital Health, Safety, & Citizenship)

- Does every student in my classroom have equitable access to the learning experiences I design?
- Have I ensured that every student in my classroom can access the edtech tools we use?

The following are some immediate, high impact steps educators can take to advance the goals of the NETP and improve the equitable and effective use of edtech in their communities.

1) Establish professional learning networks and communities with your peers on topics in the NETP.
2) Advocate directly or through your member organizations for the conditions necessary to support the effective use of technology in your classroom and community.
3) Inspire your peers and leaders with examples of incredible work taking place in other schools across the country.

4) Adopt the UDL Framework in your school.

Educators are encouraged to read the full report for more recommendations and examples of states, districts and schools that are using technology effectively to drive outcomes for learners.

Chapter 2

Parent and Family Digital Learning Guide*

Office of Educational Technology

What can this guide do for you? This "Parent and Family Digital Learning Guide" will help you, as a parent or caregiver, understand important approaches for using technology in a manner that focuses on the needs of your child. This guide provides resources that will help you as you work with your child, your child's teachers, and school leaders to prepare your child for success in digital learning.[1]

This guide is built to help parents, including those who have limited experience with digital tools, those who are familiar with these tools, and others in between. This means that each section will start with foundational pieces and build from there.

Introduction

What should my child know and how do I know if they have learned it? How can I be sure that my child is progressing and getting the help they need? How should my child use technology for learning and what is the right balance of being online vs. offline? How can my child stay connected with their friends and teachers?

* This is an edited, reformatted and augmented version of Office of Educational Technology.

[1] "Digital learning" is used throughout this guide to refer to learning that leverages digital tools and resources, regardless of where it occurs.

In: The Digital Divide: Access, Issues, and Policies
Editor: Simon L. Bech
ISBN: 979-8-89530-238-5

Parents, educators, and researchers have asked these questions for years; they are even more relevant in light of the prolonged school building closures due to the COVID-19 pandemic.

Is technology the answer to all of these questions? No, of course not. Technology is a tool. Technology, when used appropriately, can empower learning, engage and motivate students, and help make learning interactive. Teachers can use technology to personalize learning and adapt to the needs of your child, factoring in your child's strengths, interests, and weaknesses. Today's digital tools and resources support and enhance learning at home and will help you to support your child's success and develop skills for their future.

Digital tools (such as devices, apps, and platforms) can create flexible learning environments, help you and your child set clear and easy-to-understand learning goals, and keep track of progress. These tools help facilitate communication between you and your child's teacher, allowing you to work together toward ensuring that your child succeeds inside and outside of the classroom. To take full advantage of this potential, your child will need access to a device and the internet (at school and at home). Your child also needs carefully selected digital tools, resources, and guidance on how to use technology safely and appropriately. Having access, devices, internet connectivity, and digital tools is ideal, but we know this isn't the reality for everyone. In these cases, children may need to engage in remote learning—for example, paper packets with supplemental learning from a device whenever possible. This guide will focus on making the most of situations where digital learning is possible.

Part One: Benefits of Digital Learning

The following sections explain three distinct benefits of digital learning. Digital learning can help you and your child's teacher meet the specific needs of your child, understand your child's progress, and connect you and your child with your school community and beyond.

Each benefit is explained below, along with questions you may ask your child's teacher, so you can take advantage of these benefits and the resources that are available.

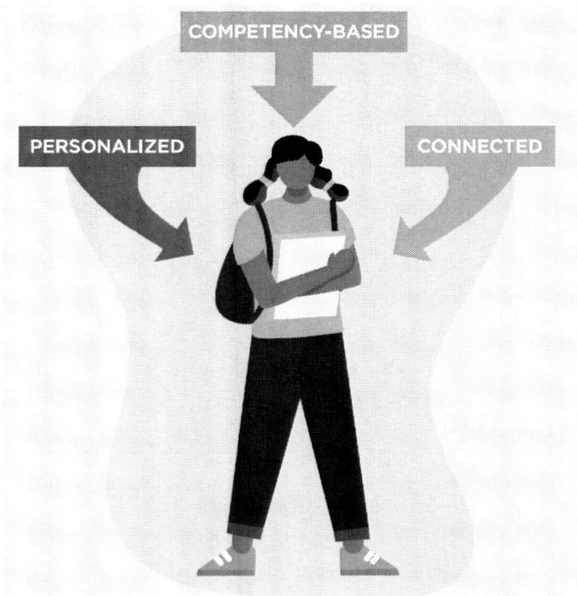

Meeting the Learning Needs of Your Child: Personalized Learning

This section in 30 seconds: You and your child's teacher can use technology and digital tools to make sure that your child is learning in the ways that work best for them. These tools can help change the way content is presented and provide flexibility, so your child has a chance to demonstrate what they have learned in the way that is most effective and appropriate for them.

A "one size fits all" approach to education does not work to address the uniqueness of each learner. Learning experiences should engage, honor, and challenge students and provide support tailored to address their individual strengths, needs, abilities, and interests. A personalized learning approach may complement Individualized Education Programs (IEPs) which are designed to guarantee supportive services to meet the needs of students with disabilities.[2] However, a personalized learning approach and an IEP are not the same thing. The requirements of an Individualized Education Program are provided in the

[2] Note that a personalized learning approach may also complement the services and accommodations provided to students with disabilities under Section 504 of the Rehabilitation Act of 1973, 34 C.F.R. § 104.33.

Individuals with Disabilities Education Act (IDEA), and those same requirements may not apply to students who don't have a documented disability.

To personalize learning, the learning experiences and resources provided should be flexible and follow a sequence that builds upon skills that develop your child's confidence and motivation. You know your child best, and helping teachers understand your child is part of personalizing learning. Teachers can use technology in powerful ways that support this personalization of learning.

Personalized learning is an educational approach that tailors learning experiences to each student's strengths, needs, skills, and interests (Morin, 2020).

Provide Multiple Means of Engagement

Learners can be motivated to learn in different ways, and a wide variety of factors can influence learning. These include:

- Relevance (e.g., can my child make connections to the materials and assignments? Can my child relate to the topics and/or apply their skills outside of school?);
- interest (e.g., does my child get excited when talking about this topic?);
- language (e.g., can my child understand and access the language in their materials and/ or assignments? Do the assignments that are given to my child help build fluency and vocabulary, even if they are learning English?);
- background knowledge (e.g., can this topic be connected to something that my child already knows or has experienced?); and
- differences in how they process information (e.g., does my child have a specific learning disability like dyslexia, dysgraphia, or dyscalculia), a sensory disability such as blindness or visual impairment, deafness or hearing impairment, or other difference in how they process or access information?).

Digital tools allow teachers to make changes based on your child's preferences. Here are four ways that technology can be used to customize learning to your child's needs and preferences:

1. *Choose your preferred learning environment.* Digital technologies allow learning to take place synchronously (i.e., at the same time), asynchronously (i.e., not at the same time), or both synchronously and asynchronously (e.g., with a mix of live interactions and assignments completed according to each student's own schedule and pace). Learning can be organized for individual, small group, and whole class interactions, which may appeal to different learners' preferences.

   Examples of Synchronous Activities
   - A scheduled class in a school
   - Live video conferencing with interactive participation
   - A scheduled online live chat session
   - A scheduled time during which teachers or tutors are available

   Examples of Asynchronous Activities
   - Completing assigned homework
   - Viewing a library or playlist of videos
   - Engaging in individual or group activities where students choose the time to participate
2. *Uncover new learning opportunities.* Many technology applications can support partner or group work and facilitate feedback from peers and teachers. Such applications can also help your child find new things to learn. For example, many sources of information are available online, such as from museums and libraries, historical sites, scientific laboratories, and other sources from the web that support curiosity, inquiry, and research. These tools can also help your child access digital books, simulations, games, interactive content, and online explorations. We have listed several examples in the resources at the end of this section.
3. *Support creative means of expression.* Your child can learn to use digital tools for organizing, researching, writing, publishing, and creating media on topics that are important and interesting to them. Students can also keep their own personal portfolio, a record of their learning, and a blog or journal including reflections on their goals and learning progress.
4. *Provide fast feedback.* Technology can offer real-time assessment of learning and progress to inform and guide your child as they work.

This enables your child to self-monitor and gives you and your child's teacher information to know how best to provide support.

Provide Multiple Means of Interacting with Content

Learners differ in the ways in which they best access and comprehend information. Some students grasp information more quickly through visual or auditory means rather than printed text. Other students may need special supports to remember things or keep track of multiple-step problems that they are trying to solve.

There are two groups of students that may benefit most from this type of flexibility, although it is important to also note that these groups are not the same and may need unique supports that are relevant to their individual background:

1. If your child has any sensory disabilities (e.g., blindness or deafness) or learning disabilities (e.g., dyslexia, dyscalculia, dysgraphia), or
2. If your child speaks a language other than English or is a newcomer student, they may benefit when content and resources are presented in a variety of ways.

Under federal law,[3] websites and apps used in schools must be accessible or if necessary, schools must provide equally effective alternate access, so that no student is denied the opportunity to learn because of their language background or disability.

English Learners

"Parents or guardians may choose for their child to receive services to learn English if their child is identified as needing these services. School districts and schools are required by federal law to provide these services. Schools must ensure meaningful communication with limited English proficient [students?]" (NCELA, 2018, pg. 2).

[3] Section 504 of the Rehabilitation Act of 1973 (Section 504) and Title II of the Americans with Disabilities Act of 1990 (Title II).

Additionally, your child may differ in the ways that they can best demonstrate what they know.[4] Your child may be able to express themselves well in written text but struggle with speech, or vice versa. Children may be able to show what they have learned through illustration better than following conventions of text on pages and margins. With the right tools and accommodations in testing and throughout the learning process, all students can have multiple means of accessing content and demonstrating content mastery.

Accessibility

The Office for Civil Rights (OCR) at the U.S. Department of Education has stated: "'Accessible' refers to information or technology that, at a minimum, affords a person with a disability the opportunity to acquire the same information, engage in the same interactions, and enjoy the same programs and activities as a person without a disability in an equally effective and equally integrated manner, with substantially equivalent ease of use."[5] The technology that your student uses should support accessibility such as text to speech, speech to text, closed captions, and translation tools, and resources should include multiple media formats such as text, audio, and video. Content can be presented in short or longer format to accommodate attention spans and other disability-related needs.

---

[4] Unless otherwise noted this guide does not address schools' responsibilities to provide services or modifications to students with disabilities under the Individuals with Disabilities Education Act (IDEA), Section 504 of the Rehabilitation Act of 1973, or Title II of the Americans with Disabilities Act (ADA). Information about the IDEA is available at https://osepideasthatwork.org/. Information about Section 504 and Title II is available at www.ed.gov/ocr. The Department recognizes the need for additional flexibility in the provision of educational services during the national emergency caused by COVID-19. For more information, please see the Department's web page COVID-19 ("Coronavirus") Information and Resources for Schools and School Personnel, at https://www.ed.gov/coronavirus?src=feature. The resources listed on this page include the following: "Questions and Answers on Providing Services to Children with Disabilities During the COVID-19 Outbreak" (March 12, 2020); "Fact Sheet: Addressing the Risk of COVID-19 in Schools While Protecting the Civil Rights of Students" (March 16, 2020); and "Supplemental Fact Sheet Addressing Serving Children with Disabilities During COVID-19 National Emergency" (March 21, 2020).

[5] Resolution Agreement: South Carolina Technical College System, OCR Compliance Review No. 11-11-6002.

Questions to Ask Teachers and School Leaders

What technology tools, resources, and apps do you recommend for my child? What educational enrichment websites do you recommend?

What audio books do you recommend for my child?

What assessments do you use to help us know where my child needs further instruction?

What should my child do if they finish their work quickly or if they are struggling with content?

If my child has a disability and needs additional support while learning remotely, are there assistive technology devices, services, or other resources that can assist my child?

Are the materials, technology tools, and applications that my child uses accessible while my child is learning remotely?

Are there culturally relevant materials and resources available to my child?

Resources

Guides with Tips and Tricks

- View other guides and resources funded by the U.S. Department of Education, including Family Guide to At-Home Learning from the Ceedar Center, and Parents: Supporting Learning During the COVID-19 Pandemic from the IRIS Center.
- Find more resources lists compiled by Comprehensive Center Network, funded by the U.S. Department of Education.
- Career Hacks for Workforce Readiness increases learners' workforce readiness by building strengths in key interpersonal skills, such as problem solving, leadership, communication, teamwork and collaboration, and critical thinking (produced by WGBH).
- More information on personalized learning is available from organizations such as Understood.org and KnowledgeWorks.org.
- Websites such as Edutopia, Understood.org, and state education departments offer helpful family resources to meet your child's needs at home.

- The U.S. Department of Education has also created useful resources for family learning at home. See Talk, Read, and Sing Together Every Day!
- Make the most of screen time. You can find out what's appropriate for your child's age, find tips on setting screen-time limits, and help your child develop positive habits with technology. Examples of how to do this can be found on Common Sense Media, among others.

Digital Tools

- The U.S. Department of Education has also funded the creation of tools that help provide students flexibility in accessing educational resources. Bookshare helps make reading easier for people with reading barriers. iCanConnect provides educational equipment to people with significant vision or hearing loss.
- Here are some examples of learning apps, games, and websites for your kids by age from Common Sense Media.
- Hundreds of digital books by topic, grade, and language are available at, for example, Unite for Literacy, Storynory, Lit2Go, and Story Shares.
- Hats & Ladders uses proven game mechanics, up-to-date occupational data, and personalized instruction to empower teens and young adults with career-building experiences, skills, and opportunities.
- Accessibility is explained and features presented at Apple Inc., Google, and Microsoft.

Instructional Activities

- Summertime offers special learning opportunities, such as Summer Learning Week with the National Summer Learning Association and virtual math summer camp (available in English and Spanish) with Camp Khan.
- Khan Academy offers sample home learning schedules with grade-level activities.
- Examples of learning activities designed for summer, but can be applicable at any time, are available at EdNavigator: Resource Bundle on Summer Learning.

- Discover free learning activities online, such as a live webcam of the National Zoo, Smithsonian museums, NASA's faraway place, or how to do science experiments in the kitchen.
- Online resources and daily events are curated along with virtual field trips at Wide Open School, among others.

Understanding Your Child's Progress: Competency-Based Learning

This section in 30 seconds: The time it takes to master content and develop skills can be different from child to child; however, children learn best when the support they receive is customized for each new skill. In a competency-based system, students are empowered to make more decisions in their learning and, as a result, may be more engaged.

What is it? Competency-based learning (also known as performance-based, mastery-based, or proficiency-based education) is an approach in which the teacher builds a structure around the difference in pace of each student. The class is set up to ensure that students progress after showing mastery of the skills and competencies. For example, rather than a math teacher allowing only one week for all students to learn two-digit addition before moving on to a new topic, the teacher sets the expectation that each student will be able to solve two-digit math problems using addition, but that they can work at their needed pace to demonstrate mastery.

In this approach, teachers organize the learning environment to support the strengths, weaknesses, and unique abilities of each student who learn in different ways and at different paces. While each student is tracking their own progress, they are not alone in their learning. Students still work with their peers and get support from members of their learning community. Technology can help teachers (or parents) provide the variety of support that each student will need to progress and help students know when they have gained a specific competency.

Goals of Competency-based Education at a Glance:

Students progress based on evidence they have learned a concept, not the amount of time they "sit" in the class.

Students are empowered to make decisions about their learning, including how they will demonstrate what they learned.

Assessment is a positive experience for students that provides timely, relevant, and actionable information.

Students receive different support based on their individual learning needs.

Strategies to ensure equity for all students are embedded in the learning experience.

Expectations for learning are clear and measurable.

Why do some find it beneficial? A competency-based system can be particularly flexible in working with disruptions. Competency-based systems value flexible learning environments where learning may happen at different times and different spaces. The development of new skills can be independent of location and students have the ability to pause or move ahead with their learning as needed.

How can you support your child? Your child's school may not have adopted a full competency system, but the principles can still be beneficial for you in helping support your child's progress. You should work closely with your child's teacher to find out what is required for each subject and what you can do to support the mastery of key skills. Additionally, various websites which we have included below provide guidelines for assessing the development of your child. Finally, share what you have noticed about your child's progress to help their teachers know more about your child's strengths and needs.

Questions to Ask Teachers and School Leaders

What are the learning expectations for this subject or academic year? Can you show me examples of grade-level work?

What can I do at home to help my child with grade-level class work? What resources do you recommend?

Is my child on track to promote to the next grade or graduate on time? If not, what can they do to get back on track?

In the case of school building closures, ask:

- Which assignments/activities are mandatory and which allow for choice/flexibility?
- What should my child do if they complete a task earlier than expected? What should my child do if they need more time?
- How can my child demonstrate and keep track of what they have learned and what they still need to learn?
- How will my child be graded?

Resources

Be A Learning Hero is a website that provides resources to help keep your child on track including math, reading, life skills, planning for college, and more.

This Readiness Check allows you to see how your student has progressed with important math and reading skills. This tool also connects to books, videos, and other resources to help students review content they have learned and practice key skills.

GreatSchools Milestones show examples of grade-level reading, writing, and math skills. The NBC News Learn Parent Toolkit shows examples of what important math, English, and social-emotional skills look like by age.

Show What You Know: A Parent's Guide To The Global Shift to Competency explains additional benefits of competency-based learning.

Connect with Your Community and Beyond: Developing Partnerships

> This section in 30 seconds: Students are more engaged when parents and families are involved in education. Using digital learning resources provides new opportunities for your family to develop a strong partnership with your school. Technology can help you and your child stay connected to your local community, your child's school and teachers, and other parents and children.

Social Emotional Support from Your Local Community

In a national survey of parents related to COVID-19, the top concern for parents during school closures is that their child is missing important social interactions at school and with friends (Learning Heroes, 2020). Emotions and social relationships are essential components of learning. Schools provide counseling services and community spaces and play a pivotal role in the social development and mental well-being of students.

If your school is providing instruction virtually or your child is learning from home, technology can help support social connections by providing multiple means of connection with teachers and peers. Consider these examples of ways technology can help. You and your child could:

Hold video conferences to stay connected to teachers and peers.

Take pictures of their work or their creations and share them with their teacher or classmates.

Get to know their teacher and classmates better by exchanging pictures, stories, and special memories.

Practice writing by sending letters and e-mails to friends and relatives.

Set up virtual playdates for your younger child and make sure your older child has time to talk with friends.

Set up video chats with grandparents and other family members.

Social connections can reduce the impact of stress while also helping children develop communication, problem-solving, and empathy skills. For example, time with friends helps your child build relationships and talk with others who understand and relate to their feelings.

Learning Resources and Support from Your School Community

Two-way communication with your school community is essential. Find the district website and learn where and when updates are posted. See if information from your child's teacher, including assignments, are posted online. Establish the best way for you to provide information or ask questions, through phone, e-mail, text messaging, or other means.

Virtual communication can help you:

Better understand your child's progress and different subjects they are learning

Learn about opportunities from device distribution to enrichment programs to exam preparation

Know right away if there are any issues, academic or non-academic Share what you know works best to support your child

A recent study about the impacts of COVID-19 shows that the majority of parents nationally say they plan to share what they noticed about their child's learning during school closures with their child's teacher (Learning Heroes, 2020). Staying connected to school communities will help parents and families while better supporting their children in their learning environment moving forward.

Ways Your Child's Teacher Might Use the Technology Available to Them to Facilitate Connections and Collaboration Include:

Having students share their projects and essays by creating a website or photo gallery of their work.

Providing opportunities for students to share experiences, engage in digital class discussions and small group work, and support one another.

Providing avenues for students to share questions, comments, and concerns that are related to instruction, as well as those related to how they are feeling.

Making space for informal connections and personalized support by regularly scheduling a virtual meeting with you, your child, or both of you.

Tools supporting two-way family and school communication include the school website, video conferencing, phone, text messaging, email, online office hours, and online surveys.

Learning Resources and Support from beyond Your Local Community

Your child can expand their community by connecting with other peers and educators outside their school, city, state, and country to share ideas and collaborate on projects. Technology can give your child opportunities to engage in research and problem-solving activities, including with other learners in their class or even around the world.

Access to Virtual Learning Schools

Your child may benefit from virtual learning courses provided by your school, district, or state. This may include full courses that are self-paced, access to a virtual classroom that provides teachers, content, and assessments, or some combination. If your school is closed and/or the options that it provides do not meet the particular needs of your child, a virtual school may provide access to what your child needs to continue progressing through their courses.

> Virtual learning refers to online learning that takes place outside of the school or brings what is outside of the school into the school. It uses an online environment to connect students who may be physically located in one place with a course or learning opportunity located somewhere else (CORE Education, 2020).

Some states have online K–12 schools that are operated by the state or district. These can be helpful during school building closures and even at other times. Online schools may offer courses that your child may not otherwise have in their schools, and, if necessary, can also help your child make up credits to continue toward graduation.

Questions to Ask Teachers and School Leaders

How often will my child have a one-on-one check-in with their teacher or other school personnel?

When and where are important school and class updates posted?

What is the best way for me to provide information or ask questions? Through email, text message, or other means?

Who do I ask to provide me with an interpreter at the school? Is there someone in the school who works with families?

What supports (e.g., a counselor) are available to help my child cope with their emotions and mental health?

Is there a virtual school option through my district or state? What courses are available?

Resource

Guides with Tips and Tricks

- Learn more about family engagement from, for example, Understood.org.
- The Institute for Education Sciences has created an introduction to "Supporting young children's learning and well-being at home: A COVID-19 resource for teachers, parents, and caregivers."
- Learn more about federal laws that apply to your local school through the "Understanding the Every Student Succeeds Act: A Parent's Guide to the Nation's Landmark Education Law."
- Visit the Home School Legal Defense Association to learn more about connecting to the homeschooling community, including state-level requirements such as testing and mandatory subjects.
- Learn to help children and teenagers adapt to new circumstances and manage anxiety, stress, and boredom with podcasts, videos, and articles.
- Explore the value of gratitude to help your child develop empathy, improve sleep, and manage trauma.
- The Ultimate Guide to Online School is a resource that explains how to switch to online school if schools are closed and not offering instruction and you decide it's the best option for your child.

Digital Tools

- Download a helpful parent-teacher letter from Prepared Parents.

- For grades K–8, using a tool, such as this "Puzzle to Plan" tool, helps support home learning and home-to-school coordination. For high school, review subject and credit completion requirements with your child and create a plan together.
- "The Reality of Virtual Schools" from non-profit GreatSchools offers some things parents should know about the alternative to brick-and-mortar education.
- Find fun (and free) interactive resources to set your child up for success in the new school year and partner with teachers from Learning Heroes or other similar websites.

Part Two: Enabling Digital Learning

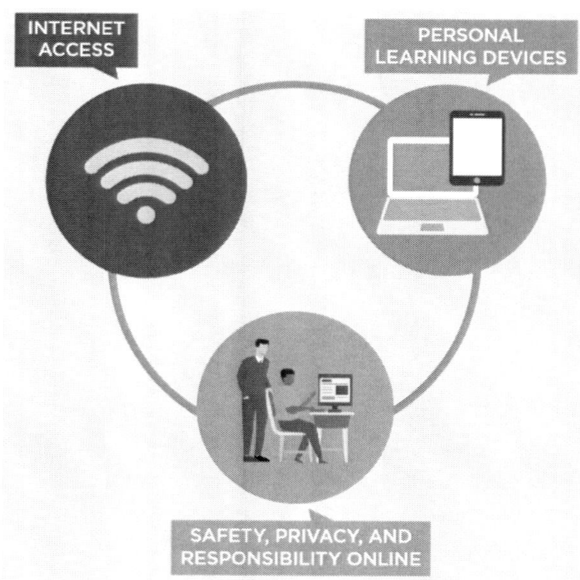

To take advantage of the benefits of digital learning, your child needs access to a personal learning device, such as a laptop, and access to the internet at home.

Ensuring access to a device and the internet also facilitates a more seamless transition between school and home. Your child can access online platforms that record progress and provide digital learning activities and resources.

Having full access is ideal, but we know this isn't the reality for everyone. If you child has no device (or only a smartphone), use the sections below as you find ways to obtain a device that will meet their learning needs.

Ensuring Your Child's Access: Personal Learning Devices

In order for your student to have access to a personal learning device, several options may be available.

Learn about device distribution opportunities. Reach out to your child's teacher or counselor to ask about access to a digital device, such as a laptop or tablet. Even if you already have a computer at home, each child should have their own reliable device so they can fully participate in digital learning at the same time when needed.

Get technical support. Ask your school for support if you have trouble with the device or need help setting it up. Schools may be hosting virtual town halls or other events for parents and families.

Learning can take place offline, too. Ask your child's teacher or local library for activities students can do without a screen, so that they can continue learning if a device is not available and maximize meaningful use of screen time when a device is available.

Ensuring Your Child's Access: Internet Service

Streaming and downloading content and participating in video conferences requires a high-speed, reliable internet connection. Although many public spaces offer internet access, obtaining access at home is critical for supporting continuity of learning. If you do not have access to the internet to support your child's learning, some options may be available to you.

Discover school- or community-provided internet access. Some schools provide internet hotspots for students to check out, and some communities have open access to a community-based network. Check with your school and public library to learn about options in your community. The resources section below provides additional sources for finding internet access options in your community.

Learn about your internet access. If you already have service, make sure it can support the increased online activity and that you understand any data limits (if applicable).

Ensuring Your Child's Safety, Privacy, and Responsibility Online

Get to know your rights and learn what information is being collected or shared about your child.

Your child should be learning safe and responsible online practices. We offer the sections below as helpful places to start discussing internet security and privacy with your child. Reach out to your school with questions or feedback.

Security Settings

Turn on the security features on any device your child may use for learning activities. These can be found in the device's general settings under the privacy menu. These features can:

Restrict access to offensive or inappropriate content Require approval for downloads

Limit time spent on certain apps

Digital Citizenship

Talk with your child about how to be a responsible digital citizen. Remind your child that virtual communities are an extension of their classrooms, and the same basic rules apply, such as treating others with respect. Let your child know that they should tell you, their teacher, or a family member if they or a classmate are being bullied or are worried about any troubling content, encounters, or activities online.

Password Management

Make sure you and your child have all the information to find their learning resources. Keep track of log-in and password information and URLs for each platform they use. Consider using a password manager in your internet browser or keep passwords written down in a safe place. Change passwords regularly.

Video Conferencing

Talk with your child's teacher if you aren't comfortable with your child using the video feature during virtual lessons. Many platforms allow you to use virtual backgrounds or images to protect the privacy of your home. If the school plans to record a lesson or take screenshots during a lesson and you are uncomfortable, ask if your child can be off-camera or watch the recorded lesson later.

Privacy Policies

Keep in mind that many schools have different agreements with companies to protect the privacy of students, and checking with your school is always an important first step. Schools may use certain digital learning tools without your consent as long as the use of these tools aligns with state and federal law.

Federal Laws Governing Privacy and Safety: FERPA, IDEA, and COPPA

The Family Educational Rights and Privacy Act, known as FERPA, is a federal law that, among other things, generally prohibits FERPA-covered educational agencies (e.g., school districts) and institutions (i.e., schools) from disclosing personally identifiable information (PII) from the education records of a student without the prior written consent of the student's parent or the "eligible student" herself or himself (i.e., the student if he or she is 18 years or older or attends an institution of postsecondary education).[6] FERPA also generally provides parents and eligible students with the right to inspect and review their education records, and the right to seek to amend information in their education records that is inaccurate, misleading, or in violation of the student's rights of privacy.[7] For more information regarding FERPA, please visit the U.S. Department of Education's Student Privacy Policy Office's website at: https://studentprivacy.ed.gov.

---

[6] 20 U.S.C. §§ 1232g(b), (h), (i), and (j), and 34 CFR Part 99, Subpart D. FERPA contains specific exceptions to this general consent requirement which are set forth in 20 U.S.C. § 1232g(b)(1)-(b)(3), (b)(5), (b)(6), (h), (i) and (j), and 34 CFR § 99.31.

[7] 20 U.S.C. §§ 1232g(a)(1)(A) and (a)(2), and 34 CFR Part 99, Subparts B and C.

Of note, the U.S. Department of Education recently released guidance to parents on FERPA in April of 2020 entitled, "The Family Educational Rights and Privacy Act: Guidance for Parents," which is available at https://studentprivacy.ed.gov/sites/default/files/resource_document/file/FERPAGuidanceForParents.pdf.

The Individuals with Disabilities Education Act (IDEA) also protects PII in education records of children with disabilities eligible under the IDEA, and generally requires the prior consent of the parent for disclosure of PII to third parties. The IDEA generally incorporates the FERPA exceptions to the prior written consent requirement. The U.S. Department of Education released guidance to parents on FERPA in April of 2020.

The Children's Online Privacy Protection Act, known as COPPA, generally gives parents control over what information is collected about their children online. Under COPPA, schools may in certain circumstances provide consent on behalf of parents to the collection of student personal information. The FTC recently clarified, "Schools can consent on behalf of parents to the collection of student personal information—but only if such information is used for a school-authorized educational purpose and for no other commercial purpose. This is true whether the learning takes place in the classroom or at home at the direction of the school." Guidance from the FTC is available at: https://www.ftc.gov/news-events/blogs/business-blog/2020/04/coppa-guidance-ed-tech-companies-schools-during-coronavirus.

Questions to Ask Teachers and School Leaders

What apps or websites are being used in my child's classroom?

- Do they require students to have an account?
- How do I keep track of usernames and passwords?
- What data (information) about my child does the platform receive when my child uses the app or website?
- How is my child's information secured?
- How is my child protected from distracting or inappropriate content online?

Are there forms to sign to give consent for my child to use digital learning tools?

How does the school manage privacy policies of applications being used for learning?

Will my child with an IEP or special education services be supported over video? If so, will it be recorded? Who will have access to the recording, and how long will it be stored?

Will my English Learner (EL) be supported over video? What additional resources or language accommodations will be available for my child?

Does your school's website have sections discussing student privacy policies and what education technology is being used?

Resources

Guides with Tips and Tricks

- Help your child build a positive online identity. Check out the resources on Learning Keeps Going, which has guides and tips for developing a positive online identity.
- Reinforce that online actions matter. What your child posts, writes, and likes becomes permanent. Find more tips from Google at Be Internet Awesome.
- Build your child's digital citizenship skills with family tips and activities from Common Sense Digital Citizenship resources organized by grade level in Spanish and English.
- StopBullying.gov provides information and tips for preventing and handling cyberbullying.
- Meeting in virtual classrooms can help students stay connected to their school community, but it's still important for parents to make sure their online interactions are safe. Check out these tips from Common Sense Media for knowing who your child is talking with online.
- The Future of Privacy Forum maintains a list of developers who have signed the Student Privacy Pledge.
- The Children's Internet Protection Act (CIPA) was enacted by Congress in 2000 to address concerns about children's access to

obscene or harmful content over the internet, and a consumer guide provides information on how to protect your child.

- For additional information on online safety concerns and ways of protecting your child online, see "Cyber Safety Considerations for K-12 Schools and School Districts."

Digital Tools

- You can find free or low-cost internet service options in your area using the zip code search tool at EveryoneOn or explore the options compiled and explained by the National Digital Inclusion Alliance.
- Wide Open School offers digital training, as well as great online and offline learning resources and events for students of all ages.
- Download a browser plug-in that limits tracking and advertisements to protect your child's information. Tools like Adblock Plus and Disconnect provide step-by-step instructions.
- Websites like Polisis publish privacy policies for apps or websites your child might be using. Common Sense Media may have reviewed the tool's privacy policies and practices.

How to File a Discrimination Complaint with the Office for Civil Rights

Educational institutions have a responsibility to protect every student's right to learn in a safe environment free from discrimination. The U.S. Department of Education's Office for Civil Rights (OCR) enforces several federal civil rights laws that prohibit discrimination in programs or activities that receive federal financial assistance from the U.S. Department of Education (ED). Discrimination on the bases of race, color, and national origin is prohibited by Title VI of the Civil Rights Act of 1964; sex discrimination is prohibited by Title IX of the Education Amendments of 1972; discrimination on the basis of disability is prohibited by Section 504 of the Rehabilitation Act of 1973 and Title II of the Americans with Disabilities Act of 1990 (Title II prohibits discrimination on the basis of disability by public entities, whether or not they receive federal financial assistance); and age discrimination is prohibited by the Age Discrimination Act of 1975.

These civil rights laws extend to all state education agencies, elementary and secondary school systems, colleges and universities, vocational schools, proprietary schools, state vocational rehabilitation agencies, libraries and museums that receive federal financial assistance from ED. Programs or activities that receive ED funds must provide aids, benefits, or services in a nondiscriminatory manner in an environment free from discriminatory harassment that limits educational opportunities. Such aids, benefits, or services may include, but are not limited to, admissions, recruitment, financial aid, academic programs, student treatment and services, counseling and guidance, discipline, classroom assignment, grading, vocational education, recreation, physical education, athletics, housing, and employment.

Anyone who believes that an education institution that receives federal financial assistance has discriminated against someone on the basis of race, color, national origin, sex, disability, or age may file a complaint with OCR. The person or organization filing the complaint need not be a victim of the alleged discrimination but may complain on behalf of another person or group. Generally, a complaint must be filed within 180 calendar days of the date of the alleged discrimination. Complainants may file a complaint by mail or facsimile with the appropriate regional office (https://www2.ed.gov/about/offices/list/ocr/addresses.html), e-mail (ocr@ ed.gov), or by using OCR's electronic complaint form (https://www2.ed.gov/about/offices/list/ocr/complaintintro.html).

Legal Disclaimer

This document contains resources that are provided for the user's convenience. The inclusion of these materials is not intended to reflect their importance, nor is it intended to endorse any views expressed, or products or services offered. These materials may contain the views and recommendations of various subject matter experts as well as hypertext links, contact addresses, and websites to information created and maintained by other public and private organizations.

The opinions expressed in any of these materials do not necessarily reflect the positions or policies of the U.S. Department of Education. The U.S. Department of Education does not control or guarantee the accuracy, relevance, timeliness, or completeness of any outside information included in these materials.

Other than statutory and regulatory requirements included in the document, the contents of this guidance do not have the force and effect of law and are not meant to bind the public. This document is intended only to provide clarity to the public regarding existing requirements under the law or agency policies.

References

English Learner Family Toolkit: Attending Schools in the United States. (2018). National Clearinghouse for English Language Learners. Retrieved from https://ncela.ed.gov/ files/family_toolkit/EL-Family-Tool-Kit-Attending-Schools-in-the-US.pdf.

Family Educational Rights and Privacy Act. (2020, April). Guidance for Parents. Retrieved from https://studentprivacy.ed.gov/sites/default/files/resource_document/file/ FERPA GuidanceForParents.pdf.

Federal Trade Commission. (2020). Children's Privacy. Retrieved from https://www.ftc.gov/tips-advice/business-center/privacy-and-security/children%27s-privacy.

Immordino-Yang, M. H., Darling-Hammond, L., & Krone, C. (2018). The Brain Basis for Integrated Social, Emotional, and Academic Development. The Aspen Institute. Retrieved from https://assets.aspeninstitute.org/content/uploads/2018/09/Aspen_ research_FINAL_web.pdf.

Introduction to Competency-Based Education. (2020). Aurora Institute. Retrieved from https://aurora-institute.org/our-work/competencyworks/competency-based-education/.

Kaufman, T. (n.d.). Family Engagement and Student Success: What the Research Says. Understood. Retrieved from https://www.understood.org/en/school-learning/for-educators/ partnering-with-families/family-engagement-and-student-success.

Learning Heroes. (2020). Parents 2020: COVID-19 Closures—A Redefining Moment for Students, Parents, and Schools [Webinar]. Retrieved from https://bealearninghero. org/research/.

Morin, A. (n.d.). Personalized Learning: What You Need to Know. Understood. Retrieved from https://www.understood.org/en/school-learning/partnering-with-childs-school/instructional-strategies/personalized-learning-what-you-need-to-know/.

Schifferle, L. W. (2020, April). COPPA Guidance for Ed Tech Companies and Schools during the Coronavirus. U.S. Federal Trade Commission. Retrieved from https://www.ftc.gov/news-events/blogs/business-blog/2020/04/coppa-guidance-ed-tech-companies-schools-during-coronavirus.

Virtual Learning. (2020). Core Education. Retrieved from https://core-ed.org/research-and-innovation/ten-trends/2013/virtual-learning/.

Chapter 3

The Persistent Digital Divide: Selected Broadband Deployment Issues and Policy Considerations*

Colby Leigh Rachfal

Abstract

Access to high-speed internet—known as broadband—has become a topic of increasing significance over the past few decades, with extra urgency in recent years due to the Coronavirus Disease 2019 (COVID-19) pandemic. Deployment of broadband is not uniform across the United States. Some areas lack broadband entirely—creating a so-called digital divide between those who have access to broadband service and those who do not.

Although some public entities (e.g., municipalities) provide broadband service, broadband is primarily deployed by the private sector. Private sector providers typically make their deployment decisions based on economic criteria, such as whether an area will provide a sufficient return on investment. They may therefore choose not to serve communities that have a lower population density (i.e., rural or remote areas) if they conclude that the cost to provide service would outweigh the returns. The terrain in some rural or remote areas may also make some technologies—such as fiber optic cable—more expensive to deploy. In such cases, it may not make economic sense for providers to deploy broadband in the absence of some type of subsidy to offset their costs.

* This is an edited, reformatted and augmented version of Congressional Research Service, Publication No. R47506, dated April 18, 2023.

In: The Digital Divide: Access, Issues, and Policies
Editor: Simon L. Bech
ISBN: 979-8-89530-238-5

Federal support for broadband deployment comes primarily from three agencies—the Federal Communications Commission (FCC), the U.S. Department of Agriculture, and the National Telecommunications and Information Administration (an agency in the Department of Commerce). Other federal agencies have programs that fund broadband deployment as one among many possible activities, but in most cases broadband is not the primary eligible funding activity. The federal government has been providing support for broadband deployment for decades; progress has been made, but the digital divide persists. To deploy federal resources effectively, an accurate national picture of where broadband is and is not available is key. The FCC has responsibility for mapping broadband availability, but ensuring the accuracy of the data has been challenging, and the federal government does not know precisely where broadband has and has not been deployed. Another issue is that broadband takes time to deploy, especially if there are supply chain problems, labor shortages, or delays in administration of federal funding.

The digital divide puzzle is complex and has many pieces. Additional funding for broadband deployment may not alone be enough to close it. The 118th Congress may also assess whether regulatory policies are helping or hindering broadband deployment and weigh how changes in regulatory policies could help. Possible considerations include

- the sufficiency of federal broadband funding and whether more is needed,
- the numerous federal agencies and programs involved in promoting broadband deployment, which could lead to coordination issues or duplication of effort,
- the FCC's minimum broadband speed benchmark and whether raising the speed benchmark could inadvertently create a new digital divide,
- the potential for prioritization of unserved areas to ensure ubiquitous broadband availability, and
- the potential application of rural electrification strategies to rural broadband deployment.

Policy options proposed in bills currently under consideration by the 118th Congress include, for example, prioritizing the processing of applications for rural broadband projects located in areas with the shortest construction seasons (H.R. 43), amending the Internal Revenue Code of 1986 to exclude certain broadband grants from gross income (H.R. 889/S. 341), determining whether the lack of network equipment significantly impacted the deployment of broadband (S. 690), and ensuring that broadband maps are accurate before funds are allocated under the Broadband Equity, Access, and Deployment Program (S. 1162).

Introduction to Broadband and the Digital Divide

Broadband is high-speed internet service that is faster than traditional dial-up internet service and offers an "always on" connection. It can be delivered through various technologies, such as

- digital subscriber line (DSL), which uses copper telephone wires to transmit data;
- cable modem, which uses the same coaxial cables used for cable television;
- fiber optic cable, which uses pulses of light shot by lasers through thin strands of glass;
- wireless, which uses a radio connection between a user's device, such as a laptop or phone, and a service provider's terrestrial antenna; and
- satellite, which uses a radio connection between a user's device and a service provider's space-based antenna.[1]

The Federal Communications Commission (FCC)—an independent agency over which Congress has oversight—has set a minimum speed benchmark as its definition of broadband. The benchmark, adopted in 2015, is 25 megabits per second (Mbps) to download data and 3 Mbps to upload data. This benchmark is referred to as "25/3."[2]

Broadband has become increasingly important as aspects of everyday life continue to move online. This trend became especially apparent during the Coronavirus Disease 2019 (COVID-19) pandemic, with activities such as school and work moving from in-person to online. However, not everyone in the United States has equal access to broadband. The gap between those who have access to broadband and those who do not is referred to as the digital divide. The term originated at the National Telecommunications and

---

[1] Federal Communications Commission, "Types of Broadband Connections," June 23, 2014, available at https://www.fcc.gov/general/types-broadband-connections.

[2] 25/3 Mbps was an increase from the previous benchmark (4/1 Mbps), which was adopted in 2010. Tyler Cooper, *The FCC Definition of Broadband: Analysis and History*, BroadbandNow, November 2, 2021, available at https://broadbandnow.com/report/fcc-broadband-definition/.

Information Administration (NTIA) in the mid-1990s "to express the gap between 'haves' and 'have-nots' in terms of access to computers."[3] The term has evolved to include other aspects of technology access, especially broadband availability. Despite billions of federal dollars directed toward broadband deployment, discrepancies in access to broadband remain. The continuing lack of broadband access in some areas can be attributed to several factors, including terrain, population density, demography, and market characteristics.

Rural and tribal areas are most affected, but urban areas can also be.

> This report provides an overview of the digital divide in broadband deployment and issues that contribute to it persistence. The report includes a discussion of policy issues facing Congress. An Appendix lists related legislation in the 118th Congress.[4]

Why Is the Digital Divide Persistent?

Since 1999, the FCC has issued 16 reports that provide a snapshot and assessment of broadband deployment.[5] Table 1 shows percentages of Americans in urban, rural, and tribal areas with access to fixed[6] broadband at speeds of 25 Mbps/3Mbps, since the adoption of the minimum speed benchmark in 2015, as presented in the FCC's *Fourteenth Broadband Deployment Report*.[7] Although the percentage of Americans that lack access to broadband has been shrinking, 100% access to broadband for all Americans in urban, rural, and tribal areas across the United States is still elusive, as

---

[3] Advay Chandra, *What Is Digital Divide and Why Must We Understand That Term?*, Learning Spaces, May 10, 2021, available at https://learningspacesglobal.org/what-is-digital-divide/.

[4] This report focuses on the digital divide as it pertains to broadband deployment. Broadband adoption and affordability issues, which are another aspect of the digital divide, are outside the scope of this report. For more information on broadband adoption and affordability, see CRS Report R46108, *Demand for Broadband in Rural Areas: Implications for Universal Access*, by Brian E. Humphreys.

[5] Of the 16 reports, 14 have a national focus, while two have a rural focus. An archive of these reports is available at Federal Communications Commission, *Broadband Progress Reports*, available at https://www.fcc.gov/reports-research/reports/broadband-progress-reports.

[6] Fixed broadband includes DSL, fiber, cable, fixed wireless, and fixed satellite, but not mobile wireless or satellite.

[7] Federal Communications Commission, *Fourteenth Broadband Deployment Report*, January 19, 2021, p. 20, available at https://docs.fcc.gov/public/attachments/FCC-21-18A1.pdf.

certain factors may contribute to areas perpetually remaining unserved with broadband.

Table 1. Percentage of Americans with access to fixed broadband at the minimum speed benchmark of 25/3 Mbps

	2015	2016	2017	2018	2019
All U.S.	89.9%	91.9%	93.5%	94.4%	95.6%
Urban	96.7%	97.7%	98.3%	98.5%	98.8%
Rural	61.5%	67.8%	73.6%	77.7%	82.7%
Tribal	57.8%	63.1%	67.9%	72.3%	79.1%

Source: Federal Communications Commission, Fourteenth Broadband Deployment Report, January 19, 2021, p. 20, available at https://docs.fcc.gov/public/attachments/FCC-21-18A1.pdf.

Notes: The FCC's Fourteenth Broadband Deployment Report with data as of December 31, 2019, is the most recent report.

Some challenges that may contribute to the persistence of the digital divide include

- the federal government does not know precisely who has broadband access and who does not;
- broadband can be difficult and costly to deploy;[8]
- broadband takes time to deploy, and
- supply chain problems, labor shortages, or delays in the administration of federal funding can exacerbate broadband deployment issues.[9]

The following sections address each of these challenges.

Broadband Availability Data and Mapping Challenges

Pinpointing where broadband is and is not deployed across the United States has been challenging. Estimates of how many Americans lack access to

---

[8] Christopher Ali, *Everything You Wanted To Know About Broadband (But Were Afraid to Ask)*, Benton Institute for Broadband & Society, August 31, 2020, available at https://www.benton.org/blog/everything-you-wanted-know-about-broadband-were-afraid-ask.

[9] NBC5, "Lots of Broadband Money, but US Expansion Finds Speed Bumps," April 16, 2022, available at https://www.mynbc5.com/article/lots-of-broadband-money-but-us-expansion-finds-speed-bumps/39741440.

broadband vary—ranging, for example, from the FCC's estimate of 14.5 million[10] to an estimate by BroadbandNow of 42 million[11] to Microsoft's estimate of 157.3 million.[12] Without an accurate figure, it is difficult for policymakers to know how much funding would potentially help close the divide—and where to direct it. FCC Chairwoman Jessica Rosenworcel stated in a June 30, 2022, blog post:

> For as long as people have been talking about the digital divide, there have been complaints that we lack detailed maps to tell us exactly where broadband is—and is not—available. This has been a constant source of frustration for policymakers trying to deploy resources to build broadband in more places as well as consumers, who knew with greater accuracy than Washington about their what broadband service was available where they lived or worked.[13]

The FCC has had primary responsibility for developing a comprehensive map of broadband access in the United States since 2018,[14] but the data and methodology used to compose the map may have overstated availability. For example, an entire census block[15] was considered as served if at least one

---

[10] Federal Communications Commission, *Fourteenth Broadband Deployment Report*, January 19, 2021, available at https://www.fcc.gov/reports-research/reports/broadband-progress-reports/fourteenth-broadband-deployment-report.

[11] John Busby, Tyler Cooper, and Julia Tanberk, "BroadbandNow Estimates Availability for All 50 States; Confirms That More Than 42 Million Americans Do Not Have Access to Broadband," BroadbandNow, October 13, 2022, available at https://broadbandnow.com/research/fcc-broadband-overreporting-by-state.

[12] Charlotte Edmond, "Airband: The Initiative to Bring the Internet to Everyone," Microsoft, September 1, 2020, available at https://news.microsoft.com/on-the-issues/2020/09/01/airband-initiative-rural-broadband-digital-divide/.

[13] Chairwoman Jessica Rosenworcel, *Status Update: Mapping Where Broadband Is—and Is Not—Available in the U.S.*, Federal Communications Commission, June 30, 2022, available at https://www.fcc.gov/news-events/notes/2022/06/30/ status-update-mapping-where-broadband-and-not-available-us.

[14] For more background and information about broadband data and mapping, see CRS Report R45962, *Broadband Data and Mapping: Background and Issues for the 117th Congress*, by Colby Leigh Rachfal.

[15] According to the FCC, "Census blocks are the smallest unit of geography defined by the Census Bureau ... but are diverse in size. While the largest block is over 8,500 square miles (it's in Alaska), half the blocks are smaller than a tenth of a square mile (6.4 acres)." See Federal Communications Commission, *More About Census Blocks*, October 27, 2020, available at https://transition.fcc.gov/form477/Geo/more_about_census_blocks.pdf. Population does not delineate census blocks; many census blocks have no population. See U.S. Census Bureau, "What Are Census Blocks?," July 2011, available at https://www.census.gov/newsroom/blogs/random-samplings/2011/07/what-are-census-

home or business in that census block had broadband access. This policy could have consequences for efforts to address the digital divide, as the FCC's map is frequently consulted to identify areas that are completely unserved with broadband, and thus, to determine where to invest federal resources through programs such as the Rural Digital Opportunity Fund (RDOF) and the Broadband Equity, Access, and Deployment (BEAD) program.[16] Many Members of Congress have acknowledged the potential implications of inaccurate broadband data and mapping. For example, some Members have written letters on the topic to the FCC Chair.[17]

In March 2020, Congress enacted the Broadband Deployment Accuracy and Technological Availability Act (Broadband DATA Act; P.L. 116-130). This law required the FCC to change how broadband data is collected, verified, and reported. For example, the law requires specific location-level information about broadband services available throughout the country and implementation of a public challenge process in which consumers, state, local, and tribal governments, and other stakeholders (e.g., internet service providers) can submit challenges to the FCC if they believe the map required under the act—referred to as the National Broadband Map—contains inaccurate data (e.g., overstated availability of broadband service).

The pre-production version of the National Broadband Map debuted on November 18, 2022, to mixed reviews. Some stakeholders acknowledge that, although some issues persist, the map is an improvement from the previous version, and they have applauded the FCC for its efforts.[18] Some Members of Congress have expressed concerns. For example, on December 21, 2022, multiple Senators wrote a letter to Chairwoman Rosenworcel, stating,

---

blocks.html. Census blocks are grouped into block groups, which are "generally defined to contain between 600 and 3,000 people." See U. S. Census Bureau, "Glossary," April 11, 2022, available at https://www.census.gov/programs-surveys/ geography/about/ glossary.html.

16 For more information, see CRS Report R46501, *Rural Digital Opportunity Fund: Requirements and Selected Policy Issues*, by Colby Leigh Rachfal.

17 For example, see *Wyden, Barrasso and 12 Bipartisan Senators Urge FCC to Ensure Rural, Tribal Communities Receive Fair Share of Federal Broadband Grants*, March 22, 2023, available at https://www.wyden.senate.gov/news/ press-releases/wyden-barrasso-and-12-bipartisan-senators-urge-fcc-to-ensure-rural-tribal-communities-receive-fair-share-of-federal-broadband-grants, and *Rep. Allen Leads Bipartisan Georgia Delegation Letter to FCC on Broadband Map*, July 12, 2021, available at https://allen.house.gov/news/documentsingle.aspx?DocumentID=4762.

18 Kristi Eaton, "New FCC Broadband Map of the U.S. Is 'A Step in the Right Direction,'" *The Daily Yonder*, December 12, 2022, available at https://dailyyonder.com/new-fcc-broadband-map-of-the-u-s-is-a-step-in-the-right-direction/2022/12/12/.

> We have heard from constituents, state and local governments, and service providers alike of continuing concerns about the accuracy of the map, ranging from persistent issues with missing or incorrect serviceable locations to potentially overstated claims of coverage by providers.[19]

Additionally, news outlets have reported that some providers may have submitted false broadband availability data to the FCC.[20] The digital divide will be difficult to close unless areas unserved with broadband are accurately identified. Congress may consider additional legislative actions, such as enhancing accountability protocols for data submitted by providers, penalizing providers that provide false or inaccurate data, or increasing the frequency of updates to the National Broadband Map.[21]

To assist with improving the accuracy of the map, state and local governments have been encouraging residents to check their address on the National Broadband Map and challenge incorrect information.[22] The map is to be updated at least twice a year with the resolution of consumer challenges, along with updated service provider data on availability.[23] Although the

---

[19] Letter from Senators Shelley Moore Capito, Jacky Rosen, Roger Wicker, John Thune, Tammy Baldwin, John Barrasso, Michael F. Bennet, Sherrod Brown, Benjamin L. Cardin, Catherine Cortez Masto, Mike Crapo, Tammy Duckworth, Dick Durbin, Joni Ernst, Dianne Feinstein, Chuck Grassley, Cynthia Lummis, Roger Marshall, Jerry Moran, Kyrsten Sinema, Dan Sullivan, Joe Manchin, Robert Menendez, Deb Fischer, Jon Tester, and Todd Young to the Honorable Jessica Rosenworcel, Federal Communications Commission Chairwoman, December 21, 2022, available at https://www.feinstein.senate.gov/public/_cache/files/7/3/739aa0e3-bfa9-4601-a7c8-f3dc3f08dcbe/177487E8F5C7D6FF8794BB957E97B483.12-21-2022-final-signed-capito-rosen-broadband-accuracy-and-accountability-letter1.pdf.

[20] Jon Brodkin, "Starlink, Verizon, and T-Mobile Made Shaky Claims on FCC Coverage Map," *arsTechnica*, February 13, 2023, available at https://arstechnica.com/tech-policy/2023/02/starlink-verizon-and-t-mobile-made-shaky-claims-on-fcc-coverage-map/.

[21] For more information, see CRS In Focus IF12298, *FCC's National Broadband Map: Implications for the Broadband Equity, Access, and Deployment (BEAD) Program*, coordinated by Colby Leigh Rachfal.

[22] Guy McCarthy, "Tuolumne County Urges Residents to Provide Input on FCC National Broadband Map," *The Union Democrat*, December 8, 2022, available at https://www.uniondemocrat.com/news/article_782e921a-767e-11ed-be09-23496a9e614a.html.

[23] According to a March 23, 2023, Notes from the FCC post by Chairwoman Jessica Rosenworcel, "In the past four months, our mapping team has processed challenges to availability data for over 4 million locations. In other words, on average, we are addressing availability challenges to tens of thousands of locations every single day. Every two weeks, our public map is updated to reflect all availability challenges that have been resolved." See Chairwoman Jessica Rosenworcel, *The National Broadband Map—Getting Better All the Time*, Federal Communications Commission, March 23, 2023, available at

challenge process may result in more accurate data, it remains to be seen whether national mapping of where broadband is and is not available will continue to pose a challenge. This issue has been a particular focus of congressional interest in light of the $42.45 billion BEAD program, which is required by law to use the National Broadband Map to determine how much BEAD funding a state is to receive based on the state's share of unserved locations.

State Variability and Cost to Deploy

Areas of the United States vary dramatically in terms of landform, climate, and settlement patterns. There are mountains in the West, semi-arid grasslands in the Great Plains, and wilderness in Alaska. Such variations can present challenges in deploying broadband. Climatic variations, for example, may allow the deployment of buried cables all year in some places (e.g., some parts of California), while others may have ground that is frozen for long periods (e.g., Michigan) and may therefore have to pause deployment efforts at certain times of year. In the 118th Congress, the Rural Broadband Window of Opportunity Act (H.R. 43) would require the FCC to prioritize the processing of applications for certain rural broadband expansion projects that are located in areas with the shortest construction seasons (generally areas with long winters and heavy snowfall).

Of the technologies used to deliver broadband, fiber is typically preferred by both consumers and providers due to its reliability (fiber cables are typically buried underground) and scalability (i.e., flexibility to accommodate higher speeds in the future).[24] Additionally, fiber can provide symmetrical speeds of up to 1,000 Mbps and lower latency (i.e., lag time) than other technologies.[25] However, geography can make laying fiber challenging as, in many cases, deploying fiber requires subsurface digging to bury conduit and physically connecting each household.

---

https://www.fcc.gov/news-events/notes/2023/03/23/national-broadband-map-getting-better-all-time.

[24] Fiber Broadband Association, *Fiber Broadband Association Releases Broadband Experience Index*, October 21, 2019, available at https://www.fiberbroadband.org/blog/fiber-broadband-association-releases-broadband-experience-index.

[25] Tyler Cooper, "DSL vs. Cable vs. Fiber: Which Internet Option Is the Best?," BroadbandNow, May 6, 2022, available at https://broadbandnow.com/guides/dsl-vs-cable-vs-fiber. Broadband speed is symmetrical if upload speed and download speed are the same.

Returns on investment typically drive broadband deployment decisions. Areas in which it is difficult and expensive to deploy broadband (e.g., mountains) often make little economic sense for providers.[26] According to Pew Charitable Trusts, "cost is one obstacle to extending broadband internet to everyone who wants it. The companies providing the services need adequate returns to justify their investment in the necessary fiber, towers, and cables."[27]

Cost estimates of fiber deployment can range from less than $20,000 per mile to more than $300,000 per mile, depending on location.[28] To deploy fiber, technicians lay conduit underground or between poles, splice and join conduit, and connect conduit to network equipment such as routers and end-use modems. According to Forbes, "about every 40 to 60 miles, the [fiber] connection must be re-amplified[29] at an in-line amplification (ILA) shelter.... ILAs can be costly to build and maintain. This issue is one of the reasons why fiber is not available everywhere."[30]

Fiber also requires middle mile infrastructure, which "is the physical mid-section of the infrastructure required to enable [last mile] internet connectivity for homes, businesses, and community institutions."[31] In rural or remote areas, it can be "more difficult for providers to deploy service, increasing capital expenditure costs (e.g., construction equipment, labor) and the likelihood of needing to build longer middle mile infrastructure to reach the internet core [network]."[32]

Figure 1 depicts the role of middle mile infrastructure in enabling last mile connectivity.

---

[26] Anna Read, *How Can the United States Address Broadband Affordability?*, The Pew Charitable Trusts, April 29, 2022, available at https://www.pewtrusts.org/en/research-and-analysis/articles/2022/04/29/how-can-the-united-states-address-broadband-affordability.

[27] Joyce Winslow, *America's Digital Divide*, Pew Charitable Trusts, July 26, 2019, available at https://www.pewtrusts.org/en/trust/archive/summer-2019/americas-digital-divide.

[28] Vantage Point Solutions, *Cost of Bringing Broadband to All*, August 1, 2022, p. 7, available at https://www.fcc.gov/ ecfs/document/10801232791699 3/2.

[29] "Amplification boosts the signal in the optical fiber ... (i.e., it increases the distance over which the data between two sites can be transmitted)." See Smartoptics, *Managing Amplification and Dispersion in the Optical Network*, available at https://www.smartoptics.com/article/managing-amplification-dispersion-network/.

[30] Raymond Nelson, "The Future of Fiber," *Forbes*, April 18, 2018, available at https://www.forbes.com/sites/forbestechcouncil/2018/04/18/the-future-of-fiber/?sh=201e5ffb2bc9.

[31] California Department of Technology, *Middle-Mile Broadband Initiative FAQ*, available at https://cdt.ca.gov/middle-mile-advisory-committee/middle-mile-faq/.

[32] National Telecommunications and Information Administration, *Economics of Broadband Networks*, available at https://broadbandusa.ntia.doc.gov/sites/default/files/2022-03/Economics%20of%20Broadband%20Networks%20PDF.pdf.

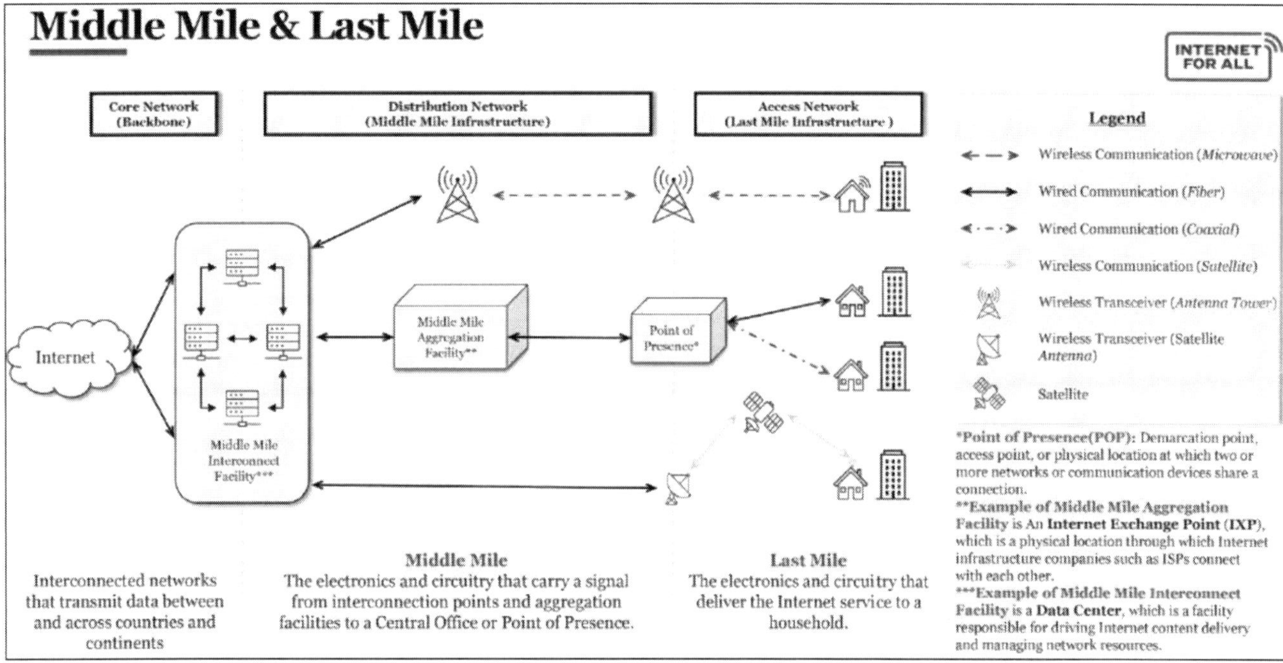

Source: National Telecommunications and Information Administration, Introduction to Broadband and High Speed Internet, Fall 2022, p. 17, available at https://broadbandusa.ntia.doc.gov/sites/default/files/2022-12/Introduction_to_Broadband_and_High_Speed_Internet_FINAL_0.pdf.

Notes: This figure is included for illustrative purposes.

Figure 1. Core Network, Middle Mile, and Last Mile Infrastructure.

According to Fierce Telecom, "middle mile access is a huge issue that drives up the cost of rural fiber deployments."[33] Further, much of the middle mile infrastructure needed across the United States for last mile connectivity does not currently exist. According to Matthew Rantanen, technology and telecommunications co-chairman of the National Congress of American Indians,

> The middle-mile fiber is missing. We did the math, got maps from carriers and tribes, worked with the GIS [geographic information system] folks and anchor institutions— there's about 8,000 missing miles in the Lower 48 states, 1,800 just in California. That's a billion-dollar problem on its own just in the Lower 48.[34]

A consideration for Congress is whether the government might consider funding middle mile infrastructure that would be too costly for private providers without subsidies. While Congress provided $1 billion in funding for middle mile infrastructure in the Infrastructure Investment and Jobs Act (IIJA; P.L. 117-58)—which is being administered by the National Telecommunications and Information Administration (NTIA)[35]—whether that funding resolves the lack of middle mile infrastructure, or whether additional funding might be needed remains to be seen.

Fiber is not the only broadband technology that may be costly to deploy. Many providers, including winners from the FCC's Rural Digital Opportunity Fund (RDOF) auctions, are using a technology called fixed wireless access (FWA), which "is a way of providing wireless connectivity through radio links between two fixed points."[36] According to Fierce Telecom, "while FWA deployments are generally cheaper than fiber … in a place like Alaska, even getting a tower built is going to be much more expensive given the rural nature

---

[33] Diana Goovaerts, "FBA CEO Says 'No One Too Expensive to Reach' with Fiber," Fierce Telecom, September 28, 2022, available at https://www.fiercetelecom.com/broadband/fba-ceo-says-no-one-too-expensive-reach-fiber.

[34] Robert Chaney, "Broadband Funding for Native Communities Could Finally Connect Some of America's Most Isolated Places," *MIT Technology Review*, September 21, 2022, available at https://www.technologyreview.com/2022/ 09/21/1059682/pandemic-broadband-funding-native-communities-blackfeet-internet-access/.

[35] National Telecommunications and Information Administration, *Enabling Middle Mile Broadband Infrastructure Program*, available at https://broadbandusa.ntia.doc.gov/enabling-middle-mile-broadband-infrastructure-program.

[36] everythingRF, "What Is Fixed Wireless Access?," May 28, 2020, available at https://www.everythingrf.com/ community/what-is-fixed-wireless-access.

of the roads, lack of rural electricity at a tower site, and mountain topography."[37]

In places where fiber or FWA may not be feasible to deploy—due to cost or geography—other technologies may be able to step in and help fill the gap. For example, broadband provided by satellites in low Earth orbit (LEO) may hold promise, especially in remote or rural areas. LEO satellites, which are positioned at a much lower altitude than geostationary (GEO) satellites, have the potential to deliver broadband speeds closer to those that can be achieved with fiber, as well as lower lag times or latency. However, there are many unknowns—for example, whether LEO satellites can consistently provide the anticipated lower latency and higher speeds.[38] Although fiber may be the preferred technology by consumers and providers, other technologies may be best suited for particular areas (e.g., LEO satellites in remote areas) and each community has different challenges a particular technology might be able to address. An additional consideration for Congress could be whether some states (e.g., ones that have challenging terrain) may require uniquely tailored plans to close the digital divide.

Network Construction Time and Other Potential Delays

Many policymakers see closing the digital divide as urgent, but the time it takes to deploy broadband infrastructure may pose a challenge in providing an immediate solution. According to Dgtl Infra Real Estate 2.0,

> As a general rule, fiber construction takes 6 to 10 months for a network to become operational, after the beginning of a build-out. However, the construction timeline for a new fiber optic network varies depending upon the number of route miles to be constructed, the number of homes or premises targeted for connection to the network, and the general deployment of the network.[39]

---

[37] Diana Goovaerts, "The Cost of Running Fiber in Rural America: $200,000 per Passing," Fierce Telecom, September 27, 2022, available at https://www.fiercetelecom.com/broadband/cost-running-fiber-rural-america-200000-passing.

[38] For more information see CRS Report R46896, *Low Earth Orbit Satellites: Potential to Address the Broadband Digital Divide*, by Colby Leigh Rachfal.

[39] Jonathan Kim, *Fiber Optic Network Construction: Process and Build Costs*, Dgtl Infra, July 28, 2022, available at https://dgtlinfra.com/fiber-optic-network-construction-process-costs/.

Broadband can take even longer to deploy if an entity is receiving federal funding to construct a network. For example, the FCC's RDOF was announced in January 2020, with a reverse auction[40] held in December 2020. Following the auction, the FCC began reviewing long-form applications[41] from winning bidders. It did not begin approving disbursement of support until July 2021. Approvals are still ongoing as of the publication of this report. Similarly, a January 24, 2023, Government Accountability Office (GAO) report found that announcement of awards for NTIA's Broadband Infrastructure and Tribal Broadband Connectivity Programs took longer than anticipated. For example, award announcements for the Tribal Broadband Connectivity Program were expected in November 2021, but as of September 2022, awards were still being announced on a rolling basis.[42] Further, because of construction milestones—typically measured in years— communities may have to wait years after an award is announced before they actually receive broadband service. For example, funding recipients under RDOF have eight years to serve all locations (i.e., homes and businesses).[43]

Factors other than construction and administrative delays can also slow deployment. For example, workforce challenges—such as labor shortages—may contribute to the length of time to construct a network. Stakeholders have differing perspectives on whether broadband workforce shortages will pose a challenge to closing the digital divide. A December 15, 2022, GAO report "found that thousands more skilled workers will be needed to deploy broadband and 5G funded by recent federal programs. ... We found mixed evidence on whether there's a shortage of these workers."[44]

Congress may consider whether to direct federal agencies to collect additional data on the broadband workforce to help determine whether a workforce shortage exists, and, if so, how that might negatively affect efforts

---

[40] In a reverse auction, the lowest bidder wins.

[41] According to the FCC, "winning bidders must provide in their long-form applications additional information about qualifications, funding, and the network that they intend to use to meet their obligations." See Federal Communications Commission, *Auction 904: Rural Digital Opportunity Fund*, available at https://www.fcc.gov/auction/904/factsheet.

[42] Government Accountability Office, *Broadband Funding: Stronger Management of Performance and Fraud Risk Needed for Tribal and Public-Private Partnership Grants*, January 24, 2023, available at https://www.gao.gov/ products/gao-23-105426.

[43] Federal Communications Commission, *Auction 904: Rural Digital Opportunity Fund*, available at https://www.fcc.gov/auction/904/factsheet.

[44] Government Accountability Office, *Telecommunications Workforce: Additional Workers Will Be Needed to Deploy Broadband, but Concerns Exist About Availability*, December 15, 2022, available at https://www.gao.gov/products/ gao-23-105626.

to close the digital divide. Additionally, Congress could consider directing the FCC, NTIA, and the U.S. Department of Agriculture (USDA) to collect information from grant recipients on any difficulties experienced in securing skilled technicians for deployment projects as part of reporting requirements.[45] If Congress determines there is a workforce shortage, potential options to address the issue may include federal funding for training programs to produce more workers with the needed broadband skills or incentivizing companies to provide higher pay to attract the needed workers (for example, prioritizing federal funding applications for companies that meet or exceed a certain pay threshold). Initiatives such as these may take years to develop, which can make it challenging to address workforce shortages in a timely manner (e.g., if it takes time to set up a training program and train a useful number of workers, the shortage may have resolved itself by the time the training is completed).

Broadband providers may continue to face shortages in the supply chain (e.g., fiber optic cable, electronic equipment) which can add time to deployment.[46] For example, in 2021, AT&T stated that it had planned to build fiber to 3 million homes, but would only actually build to around 2.5 million, mainly due to supply chain issues.[47] Supply chain issues could delay Vermont's plan to bring fiber optic service to every home on the electric grid within five years, as wait times for some materials are now one year.[48] Supply chain issues can be attributed to multiple factors. For example, the COVID-19 pandemic increased demand for broadband with the shift to telework and distance learning activities. At the same time, production was stalled "as factories were forced to limit shifts or close."[49] Further, with the influx of

---

[45] For more information see CRS In Focus IF12111, *Bridging the Digital Divide: Broadband Workforce Considerations for the 118th Congress*, by Colby Leigh Rachfal.

[46] Cathy Cash, "Down to the Wire: A Perfect Storm of Shortages Threatens to Douse Rural Broadband Progress," *Rural Electric Magazine*, August 1, 2021, available at https://www.cooperative.com/remagazine/articles/pages/kinks-in-the-chain-a-perfect-storm-of-shortages-threatens-to-douse-rural-broadband-progress.aspx.

[47] Deborah Kish, "The Vicious Cycle of the Supply Chain in Fiber Broadband—Is an End in Sight?," *Broadband Communities Magazine*, November 2021, available at https://www.bbcmag.com/community-broadband/the-vicious-cycle-of-the-supply-chain-in-fiber-broadband-is-an-end-in-sight.

[48] Fred Thys, "Supply Issues Drive Vermont Broadband Timeline," *Valley News*, April 24, 2022, available at https://www.vnews.com/broadband-rollout-may-take-longer-than-helped-46069936.

[49] Cathy Cash, "Down to the Wire: A Perfect Storm of Shortages Threatens to Douse Rural Broadband Progress," *Rural Electric Magazine*, August 1, 2021, available at https://www.erative.com/remagazine/articles/pages/kinks-in-the-chain-a-perfect-storm-of-shortages-threatens-to-douse-rural-broadband-progress.aspx.

federal funding for broadband— particularly in the IIJA—many providers are competing for materials at the same time.[50] Some Members of Congress introduced legislation in the 117th Congress seeking to address supply chain issues. For example, the Network Equipment Transparency Act (S. 3692) would have required the FCC to determine (every two years) whether the lack of network equipment significantly impacted the deployment of broadband. That legislation has been reintroduced as S. 690 in the 118th Congress.

Policy Issues for Congress

In addition to the oversight issues already discussed, Congress may seek to address a number of other topics:

- the adequacy of funding provided to date, and potential needs for additional funds;
- the numerous federal entities and programs involved in the broadband landscape and whether to reduce or combine programs, or move programs under a single federal agency;
- the FCC's minimum broadband speed benchmark—and determining whether raising the benchmark could create a "new" digital divide, including the dilemma of whether to prioritize federal funding solely for unserved areas; and
- the potential application of rural electrification efforts to rural broadband connectivity and limitations on cooperatives and municipalities.

Each of these issues is discussed in greater detail below.

Potential Funding

Congress has provided billions of dollars to close the digital divide—most recently, the $65 billion broadband investment in the IIJA (P.L. 117-58).

---

50 Alex Goldman, *Supply Chain Will Challenge US Fiber, Fixed Wireless Rural Broadband Rollouts*, Fiber Broadband Association, December 10, 2021, available at https://optics.fiberbroadband.org/Full-Article/supply-chain-will-challenge-us-fiber-fixed-wireless-rural-broadband-rollouts-1.

However, it remains to be seen whether the funding allocated in the IIJA for broadband will close the digital divide. In 2017, the FCC's Office of Strategic Planning and Policy Analysis estimated that it would cost approximately $80 billion to connect every U.S. household to fiber—with the cost to connect the last 2% of households (mostly in remote areas) estimated at approximately $40 billion.[51]

Some critics do not believe the $65 billion allocated by the IIJA will be enough to close the digital divide. Estimates vary with respect to how much additional funding would be needed. According to a Tufts University study, "at least $240 billion is needed to close the digital divide—$175 billion more than the $65 billion allocated."[52] A study conducted by America's Communications Association Connects (ACA Connects) estimates that it could take between $20 billion and $198 billion to connect all homes and businesses to broadband service—with higher broadband speeds involving higher costs.[53] Another study by Vantage Point Solutions (VPS) found the cost could exceed $400 billion.[54]

An article by Techdirt states, "an analysis of broadband deployment by the [Wall Street] Journal found, unsurprisingly, that funding has been thrown numerous times at the same regions that are still … somehow waiting for modern-era broadband to arrive."[55] Mapping broadband availability may help; however, according to the VPS report, "even if the number of locations that need upgrades to receive broadband were known precisely, it remains a difficult task to determine the cost to construct broadband networks

[51] Paul de Sa, *Improving the Nation's Digital Infrastructure*, Federal Communications Commission, January 17, 2017, p. 2, available at https://docs.fcc.gov/public/attachments/DOC-343135A1.pdf.

[52] Bhaskar Chakravorti, "How to Close the Digital Divide in the U.S.," *Harvard Business Review*, July 20, 2021, available at https://hbr.org/2021/07/how-to-close-the-digital-divide-in-the-u-s.

[53] Cartesian, *Addressing Gaps in Broadband Infrastructure Availability and Service Adoption*, June 2021, p. 11, available at https://acaconnects.org/index.php?checkfileaccess=/wp-content/uploads/2021/06/Addressing-Gaps-in-Broadband-Infrastructure-Availability-and-Service-Adoption-ACA-Connects-and-Cartesian-June2021.pdf.

[54] Vantage Point Solutions, *Cost of Bringing Broadband to All*, August 1, 2022, p. 3, available at https://www.fcc.gov/ ecfs/document/1080123279169993/2.

[55] Karl Bode, "We Just Keep Throwing Billions at Telecom Monopolies in Exchange for Half-Completed, Shitty Broadband Networks," Techdirt, June 17, 2022, available at https://www.techdirt.com/2022/06/17/we-just-keep-throwing-billions-at-telecom-monopolies-in-exchange-for-half-completed-shitty-broadband-networks/.

throughout the United States."[56] The report further states, "underground fiber construction may cost less than $20,000 per mile in some areas, but be more than $300,000 per mile in other areas. Not only do these factors make estimating construction costs in a given region difficult, but they also change over time."[57] Determining how much funding might be needed to close the digital divide is a dynamic issue and may be a continuing debate for the 118th Congress.

Federal Agencies and Programs

The primary agencies providing federal support for broadband deployment are the FCC, NTIA, and USDA. Other federal agencies may also provide funding for broadband deployment. For example, the U.S. Department of the Treasury Capital Projects Fund allows the use of its funding for broadband infrastructure projects, among many other eligible uses. The number of federal entities involved in broadband deployment efforts has been an issue of concern among some Members of Congress.[58] A May 2022 GAO report found that "federal broadband efforts are fragmented and overlapping, with more than 100 programs administered by 15 agencies."[59] According to NTIA's BroadbandUSA federal funding site, 63 of these programs are for broadband deployment purposes.[60]

The number of these programs may make coordinating among agencies challenging. For example, although NTIA, FCC, and USDA have an interagency agreement to coordinate broadband deployment federal funding, there is no coordinated map or effort to track where the funding from all possible agencies and programs is going to build out broadband.[61] This could

---

[56] Vantage Point Solutions, *Cost of Bringing Broadband to All*, August 1, 2022, p. 7, available at https://www.fcc.gov/ ecfs/document/108012327916993/2.

[57] Ibid., p. 7.

[58] Template letter from Senator John Thune, December 6, 2022, available at https://www.thune.senate.gov/public/_cache/files/0d7fef2d-7031-4224-be1f-d92ff 4bc26a7/5A4B462A12E9BA0612544839342F2BF1.12.6.22-broadband-oversight-letter.pdf.

[59] Government Accountability Office, *Broadband: National Strategy Needed to Guide Federal Efforts to Reduce Digital Divide*, May 31, 2022, available at https://www.gao. gov/products/gao-22-104611.

[60] National Telecommunications and Information Administration, *Federal Funding*, available at https://broadbandusa.ntia.doc.gov/resources/federal/federal-funding.

[61] U.S. Department of Agriculture, *USDA, FCC, and NTIA Announce Interagency Agreement to Coordinate Broadband Funding Deployment*, June 25, 2021, available at

lead to a potentially unclear picture of where the digital divide is being addressed—and by what federal programs—and where it is not. A result could be duplication of efforts—leaving some areas well served with broadband, while others remain unserved or underserved. Congress might consider requiring broadband service providers to include data on broadband buildout using federal funding as part of FCC reporting requirements for incorporation as a layer into the National Broadband Map. Congress could also require entities to report this information to the FCC for incorporation into the National Broadband Map as part of conditions of accepting a broadband grant.

The telecommunications industry has weighed in on the multitude of programs that fund broadband infrastructure (and other broadband activities). According to a January 6, 2023, industry association response to a December 6, 2022, letter from Senator John Thune,

> part of the reason that so many broadband programs exist is precisely because Congress has far too often in the past sought to create new programs from whole cloth rather than examining which programs have worked best in the past and seeking to leverage and build upon those initiatives instead.[62]

A consideration for Congress might be whether to assess the success of federal broadband programs—for example, maintaining programs that have been successful and potentially eliminating or consolidating programs that have been less successful. One approach could be to establish criteria for program success, e.g., a minimum percentage of unserved locations a program must connect to broadband service to be considered successful. Another option could be combining existing programs that may fund similar purposes. This idea had been proposed in the 117th Congress for two programs at the USDA—the Broadband Internet Connections for Rural America Act (H.R. 4374) and the Broadband for Rural America Act (H.R. 3369). Both bills would have combined the ReConnect Program and the Rural Broadband Access Program into one program called the ReConnect Rural Broadband Program. Consolidating programs across agencies may also present challenges. According to a May 2022 GAO report,

---

https://www.usda.gov/media/press-releases/2021/06/25/usda-fcc-and-ntia-announce-interagency-agreement-coordinate.

[62] Shirley Bloomfield, *Letter to Senator John Thune*, NTCA—The Rural Broadband Association, June 6, 2023, available at https://www.ntca.org/sites/default/files/documents/2023-01/ThuneReply.pdf.

> Programmatic differences, whether from changes over time or the development of new programs, have limited agencies' ability to align programs to address broadband needs in a complementary way, according to agency officials. Programs have their own definitions, eligibility criteria, and other requirements—which may be established in statute or through agency administrative processes.[63]

Further, the report states that, "The federal government has used a variety of mechanisms for coordination, but no current national strategy exists to provide clear roles, goals, objectives, and accountability to agencies or synchronize the numerous interagency coordination efforts."[64] To reduce the number of federal agencies involved, Congress may weigh whether all programs that provide funding for broadband could be consolidated under a single federal agency—for example the FCC, NTIA, or USDA. This would potentially eliminate the need for federal agency coordination and reduce the possibility of duplicative efforts. Consolidating broadband efforts under a single agency might also provide an avenue for a single national strategy in closing the digital divide. On the other hand, consolidation could be challenging because different agencies have different missions and priorities and may fall under different authorizing committees and appropriations subcommittees.

A potential counterpoint to consolidation is that a single agency may not have the staff or resources to handle the already-existing large number of broadband initiatives and Congress may need to provide the selected agency with additional appropriations for this purpose. This also may require Congress to make legislative changes to aid in aligning broadband efforts under a single agency, for example, codifying a single definition for "rural" or "unserved" for usage across all programs. This could also aid in the creation of a common application process for entities applying to broadband programs, which may streamline the application process across programs and encourage more entities to apply for funding. According to GAO,

> We've also noticed that many potential recipients of broadband funding in underserved areas struggle to identify which of the many federal programs meets their needs, and have difficulty navigating the programs' complex

[63] Government Accountability Office, *National Strategy Needed to Guide Federal Efforts to Reduce Digital Divide*, May 2022, p. 21, available at https://www.gao.gov/assets/gao-22-104611.pdf.

[64] Ibid., p. 31.

application processes. These issues may all be hampering the federal government's ability to increase broadband access in these areas.[65]

Congress could also choose to leave federal broadband programs in place within their current agencies.

FCC Minimum Broadband Speed Benchmark and Prioritization of Unserved Versus Served Areas

Section 706(a) of the Telecommunications Act of 1996 (P.L. 104-104) directs the FCC to determine whether broadband is deployed to all Americans on a reasonable and timely basis. As part of this effort, the FCC sets a minimum broadband speed benchmark to define what it considers broadband service. In 2015, the FCC set that benchmark speed to 25 Mbps/3 Mbps, which remains in place today.

The definition of what constitutes broadband service can have implications for federal policies targeted toward closing the digital divide. For example, on July 15, 2022, Chairwoman Rosenworcel proposed increasing the minimum broadband benchmark speed to 100 Mbps/20 Mbps.[66] According to the FCC's Fourteenth Broadband Deployment Report, approximately 14.5 million Americans do not have access to broadband at speeds of 25/3 Mbps—meaning these areas are considered as unserved.[67] If the FCC were to raise the broadband speed benchmark, any areas that have 25/3 Mbps, but are not served with the new minimum speed benchmark, would be considered unserved with broadband. This could exacerbate the digital divide, as federal funds intended to provide service to areas without 25/3 Mbps service might be redirected to upgrade speeds in areas that already have 25/3 Mbps service but do not meet the new faster benchmark.

---

[65] Government Accountability Office, *Closing the Digital Divide for the Millions of Americans Without Broadband*, February 1, 2023, available at https://www.gao.gov/blog/closing-digital-divide-millions-americans-without-broadband.

[66] Federal Communications Commission, *Chairwoman Rosenworcel Proposes to Increase Minimum Broadband Speeds*, July 15, 2022, available at https://www.fcc.gov/document/chairwoman-rosenworcel-proposes-increase-minimum-broadband-speeds.

[67] Federal Communications Commission, *Fourteenth Broadband Deployment Report*, January 19, 2021, p. 2, available at https://www.fcc.gov/reports-research/reports/broadband-progress-reports/fourteenth-broadband-deployment-report.

On the other hand, raising the FCC's minimum speed benchmark might make it more likely that the FCC would find that broadband deployment is not occurring in a reasonable and timely fashion. This could cause the FCC to take further action in the form of new broadband programs or initiatives to speed deployment, or regulatory action—such as streamlining infrastructure deployment rules.[68]

In many cases, federal broadband programs outside the FCC have set other speed thresholds for networks built using federal funds. For example, while the Treasury Department uses a 100/100 Mbps standard for capital projects funded through the American Rescue Plan Act of 2021 (P.L. 117-2),[69] the NTIA's BEAD program requires grant recipients to build to a minimum of 100/20 Mbps.[70] Different agencies setting varying speed thresholds may cause inconsistencies in closing the digital divide. Congress might consider specifying a single benchmark as the standard for all federal agencies administering broadband programs, or directing all agencies to use the FCC benchmark.

Some policymakers believe that those who currently lack broadband entirely should be prioritized to prevent duplication in areas that already have some level of broadband access. For example, on February 4, 2022, some Members of Congress wrote to NTIA, urging the agency to prioritize projects targeted at unserved areas.[71] In response to the proposed RDOF, in 2019, the Pennsylvania Public Utility Commission urged the FCC to prioritize unserved areas.[72] A provision to connect areas unserved by broadband was proposed in

---

[68] For more information see CRS In Focus IF11875, *Raising the Minimum Fixed Broadband Speed Benchmark: Background and Selected Issues*, by Colby Leigh Rachfal.

[69] U.S. Department of Treasury, *Guidance for the Coronavirus Capital Projects Fund for States, Territories & Freely Associated States*, September 2021, p. 3, available at https://home.treasury.gov/system/files/136/Capital-Projects-Fund-Guidance-States-Territories-and-Freely-Associated-States.pdf.

[70] National Telecommunications and Information Administration, *Broadband Equity, Access, and Deployment Program*, Notice of Funding Opportunity, pp. 64-65, available at https://broadbandusa.ntia.doc.gov/sites/default/files/2022-05/BEAD%20NOFO.pdf.

[71] Letter from Senators Steve Daines, Charles E. Grassley, Thom Tillis, John Barrasso, Marco Rubio, Mike Braun, James Lankford, Cynthia M. Lummis, James E. Risch, Lindsey O. Graham, Tommy Tuberville, John Kennedy, Mike Crapo, Ted Cruz, John Boozman, Richard Burr, John Cornyn, James M. Inhofe, and Roger Marshall to Assistant Secretary Alan Davidson, February 4, 2022, available at https://www.grassley. senate.gov/imo/media/doc/ grassley_et_al.tontiabroadbandfunding.pdf.

[72] Pennsylvania Business Report, *PUC Urges Federal Communications Commission to Prioritize Unserved Areas in Broadband Access Expansion Efforts*, October 16, 2019, available at https://pennbizreport.com/news/14442-puc-urges-federal-communications-commission-to-prioritize-unserved-areas-in-broadband-access-expansion-efforts/.

the 117th Congress in the Connect Unserved Americans Act of 2022 (S. 3587/H.R. 7060). Among other things, the bill would have increased the percentage (from 50% to 80%) of rural households that a project must serve to receive a grant or loan through the Rural Utilities Service's Distance Learning, Telemedicine, and Broadband program.

Congress may weigh which aspect/definition of the digital divide it wishes to prioritize—whether to prioritize funding for areas without 25/3 Mbps broadband ahead of funding upgrades of existing 25/3 Mbps networks to faster speeds. Congress may also take population density and number of connections into account—for example, should Congress prioritize federal funds that might connect thousands of households in an area versus hundreds of households in an area.

Applying Tools from Rural Electrification and Limitations on Cooperatives and Municipalities

How to connect rural areas to services has faced the United States in the past in the context of electricity. According to the USDA, "in 1936, nearly 90% of farms lacked electric power because the costs to get electricity to rural areas were prohibitive."[73] Similar to broadband deployment, "running wires into the countryside where there might be only a few people per square mile seemed uneconomical for either investors or taxpayers."[74] In response, the Rural Electrification Act of 1936 (REA; P.L. 74-605) was enacted, which allowed the federal government to make low-cost loans to nonprofit cooperatives.[75] The REA helped bring electricity to rural areas, as by 1950, nearly 80% of U.S. farms had electric service.[76]

---

73 Brandon McBride, *Celebrating the 80th Anniversary of the Rural Electrification Administration*, U.S. Department of Agriculture, February 21, 2017, available at https://www.usda.gov/media/blog/2016/05/20/celebrating-80th-anniversary-rural-electrification-administration.

74 Harold D. Wallace Jr., *Power from the People: Rural Electrification Brought More Than Lights*, National Museum of American History, February 12, 2016, available at https://americanhistory.si.edu/blog/rural-electrification.

75 National Park Service, *Rural Electrification Act*, August 8, 2021, available at https://www.nps.gov/home/learn/historyculture/ruralelect.htm.

76 Brandon McBride, *Celebrating the 80th Anniversary of the Rural Electrification Administration*, U.S. Department of Agriculture, February 21, 2017, available at https://www.usda.gov/media/blog/2016/05/20/celebrating-80th-anniversary-rural-electrification-administration.

Some policymakers have drawn parallels between rural electrification and rural broadband deployment, arguing "that something similar [to rural electrification] needs to happen to create widespread changes to the issue of rural internet availability."[77] For example, according to a 2018 statement by FCC Chairwoman (then Commissioner) Rosenworcel, "We were able to get electrification to happen in rural, hard-to-reach parts of this nation … we need to be able to do the same with broadband."[78] A July 2021 White House fact sheet stated, "broadband internet is the new electricity. It is necessary for Americans to do their jobs, to accelerate precision agriculture, to participate equally in school learning and health care, and to stay connected."[79]

Cooperatives[80] played the main role in rural electrification. Similar to broadband, "power companies thought rural America too spacious and sparsely populated to provide the necessary returns on investment."[81] Similarly, "there has been a growing trend among electric cooperatives, which electrified these same rural parts of the country in the 1930s and 1940s, to do it again for broadband."[82] According to Pew Charitable Trusts, "A key challenge for electric cooperatives seeking to provide broadband services is securing funding or financing for deployment. Because they do not have as

---

[77] Sky Lebron, "Rural Broadband Remains Scarce Across North Central Florida. Here's What That Means for People Without It," WUFT, January 5, 2022, available at https://www.wuft.org/news/2022/01/05/rural-broadband-remains-scarce-across-north-central-florida-heres-what-that-means-for-people-without-it/.

[78] Marguerite Reardon, "FCC Leaders Say We Need a 'National Mission' to Fix Rural Broadband," CNET, October 24, 2018, available at https://www.cnet.com/tech/services-and-software/fcc-leaders-say-we-need-a-national-mission-to-fix-rural-broadband/.

[79] The White House, *FACT SHEET: Bipartisan Infrastructure Framework Creates Economic Opportunities for Rural America*, July 8, 2021, available at https://www.whitehouse.gov/briefing-room/statements-releases/2021/07/08/fact-sheet-bipartisan-infrastructure-framework-creates-economic-opportunities-for-rural-america/.

[80] According to The Pew Charitable Trusts, "Electrical cooperatives are private, nonprofit organizations that provide electricity to customers in their service areas. They are customer-owned and operate on a cost-of-service basis, returning extra profits as dividends to members or to be invested in infrastructure." See Lily Gong and Anna Read, *States Considering Range of Options to Bring Broadband to Rural America*, The Pew Charitable Trusts, March 29, 2022, available at https://www.pewtrusts.org/en/research-and-analysis/articles/2022/03/29/states-considering-range-of-options-to-bring-broadband-to-rural-america.

[81] Christopher Ali, *The Legacy of the Rural Electrification Act and the Promise of Rural Broadband*, LPE Project, July 12, 2021, available at https://lpeproject.org/blog/the-legacy-of-the-rural-electrification-act-and-the-promise-of-rural-broadband/.

[82] Marguerite Reardon, "Electric Cooperatives Could Be the Key to Solving the Rural Digital Divide," CNET, February 9, 2020, available at https://www.cnet.com/tech/mobile/electric-cooperatives-could-be-the-key-to-solving-the-rural-digital-divide/.

much capital as traditional internet service providers, cooperatives often turn to state and federal programs for additional funding for these projects."[83]

Cooperatives may have difficulties in accessing federal funding for broadband. According to NTIA's BroadbandUSA federal funding site, out of over 90 programs, cooperatives may potentially be eligible for 15 funding opportunities. Among these is the USDA's ReConnect program, which offers loans, grants, and loan-grant combinations for broadband deployment in rural areas.[84] A consideration for Congress may be whether to expand eligibility criteria for cooperatives for other federal broadband programs or whether to create a new broadband program that prioritizes cooperatives as eligible recipients.

Municipal broadband is another avenue Congress could potentially look to in filling rural broadband gaps. Some public entities, such as municipal governments, have stepped in to provide broadband services to areas unserved by private sector providers. A patchwork of state laws on municipal broadband exist, with 28 states allowing municipalities to deploy broadband and 22 states either explicitly prohibiting it or having regulations that could make establishing municipal broadband networks challenging. As one of many various options, Congress could weigh granting the FCC explicit authority to preempt state laws to remove potential barriers to municipal broadband investment in unserved areas.[85] Additionally, legislation has been introduced in the 118th Congress (H.R. 2252) that would amend the Telecommunications Act of 1996 (P.L. 104-104) to allow State and local governments, public-private partnerships, and cooperatives to provide broadband services.

Arguments can be made both for and against broadband provided by cooperatives (and municipal networks, discussed further below). According to an analyst at the Rockefeller Institute of Government of the State University of New York:

> Though municipal broadband and cooperatives have been growing in popularity, they have also been a topic of heated debate. Proponents argue

---

[83] Lily Gong and Anna Read, *States Considering Range of Options to Bring Broadband to Rural America*, The Pew Charitable Trusts, March 29, 2022, available at https://www.pewtrusts.org/en/research-and-analysis/articles/2022/03/29/states-considering-range-of-options-to-bring-broadband-to-rural-america.

[84] U.S. Department of Agriculture, *Program Overview*, available at https://www.usda.gov/reconnect/program-overview.

[85] For more information see CRS Report R47225, *Expanding Broadband: Potential Role of Municipal Networks to Address the Digital Divide*, by Colby Leigh Rachfal.

> that these models are more democratically accountable and will lead to increased competition as well as higher-quality, more affordable, and wider-reaching service than that provided by their private-sector counterparts. Conversely, detractors say these models may not be financially sustainable and could potentially crowd out private investment. Additionally, some argue that lack of expertise makes governments ill-suited to take on the tasks of operating and maintaining commercial broadband networks and that failure comes at the expense of taxpayers.[86]

Both federal and state efforts have tried to replicate aspects of—or expand on—the REA for rural broadband efforts. For example, the New Deal Rural Broadband Act of 2017 (H.R. 800, 115th Congress) would have amended the REA to establish a rural broadband office within the USDA and also authorize new grants and loans for developing broadband in rural, underserved, and tribal areas. On the state level, in 2021, the Vermont legislature passed H. 360, which has been referred to as Vermont's "rural electrification project" for broadband.[87] H. 360 focuses on "bringing regional, community-minded solutions to address a problem where the marketplace has failed" and "requiring connectivity solutions to serve all, not just the most profitable neighborhoods."[88] This effort includes Vermont's communications union districts—"a type of municipality where multiple towns could partner together to develop coordinated, regional solutions for broadband connectivity."[89]

Conclusion

The primary means the United States has for encouraging broadband deployment by broadband service providers is subsidizing them to serve areas that they would otherwise find uneconomical to serve. Funding is a key factor in the digital divide and debates continue about how much funding would potentially help close it. In addition, providing additional funding on top of what has already been allocated may not alone close the divide, as it

---

86 By Kevin Schwartzbach, *Should States Fund Municipal Broadband and Cooperatives?*, Rockefeller Institute of Government , March 24, 2022, available at https://rockinst.org/blog/should-states-fund-municipal-broadband-and-cooperatives/.

87 Tim Briglin and Laura Sibilia, *Briglin & Sibilia: Vermont's Rural Electrification Project for Broadband*, VTDigger, April 4, 2021, available at https://vtdigger.org/2021/04/04/briglin-sibilia-vermonts-rural-electrification-project-for-broadband/.

88 Ibid.

89 Ibid.

encompasses additional complex policy issues. In this regard, Congress may investigate whether existing regulatory policies are helping or hindering broadband deployment in unserved areas.[90]

In addition to funding, Congress may weigh other proposals intended to address the persistence of the digital divide, such as whether to reduce or combine any of the multitude of federal entities and programs involved in the broadband landscape, or to move programs under a single federal entity. Additionally, Congress could examine whether prioritizing federal funding solely for areas completely unserved with broadband might close the existing gap more quickly than devoting some funds to upgrades in areas that already have some service. Congress also may examine whether raising the FCC's minimum broadband speed benchmark could exacerbate the existing digital divide by increasing the number of households that are considered unserved. Congress could also consider whether the application of some aspects of past rural electrification efforts, such as encouraging deployment cooperatives or municipalities in rural areas, could be applicable to rural broadband connectivity.

If the 118th Congress chooses to consider solutions to the persistence of the digital divide, it has a variety of potential options to weigh. Examples of proposals related to broadband deployment in legislation currently before Congress include

- prioritizing the processing of applications for certain rural broadband expansion projects that are located in areas with the shortest construction seasons;
- amending the Internal Revenue Code of 1986 to exclude certain broadband grants from gross income; and
- amending the REA (P.L. 74-605) to provide requirements on the use of assistance for broadband deployment.

The Appendix contains a summary of legislation introduced in the 118th Congress.

---

[90] U.S. House of Representatives, 118th Congress, *Authorization and Oversight Plan of the Committee on Energy and Commerce*, February 2023, p. 11, available at https://d1dth6e84htgma.cloudfront.net/E_and_C_Authorization_and_Oversight_Plan_118_FINAL_e858cde3ea.pdf.

Appendix. Legislation in the 118th Congress

At the time of publication, 16 bills have been introduced in the 118th Congress that relate to the deployment of broadband in some capacity, with 10 originating in the House and 6 in the Senate.[91]

Introduced in the House

H.R. 43. As introduced on January 9, 2023, the Rural Broadband Window of Opportunity Act would require the Federal Communications Commission to prioritize the processing of applications for certain rural broadband expansion projects that are located in areas with the shortest construction seasons (e.g., areas with long winters and heavy snowfall). Referred to the House Energy and Commerce Committee.

H.R. 827. As introduced on February 2, 2023, the Home Internet Accessibility Act, among other things, would require the Comptroller General to submit to Congress a report on the capacity of federally assisted housing to support broadband service.

H.R. 889. As introduced on February 9, 2023, the Broadband Grant Tax Treatment Act would amend the Internal Revenue Code of 1986 to exclude certain broadband grants from gross income. Referred to the House Ways and Means Committee. Companion bill to S. 341.

H.R. 922. As introduced on February 9, 2023, the RURAL Broadband Act of 2023, among other things, would amend the Rural Electrification Act of 1936 to provide requirements on the use of assistance for broadband deployment. Referred to the House Agriculture Committee and the House Energy and Commerce Committee.

H.R. 1178. As introduced on February 24, 2023, the Broadband Stock Acquisition in Local Exchanges Act, among other things, would allow an investment tax credit for 30% of expenditures to purchase, maintain, or improve property to provide voice telephone service or broadband internet access in rural empowerment zones.

---

[91] On April 13, 2023, CRS conducted a search of legislation in the Congress.gov database to identify legislation introduced in the 118th Congress that relates to deployment of broadband. CRS used search term "broadband," selected the 118th Congress (2023-2024), and selected bills (H.R. or S.).

H.R. 1241. As introduced on February 28, 2023, the Broadband Incentives for Communities Act would establish a competitive grant program at the National Telecommunications and Information Administration to assist local governments in providing efficient review and approval of zoning and permitting applications that facilitate the deployment of broadband infrastructure. Referred to the House Energy and Commerce Committee.

H.R. 1752. As introduced on March 23, 2023, the E-BRIDGE Act would amend the Public Works and Economic Development Act of 1965 to provide for a high-speed broadband deployment initiative.

H.R. 1812. As introduced on March 27, 2023, the Reforming Broadband Connectivity Act of 2023, among other things, would require the Federal Communications Commission to complete a rulemaking to reform the contribution system of the Universal Service Fund, including by expanding the contribution base of the Universal Service Fund. Companion bill to S. 975.

H.R. 2285. As introduced on March 29, 2023, the bill would provide for a limitation on availability of funds for U.S. Department of Agriculture, Rural Utilities Service, Distance Learning, Telemedicine, and Broadband Program for fiscal year 2024.

H.R. 2252. As introduced on April 10, 2023, the bill would amend the Telecommunications Act of 1996 to preserve and protect the ability of state and local governments, public-private partnerships, and cooperatives to provide broadband services.

Introduced in the Senate

S. 275. As introduced on February 7, 2023, the Rural Broadband Protection Act of 2023 would require the Federal Communications Commission to establish a process to vet applicants seeking funding under the high-cost universal service programs. Applicants would be required to provide a proposal for deploying a broadband network, containing enough detail and documentation for the Federal Communications Commission to ascertain whether the applicant has the technical capabilities to deploy the proposed network and deliver services. Referred to the Senate Commerce, Science, and Transportation Committee.

S. 341. As introduced on February 9, 2023, the Broadband Grant Tax Treatment Act would amend the Internal Revenue Code of 1986 to exclude certain broadband grants from gross income. Referred to the Senate Finance Committee. Companion bill to H.R. 889.

S. 690. As introduced on March 7, 2023, the Network Equipment Transparency Act would require the Federal Communications Commission to determine (subject to available data) whether the lack of network equipment significantly impacted the deployment of broadband and other advanced telecommunications capability. The bill would also require the FCC to include this determination in its biennial report on the state of the communications marketplace.

S. 856. As introduced on March 16, 2023, the Funding Affordable Internet with Reliable Contributions Act would require the Federal Communications Commission to study and report on the feasibility of funding the Universal Service Fund through contributions from edge providers (i.e., providers of online content or services, such as search engines).

S. 975. As introduced on March 27, 2023, the Reforming Broadband Connectivity Act of 2023, among other things, would require the Federal Communications Commission to complete a rulemaking to reform the contribution system of the Universal Service Fund, including by expanding the contribution base of the Universal Service Fund. Companion bill to H.R. 1812.

S. 1162. As introduced on March 30, 2023, the bill would ensure that broadband maps are accurate before funds are allocated under the Broadband Equity, Access, and Deployment Program based on those maps.

Disclaimer

Chapter 4

Closing the Digital Divide in Rural America*

Committee on Agriculture

Wednesday, June 21, 2023
House of Representatives,
Committee on Agriculture,
Washington, D.C.

The Committee met, pursuant to call, at 10:03 a.m., in Room 1300 of the Longworth House Office Building, Hon. Glenn Thompson [Chairman of the Committee] presiding.

Members present: Representatives Thompson, Lucas, Crawford, LaMalfa, Rouzer, Bost, Johnson, Baird, Mann, Feenstra, Miller of Illinois, Rose, Molinaro, De La Cruz, Langworthy, Duarte, Nunn, Van Orden, Chavez-DeRemer, Miller of Ohio, David Scott of Georgia, Costa, McGovern, Adams, Spanberger, Brown, Davids of Kansas, Caraveo, Salinas, Perez, Davis of North Carolina, Budzinski, Sorensen, Crockett, Jackson of Illinois, and Craig.

Staff present: Nick Rockwell, Paul Balzano, Adele Borne, Wick Dudley, Erin Wilson, John Konya, DeShawn Blanding, Kate Fink, John Lobert, Ashley Smith, and Dana Sandman.

---

* This is an edited, reformatted and augmented version of Hearing before the Committee on Agriculture, House of Representatives, One Hundred Eighteenth Congress, First Session, Serial No. 118–17, dated June 21, 2023.

In: The Digital Divide: Access, Issues, and Policies
Editor: Simon L. Bech
ISBN: 979-8-89530-238-5

Opening Statement of Hon. Glenn Thompson, a Representative in Congress from Pennsylvania

The CHAIRMAN. Morning, welcome to the House Agriculture Committee hearing room, as we gavel in this morning, we just pause and—kind of tradition, what we have with the Agriculture Committee, and give thanks for what we are provided. And so, I will take the privilege of leading that prayer here this morning, and then we will get gaveled in right after that.

Heavenly Father, we love you so much. We thank you for all that you provide for us. Lord, we thank you for the privilege that each and every one of us have of serving on this Committee, Lord, to be stewards of what you provide us as we lift up those who provide for this nation all the things that are essential, food, fiber, building materials, energy resources, and, quite frankly, the technology, and all the resources that you have provided us to capitalize for the benefit of the lives of those who live in rural America, and, quite frankly, throughout this country. And so, we ask your blessings over these proceedings, and I pray this in the name of my savior, Jesus Christ. Amen. All right.

So the Committee will come to order. Welcome, and thank you for joining today's hearing entitled, *Closing the Digital Divide in Rural America.* After brief opening remarks Members will receive testimony from our witnesses today, and then the hearing will be open to questions. So let me start off.

Throughout this Congress the House Committee on Agriculture has had countless discussions on ways that we can empower our farm families and build a robust rural economy, and a pillar of these discussions is providing rural communities with access to high-speed, affordable, and reliable broadband internet connectivity. The digital divide has left many Americans unable to access dependable, fast internet service. Disconnected Americans lose opportunities to grow their businesses, acquire new skills, or even engage in daily activities. And while I am fortunate to live in an area which offers quality internet service, although I will say not a regular basis to my home, my district is not immune to these challenges.

I represent 18 counties, totaling 1⁄3 of the land mass in rural Pennsylvania, and I can tell you there exists a checkerboard of connectivity. Americans without high-speed internet access are slipping further behind as more and more aspects of American society are conducted online. Despite decades of effort, and billions of dollars spend, too many communities are still on the wrong side of the divide. With its unique reach, expertise, and experience serving rural America, USDA's Rural Utilities Service, or RUS, is well positioned to serve a leading role in our nation's rural broadband strategy.

Contrary to other Federal agencies working to close the digital divide, USDA is the only Federal agency that has offices and devoted staff in all 50 states, enabling constituents to have direct access to those who are reviewing, implementing, and managing connectivity programs that meet the needs of rural communities. The House Committee on Agriculture has worked hard on a bipartisan basis to close the connectivity gap, including through the 2018 Farm Bill. These modifications were the result of years of work to create policies and programs that address the difficulties faced by rural communities.

Sadly, too many of those policies and programs remain dormant. These include programs and policies that address qualifying areas, long-term network viability, support for our most remote communities, and program integrity. However, last Congress, this Committee introduced, marked up, and passed unanimously bipartisan legislation, H.R. 4374, the Broadband Internet Connections for Rural America Act, or BICRAA, which set the stage for an historic commitment and investment in rural broadband, and for us to finally close the digital divide.

Specifically, the bill codified the ReConnect Program and merged it with USDA's existing retail rural broadband program, provided last minute technical and financial assistance to rural communities seeking to improve their broadband service, ensured accurate mapping of broadband connectivity in rural areas, promoted borrower accountability, and protecting taxpayers with new tools to ensure promised services are delivered to rural communities. It also increased resources available to build-out middle-mile infrastructure, and allocated funds to invest in distance learning and telemedicine capabilities.

While this bill did not receive floor consideration in the 117th Congress, it will be the foundation for the broadband subtitle in the 2023 Farm Bill, which brings us to today, where we will hear directly from stakeholders about the importance of USDA's broadband programs. It is also an opportunity to discuss important policy ideas, including minimum eligibility requirements, build-out speed requirements, workforce and supply chain issues, broadband mapping, and agency coordination, as well as precision agriculture programs.

Now, I have always said the best policies come when we work together, and I look forward to continuing to work with the Ranking Member on crafting the broadband provisions for the 2023 Farm Bill. Together, we can provide the Department of Agriculture the tools it needs to bring broadband connectivity to rural America quickly, and responsibly, and with sustainability. Simply put, we must meet the current and future needs in rural America.

We have a great panel of witnesses today who understand the challenges and the complexity of rural broadband networks, bringing innovative solutions to life, and most importantly, serve their communities. I appreciate each of them for making time to be with us today, and I look forward to the conversation.

[The prepared statement of Mr. Thompson follows:]

Prepared Statement of Hon. Glenn Thompson, a Representative in Congress from Pennsylvania

Throughout this Congress, the House Committee on Agriculture has had countless discussions on ways we can empower our farm families and build a robust rural economy. A pillar of these discussions is providing rural communities with access to high-speed, affordable, and reliable broadband internet connectivity.

The digital divide has left many Americans unable to access dependable, fast internet service. Disconnected Americans lose opportunities to their grow businesses, acquire new skills, or even engage in daily activities.

While I am fortunate to live in an area which offers quality internet service to my home, my district is not immune to these challenges.

I represent 18 counties, totaling 1/3 of the landmass in rural Pennsylvania. I can tell you, there exists a checkerboard of connectivity.

Americans without high-speed internet access are slipping further behind as more and more aspects of American society are conducted online.

Despite decades of effort and billions of dollars spent, too many communities are still on the wrong side of the divide.

With its unique reach, expertise, and experience serving rural America, USDA's Rural Utilities Service or RUS is well-positioned to serve as a leading role in our nation's rural broadband strategy.

Contrary to other Federal agencies working to close the digital divide, USDA is the only Federal agency that has offices and devoted staff in all 50 states, enabling constituents to have direct access to those who are reviewing, implementing, and managing connectivity programs to meet the needs of rural communities.

The House Committee on Agriculture has worked hard on a bipartisan basis to close the connectivity gap, including through the 2018 Farm Bill.

These modifications were the result of years of work to create policies and programs that address the difficulties faced by rural communities.

Sadly, too many of those policies and programs remain dormant.

These include programs and policies that address qualifying areas, long-term network viability, support for our most remote communities, and program integrity.

However, last Congress, this Committee introduced, marked up, and passed unanimously bipartisan legislation, H.R. 4374, the *Broadband Internet Connections for Rural America Act* or *BICRAA,* which set the stage for a historic commitment and investment in rural broadband, and for us to finally close the digital divide.

Specifically, the bill:

- Codified the ReConnect program and merged it with USDA's existing retail rural broadband program;
- Provided last mile technical and financial assistance to rural communities seeking to improve their broadband service;
- Ensured accurate mapping of broadband connectivity in rural areas;
- Promoted borrower accountability and protecting taxpayers with new tools to ensure promised services are delivered to rural communities;
- Increased resources available to build-out middle-mile infrastructure; and
- Allocated funds to invest in distance learning and telemedicine capabilities.

While this bill did not receive floor consideration in the 117th Congress, it will be the foundation for the broadband subtitle in the 2023 Farm Bill.

Which brings us to today, where we will hear directly from stakeholders about the importance of USDA broadband programs. It is also an opportunity to discuss important policy ideas, including minimum eligibility requirements, build-out speed requirements, workforce and supply chain issues, broadband mapping and agency coordination, as well as precision agriculture programs.

I have always said the best policies come when we work together. I look forward to continuing to work with the Ranking Member on crafting the broadband provisions for the 2023 Farm Bill.

Together, we can provide the Department of Agriculture the tools it needs to bring broadband connectivity to rural America quickly and responsibly, and with sustainability. Simply put, we must meet the current and future needs in rural America.

We have a great panel of witnesses today who understand the challenges and complexity of rural broadband networks, bring innovative solutions to life, and most importantly, serve their communities.

I appreciate each of them for making time to be with us today and look forward to the conversation.

The CHAIRMAN. I would now like to welcome the distinguished Ranking Member, the gentleman from Georgia, Mr. Scott, for any opening remarks he would like to make.

Opening Statement of Hon. David Scott, a Representative in Congress from Georgia

Mr. DAVID SCOTT of Georgia. Well, thank you very much, Mr. Chairman, for convening today's hearing. Expanding high-speed, reliable, and affordable broadband access in rural America is a top priority of mine in this farm bill. I appreciate the opportunity to once again join forces with you, Mr. Chairman, to highlight its importance and chart a path to finally bring high quality internet service to every single part of rural America. Now is the time.

High-speed, reliable, and affordable broadband is something each of us here in Congress count on daily to stay in touch with loved ones, conduct business, schedule appointments, make purchases, and to stay informed. In addition to day to day uses, broadband addresses other longstanding inequities through expanding access to healthcare, educational, and workforce development opportunities. Broadband is now an integral part of our daily lives, but most areas in rural America go without broadband, and that must change now.

Friends, it is also very important for us to know that the United States Department of Agriculture has a long history of serving rural America through making sure that rural America has the resources and investments necessary to support modern infrastructure, all the way back to 1935. Remember, some of us do, when the Rural Electrification Administration was created under the Department of Agriculture to bring electricity to rural areas? And the Rural Electrification Administration now operates under the Rural Utilities Service moniker, reflecting that the agency provides an array of loans, grants, and loan guarantees to deliver rural broadband, in addition to electricity and drinking water, to our rural communities.

And since its enactment just before the 2018 Farm Bill, the ReConnect Program, administered by the USDA, has delivered a total of $3.86 billion to create and improve high-speed internet access to rural customers. As the primary program used to deliver broadband and financial funding to rural America, I look forward to working with my House and Senate Agriculture colleagues to codify and provide permanence for this program through our upcoming 2023 Farm Bill.

And as we consider changes to broadband programs in the 2023 Farm Bill, it is my priority to ensure that these programs support reliable delivery of high-speed, reliable, and affordable broadband that can support modern uses, such as telehealth, precision agriculture, distance learning, and our remote work jobs and business opportunities, as well as many other potential future uses not yet even imagined. To ensure responsible and effective use of the historic Federal investments in broadband, any investments made must support future-proof and scalable broadband networks. That means establishing progressive standards for speed, as well as including considerations for affordability of broadband services, and overall network capacity.

And, finally, I would like to discuss Federal agency coordination. The bipartisan infrastructure bill (Pub. L. 117–58) signed into law provided $65 billion for broadband, with the bulk of that going to NTIA's BEAD Program. As implementation of that program is ongoing, it is of utmost importance that any Federal agencies working to expand broadband coverage establish open lines of communication and continue to coordinate resources and projects. As the only Federal agency with the sole mission of serving rural America, USDA Rural Development must take the leading role in expanding high-speed internet to each and every part of our rural communities.

I look forward to hearing from the distinguished panel of witnesses that sits before us today on these issues, and any other thoughts you all may have to improve USDA broadband programs and deliver high quality broadband to rural communities now. Thank you, Mr. Chairman.

The CHAIRMAN. I thank the gentleman. The chair would request that other Members submit their opening statements for the record so that witnesses may begin their testimony, and to ensure that there is ample time for questions. Welcome once again to our distinguished panel that we have here. A pretty impressive panel for this topic, Mr. Ranking Member.

Mr. DAVID SCOTT of Georgia. Yes.

The CHAIRMAN. Our first witness today is a former colleague in Congress, the Honorable Jim Matheson, who is the Chief Executive Officer of the National Rural Electric Cooperative Association. Our next witness, who is Mr. James Assey, Executive Vice President of NCTA, the Internet and Television Association. Our third witness today is Mr. David Zumwalt, the President and Chief Executive Officer of the Wireless Internet Service Providers Association. Our fourth witness today is Mr. Tom Stroup, President of the Satellite Industry Association. Our fifth witness is Mr. Bill Hurley, Chair of the Agriculture Sector Board for the Association of Equipment Manufacturers. And our sixth, and final, witness today is Mrs. Shirley Bloomfield, the Chief Executive Officer of NTCA, the Rural Broadband Association.

So, thank you, all of our impressive witnesses, for joining us today, and we are now going to proceed to your testimony. You will each have 5 minutes. The timer in front of you will count down to zero, at which point your time has expired, and hopefully we could wrap up whatever point that you are in the middle of. Mr. Matheson, Congressman, please begin when you are ready. Welcome back.

Statement of Hon. Jim Matheson, Chief Executive Officer, National Rural Electric Cooperative Association, Arlington, VA

Mr. MATHESON. It is good to be here, thank you. Thank you, Chairman Thompson, Ranking Member Scott, and Members of the Committee for this opportunity. I am Jim Matheson, CEO of the National Rural Electric Cooperative Association, also known as NRECA. NRECA is the national service association for 900 electric co-ops that serve 42 million people in 48 states, and as cooperatives, they are owned by the consumers that they serve, and that gives us an interesting perspective on meeting consumer needs, because the consumers are the owners of the utility. Their mission, of course, is to provide low-cost, reliable power to their members, and it has been that way since the 1930s. They have a longstanding commitment also to improve their communities in which they serve, and they are actively engaged in many rural economic development efforts that go beyond electrification.

Now, today more than 200 of our members, 200 electric co-ops, are involved in rural broadband deployment efforts. They recognize the impact that reliable high-speed internet will have on their communities, and they also recognize the challenges of deploying that in low density, rural, and remote areas. For many cooperatives, the story of rural broadband development today mirrors the story of rural electrification nearly 100 years ago. The cost of building and maintaining networks in sparsely populated areas, in difficult terrain, can be prohibitive for many providers. It is a cost-intensive process, with little return on investment. Since cooperatives are owned by the people they serve, they understand the need for broadband in these areas, and the challenges associated with deploying the infrastructure, which is why some of our members have chosen to include broadband in their book of business.

So as this Committee works to develop the next farm bill, electric cooperatives think there are great opportunities to make improvements to broadband programs at USDA. Specifically, we encourage the Committee to make the ReConnect Program permanent and easier to access, provide robust funding for rural broadband through USDA, prioritize symmetrical speeds and scalable networks, and invest in middle-mile infrastructure.

An affordable and reliable internet connection is critical for growth and development of rural America, we all know that. Broadband is no longer a luxury, but instead it is a necessity for business, for education, for healthcare across the whole country. Internet-based services are a routine part of modern life, and it is increasingly clear the bandwidth and capacity must meet the needs not just of today. They need to anticipate the needs of tomorrow. Last Congress this Committee advanced the Broadband Internet Connections for Rural America Act, which would make USDA's ReConnect Program permanent, and would provide consistent funding moving forward. As discussions continue around the future of this and other broadband programs at USDA, let me offer just some— a few recommendations.

First, Congress should prioritize scalable, future-proof networks in any future rounds of Federal funding. Without the ability for networks to grow in response to increased bandwidth needs and consumer demands, the challenge of solving the broadband gap in rural America won't go away. In urban areas, gigabit speed networks are becoming increasingly common, yet in many cases the discussion about rural access seems to focus on what is good enough. Broadband services should be equitable no matter where an individual chooses to live, and taxpayer dollars will be best spent supporting networks and technologies that can meet both current and future needs.

Second, the definition of an *area unserved by broadband* should be raised to include areas that do not have at least 100/100 megabits per second. Building networks in low density, hard to reach areas is challenging, but

Congress must prioritize networks that can meet consumer demand and ensure the residents of these areas are able to receive a quality service regardless of whether they are considered unserved or underserved.

Third, the time-consuming and difficult application process should be streamlined. The submission portal is not user-friendly, and some have commented that attempting to fill out the program application is like having a second job. For small providers with limited resources, this is incredibly challenging, and could be prohibitive. And finally, the Committee should once again authorize a middle-mile program at USDA. Access to this infrastructure can make a big difference in reducing the cost to deploy last mile networks in rural areas. However, many rural providers lack access to a robust middle-mile connection.

Electric cooperatives are increasingly deploying fiber infrastructure as part of their electric utility network, which enables a high bandwidth, low latency internal communication system to support electric utility operations. Beyond lowering energy costs, a fiber backbone allows co-ops to expand other technology offerings, such as distributed energy resources, electric vehicle access, or expanding retail broadband. Leveraging excess fiber capacity from their internal communication systems to provide middle-mile access to other third party providers, such as local cable providers, small telephone companies, and wireless internet service providers enables a critical link between the internet service provider's local network and the broader internet ecosystem.

Let me just close by saying rural electric cooperatives are deeply committing to bridging the digital divide and connecting rural homes and businesses with reliable and sustainable high-speed broadband service. As this Committee considers opportunities to expand broadband access in rural America, I do appreciate the opportunity to provide the cooperative perspective on USDA's broadband programs. NRECA and the nation's electric cooperatives look forward to working with this Committee, and others in Congress, to address these issues and close the digital divide once and for all. Thank you.

[The prepared statement of Mr. Matheson follows:]

Prepared Statement of Hon. Jim Matheson, Chief Executive Officer, National Rural Electric Cooperative Association, Arlington, VA

Chairman Thompson, Ranking Member Scott, and Members of this Committee. Thank you for inviting me to testify today. My name is Jim Matheson and I serve as the Chief Executive Officer of the National Rural Electric Cooperative Association. NRECA is the national service organization for more than 900 rural electric cooperatives that provide electric service to approximately 42 million people across 48 states. Rural electric cooperatives are member-owned, not-for-profit, and formed to provide safe, reliable electric service to their member-consumers at the lowest reasonable cost. They have a longstanding commitment to improving the communities in which they serve, and many are actively engaged in rural economic development efforts that go beyond electrification.

Today, more than 200 electric cooperatives are involved in rural broadband deployment efforts, recognizing the impact that a reliable high-speed internet connection can have on their communities and the challenges of deploying this infrastructure in low density, rural, and remote areas. For many cooperatives, the story of rural broadband deployment today mirrors the story of rural electrification nearly 100 years ago. The cost of building and maintaining networks in sparsely populated areas with difficult terrain is prohibitive for many providers. It is a cost-intensive process with little return on investment. Since cooperatives are owned by the people they serve, they understand the need for broadband in these areas and the challenges associated with deploying this infrastructure, which is why some have chosen to expand their services to include broadband.

As this Committee works to develop the next farm bill, electric cooperatives believe there are great opportunities to make improvements to broadband programs at the U.S. Department of Agriculture. Specifically, we encourage the Committee to:

- Make the ReConnect program permanent and easier to access
- Provide robust funding for rural broadband through USDA
- Prioritize symmetrical speeds and scalable networks in any future rounds of Federal funding
- Invest in middle-mile infrastructure

Broadband Is Critical for Rural America

An affordable and reliable internet connection is critical for the growth and development of rural America. Broadband is no longer a luxury, but instead a necessity for business, education, and healthcare access across the country. The Coronavirus pandemic highlighted the ongoing disparity between urban and rural access to a broadband connection and made clear how critical a high-speed internet connection is for rural economic development and quality of life. Without these connections, families may choose not to return to the small towns where they grew up, businesses choose to locate elsewhere, and farmers struggle to access the latest technologies that help lower input costs and improve yields. Internet based services are a routine part of modern life, and it is increasingly clear that bandwidth and capacity must meet the needs of today and anticipate the needs of tomorrow.

For many rural communities, the U.S. Department of Agriculture (USDA) has been a longtime trusted partner for rural economic development efforts. Rural electric cooperatives have been partnering with the agency for more than 80 years on efforts to build reliable electric networks in rural areas. What started in the 1930s as a partnership between rural communities and the Rural Electrification Administration has evolved into a much-needed, modern financing tool to build, maintain, and modernize electric, water, and telecommunications infrastructure through today's Rural Utilities Service (RUS). Federal programs administered by RUS are designed to address the unique challenges facing rural communities, such as low population densities and vast terrain, providing financing and technical assistance to improve the quality of life in hard-to-reach areas.

Many cooperatives have started deploying broadband in their service territories in large part because no one else will do it. Since cooperatives are owned by the people they serve, they understand the need for broadband in their rural service areas and the challenges associated with deploying this infrastructure. Electric cooperatives of all sizes are entering the broadband business due to demand from their members, who in many instances have no other alternative for a reliable internet connection. Despite these challenges, many cooperatives have built reliable, future proof networks capable of providing symmetrical speeds to both consumers and businesses.

For electric cooperatives, investments in broadband have produced significant benefits both internally and externally. Electric cooperatives are increasingly deploying fiber optic infrastructure as part of their electric network builds, which enables a high bandwidth, low latency internal communications system to support utility operations. Via this infrastructure, co-ops can monitor their systems in real time, improve response times to outages, and better manage utility resources. It also allows the co-op to improve the resiliency of the electric network and deploy smart grid technologies, such as advanced metering infrastructure, which can help reduce the overall costs to consumers. Beyond lowering energy costs, a fiber backbone allows co-ops to expand other technology offerings, such as distributed energy resources, electric vehicle access, or retail broadband service.

Through USDA's Electric Loan Program, electric cooperatives and other utilities can invest in smart grid technologies to improve grid security and reliability. The program allows recipients to use up to ten percent of the loan to construct broadband infrastructure in areas lacking a minimum acceptable level of broadband. This program correctly recognizes the dual-use nature of assets used for broadband communications services and electric cooperative smart grid technologies.

While retail broadband offerings have been successful for some cooperatives, others are choosing not to provide retail service, but instead are leveraging excess fiber capacity from their internal communications systems to provide middle-mile broadband access to other third-party providers, such as local cable providers, small telephone companies, and wireless internet service providers. This provides a critical link between the internet service provider's local network and the broader internet ecosystem. Access to this infrastructure can make a big difference in reducing the cost to deploy last mile networks in rural areas, however many rural providers lack access to a robust middle-mile connection. In the 2018 Farm Bill, this Committee recognized the importance of middle-mile networks and authorized a program at USDA to expand middle-mile infrastructure into rural areas. Unfortunately, the program has not moved forward. We encourage the Committee to consider reauthorizing the program, as strong middle-mile access is critical to last mile deployment and ensuring that every American receives reliable internet access.

As electric utilities, cooperatives own and maintain utility poles and rights-of-way for the safe and reliable distribution of electricity to their members. Ensuring the safe, affordable, and reliable delivery of electricity is the first priority for every electric cooperative. When safety, space and capacity allow, co-ops lease out excess space on their poles for the delivery of telecommunications services by third party providers, or even their own broadband subsidiary. This relationship provides communications companies with cost-based access to an existing pole distribution network for a small fraction of the significant costs that co-ops have incurred to build and maintain these systems.

Some within the communications industry have called for a one-size-fits-all rate for cooperative pole attachments. NRECA and all electric cooperatives strongly encourage the Committee to reject any proposals that would implement this type of regulation. As locally owned and democratically governed entities, electric cooperatives work in good faith to negotiate reasonable rates for pole attachments so that the burden of financing rural broadband deployment does not unfairly fall on rural electric customers. On average, electric co-ops serve seven customers per mile, compared to approximately 34 customers per mile served by larger investor-owned utilities. A one-size-fits-all approach does not accurately reflect the unique cost of building and maintaining a pole distribution network in low density, hard-to-reach rural areas that can differ from state to state and co-op to co-op.

The "Broadband Internet Connections for Rural America" Act

Last Congress, this Committee advanced the Broadband Internet Connections for Rural America Act,[1] which would make USDA's ReConnect program permanent and provide consistent funding moving forward. As discussions continue around the future of this and other broadband programs at USDA, I'd like to offer some recommendations.

First, Congress must prioritize scalable, future-proof networks in any future rounds of Federal funding. Without the ability for networks to grow in response to increased bandwidth needs and consumer demands, the challenge of solving the broadband gap in rural America will persist. In urban areas, gigabit speed networks are becoming increasingly common, yet in many cases the discussions around rural access seem to focus on what is "good enough." Broadband services should be equitable no matter where an individual chooses to live, and taxpayer dollars will be best spent supporting networks and technologies that can meet current and future needs, rather than investing in standards that are or soon will be obsolete.

Second, the definition of an area unserved by broadband should be raised to include areas that do not have at least 100/100 Mbps. Building networks in low density, hard to reach areas is challenging, but Congress must prioritize

[1] *https://www.congress.gov/117/bills/hr4374/BILLS-117hr4374rh.pdf.*

networks that can meet consumer demand and ensure that residents in these areas are able to receive quality service regardless of whether they are considered unserved or underserved.

Third, the program must be streamlined. The ReConnect application process is time consuming and difficult. The submission portal is not user friendly, and some have commented that attempting to fill out the program application is like having a second job. For small providers with limited resources, this is incredibly challenging and can be prohibitive. The application also lacks so-called "safeguards," meaning that if an applicant forgets to attach necessary information, such as their audited financial statement, the application platform will still certify and allow the applicant to submit rather than giving a warning that the required documentation has not been submitted. If that happens, there is no ability to go back and submit the missing documentation, which disqualifies the application. As Congress considers opportunities to modify or improve the application process moving forward, providing pathways to correct easily rectifiable errors or omissions would be helpful.

The Broadband Internet Connections for Rural America Act also includes robust funding for the USDA Community Connect Program. While a smaller and less popular program than ReConnect, cooperatives who have used this program have found it to be easy to manage and are typically able to complete the project within the program's 3 year build requirement. The program also includes an 80/20 grant/match ratio that is incredibly helpful for projects in low density rural footprints. However, one of the challenges that cooperatives have faced with the program is the requirement to facilitate a community center within the proposed funded service area. Due to the inherent rurality of these areas, there are not typically existing facilities conducive to hosting such a site. Flexibility to allow the community center to be facilitated in areas adjacent to and within a reasonable distance of the proposed funded service area could provide the dual benefit of expanding broadband access in rural areas while also facilitating an internet connection at an existing community facility, such as a library.

Prioritize Scalable, Future-Proof Networks

For many rural consumers, the promise of a broadband connection has gone unfulfilled. Recent Federal programs have defined "unserved" as areas lacking service at 25/3 megabits per second (Mbps) and "underserved" as areas lacking service at 100/20 Mbps. However, the Federal Communications Commission (FCC) today still defines broadband as 25/3 Mbps—a definition that was put in place nearly 10 years ago with limited consideration of raising that definition to be more reflective of current consumer demands. This must change. According to recent reports,[2] nearly 70% of U.S. homes receive internet service offering speeds of 200 Mbps or more, and more than 25% of homes are subscribing to gigabit or faster speeds. Other reports indicate that we are trending toward multi-gigabit networks by 2030.[3] It is clear that technology and user demand for bandwidth are exponentially increasing, which is why networks built in rural areas must be able to keep up with these growing demands.

The FCC has recognized this fact itself. In the FCC's 2021 Section 706 Report,[4] it noted that, as of December 2019, the vast majority of Americans had access to fixed terrestrial broadband service at 250/25 Mbps. Specifically, the Report states, "Between 2018 and 2019 . . . the deployment of 250/25 Mbps also increased from approximately 86% to over 87% of the population." If over 87% of the population has access to fixed terrestrial broadband service at 250/25 Mbps, it is difficult to comprehend why the Commission continues to maintain that the current dated definition of 25/3 Mbps is sufficient. This fact also begs the question of why most broadband programs and general consensus has landed on updating the definition of broadband to 100/20 Mbps, a definition that is well below what more than 87% of the population had access to in 2019. The Universal Service provisions in the 1996 Telecommunications Act requires comparable services at comparable rates between urban and rural areas. Rural communities should not be treated as second class citizens and be relegated to "good enough" broadband.

For farm communities, adoption of precision agriculture technology enables farmers and ranchers to optimize their operations, lower input costs, and increase product yields. Incorporating new technologies into farming operations allows for the adoption of automatic irrigation, soil health monitoring, improved weather forecasting, and real time monitoring of facilities. Some applications, such as the use of sensors in farm equipment, require low bandwidth but a wide range of field coverage. Other tools, such as the use of drones for the application of fertilizer or herbicides, require high

---

[2] *https://openvault.com/wp-content/uploads/2023/02/OVBI_4Q22_Report.pdf.*

[3] *https://www.fiercetelecom.com/telecom/fba-tips-household-broadband-speed-need-to-surpass-2-gbps-by-2030.*

[4] *https://www.fcc.gov/document/fcc-annual-broadband-report-shows-digital-divide-rapidly-closing.*

bandwidth and low latency. New technologies to aid and improve agricultural operations are constantly being developed and released to market, creating a growing demand for bandwidth in and around the farm and underscoring why a robust and scalable network connection is essential.

As Congress looks at USDA's broadband programs via the upcoming farm bill, scalable, future proof networks must be prioritized. The economics of deploying reliable, high-speed internet infrastructure in rural and remote areas is challenging for any provider, with low population densities and difficult terrain presenting little opportunity for return on investment. However, consumer demands for broadband speeds and capabilities continue to grow.[5] With that in mind, minimum build to speeds in any future rounds of Federal funding should be at least 100/100 Mbps symmetrical, and reevaluated on a consistent and regular basis to ensure that rural communities and families receive adequate broadband service both now and into the future. This will also eliminate the need for Congress to fund incremental network upgrades down the line.

Recently, Reps. Zach Nunn and Angie Craig introduced the ReConnecting Rural America Act, a bill that would codify the ReConnect program, prioritize symmetrical network speeds, and would provide the flexibility for the Secretary of Agriculture to reevaluate the minimum acceptable level of broadband service provided to rural areas. These flexibilities are important in ensuring that rural communities and families receive adequate broadband service now and into the future.

Reevaluate How Overbuilding Is Defined

Duplicating Federal support to build broadband networks is a serious concern. However, the level of service that federally supported networks provide must be considered when discussing the topic of overbuilding. As previously discussed, Federal programs acknowledge anything under 25/3 Mbps to be considered "unserved," and anything under 100/20 Mbps to be considered "underserved," yet it was only recently that these standards were adopted for some broadband programs. For example, the 2018 Connect America Fund Auction at the FCC allowed providers to bid in a 10/1 Mbps speed tier, and those winning providers will continue to receive support through 2028.

5 *https://www.broadbandtechreport.com/test/article/14293999/openvault-finds-usagebased-broadband-consumption-on-par-with-flatrate.*

Similarly, the first two rounds of ReConnect, which made awards in 2019 and 2020, respectively, had a minimum build to requirement of 25/3 Mbps.[6] Federal programs do not move quickly, which is why future-looking standards must be put in place.

Any discussion of reforms or constraint against overbuilding should be coupled with an evaluation of ongoing Federal support programs, and the quality of service those programs are supporting. Rural Americans should not be relegated to sub-par, "good enough" broadband service simply because an area is already receiving or has a commitment to receive support to build a network that does not meet current Federal definitions of broadband or consumer demands. Similarly, continuing to provide Federal support for networks that no longer meet the definitions of "served" is not good public policy nor is it a good use of taxpayer dollars. Instead, this will leave many rural residents without adequate service unless another ISP is willing to tackle the high costs associated with building this infrastructure in hard-to-reach areas without any additional support.

Permitting Reform Is Needed

The National Environmental Policy Act (NEPA) regulations present a significant challenge to rapid infrastructure deployment, often delaying projects and driving up costs. Co-ops face NEPA requirements when seeking a variety of Federal permits, approvals, and financial assistance, such as access to power line rights of way on Federal lands. In some instances, NEPA has been applied differently by Federal agencies, or even within different field offices of an agency.

For example, when a cooperative in Colorado won a USDA ReConnect award to provide broadband service, they planned to use existing electric infrastructure for the project and did not anticipate any permitting problems. However, the project sought to cross land managed by the U.S. Interior's Bureau of Land Management (BLM), which required full oversight and review of the proposed USDA funded infrastructure project simply because the project involved broadband service rather than electric service. As a result, the co-op was required to undergo an expensive, time consuming, and onerous permitting process through BLM that added months of delay and an unanticipated, and unbudgeted, $800,000 to the project. For electric service,

---

6 *https://www.rd.usda.gov/sites/default/files/foa_2_awards_report_508c.pdf.*

the existing rights of way are sufficient, and the co-op can upgrade their facilities without the added time and expense. But because this co-op was attaching broadband infrastructure to their existing poles in the existing right of way, BLM treated the project as a greenfield build which triggered a full environmental review.

In many instances, existing rights-of-way and easements only apply to electric service and not to broadband, which impacts not only cooperatives deploying broadband but any electric utility seeking to lease out excess fiber capacity to third-party telecommunications providers. Many cooperatives are including fiber to support electric operations or implement smart grid technologies. Fiber installed to support electric operations is typically allowed in electric utility rights of way, but if a co-op leases excess fiber to a third party for retail broadband, or chooses to provide retail broadband themselves, it could trigger a violation. Often, the utility must renegotiate the right of way or easement agreement with each state or Federal agency, local jurisdiction, or private landowner, which can take years and can cost millions of dollars.

The National Broadband Map Still Presents Challenges

In November 2022, the Federal Communications Commission (FCC) released the pre-production drafts of the National Broadband Maps, which are required to be used by the National Telecommunications and Infrastructure Administration (NTIA) to calculate how much states will receive in BEAD based on the number of unserved and underserved locations in each state. The maps released by the FCC display a more granular, location by location picture of where broadband service exists across the country and are a significant step forward from the previous maps, which tracked broadband deployment on a Census block level basis.

As part of the ongoing mapping process, the FCC collects self-reported, location level data from Internet Service Providers (ISPs) through the Broadband Data Collection (BDC), which happens twice per year. This data reflects the advertised availability of broadband service or where it could be installed, as reported by the ISPs in those areas. Once the maps were released, the FCC invited the public to review the data displayed and submit challenges highlighting inaccuracies.

NRECA worked to organize a multi-pronged response to the new maps, coordinating with cooperatives to submit over 260,000 availability challenges across multiple states, in addition to a grassroots education campaign to help cooperative members understand the map data and how to submit an individual challenge. Given the historic amount of funding made available through the upcoming BEAD program, it is critically important to NRECA and its members that this data is correct. Inaccuracies could mean that cooperative members miss their chance at a broadband connection through this historic funding opportunity.

Despite significant progress in improving the map's accuracy over the past 6 months, it is clear that there are still discrepancies between what the map displays and the realities on the ground. The continued reliance on advertised speeds instead of actual speeds opens the door to gamesmanship with mapping data and could prevent rural areas from receiving a high-speed internet connection.

Continued coordination between the FCC, NTIA, and [USDA] on broadband mapping initiatives would help ensure map accuracy. USDA is a uniquely focused agency with substantial knowledge of rural issues and areas, and has relationships with rural communities. USDA is a valuable partner for communities seeking to access and implement Federal programs, and increasingly the agency is playing a key role in helping to connect rural areas with the broadband resources they need to thrive. Given their rural focus, increased coordination with USDA on mapping accuracy and challenges could prove beneficial to ensuring rural communities are accurately reflected in mapping updates.

Conclusion

Rural electric cooperatives are deeply committed to bridging the digital divide and connecting rural homes and businesses with reliable and sustainable high-speed broadband service. As this Committee considers opportunities to connect all rural communities, I appreciate the opportunity to provide the cooperative perspective on USDA's broadband programs, and your attention to this important and timely issue. NRECA and the nation's electric cooperatives look forward to working with this Committee and others in Congress to address these issues and close the digital divide once and for all.

The CHAIRMAN. Thank you, Mr. Matheson. Mr. Assey, please begin when you are ready.

Statement of James M. Assey, Jr., J.D., Executive Vice President, NCTA—The Internet and Television Association, Washington, D.C.

Mr. ASSEY. Thank you, Chairman Thompson, Ranking Member Scott, and Members of this Committee. It is a distinct pleasure and honor to appear before you today on this important topic. As we review our current and future efforts to close the digital divide across rural America, it is worth reflecting on the journey. A journey that, perhaps informed by our own experiences during the COVID pandemic, that is propelled by our growing understanding that broadband and high-speed connectivity are increasingly central to how we learn, how our families connect, how our businesses operate, and generally how we participate in a 21st century society.

That journey started long ago. It has been fueled over time by competition and private capital investment that has resulted in the rapid growth of networks across much of the country. Over the last decade the cable industry alone has invested over $185 billion to build and expand both the reach and the capabilities of its networks. Today, 86 percent of the country has access to wired broadband from a cable and/or fiber provider. Two cable companies alone, Charter and Comcast, reach roughly 1⁄3 of all rural homes and businesses, and 99 percent of the homes passed by cable networks in rural America can receive internet service at speeds of 100 megabits or better.

Yet, despite such significant progress, we know our journey is not yet complete. There are still significant areas where broadband's ubiquity is frustrated by the unique economic challenges of low population density and high cost to construct and operate networks. Government programs, like those administered under the Department of Agriculture's Rural Utilities Service, have the potential to overcome these obstacles, offering assistance that will incent further investment in rural communities. But without careful design, such programs can also result in government spending that may benefit individual companies but does little to shrink the universe of the unserved.

As we think about the next chapter of this journey, we should recognize some advantages and some challenges that we face. On the plus side of the ledger, Congress has recently provided an unprecedented amount of resources to shrink the digital divide. At just the Federal level over $160 billion has been allocated over the past 4 years to aid broadband expansion. Some of this funding is already flowing to broadband projects, but far more is expected in the future. In addition to more funding, we are building better broadband maps that help us develop a common understanding of areas without service, and we are seeing early signs of better coordination among competing agencies that are tasked with similar objectives. These developments give us hope that we are poised to make significant strides over the next few years in reducing the rolls of the unconnected. But along with such opportunity comes risk.

Indeed, history has shown us that, in the absence of proper program design, focus, and coordination, there remains a high risk that resources will be squandered, and that good intentions will fail to translate into broadband connections for those most in need. For that reason, as the Committee considers new legislation addressing RUS broadband programs, it should recognize that future actions to close the digital divide may have less to do with a call for new capital, and more to do with the direction needed to ensure a proper program design and administration. In particular, we would urge the Committee to consider the following areas of reform.

First, the need for greater clarity and focus in directing funding distributions to unserved areas. Second, the need to modernize application requirements, that would encourage participation among qualified providers. Third, the need to eliminate status-based scoring priorities, and other preferences that thwart fair competition. And last, the need to address execution challenges, like permitting, and access to utility poles, that can stall the efficient completion of construction projects.

Many of these challenges are reflected in the Rural Internet Improvement Act (H.R. 3216) sponsored by Representatives Cammack, Soto, Jackson, and Gluesenkamp Perez. This bill appropriately recognizes the need for prioritizing funding to unserved areas, and suggests other reforms that will improve the focus, fairness and efficiency of existing RUS programs. With proper oversight and efficient administration, the next 5 years offer us the best chance yet to shrink the digital divide and bring the benefits of broadband to all. We in the cable industry look forward to working with you, the Members of this Committee, on that journey. Thank you.

[The prepared statement of Mr. Assey follows:]

Prepared Statement of James M. Assey, Jr., J.D., Executive Vice President, NCTA—The Internet and Television Association, Washington, D.C.

Chairman Thompson, Ranking Member Scott, and Members of the Committee, thank you for inviting me to discuss our members' experience with USDA's broadband funding programs and our suggestions to make these programs even more successful. My name is James Assey, and I am the Executive Vice President of NCTA—The Internet and Television Association ("NCTA"). NCTA represents the nation's largest broadband providers, which construct and operate fiber-rich highspeed internet networks that reach over 77% of the U.S. population, including a large and growing number of rural homes and businesses.

Over the last few years, our nation's response to challenges arising from the pandemic has put a renewed urgency and spotlight on the importance of ensuring every American can access the internet through a high-speed connection. In common cause, our industry has risen to that challenge, accelerating the pace of innovation and forging new broadband connections both throughout and outside their traditional service areas. Collectively, cable ISPs have invested more than $185 billion in private capital over the last decade to build and upgrade networks across America, including $21.7 billion in 2022 alone. This capital has extended the collective reach of cable broadband networks, adding about 6.4 million households between December 2018 and December 2021, nearly a third of which are rural households.

But, just as important, this massive investment has revolutionized the capabilities of these networks and their value to consumers, leveraging new technology and rapid innovation to launch the development of cable's 10G platform that is bringing 'speed at scale' to millions across America. Currently, 99% of U.S. homes passed by cable are capable of receiving a 1 Gigabit service from their cable ISP. And with even more scalable, technological innovation on the horizon, the future, wide-scale diffusion of networks offering 10 Gigabit connections to U.S. households is well within view.

The dividends of these investments are not only collected in urban and suburban environments, but also increasingly in rural communities where the high-speed capabilities of cable broadband networks are bringing world-class broadband to rural communities throughout the country. Charter and Comcast alone serve nearly a third of all rural homes and businesses. In fact, when robust, high-speed broadband is available in rural America, it is more likely to be from a cable provider than any other platform:

Rural units served (total U.S. rural units = 36.7 million)

Tech	Number of Rural Units Served (millions)	Service Available at 100/20 or better (millions)	Service Available at 1 Gig or better (millions)	% of Rural Footprint at 1 Gig or better
Cable	17.5	17.1	16.4	94%
Telco †	20.1	5.5	4.4	22%
Fixed wireless	29.0	4.8	0.5	2%

† including copper, fiber, and fixed wireless.
Source: FCC *National Broadband Map.*

Despite this growth and these significant advances, we know that the job is not yet done and the challenges ahead are formidable. Unserved communities generally lack broadband facilities for one primary reason—they are prohibitively expensive to serve. The cost of deploying infrastructure over expansive, difficult terrain is often exponentially higher than other areas. At the same time, the potential revenue to offset those expenses is inversely less where fewer people and businesses reside. Government funding is essential to offsetting these dynamics and incenting companies to serve those communities.

At USDA, one of the most promising programs to help cable and other ISPs reach unserved households in rural areas had been the Rural eConnectivity program run by the Rural Utilities Service ("RUS"), better known as the "ReConnect" program. Unlike other RUS broadband funding programs, this program was, at its creation, tightly focused on helping to direct capital investment in building broadband networks in unserved areas through a competitive process that, in distinction to past practice, allowed all providers to participate and compete on a level playing field. Over the last 5 years, the cable industry worked extensively with RUS and Congress to make significant improvements to the ReConnect program, making it easier and more attractive for competitive providers, who were not traditional recipients for RUS support, to participate. Some progress has been made. For example, RUS has taken needed action to modernize outdated application and data requirements that were overwhelming for many would-be applicants to assemble, especially for providers with nationwide operations.

Unfortunately, more recent updates have created new obstacles. Changes to the program have made winning funding awards extremely difficult for cable ISPs, and have clouded the program's focus away from unserved areas. Specifically, RUS has changed the scoring methodology for the program and injected new bias so that certain providers—in particular, municipalities, nonprofits and cooperatives—get an automatic significant scoring preference, as do those that build using unionized contract labor. Additional points are awarded for those providers willing to agree to onerous open access mandates, which most providers are not willing to do.

These calculated changes impede fair competition and have made it extremely difficult for cable ISPs to secure funding, even when they seek to serve areas where no one else wants to deploy. In addition, the agency's action in significantly relaxing the required minimum percentage of unserved homes required of project applications has created new problems and drawn dollars away from areas where they are most needed. Indeed, scarce resources that should be directed toward bringing service to unserved households are instead being used to subsidize network overbuilds in ways that further challenge the economics of serving remote areas, and worse, do nothing to reduce the number of unserved households.

Beyond considering the internal changes required to promote greater efficiency and effectiveness of RUS programs, the next Farm bill must also grapple with the external challenges of encouraging greater coordination and consistency among a number of Federal and state agencies that will similarly focus on closing the digital divide. To promote efficiency and minimize waste, it will be more important than ever that we direct greater coordination and collaboration among Federal and state agencies engaged in similar efforts. With so many billions of Federal funding dollars being focused on broadband expansion over the next several years, we believe that it is more important than ever to get these programs right and to put controls in place that will prevent inefficiency and waste.

As the Committee considers these issues, we believe that matters addressed in the Rural Internet Improvement Act, introduced by Representatives Cammack, Soto, Jackson and Perez, would go a very long way toward making needed changes and establishing clear Congressional direction. Most notably, the Rural Internet Improvement Act provides important protections against overbuilding, modernizes eligibility rules, reduces excessive data burdens in both the application and funding phases, and calls for substantially increased coordination among the various agencies distributing broadband funding.

Cable's Decades Long Commitment to Rural America

Before discussing cable's experience with USDA funding programs, I want to underscore that cable ISPs have made it their mission to ensure that our most rural communities are at the leading edge of technology.

Our growth in recent months has included important progress in reaching previously unserved areas, thanks both to cable's commitment to invest in rural areas and to partnerships with the FCC, through its CAF II and RDOF auctions, and with the states we serve. For example:

- *Cable's Private Investment in Rural Areas*
  - Comcast invest billions of dollars every year to expand and evolve its network—more than $20 billion from 2018–2022 alone, and $33 billion in the past decade. Comcast added 813,000 new passings in 2021, and an additional 840,000 in 2022, including many in rural areas. The company recently announced that it is further accelerating connecting more homes, by planning to pass one million additional new addresses in 2023, bringing the total new passings in just 3 years to 2.65 million homes.
  - Charter also continues to invest billions of dollars every year to expand and evolve its network—more than $40 billion from 2018–2022 alone. Charter has also committed to significant expansion in rural areas in states across the country. In March, Charter announced a $12 million commitment to rural broadband expansion in Maine, which will bring gigabit-speed broadband access to over 3,500 unserved homes and small businesses in several towns in Somerset and Oxford counties. Concurrently, Charter announced an investment of approximately $70 million in Maine, part of a company-wide network evolution that will enable the delivery of symmetrical and multiple gigabit speeds across the state. This 100% Charter-funded investment is expected to be substantially complete across the company's Maine service area, which comprises more than 700,000 homes and businesses, by the end of 2025.
- *Cable's Partnerships with Government to Bring Service to Unserved Areas*
  - Charter Communications plans to build nearly 100,000 miles of new U.S. broadband infrastructure through its RDOF expansion alone—a distance that would circle the equator more than four

times. As part of that commitment, Charter announced a $5 billion investment that will connect more than one million unserved, mostly rural homes and small businesses to reliable, highspeed broadband service at speeds up to a gigabit per second. While the RDOF funds will go a long way to connecting people, approximately $4 of every $5 of this build-out will come from private capital invested by Charter— they and other cable ISPs are investing their own funds to connect people in rural areas.

- In addition to RDOF and Federal programs, Charter has participated in dozens of state broadband funding rounds and hundreds of local funding opportunities, earning subsidies to build to more than 300,000 locations since 2021. For example, through Louisiana's Granting Unserved Municipalities Broadband Opportunities ("GUMBO") program, which was funded through the ARPA, Charter was awarded more than $10 million in grants to support broadband expansion across three Louisiana parishes. Upon completion, this investment will deliver high-speed internet access to more than 2,000 currently-unserved homes and businesses.
- Comcast has been awarded grants from Federal, state and local programs in 24 states, including multiple awards to build-out its gigabit broadband network to homes that are unconnected to broadband today, including more than 30,000 unserved homes in Georgia and over 51,000 in Florida.
- Comcast has also been awarded funds from Pennsylvania's Unserved HighSpeed Funding State Program to reach unserved homes in Lycoming, Armstrong and Union counties, as well as from the Build Illinois Bond Fund, ARPA/Connect IL Round 2 to bring service unconnected homes in Whiteside county.
- In 2022, Cox committed hundreds of millions of dollars to expand its fiber infrastructure to provide best-in-class high-speed internet to un and under-served areas. This included establishing a Market Expansion Team ("MET"), which is solely focused on expanding Cox's network to un and underserved areas beyond the existing service area. The MET supports Cox's focus on advancing digital equity by bringing Cox's robust network to communities without broadband in a world where communities need to be connected to thrive. Since 2022, Cox has successfully

    secured nearly $100 million in grant funds and matched that with more than $100 million in private capital to extend services to almost 50,000 homes in eight states, in addition to many wholly self-funded projects. Through these partnerships, Cox has activated service in about 30 previously unconnected communities with more currently under construction, and that's just the beginning. Looking ahead 12 months, Cox plans to more than double that number.
  - Mediacom was awarded $13.4 million in grant funding from the State of Alabama, to help extend broadband to nearly 20,000 locations there. Its new locations will span multiple counties, including locations in northwest Baldwin County, southwest Escambia County, and Mobile County.
  - In Sherburne County, Minnesota, Midco is utilizing private capital, RDOF funds and local partnerships with the county and six townships to complete several broadband expansion projects. From 2020–2024, nearly 10,000 homes and businesses in the county will be connected with over 1.5 million of new broadband infrastructure constructed. In total, Midco's investment in Sherburne County since 2020 is over $32 million.
  - In Alaska, GCI is deploying fiber to some of the most remote communities in the country. GCI paired $25 million in ReConnect funds with over $50 million of its own capital to support its Alaska United—Aleutians Fiber Project, which provided terrestrial broadband service for the first time to Unalaska/ Dutch Harbor and five other communities—King Cove, Sand Point, Akutan, Chignik Bay, and Larsen Bay. GCI also has been awarded a $31 million ReConnect grant in support of its Lower Kuskokwim Fiber Expansion Project, which will bring fiber-optic infrastructure to five Yukon-Kuskokwim Delta communities in Western Alaska.
- *Cable's Innovative Solutions to Support Rural Communities*
  - Nestled alongside a pond and horse farm in rural Eastover, South Carolina, is Camp Cole—a fully accessible camp and retreat facility for children, teens, and adults facing serious illnesses and other physical, mental, and emotional health or life challenges. Internet connectivity is critical to providing many campers with the resources they need, including monitoring medical devices, conducting video calls with doctors and care providers, and

ensuring counselors can communicate across the campus. During construction of the Camp Cole facility, camp staff reached out to Charter about getting the rural property online. Within a few short months—and at virtually no cost to them— Camp Cole was connected to Charter's high-speed Spectrum Internet, and today campers and staff enjoy 300 Mbps speeds across the property.

- In Colorado, Charter has used various wireless technologies such as 5G, WiFi, and Citizens Broadband Radio Spectrum ("CBRS") spectrum to deliver service to transform how Wells Bridge Farm does business. Wells Bridge Farm was able to deploy a WiFi network and enable connected sensors to provide enhanced security to the farm's main gate and real-time glimpses into what was occurring on the farm, and with the animals, offering opportunities for proactive care for the horses and enhanced productivity for the farm. The success of this wirelessly connected smart farm now paves the way for similar digital solutions in other communities.
- Midco relies on an existing broadband network to connect relay towers, thereby extending a signal miles beyond where the physical wires stop. Midco uses traditional towers, as well as grain elevators or water towers, to reach homes or farms miles away from those wired networks. This means they can still receive broadband service without the need for an ISP to lay miles and miles of fiber in challenging terrain. Midco, which serves communities throughout South Dakota, North Dakota, Minnesota, Kansas, and Wisconsin, has championed the use of fixed wireless for precision agriculture. Some of these communities have fewer than 100 people, with miles and miles of land separating one neighbor from the other.

These examples underscore cable's commitment to expand networks and reach those areas that need it most.

While cable ISPs are reaching new homes with broadband fiber every day, they also remain keenly aware that government funding will be needed to reach places where challenging terrain or other factors make private investment alone too uneconomical. For broadband to reach rural America as quickly as possible, it is critical that funding programs be technology-neutral, encourage the broadest participation of qualified broadband providers, and be as flexible as possible. And that leads me to our current concerns about the current direction of the ReConnect Program and other broadband funding programs administered by RUS.

Restoring Program Focus and Continuing Needed Coordination Will Help Rural America

As further rural build-out intensifies in the coming years to reach more unserved communities, the effectiveness of RUS broadband programs will depend on Congressional action to restore a clarity of purpose and to promote coordinated and consistent action that promotes fair competition. Recent changes to the ReConnect program have significantly shifted the focus of this program away from the portions of rural America lacking broadband access. This shift should be reversed.

First, Congress should act to restore ReConnect's focus on unserved areas and establish a common understanding of what it means to be "unserved." While the original ReConnect program required that at least 90% of households in a project area qualify as unserved to be eligible for funding, the most recent round of funding significantly relaxed this requirement and considered areas to be eligible for funding even when as many as 50% of households already had access to broadband service. The most likely result of this change is that monies will be diverted from the areas that are 90% unserved, which are typically the hardest areas to serve, and those areas will remain unserved.

The agency also has changed the speed thresholds used to determine when an area already has "sufficient" access to broadband service, which has clouded the agency's commitment to focus scarce resources first on reducing the number of households without any acceptable broadband connectivity. When eligibility is restricted to areas that do not receive a basic level of broadband service, such as 25/ 3, we know that funding will be used to bring broadband where it did not previously exist. But when areas with some level of service are defined as eligible for funding on a par with those with nothing, providers will naturally pursue those projects that are less expensive to deploy broadband to, i.e., those with better potential economic return, while those areas most in need of assistance will again end up at the back of the line.

This needs to change. There should be an absolute priority for qualified applications to extend service to areas without 25/3 service, and most funding should be put to that use. For example, you could provide that 75% of the funding needs to be for projects without 25/3, or you could provide that no funding could be granted for projects in underserved areas (those that have service that is between 25/3 and 100/20 speeds) until at least 80% of areas lacking 25/3 have been covered.

Additionally, RUS does not sufficiently take into account where areas are already being built out due to awards from other government programs when it determines which areas should be considered unserved. Allowing government broadband programs to grant funding in places where other government awards have already been committed for broadband construction dangerously decreases the effectiveness of the program. For example, NCTA member Midco was overbuilt by two ReConnect awards in rural South Dakota, even though it was already building a fixed wireless network serving those areas that was being partially funded by an FCC grant. Because Midco had not yet finished construction, the area was still considered "unserved," and so its challenges to those funding awards were denied. Programs need to be coordinated so that there is a common understanding of eligibility, one that takes into account areas already funded for deployment.

Second, Congress should direct RUS, in reviewing applications, to limit scoring preferences to those that relate to applicant experience or platform performance. Points for being a particular type of entity (*e.g.,* an electrical or gas cooperative), or for agreeing to assume extra regulatory obligations (*e.g.,* particular wage standards) do nothing to ensure that broadband networks will reach rural America quickly and will be run well, and are simply inappropriate vehicles for directing funding to favored providers.

Third, as it has in other broadband programs, Congress should ensure that performance standards (sometimes referenced as "build to" speed requirements) retain some element of flexibility to produce solutions that are forward-leaning, but also robust and cost-effective. As we have seen in the context of the FCC's RDOF auction, an open competitive process for subsidy awards can be structured to incent extremely robust and scalable platform solutions, but too high a performance threshold can also lead to situations where requirements preclude some areas from attracting willing providers. Programs need flexibility to accommodate different technological solutions, and guidelines for identifying those areas where flexibility can and should be accommodated. States may offer a helpful guide in delineating such areas. The BEAD Program, for example, allows states to designate an "Extremely High Cost Per Location Threshold," above which the state can pick a proposal using an alternative technology when doing so would be less expensive, ensuring that the very highest cost areas are not ignored if they cannot be served effectively by fiber. *Fourth,* there are significant, burdensome data requirements in the ReConnect program, such as those designed to evaluate an applicant's financial viability. The application process should be simplified by limiting the amount of data to what is truly required to evaluate an applicant's viability. For financial requirements, RUS should allow applicants to demonstrate financial viability in various ways beyond an exclusive first lien on grant-funded assets. For example, an applicant should be permitted to rely on a bond rating performed by an expert credit rating agency to establish their financial viability.

Finally, with numerous Federal agencies and nearly all states dedicating funding to broadband deployment, it is increasingly important to ensure that all relevant agencies, and to the extent possible state programs that are awarding grants for build-out, are aware of current awards so as to ensure that government support is coordinated and being used efficiently to reduce the number of unserved households and to help achieve the goal of universal connectivity. The recent Memorandum of Understanding Regarding Information Sharing between the FCC, U.S. Department of Agriculture, the National Telecommunications and Information Administration of the U.S. Department of Commerce, and the U.S. Department of the Treasury is an important first step towards reaching that goal, but further actions will be required in the coming years as the pace of grant activity and broadband construction intensifies.

One important aspect of coordination would be to take steps to make the programs, their eligibility standards, and their requirements as consistent as possible. Entities seeking funding should not be able to "forum shop" for the least restrictive program. NCTA member Midco faced a situation where they successfully challenged a provider under the ReConnect program from overbuilding their network in rural North Dakota, but the applicant responded by applying for funding in that same area under the ARPA Capital Projects Fund program, and succeeded in obtaining funds to overbuild Midco's existing service.

To avoid this result, government entities awarding funding for broadband infrastructure (including RUS) should promptly report those awards to the Federal Communications Commission, so that maps used for granting broadband funding are consistent, and everyone works off a common data set in determining areas eligible for funding. Ideally, maps should show all areas where Federal, state, or local funding has been awarded pursuant to enforceable commitments, so that remaining dollars can be targeted at the areas not yet covered. Programs should work together towards the common goal of connecting more Americans and reducing the rolls of the unserved.

Why the Rural Internet Improvement Act Would Improve RUS's Broadband Programs

As the Committee considers a new farm bill, one promising piece of legislation to draw from is the Rural Internet Improvement Act of 2022. It would make many key improvements to the ReConnect program, enhancing participation and results, so that broadband reaches rural America faster. In particular, it would—

- Target funding to the neediest rural areas, by limiting all types of funding to areas in which at least 90% of households lack access to broadband, with the highest possible priority for applications proposing to serve areas without 25/ 3 service.
- Update the minimum build-out speed requirements to 100/20, which is a reasonable speed that allows for different technological solutions.
- Protect against wasted dollars by excluding funding in areas where a provider has been granted funding under another Federal, state, or local broadband funding program, or where a provider is otherwise required to build broadband by a Federal, state or local government entity (except that the provider who secured such funding could obtain additional ReConnect funding if they used such funding for different, non-duplicative expenses, or they agreed to build broadband with faster speeds or expedited deployment milestones than were originally required).
- Simplify the application process, by limiting the amount of data required in applications to the greatest extent practicable, including allowing applicants to demonstrate financial viability in the least burdensome way and requiring the Secretary to establish means by which applicants can offer various forms of loan collateral and security, not just an exclusive first lien on grant-funded assets. For example, it would allow a company with a sufficient bond rating to use the bond rating to establish their financial viability, and would generally require a much closer look at whether all the data required to apply for funding is really relevant and necessary.
- Establish better communication between Federal agencies when awards are made and improve the challenge process, so that money is spent transparently and does not duplicate other agencies' efforts.

These changes would go a long way towards our shared goal of connecting rural America, and we ask you to give them careful consideration to incorporating them into any program revisions. We also urge that you avoid any changes that would compromise program efficiency and sacrifice needed focus, and that you ensure that RUS give all applicants equal consideration, even if they are not prior borrowers. If ReConnect is reoriented to its original focus, it can succeed in making meaningful contributions to bringing broadband to rural Americans currently lacking service.

* * *

In closing, I commend the Committee for its focus on ensuring that the billions of dollars being spent on broadband deployment benefits all Americans—including those in rural America. Progress has been made in some Federal and state programs to target funding at unserved areas, largely by improving the design of those programs to better identify unserved areas and by defining broadband service in a way that prioritizes people living in hard-to-reach areas that may require a menu of technologies to serve each and every household. We hope that the ReConnect program and other new programs will be changed so that they are implemented with similar goals and guardrails in place. Thank you again for inviting me here today, and we look forward to working with you on these important issues.

The CHAIRMAN. Thank you, Mr. Assey. Mr. Zumwalt, please begin when you are ready.

Statement of David M. Zumwalt, President and Chief Executive Officer, Wireless Internet Service Providers Association, Washington, D.C.

Mr. ZUMWALT. Thank you, Chairman Thompson, Ranking Member Scott, and Members of this Committee. Thank you for convening this important hearing. My name is David Zumwalt, and I am the President and CEO of WISPA—Broadband Without Boundaries, representing nearly 1,000 members that provide connectivity to unserved and underserved communities across the country.

Wireless Internet Service Providers, or WISPs, serve nine million Americans nationwide and deploy a variety of technologies, including fiber, as well as wireless, to deliver reliable broadband services. Most of their subscribers live and work in rural areas that other providers have historically overlooked or chosen not to serve.

WISPs and entrepreneurial community businesses, are often putting up their own capital to serve their neighbors. They come in many sizes, and their importance is enormous to the communities they serve. They live there, bank there, send their children to school there, and in some cases farm there. They are the hometown ISPs.

At the outset of the pandemic, WISPs were quick to adapt to changes in consumer demand to meet our nation's essential connectivity needs. WISPs know all too well that the digital divide is a long way from being closed. These challenges are particularly acute for our nation's farmers, who are facing higher costs and difficult supply chain issues. Connectivity is more critical than ever, and many applications, such as precision agriculture, require wireless broadband. Every American, regardless of where they live, should have broadband internet access. Recognizing the urgency of this moment, we are eager to stand with you in fulfilling our nation's connectivity mission.

The farm bill has been assisting rural communities' transition to the digital age for many years. As such, it is critical that, going forward, the farm bill's broadband programs stay focused on those communities that are truly unserved. WISPA strongly supports the goals of the ReConnect Program, however, without careful structuring and a clear process, the program risks undermining our shared goals of connecting rural communities quickly. RUS's most recent funding round exemplifies some of these issues.

First, ReConnect should not establish, as gating criteria, a requirement that applicants must provide 100 megabit per second symmetrical service. At present, ReConnect funded projects must be capable of delivering this symmetrical service to every location. In our experience, rural consumers are not asking for 100 megabits per second upload speeds, nor does it represent what urban subscribers are actually using today. To make symmetry a requirement would effectively prevent many providers from even applying for funding, leaving communities unconnected. It would force many communities to wait longer for service when they could have reliable broadband much sooner by utilizing the right tool for the right job, an assortment of proven technologies that can get the job done.

If requirements such as symmetrical speeds are locked in statute, RUS will be precluded from having the flexibility it needs. Lack of flexibility may leave many areas unserved, or force those awarded to wait years longer for service, which is counter to the purpose of the program. USDA has defined *sufficient access to broadband* as any rural area in which households have fixed terrestrial broadband service of 100 megabit downstream and 20 megabit upstream. This is reasonable, and aligns with industry experience, and should be the standard for the farm bill. By contrast, a 100/100 requirement will deflect funding to communities with more than sufficient broadband already, leaving out places that lack any broadband at all. It makes no sense to divert taxpayer dollars from where they are needed most to overbuild areas that are already connected.

This leads to our second recommendation. Subsidizing overbuilding in areas where local providers are already delivering reliable broadband distorts the market. It wastes taxpayer dollars and slows our whole of national effort to bridge the digital divide. Every community is different, and therefore requires different solutions. Placing a thumb on the scale to benefit one type of technology or provider, or to fund areas subsidized with other government funding, does no favors for Americans who are in urgent need of broadband access today. It increases the time unserved communities must wait for connectivity at the financial and societal expense of those communities.

Every community, regardless of size, location, or geography, deserves reliable broadband service. This is no small task. It will take all of us working together to ensure no community is left behind. On behalf of WISPAs members, the thousands of ISPs already at work in the digital divide, thank you again for holding this important hearing and inviting me to testify. I look forward to continuing to work with the Committee and look forward to your questions. Thank you.

[The prepared statement of Mr. Zumwalt follows:]

Prepared Statement of David M. Zumwalt, President and Chief Executive Officer, Wireless Internet Service Providers Association, Washington, D.C.

Chairman Thompson, Ranking Member Scott, and Members of the Committee, thank you for holding this important hearing and for the opportunity to testify. My name is David Zumwalt, and I am the President and CEO of the Wireless Internet Service Providers Association (WISPA)—*Broadband Without Boundaries,* representing the companies that provide connectivity to unserved and underserved households and businesses across the country.

Prior to joining WISPA, I served as Chief Operating Officer of Broadband VI, a major Internet Service Provider in the U.S. Virgin Islands whose needs for robust broadband for economic growth is unchallenged. Because of our work, in 2021, Broadband VI was awarded $84.5 million in FCC funding to supplement its private investment in Territory-wide broadband expansion. I have also served as Executive Director of the University of the Virgin Islands Research & Technology Park, a partnership of private sector, government and university stakeholders that supported the USVI's network-connected knowledge-based business sector. During my tenure, RTPark sought, but was ultimately unsuccessful in securing, $4.7 million in financing from the U.S. Department of Agriculture Rural Utilities Service (RUS) in 2008 but did secure $5.5 million in matching funds from the U.S. Department of Commerce Economic Development Administration in 2009. I have witnessed first-hand the benefits of these programs that seek to lift rural and economically challenged communities.

WISPA's nearly 1,000 members include broadband service and infrastructure providers, equipment manufacturers, and technology companies that work every day to close the digital divide in many of our country's most rural and remote communities. Our members' stories are often remarkably similar. Tired of waiting for someone else to bring broadband to them and their neighbors, they took their private capital and built a solution, connecting families, businesses, first responders and community anchor institutions.

WISPA advocates for the widespread deployment of broadband. This is best accomplished by allowing the utilization of the "right tool for the right job" so that all communities, regardless of size or location, can reap the benefits of reliable, affordable, and robust connectivity as quickly as possible.

WISPA and our members are grateful for the leadership of this Committee in promoting our shared goal of closing the digital divide with ubiquitous, reliable, and resilient broadband networks.

Importance of WISPs

WISPs serve nine million Americans, mostly in unserved, under-resourced, and Tribal territories. Our members offer cost-effective, competitive, and innovative services for these communities. WISPs deploy a variety of technologies, including fiber as well as licensed, shared, and unlicensed wireless spectrum, to deliver reliable broadband service to their customers at affordable prices, often in areas ignored by others because the deployment costs are prohibitive.

WISPs are mostly small and medium sized businesses. Many of our members have fewer than twenty-five employees, and almost 70 percent have ten or fewer full-time employees. Often investing their own private, at-risk capital, our members are truly community-based and entrepreneurial companies. According to our latest member survey, more than 75 percent of WISPA's operator members serve primarily rural areas and very often to small populations, communities that have often been passed over by the larger, national carriers. Many WISPs may be small, but to the communities they serve, their importance is enormous.

Fixed wireless broadband has proven to be a powerful and reliable tool in getting these communities online. According to a 2021 report by The Carmel Group, WISPs can deploy fixed wireless service to residential consumers at about 1/9 the capital cost of fiber-to-the-premises. These favorable economics enable WISPs to serve smaller and more remote communities, where it is not cost-effective for other technologies to be deployed.

Typical speeds that fixed wireless providers offer continue to increase as technology advances, and equipment costs become more competitive. Download speeds exceeding 1 Gbps are possible with current fixed wireless technology, with equipment available from multiple manufacturers. Our industry is one of the most dynamic, scalable and flexible in the entire broadband ecosystem, characterized by rapid, cost-effective deployment, speedy technology innovation, and many new entrants.

Moreover, fixed wireless is being deployed much more quickly than many other alternatives. The basic network elements are a tower or tall building, commercially available radio transmitters and consumer-premises equipment, and, of course, licensed and unlicensed spectrum. And WISPs don't need thousands of subscribers to make a business case; often, only a handful of potential customers will justify beginning deployment to multiple locations in an area. In sparsely populated rural areas, that's critical for consumers who should not have to continue to wait for a higher, and sometimes unattainable, critical mass of potential customers for more expensive fiber installation to their homes and businesses.

The need for fast deployment and the ability to connect rural and remote communities was never clearer than during the COVID–19 pandemic. Access to fixed wireless technology was a lifeline for many Americans. Every child who had to attend school from their bedroom, every patient who needed to access their doctor via telemedicine, every business owner who relied on

Zoom to connect with customers and suppliers—none of them could afford to wait for technology to be deployed. They needed to be online, and I am proud to say that WISPs across the country upgraded their networks where necessary to meet increased consumer demand and delivered for their communities. And they continue to do so.

In addition, investment banking firms and private equity funds have made dozens of investments in our members' businesses over the last few years. They are attracted by solid management, favorable growth potential and the large untapped rural markets that will drive new deployment and increased revenue. This trend is ongoing and, along with government funding, positions our members as significant players in the years to come.

Closing the Digital Divide

Due to the hard work and vision of this Committee, great progress is being made to connect all Americans. However, as businesses largely based in rural communities, WISPs know all too well that the digital divide is still a long way from being closed.

Despite the enormous positive impact of broadband, many Americans still do not share these benefits. There remains a substantial number of Americans who cannot fully participate in today's economy and democracy, whose children tend to lag in school, and whose communities are not able to keep pace with the economic growth potential that broadband brings. While the number of new broadband subscribers continues to grow, the rate of broadband deployment in urban, suburban, and highincome areas is outpacing deployment in rural and low-income areas. This disparity has long-term adverse economic and social consequences for those left behind. WISPA is committed to addressing this disparity.

These challenges are particularly acute for our nation's farmers, who are facing higher commodity prices and difficult supply chain issues. Connectivity, real time data, and opportunities to sell their commodities in an expedient and efficient manner are more critical than ever. And many applications used by farmers, such as precision agriculture, require wireless broadband to blanket vast acres of farmland to be useful.

Every American—regardless of where they live—should have access to the very best internet and reliability that they need. Americans in rural areas have no less a need for fast broadband than those in urban centers. The questions this Committee faces are, how do we most quickly provide the level of connectivity that rural communities need in ways that leave nobody behind? And how do we ensure that taxpayer dollars are spent in the most efficient and productive ways possible?

We cannot allow this opportunity to bridge the digital divide slip away. The NTIA BEAD program should not be the be-all and end-all for broadband deployment, and USDA can have a significant and positive impact on broadband that is complementary to that program, if the farm bill is written and implemented in a technologically neutral way that respects public and private investment. Recognizing the urgency of this moment, WISPA members stand ready to roll up their sleeves and get to work. The stakes are too high, connectivity is too important, and many rural communities have waited far too long.

WISPs' Experiences with ReConnect

The farm bill has been assisting rural communities entering the digital age for many years. For this reason, it is critical that the farm bill's broadband programs stay focused on those communities that are truly unserved. No community should be asked to wait even longer for broadband so that other communities receive upgraded network build-outs they don't actually need.

WISPA strongly supports the goals of the ReConnect program and supports the investments Congress has provided to bring broadband to more Americans, particularly those in unserved and underserved communities. However, we have seen that, without careful structuring and a clear process, the program risks undermining our shared goals of connecting rural communities with the greatest need quickly. The RUS's most recent funding round exemplifies some of these issues.

First, RUS required that any facilities to be constructed with ReConnect award funds "must be capable of delivering 100 Mbps symmetrical service to every premise in the proposed funded service area." Symmetrical service means that download speeds identically match upload speeds.

Some Members of Congress have expressed support for prioritizing symmetrical speeds. Consumers clearly value download and upload speeds differently, and it makes sense for RUS to consider them independently. To make symmetry the primary gating criteria for eligibility when consumers are not even asking for or using it when they have access to it, would prevent many providers from even applying for funding, leaving many communities out in the cold. In addition, this type of requirement would add significant time to deployment, in many cases forcing communities to wait additional years, when they could have service much quicker by utilizing other technologies.

The gap between downstream and upstream traffic has consistently grown over the last 10 years. Recently, the ratio of downstream consumption to upstream is 14 to 1. Current consumer trends demonstrate significant increases in downstream consumption while upstream traffic increases at a fraction of the rate. Today's consumers do not utilize upstream bandwidth at the same rate they use downstream and speak to it with their dollars and usage. Video streaming makes up over 80 percent of all internet traffic, 2⁄3 of which is traffic from downloads. Even popular applications that utilize relatively high upload bandwidth, such as two-way video conferencing, do not require anything near symmetrical speeds. Studies have shown video conferencing requires approximately 1⁄3 of the upstream bandwidth compared to downstream.

Networks are optimized based on consumer use patterns. The WISP industry has responded by engineering networks to favor downloads to meet their customers' demand. Even if demand for upload speeds somehow doubles down the road, it will remain far below download speed demand. Basing criteria on speculative predictions about future demand for upload speed—when, as we speak, many communities remain completely unserved—would be counterproductive, especially for an investment of this magnitude.

For these programs to be successful and cost-effective, as many broadband providers as possible should be encouraged to participate. Symmetrical service may work in some communities, but not every location is the same. Erecting artificial, unnecessary, and wasteful barriers to participation would exclude many projects that would now provide connectivity to the most remote communities. If rigid requirements, such as symmetrical speeds, are locked in statute, it precludes RUS from having the flexibility to consider projects that address other key priorities. Lack of flexibility may leave many areas unserved or force those awarded to wait years longer for service, which is counter to the purpose of the program.

Second, USDA defined sufficient access to broadband as "any rural area in which households have fixed, terrestrial broadband service defined as 100 megabits per second (Mbps) downstream and 20 Mbps upstream." The result of this requirement is that ReConnect funding will wind up going to communities with more than sufficient funding already, leaving out places that lack any broadband at all. It simply makes no sense to divert taxpayer dollars from where they are needed the most to overbuild areas that are already connected.

Simply put, subsidizing overbuilding in areas where innovative, local providers are delivering broadband, or have an enforceable commitment to do so, inequitably distorts the market. It wastes taxpayer dollars. And it still leaves many Americans without any access to broadband.

At a minimum, locations subject to an "enforceable commitment" to provide broadband service through a state or Federal program should be off-limits for initial ReConnect funding. This will address two issues. First, it will ensure that taxpayers' contributions to the FCC's Connect America Fund and Rural Digital Opportunity Fund will not be used to subsidize multiple providers in the same market—in effect, the government would be competing with itself.

Second, exempting from ReConnect funding locations subject to an existing "enforceable commitment" will protect the integrity of the programs and the reliance interests of those CAF and RDOF recipients that are hard at work investing government funding and their own capital in deploying broadband in rural communities. It will also enable them to attract outside capital on more favorable terms.

Third, RUS included as a key criterion for awarding grants "local governments, nonprofits and cooperatives." The best provider of broadband in any given community could be a local government, a not-for-profit, a cooperative or a private commercial company. We recognize the invaluable work that rural cooperatives have done in connecting their small communities. But we believe that the best way to ensure the most people are connected to the internet—especially in areas where rural cooperatives are not present—is to allow any provider who can best serve a community to access ReConnect funding. As Congress made clear in the IIJA, the government should not be in the business of picking winners and losers. The farm bill should not perpetuate this flawed industrial policy.

Each of these issues shares one thing in common: they fail to recognize that every community is different, and therefore every solution must be different. Placing a thumb on the scale to benefit one type of technology, or one kind of provider, does no favors for Americans who are in desperate need of broadband access. It simply favors certain parties and likely increases the time unserved communities must wait for connectivity, at the financial and societal expense of the American public.

For these reasons, it is important that the farm bill broadband programs remain truly technologically neutral, both explicitly and by not using proxies—such as the requirement of symmetrical 100 Mbps upload and download speeds—whereby only a single technology can meet the required standard. A failure to adhere to technological neutrality will only exponentially increase costs and further delay broadband deployment to high-cost rural areas. If the farm bill goes down that path, it will run out of money before even getting to the farms and rural residents most in need of connectivity.

Recommendations for the Next Farm Bill

As you develop the 2023 Farm Bill, this Committee has an historic opportunity to lay the groundwork for achieving our shared goal of bringing connectivity to every American. With that in mind, I would like to share some recommendations we hope the Committee will consider:

- *Base Awards on Cost Effectiveness.* Cost-effectiveness should be the primary criterion for determining which projects are funded. This will ensure that limited taxpayer resources are allocated and targeted to connecting as many rural Americans as possible. All Americans, including those who live in hard to serve areas, should have access to internet service before public funds are used to support additional networks in communities that are already connected.
- *Modernize USDA Programs.* The USDA should revise its criteria for rural broadband development grants and loans so that the limited available funding is allocated to those projects that truly deliver broadband coverage rapidly to the most Americans for the lowest possible cost. In addition to the up-front costs of deployment, these programs should consider the total costs to the end consumer, so that Federal support is not allocated to deployments that consumers will not be able to afford nor desire.
- *Do Not Provide Funding to Overbuild Broadband Networks or Networks for Which Other Subsidies (Federal and state) Have Been Approved.* Recipients of loans, grants and loan/grant combinations under this program should not be allowed to use proceeds to fund infrastructure in areas that are already served or where there is an "enforceable commitment" to serve by another provider offering a certain level of service or a provider that is the recipient of subsidies from other government support programs. Limited public resources should be directed to areas where no service is available. Operators

deploying private, atrisk capital to connect rural Americans should not face the risk of subsidized competition, and the agency should also not apply support in areas that are already subject to support through, *e.g.*, the Connect America Fund. This risk chills private investment and distorts the marketplace.

- *Prioritize Incumbent Providers for Upgrades.* Where taxpayer dollars are to be spent for areas where this Committee decides the speeds are "underserving" the community, priority should be given to those ISP's who are currently serving the community. Chances are that ISP did something no one else wanted to do, not a Co-op nor a large provider, they built a network (most likely with their own money) where no one else would—why should they be punished with government funded competition. Instead, those incumbents should be given the first opportunity to take the capital to upgrade their service to the Committee's desired level, which can most likely be done for less dollars—once again further stretching our limited taxpayer resources further.

Last Congress, this Committee passed H.R. 4347, the Broadband Internet Connections for Rural America Act. WISPA supports the goals of this legislation and commends the Committee for its commitment to connecting rural communities. WISPA supports the funding tiers included in the legislation that gives priority funding to projects in unserved communities. Focusing on unserved areas first and achieving that objective is the fastest and most cost-effective way to stretch limited Federal dollars.

We also believe that the USDA broadband deployment subsidy programs envisioned by H.R. 4347 would benefit by requiring RUS to engage in a proceeding that solicits public comments that can help to streamline the application process for the ReConnect and other USDA broadband deployment programs. In October 2022, GAO found that significant numbers of ReConnect program applicants were rejected by USDA and ReConnect program applicants who were accepted responded that they were substantially disappointed with the ReConnect application process. Their experiences with the ReConnect application process have discouraged some from applying to the program in the future.

In addition, I would like to thank Reps. Cammack, Soto, Gluesenkamp Perez, and Jackson, along with their Senate colleagues, Sens. Thune, Luja´n, Fischer, and Klobuchar, for introducing the Rural Internet Improvement Act. This bill contains several important provisions that will improve the

ReConnect program and target its funding towards areas of need. Specifically, the legislation limits funding to areas where at least 90% of households lack access to broadband service. This approach will ensure that those communities in most need of connectivity will be served first, instead of continuing to have to wait for even the most basic broadband service. I urge the Committee to consider including many of the provisions included in the Rural Internet Improvement Act in the farm bill.

Conclusion

Every community, regardless of size, location, or geography, deserves reliable broadband service. This Committee has an extraordinary opportunity to expand digital inclusion and take dramatic steps to bridge the digital divide. Industry and the government must step up and work together to meet this moment. This is no small task: it will take every tool available to ensure the rapid deployment of networks so that no community is left behind. That is why the leadership of this Committee is so critical. Your efforts are vital to ensuring that all communities can reap the benefits of robust and reliable broadband.

WISPA and its members stand ready to help every community find the right tools to connect them to the digital economy. This means diversity in approaches, modes of deployment, and paying attention to the needs of each community. WISPs provide the right tool for the right job. WISPs help drive America's innovation economy and fuels the nation's economic future.

WISPA appreciates the opportunity to partner with the Committee in addressing these important issues. We are deeply grateful for the bipartisan recognition of the importance of universal connectivity by this Committee, by Congress, by the FCC, and the Biden Administration. All have implemented policies to promote broadband deployment.

Thank you again, Chairman Thompson and Ranking Member Scott, for holding this important hearing and inviting me to testify. I look forward to continuing to work with you and the rest of the Committee to make real progress on these very important issues. I look forward to your questions.

* * *

The CHAIRMAN. Mr. Zumwalt, thank you so much for your testimony. And now, Mr. Stroup, please begin when you are ready.

Statement of Thomas A. "Tom" Stroup, J.D., President, Satellite Industry Association, Washington, D.C.

Mr. TROUP. Chairman Thompson, Ranking Member Scott, and distinguished Members of the Committee, thank you for inviting me to testify before you today. I am Tom Stroup, President of the Satellite Industry Association. Satellite communications are transforming the operation of our nation's farms and ranches. Satellites, unlike terrestrial communications, bring a range of unique attributes that benefit farmers and ranchers. This includes the ability to cover broad geographies without the need for expensive terrestrial infrastructure, as well as increased resiliency and rapid deployment. In addition, recent innovations in the satellite industry have made the delivery of high-quality, high-speed broadband and IoT connectivity to everyone, everywhere across the United States a reality.

Satellites provide service to rural and remote areas of the country, where it remains uneconomical for terrestrial services to deploy and offer both speeds and prices comparable to terrestrial alternatives. These services are available directly to the consumer today, covering all 50 states, and delivering broadband speeds of up to 200 megabits per second. Satellites enable remote farms with livestock sensors, soil monitors, and autonomous farming equipment in rural America, far beyond where terrestrial wireless and wire line can reach or make economic sense to deploy.

Precision GPS technologies allow farmers to increase crop yield by optimizing use of fertilizer, pesticides, herbicides, and applying site-specific treatments to fields. Earth imaging satellites provide high resolution imagery that allows farmers to determine when to plant, water, or fertilize crops. And satellite advances in weather forecasting help farmers prepare for drought, floods, and other adverse weather conditions.

Satellites are critical to 5G and IoT applications that will enable the next generation of farming technologies. Satellite communications allow for remote control of driverless tractors and network connectivity between equipment at large farms where equipment may not be in the same sight line. Indeed, John Deere estimates 50,000 to 100,000 of its machines will be connected to satellites by 2026.

We are at a time of tremendous innovation in the space industry, with nearly 8,000 active satellites in orbit today, and plans for tens of thousands more through the end of the decade. And individual geostationary communication satellites are launching that provide greater capacity than some existing fleets combined. Costs are dropping for both space and ground systems, which has resulted in a decrease in the cost of capacity of 90 percent over the past 8 years. Most importantly, satellite services are available now across the entire country without the need for additional build-out. As the Information Technology and Innovation Foundation notes, no single broadband technology holds all the advantages. With finite resources and widely varying topography, we need a flexible combination of all available access technologies to bridge the digital divide.

In order to further connectivity, we recommend the Committee prioritize these seven items. First, include provisions that offer financial incentives or tax breaks to satellite internet providers to encourage their participation in rural broadband expansion. Second, allocate specific funds or grants to support the development and deployment of satellite projects, particularly those focused on serving rural and remote areas. Third, ensure that legislation adopts technology-inclusive language and requirements, allowing for flexibility and inclusivity in deployment strategies. Congress should encourage competition and innovation among various broadband providers, including satellite companies, and allow affordable solutions to reach rural America where fiber build-out is not economically feasible.

Fourth, interagency collaboration is needed to simplify and streamline the regulatory processes for satellite internet providers. This includes working to adopt and implement a common set of performance targets to reflect the needs of agriculture, a recommendation supported by the Precision Ag Connectivity Task Force. Fifth, ensure sufficient spectrum resources are available for satellite, broadband, and IoT providers to deliver high-quality and high-speed services. Sixth, encourage partnerships with satellite companies and other stakeholders, such as local communities, educational institutions, and public agencies. And finally, allocate funds for research and development initiatives focused on advancing satellite technology, capacity, and affordability that will lead to increased opportunities for rural connectivity. I appreciate the opportunity to appear before you, and I am happy to answer any questions. Thank you.

[The prepared statement of Mr. Stroup follows:]

Prepared Statement of Thomas A. "Tom" Stroup, J.D., President, Satellite Industry Association, Washington, D.C.

Chairman Thompson, Ranking Member Scott, and distinguished Members of the Committee, thank you for inviting me to testify before you today. I am Tom Stroup, President of the Satellite Industry Association (SIA).[7] SIA is a U.S.-based trade association that represents the leading satellite operators, service providers, manufacturers, launch services providers, space situational awareness companies, and ground equipment suppliers.

Satellite communications are transforming the operation of our nation's farms and ranches. Satellites, unlike terrestrial communications, bring a range of unique attributes that benefit our nation's farmers. This includes the ability to cover broad geographies without the need for expensive terrestrial infrastructure, increased resiliency, and rapid deployment. In addition, recent innovations in the satellite industry have made the delivery of high quality, high-speed broadband and internet of things (IoT) connectivity to everyone everywhere across the United States a reality.

Satellite communications and services are well-poised to help our farmers meet [today's] real challenges—from addressing food insecurity, to monitoring weather and water, to overcoming supply chain challenges. Satellites are capable of providing broadband and IoT to rural and remote areas of the country where it remains uneconomical for terrestrial services to deploy, and provide both speeds and prices comparable to terrestrial alternatives. These services are available directly to the consumer today, covering all 50 states and delivering broadband offerings up to 200 megabits per second (Mbps). Satellite broadband is also used by business and government enterprises, for both fixed and mobile purposes, using a range of spectral bands to deliver assured access to broadband communications. Further, satellites are providing critical backhaul internet connectivity to local Internet Service Providers and community institutions in remote locations.

---

[7] *SIA Executive Members include:* Amazon; The Boeing Company; DIRECTV; EchoStar Corporation; HawkEye 360; Intelsat S.A.; Iridium Communications Inc.; Kratos Defense & Security Solutions; Ligado Networks; Lockheed Martin Corporation; Northrop Grumman; OneWeb; Planet Labs PBC; SES Americom, Inc.; Spire Global Inc.; and Viasat Inc. *SIA Associate Members include:* ABS US Corp.; The Aerospace Corporation; Artel, LLC; AST Space Mobile; Astranis Space Technologies Corp.; Aurora Insight; Blue Origin; Comtech; Eutelsat America Corp.; ExoAnalytic Solutions; Hughes; Inmarsat, Inc.; Kymeta Corporation; Leonardo; Lynk; Omnispace; OneWeb Technologies; Ovzon; Panasonic Avionics Corporation; Skyloom; Telesat; ULA and XTAR, LLC.

Satellite enables remote farms with livestock sensors, soil monitors, and autonomous farming equipment in rural America, far beyond where terrestrial wireless and wireline can reach or make economic sense to deploy. Precision GPS technologies allow farmers to increase crop yield by optimizing use of fertilizer, pesticides, herbicides, and applying site-specific treatments to fields. Earth imaging satellites provide regular high-resolution imagery that allows farmers to determine when to plant, water, or fertilize crops and can be used to provide crop yield estimates, conduct scout monitoring, and monitor global food security. Satellite advances in weather forecasting help farmers prepare for drought, floods, and other adverse weather conditions.

Satellites are critical to 5G and IoT applications that will enable the next generation of farming technologies. Satellite communications allow for remote control of driverless tractors, or networked connectivity between equipment at large farms where equipment may not be in the same sightline. According to John Deere CTO Jahmy Hindeman, the company is "pretty bullish on the opportunity that the commercialization of all things space is bringing to agriculture at the moment . . . The response from farmers has been overwhelmingly positive. In the sense that for many of them, I call it the 0 to 1 problem, from no connectivity in places they wished that they had it to full connectivity in those places tomorrow. We don't think in many of those cases terrestrial cell will ever be a solution."[8] John Deere estimates 50,000– 100,000 of its machines will be connected to satellites by 2026.[9]

The satellite industry today is investing constantly to ensure it can address the challenges of the future and to make its technologies available to every American. We are at a time of explosive innovation in the space industry, with nearly 8,000 active satellites on orbit today[10,11] and plans for tens of thousands more through the end of the decade, and individual geostationary communications satellites launching that provide greater capacity than entire existing fleets combined. Satellite companies are working to optimize the use of spectrum, by investing in high-throughput satellites and flexible, software

---

[8] "Manifest Space: Space Enabled Farming with Deere CTO, 5/18/23" *https://closingbell.simplecast.com/episodes/manifest-space-space-enabled-farming-with-deere-cto-5-18-23-Y23iyvUg*.

[9] Tita, Bob, "Deere Seeks Satellite Network to Connect Far-Flung Farms" *Wall Street Journal*, 1 May 2023, *https://www.wsj.com/articles/deere-seeks-satellite-network-to-connect-far-flung-farms-65c37b0f*.

[10] "NORAD GP Element Sets Current Data", CelesTrak, 14 June 2023 *https://celestrak.org/NORAD/elements/*.

[11] Up from 1,167 in 2013; see Satellite Industry Association, "2014 State of the Satellite Industry Report".

defined payloads that allow for instantaneous reallocation of spectrum resources and the mitigation of harmful interference. Costs are dropping for both space and ground systems through the use of modular satellites, digital engineering, inter-satellite links and cloud-integrated ground stations, which minimize the need for expensive ground architecture, which has resulted in a drop in cost of capacity of 90% over the past 8 years.[12] Flat panel and phasedarray antennas lower consumer costs and enable better connectivity that has been essential to the deployment of non-geostationary satellite constellations.

Most importantly, satellite services are available now across the entire country without the need for additional build-out. As the Information Technology & Innovation Foundation notes, "No single broadband technology holds all the advantages. With finite resources and widely varying topography, we need a flexible combination of all available access technologies to bridge the digital divide . . . if we try to subsidize fiber everywhere, overbuilding will crowd out private investment."[13] In some remote areas, the cost of the USDA ReConnect program's fiber build-out has allocated costs per passing of up to $204,000 per passing,[14] and according to Tarana Wireless, a full-fiber approach to BEAD would cost upward of $200B,[15] staggering amounts for communities that can receive satellite broadband today. Additionally, fiber has been plagued by supply chain and labor shortages, in many cases doubling the cost of fiber programs supported by the Rural Development Opportunity Fund.[16,17]

---

[12] Satellite Industry Association, "2023 State of the Satellite Industry Report".

[13] Brake, Doug, and Bruer, Alexandra, "Broadband Myth Series: Do We Need Symmetrical Upload and Download Speeds?", Information Technology & Innovation Foundation, 12 May 2021 *https://itif.org/publications/2021/05/12/broadband-myth-series-do-we-need-symmetrical-upload-and-download-speeds/.*

[14] Goovaerts, Diana, "The cost of running fiber in rural America: $200,000 per passing" *https://www.fiercetelecom.com/broadband/cost-running-fiber-rural-america-200000-passing.*

[15] Ferraro, Nicole," 'Fiber-only approach' to BEAD would cost over $200B, says Tarana", Light Reading, 17 Apr. 2023 *https://www.lightreading.com/broadband/fttx/fiber-only-approach-to-bead-would-cost-over-$200b-says-tarana/d/d-id/784398.*

[16] Goovaerts, Diana, "ISPs: Inflation has doubled RDOF build costs", Fierce Telecom, 24 Oct. 2024, *https://www.fiercetelecom.com/broadband/isps-inflation-has-doubled-rdof-build-costs.*

[17] Haiar, Joshua, "Inflation Drives Up Cost of Broadband Internet Projects" 11 June 2023, *https://www.mitchellrepublic.com/news/inflation-drives-up-cost-of-broadband-internet-projects.*

In order to foster further broadband and IoT connectivity, we recommend the Committee prioritize:

- *Incentives for Satellite Internet Providers:* Include provisions that offer financial incentives or tax breaks to satellite internet providers (broadband and IoT) to encourage their participation in rural broadband expansion. This could help attract more companies to invest in satellite infrastructure and services.
- *Funding for Satellite Broadband and IoT Projects: Allocate* specific funds or grants to support the development and deployment of satellite broadband and IoT projects, particularly those focused on serving rural and remote areas, including directly to farms/ranches for last acre build-out. This can help lower the financial barriers for satellite companies to expand their networks and reach underserved regions.
- *Making Requirements Technology-Inclusive:* Ensure that legislation adopts technology-inclusive language and requirements, allowing for flexibility and inclusivity in broadband and IoT deployment strategies. By avoiding prescriptive mandates that favor specific technologies, bills can encourage competition and innovation among various broadband and IoT providers, including satellite companies, and allow for the affordable solutions to reach rural America where fiber build-out is not economically feasible. This approach would enable satellite internet providers to compete on an equal footing and encourage the development of cutting-edge satellite technologies and infrastructure. Moreover, technology-agnostic requirements can also facilitate collaboration and partnerships between different types of broadband and IoT providers, enabling hybrid solutions that leverage the strengths of multiple technologies to deliver robust and reliable broadband and IoT connectivity to rural areas.
- *Streamlined Regulatory Processes:* Interagency collaboration is needed to simplify and streamline the regulatory processes for satellite internet providers. This includes working to adopt and implement a common set of performance targets to reflect the needs of Agriculture, a recommendation supported by the Precision Ag

Connectivity Task Force.[18] Additional work could involve reducing bureaucratic hurdles and improving the reporting process for programs such as the Rural Utilities Service (RUS), expediting license approvals, and promoting cooperation between government agencies to facilitate satellite deployment.

- *Spectrum Availability:* Ensure sufficient spectrum resources are available for satellite broadband and IoT providers to deliver high-quality and high-speed services. The bill could advocate for the protection of satellite spectrum and explore opportunities for sharing or repurposing underutilized spectrum bands.
- *Collaboration and Partnerships:* Encourage partnerships between satellite companies and other stakeholders, such as local communities, educational institutions, and public agencies. Collaborative efforts can help leverage existing infrastructure, share resources, and expand the reach of satellite broadband and IoT services.
- *Research and Development:* Allocate funds for research and development initiatives focused on advancing satellite technology, capacity, and affordability. This can support innovation within the satellite industry, leading to improved performance, lower costs, and increased opportunities for rural connectivity. This includes increasing awareness and recruitment efforts in STEM programs.

I appreciate the opportunity to appear before you and I am happy to answer any questions.

The CHAIRMAN. Mr. Stroup, thank you so much. Mr. Hurley, please begin when you are ready.

Statement of Bill T. Hurley, Vice President, Distribution, Americas, AGCO Corporation; Chair, AG Sector Board, Association of Equipment Manufacturers, Duluth, GA

Mr. HURLEY. Chairman Thompson, Ranking Member Scott, and distinguished Members of the Committee, thank you for the opportunity to appear before you, and for holding this hearing today. My name is Bill Hurley.

[18] "Task Force for Reviewing the Connectivity and Technology Needs of Precision Agriculture in the U.S.", 10 Nov. 2021, *https://www.fcc.gov/sites/default/files/precision-ag-report-11102021.pdf*.

I currently serve as Chair of the Ag Sector Board of the Association of Equipment Manufacturers. I am also a Vice President with the AGCO Corporation headquartered in Duluth, Georgia.

I was born and raised in Franklin, a small town in central Texas with a population of less than 2,000. My family had a small farm not far from there in a place called Ridge, where my grandmother lived. I spent a lot of time on that farm, and with my grandmother, and I vividly remember the challenges that came from the ten families sharing the party line. While we have come a long way since then, today's hearing is a reminder that we have still not fully closed the digital divide in rural America.

AEM is a North American based international trade group representing off-road heavy equipment manufacturers, with more than 1,000 companies and more than 200 product lines in the ag and construction-related sectors worldwide. The equipment manufacturing industry supports 2.3 million jobs in the United States and contributes $316 billion a year to the U.S. economy. The men and women who make the equipment that builds, powers, and feeds the world are not just welders, fabricators, and machinists. Many are farmers and ranchers, and one in three of them live and work in rural communities. Our industry is not only deeply connected to rural America, we are a big part of it.

Equipment manufacturers are proud to provide American farmers and ranchers with the next generation of innovative tools, but they cannot take advantage of the benefits of precision ag technologies without reliable and affordable connectivity across all of rural America. Precision ag leverages technologies to enhance sustainability through more efficient use of critical inputs, such as land, water, fertilizer, and pesticides. For example, at full adoption, herbicide use could be reduced by 15 percent, and water use could be decreased by 21 percent. However, today just 1⁄4 of farms in the U.S. are currently able to leverage precision ag due to the lack of high-speed connectivity.

Reliable internet access and smart policies that help farmers and ranchers adopt these cutting edge technologies will lead to a transformative shift in ag practices that drive productivity while conserving resources. A multi-faceted strategy, including fiber optic, low-Earth orbit satellites, and 5G will continue to close the rural connectivity gap, enabling farmers and ranchers to leverage important technologies and management strategies that will help them produce more with less. For these technologies to deliver their full value, we need technology-neutral development of broadband dollars.

It is imperative that all aspects of rural America are connected, from the hospital to the school, and from the farmhouse to the field. We should not prioritize one technology over the other, but rather take an all-encompassing approach. If not, many parts of rural America will be left further behind. Other game-changing technologies, such as soil and weather sensors, machine learning and autonomy, and equipment tracking rely on connectivity. The opportunity in front of us is to prioritize connectivity for the essential food supply chain across rural America *versus* entertainment streaming speed.

The 2023 Farm Bill is this Committee's opportunity to fully embrace the potential of these technologies by including two bipartisan pieces of legislation in the final package. The Precision Agriculture Loan Program Act of 2023 (H.R. 1495) establishes the first Federal Precision Ag Loan Program within the Department of Agriculture's Farm Service Agency. Loans at lower interest rates and extended terms will give small and mid-size producers the tools that they need to monitor, manage, and maximize their operations, while significantly reducing their environmental impact. The PRECISE Act (H.R. 1495, Producing Responsible Energy and Conservation Incentives and Solutions for the Environment Act) designates precision ag as an applicable practice in the EQIP Program, and allows ag technologies which do, and will continue to, play a huge role in conservation. AEM believes that these two bipartisan bills provide an all-encompassing approach for the adoption of precision ag technologies, and respectfully urges the Committee to include them in this year's farm bill.

The implementation of precision ag technologies depends on the successful deployment of broadband dollars. It is imperative that we work together to ensure that rural America has the same affordable and reliable connectivity as the rest of the country. I thank you for inviting me here to testify today, and the Association of Equipment Manufacturers, Mr. Chairman, looks forward to continuing to work with Members of this Committee.

[The prepared statement of Mr. Hurley follows:]

Prepared Statement of Bill T. Hurley, Vice President, Distribution, Americas, AGCO Corporation; Chair, AG Sector Board, Association of Equipment Manufacturers, Duluth, GA

Chairman Thompson, Ranking Member Scott, and distinguished Members of the Committee. Thank you for the opportunity to appear before you and for holding this hearing today on closing the digital divide in rural America.

Introduction

My name is Bill Hurley, and I currently serve as Chair of the Ag Sector Board of the Association of Equipment Manufacturers. I am also a Vice President with AGCO Corporation, headquartered in Duluth, Georgia.

I was born and raised in Franklin, a small town in central Texas with a population of less than 2,000 people. My family had a small farm not far from there in a place called Ridge, where my grandmother lived. I spent a lot of time on that farm, and I vividly remember the challenges that came from ten families sharing a party line. While we have come a long way since then, today's hearing is a reminder that we have still not fully closed the digital divide in rural America.

The Association of Equipment Manufacturers is the North American-based international trade group representing off-road, heavy equipment manufacturers, with more than 1,000 companies and more than 200 product lines in the agriculture and construction-related sectors worldwide. The equipment manufacturing industry supports 2.3 million jobs in the United States and contributes $316 billion a year to the U.S. economy.

The men and women who make the equipment that builds, powers, and feeds the world are not just welders, fabricators, and machinists. Some are farmers and ranchers. And one in three of them live and work in rural communities across the country, compared to just one in five people overall in the United States. Our industry is not only deeply connected to rural America—we are a big part of it.

Equipment manufacturers are proud to provide American farmers and ranchers with the next generation of innovative tools that will keep our agriculture sector competitive for generations to come. But farmers and ranchers cannot take advantage of the benefits of precision agriculture technologies without reliable and affordable connectivity across all of rural America.

The Benefits of Precision Agriculture Technology

Precision agriculture leverages technologies to enhance sustainability through more efficient use of critical inputs, such as land, water, fertilizer, and pesticides. For example, herbicide use could be further reduced by 15 percent at full adoption. Water use could decrease by 21 percent at full adoption of precision agriculture technologies.[19] Just 1/4 of farms in the United States are currently able to leverage precision agriculture technologies due to the lack of high-speed connectivity. There is a great opportunity for growth in this area. Reliable internet access and smart policies that help farmers and ranchers adopt these cutting-edge technologies will lead to a transformative shift in agriculture practices that drive productivity while conserving resources.

Precision Agriculture Connectivity Needs

A multifaceted strategy including fiber optic, low earth orbit (LEO) satellites, and 5G will continue to close the rural connectivity gap, enabling farmers and ranchers to leverage important technologies and management strategies that will help them produce more with less. For precision agriculture technologies to reach their full potential, we need technology-neutral deployment of broadband dollars. It is imperative that all aspects of rural America are connected, from the hospital to the school and from the farmhouse to the field.

We should not prioritize one technology over the other, but rather take an all-encompassing approach, or many parts of rural America will be left further behind. Other game-changing technologies such as soil and weather sensors, machine learning and machine autonomy, equipment tracking, and food traceability will increasingly rely on connectivity. The opportunity in front of us is to prioritize connectivity for the essential food supply chain across rural America *versus* entertainment streaming speed.[20]

---

[19] Association of Equipment Manufacturers, *The Environmental Benefits of Precision Agriculture in the United States* (2021), *https://newsroom.aem.org/download/977839/environmentalbenefitsofprecisionagriculture-2.pdf*.

[20] Association of Equipment Manufacturers, *The Future of Food Production* (2022), *https://www.aem.org/AEM/media/docs/Whitepaper/AEM-Future-of-Food-Production.pdf*.

Opportunities to Advance Precision Agriculture through the Farm Bill

The 2023 Farm Bill is this Committee's opportunity to fully embrace the potential of these technologies by including three bipartisan pieces of legislation in the final package:

- *The Precision Agriculture Loan Program Act* establishes the first Federal precision agriculture loan program within the Department of Agriculture's Farm Service Agency. Loans at lower interest rates and extended terms will give small and mid-sized producers the tools they need to monitor, manage, and maximize their operations, while significantly reducing their environmental impact more effectively. I would like to thank Representatives Feenstra and Panetta for introducing this bipartisan legislation.
- *The PRECISE Act* designates precision agriculture as an applicable practice in the EQIP program. Precision agriculture technologies do and will continue to play a huge role in conservation. Adoption of these technologies allows American producers to do more with less. I would like to acknowledge Representatives Finstad, Hinson, Craig, and Panetta for working together in a bipartisan fashion on this bill.

The Association of Equipment Manufacturers believes that these two bills provide an all-encompassing approach for the adoption of precision agriculture technologies, and respectfully urges the Committee to include them in this year's farm bill.

The Promoting Precision Agriculture Act builds on a recommendation from the FCC's Precision Agriculture Task Force, which the Association of Equipment Manufacturers played an integral role in creating and which includes several equipment manufacturers. This important bill directs the Department of Agriculture and the National Institute of Standards and Technology to work together with equipment manufacturers to create standards around interoperability. Having uniform standards for our industry will give American farmers and ranchers more free market options when choosing the technology solution that best fits their operations. I would like to thank Representatives Davis Mann for introducing this bill.

Conclusion

The implementation of precision agriculture technologies depends entirely on the successful deployment of broadband dollars. It is imperative that we work together to ensure that rural America has the same affordable and reliable connectivity as the rest of America.

Thank you for inviting me to testify today. The Association of Equipment Manufacturers looks forward to continued engagement with Members of this Committee as we work to close the digital divide and strengthen rural communities. I look forward to your questions.

The CHAIRMAN. Mr. Hurley, thank you so much for your testimony. I am now pleased to recognize Mrs. Bloomfield. Please begin when you are ready.

Statement of Shirley Bloomfield, Chief Executive Officer, NTCA—The Rural Broadband Association, Arlington, VA

Mrs. BLOOMFIELD. Chairman Thompson, Ranking Member Scott, Members of the Committee, good morning, and a sincere thanks for the opportunity to testify today. NTCA members across the country deploy cutting-edge broadband networks in deeply rural areas and deliver services that are just as robust in those that are available in urban markets. Eighty percent of the customers have access to fiber-to-the-home technology. These providers stand ready to help bridge the digital divide in areas that they serve today and to go beyond to keep their good work in deploying broadband to connect the rest of the world. So, building upon these efforts, I really appreciate the opportunity to share how critical this Committee's efforts are, with USDA oversight, to the deployment of broadband in rural communities.

I am Shirley Bloomfield, CEO of NTCA—The Rural Broadband Association. We represent over 850 community-based providers who are leading innovation in small town and rural America. NTCA members offer broadband, voice, and other advanced communication services across over 30 percent of the land mass, but with less than five percent of the population. This part of the country was left behind nearly a century ago by nationwide carriers, and there is no question that small rural internet service providers are a critical part of the equation as we work to provide rural Americans with affordable and reliable internet services that will meet the needs of today and withstand the test of time.

RUS, within USDA, has played a very significant role in enabling much of this deployment to date, and it is uniquely well positioned to serve and close the divide for the benefit of still unserved Americans. And it should be tasked with doing so in a way that will ensure that the divide stays closed. As Members of the Committee assess how best to structure broadband funding programs, success in these programs should be measured by actual results on the ground rather than promises made. And we should all note that what matters most to rural Americans is not merely the deployment of broadband, but the quality, reliability, and affordability of the services they receive.

As this Committee and Congress deliberates the 2023 Farm Bill, I offer some recommendations on how to close the divide. First, we should build networks in rural American that are just as robust and reliable as those available in urban areas. I encourage the Committee to make sure program requirements are driven by the long-term needs of these communities. To that end, the farm bill should maintain high-speed symmetrical broadband networks of 100/100 megabits. This threshold has been in place for several rounds of USDA's ReConnect and has led to four to five times greater demand for funding than is available. It ensures that the needs of rural consumers are met, it is the best use of limited taxpayer dollars by building it right the first time, and promotes meaningful competition among providers of all types.

So, with that in mind, this farm bill is not the time to move the program, and the rural Americans it serves, backwards. When the Federal Government helped to provide telephone, electric, and water infrastructure in rural America in the last century, we didn't set lower standards. We ensured that rural Americans did not become second class citizens, and it was an investment that has paid off many times over, as we have the strongest rural economy in the world. Second, close coordination with Federal and state agencies is essential. There are enough un and underserved Americans awaiting connectivity to not waste precious resources overbuilding government-supported networks with government funds.

Third, we urge policymakers to look local when it comes to identifying broadband solutions in rural America, and to leverage the expertise and the experience of smaller community-based providers, regardless of their corporate form, in overcoming these challenges. NTCA service providers are based in their communities and have a longstanding relationship and track record of performance. It is a very different measure of customer service when you are running into your customers in the grocery store. Last, the Committee should consider ways to streamline historical preservation requirements and environmental reviews that often result in significant delays. In fact, we still have members who were notified of winning ReConnect Round 1 who have yet to receive their funding due to these delays.

I also want to take this opportunity to thank Members of the Committee, Representatives Nunn and Craig, and other cosponsors for introducing the ReConnecting Rural America Act (H.R. 4227), which would ensure networks continue to be built at 100 symmetrical, agency coordination is strengthened, there is a level playing field with those local providers with a proven track record being strongly urged to participate. And I also want to thank Representative Feenstra for his recently introduced Rural Broadband Modernization Act (H.R. 3964), which includes many of these same very important provisions.

I thank the Committee for its leadership. We still clearly have much work to do, in both deploying networks where they remain lacking, and operating networks where they are already built, and this is where this Committee plays a really important role in helping to build and sustain broadband in rural markets that could not otherwise justify such investments. With the RUS programs, you help to provide the tools that not just help rural America survive, but to thrive. So I look forward to sharing more about what we can see on the ground, and what we are seeing on the ground, as NTCA's members continue to build smart rural communities, and to help fuel a needed rural renaissance. Thank you very much.

[The prepared statement of Ms. Bloomfield follows:]

Prepared Statement of Shirley Bloomfield, Chief Executive Officer, NTCA—The Rural Broadband Association, Arlington, VA

Introduction

Chairman Thompson, Ranking Member Scott, and Members of the Committee, good morning and thank you for the opportunity to testify about the continued role of the broadband programs overseen by the U.S. Department of Agriculture ("USDA") as part of this Committee's review of the "farm bill's" rural development programs. With the help of these and other important broadband programs, NTCA members across the country deploy cutting-edge broadband networks in deeply rural areas and deliver services that are as robust and reliable as those available in urban markets. These providers stand ready both to help close the digital divide in areas beyond those that they serve today, and to sustain their good work to date in keeping millions of rural Americans connected to the rest of the world. Building upon such efforts, I greatly appreciate you holding this hearing and the opportunity to speak to you today.

I am Shirley Bloomfield, Chief Executive Officer of NTCA—The Rural Broadband Association ("NTCA"), which represents just over 850 community-based companies and cooperatives that are leading innovation in rural and small-town America. NTCA members and companies like them offer broadband, voice, and other advanced communications services across more than thirty percent of the country's geography where less than five percent of the U.S. population resides. There is no question that small rural internet service providers are a critical part of the equation as we work to provide Americans with affordable and reliable internet services that will meet the needs of today and stand the test of time.

Every day, NTCA members work hard to deliver for rural America. Their steadfast commitment to serving the communities that they—and many of you—call home makes them America's trusted communications solution providers. On average, each member serves nine public safety entities (police, fire, *etc.*) and seven schools in their areas with fixed broadband. NTCA members have worked for decades to invest in our nation's future by deploying essential state-of-the-art communications infrastructure. Over eighty percent of their customers on average have access to 100 Mbps broadband service or better. Over sixty percent of their customers on average have access to Gigabit speeds. These accomplishments are staggering when you consider that the average population density in these areas is about seven customers per square mile, or roughly the average density for the entire state of Montana.

The Rural Utilities Service ("RUS") within USDA has played a significant role in enabling much of this deployment to date, and it is uniquely positioned to close the digital divide for the benefit of millions of still-unserved Americans—and it should be tasked with doing so in a way that will ensure that divide stays closed. As Members of this Committee assess how best to structure broadband funding programs, success in broadband programs should be measured by results rather than promises, and we should all note that what matters most to rural Americans is not the mere deployment of the network but the quality of the services they receive. Some programs in recent years have offered the promise of better broadband, with announcements asserting that tens or hundreds of thousands of Americans will be connected to broadband at some point in the future due to Program X or Initiative Y. Some of these programs will undoubtedly deliver on that promise in coming years, at least in part and in certain places. But NTCA submits that the best proofs of concept can be found—and the best lessons drawn for future program design—by looking at which programs have in fact already delivered on the promise of reliable and sustained broadband access in rural areas.

NTCA's Experience with RUS Broadband Programs

RUS telecommunications and broadband loans and grants have helped enable and unleash billions of dollars in Federal and private capital investment in rural communications infrastructure. A mix of local presence and commitment, entrepreneurial spirit, private capital, public capital through RUS financing programs, and ongoing support through the high-cost universal service fund ("USF") programs overseen by the Federal Communications Commission ("FCC") have empowered NTCA members and other community-based providers like them to deploy reliable networks and offer robust and affordable services across wide swaths of rural America.

NTCA members have been the recipients of a number of RUS loans and grant awards through programs such as the ReConnect program, the Rural Broadband program, Distance Learning and Telemedicine grants, and the Telecommunications Infrastructure program. Through ReConnect alone, 159 NTCA members have been awarded grants or grant and loan combinations to serve approximately 441,000 households, 21,000 businesses, and 14,000 farms.[21]

NTCA recommends that Congress approach proposals for new broadband programs with a thoughtful eye and a preference for leveraging proven concepts such as many of these prior efforts. In lieu of creating new initiatives that might compete or even conflict with existing efforts, Congress should consider how well-functioning existing programs, like many of those listed above, can be enhanced and expanded to achieve even better results and reach remaining unserved areas with service levels that meet the needs of users both immediately and over the life of the network that the Federal Government is helping to fund.

---

[21] *https://www.usda.gov/reconnect.*

The Case for High-Speed Internet Access in Rural America

While broadband has value universally, it is especially important for rural Americans who often must rely even more than their urban counterparts on online access given the challenges of distance and density. From telehealth, remote work, distance learning, and precision agriculture, the opportunities for rural Americans are substantial when given the ability to access high-speed, reliable internet services.

For example, telemedicine can play a crucial role in bridging the gap between veterans and the Veterans Affairs system by providing them with seamless access to telehealth services, virtual consultations, and online resources, ensuring timely and convenient healthcare support regardless of their geographical location. Nearly a quarter of the United States veteran population resides in rural communities, underscoring the importance of leveraging connectivity to deliver critical services over great distances.[22] In fact, the Veterans Health Administration, which has long been a pioneer in the use of telemedicine, conducted a pilot program which included seven hospitals, ten multi-specialty outpatient clinics and 28 community-based primary care clinics. The 900 patients in the trial were able to utilize home telehealth devices, which allowed them to self-manage their health. The results were dramatic: a 40% reduction in emergency room visits, a 63% drop in hospital admissions and an 88% decrease in nursing home bed days of care. While the total cost savings resulting from the dramatic decrease in resource utilization was substantial, perhaps even more impressive was the 94% patient satisfaction.[23] High-speed internet is not just a luxury; it is a lifeline for rural America, bringing greater telemedicine functionality and helping residents overcome the challenges of distance that make so many tasks more expensive and time consuming.

Moreover, one of the most difficult challenges facing rural America is keeping younger generations from moving away or ultimately helping them to come back home. However, thanks to the unique opportunities of teleworking and remote learning, many parts of rural America are seeing positive growth. Technology is shaping the next generation of American jobs. Manufacturing,

---

[22] "Rural Veteran Health Care Challenges." Veteran Affairs: *https://www.ruralhealth.va.gov/aboutus/ruralvets.asp*.

[23] Broderick, Andrew, "The Veterans Health Administration: Taking Home Telehealth Services to Scale Nationally," The Commonwealth Fund Case Studies in Telehealth Adoption, Jan. 2013, *http://www.commonwealthfund.org/_/media/Files/Publications/Case%20Study/2013/Jan/1657_Broderick_telehealth_adoption_VHA_case_study.pdf*, p. 5.

agriculture and health care are among sectors that are demanding more highly-skilled employees than in the past. Increased training and education opportunities are imperative for many rural areas that face demographic and economic challenges. In rural areas, broadband can be used to support secondary and post-secondary education and training: broadband-enabled services can be used to overcome instances in which small or insular areas lack sufficient economies of scale to support interest in advanced or specialized courses.

Rural broadband providers are playing vital roles, leveraging their networks and working closely with local educational institutions. For example, Rainbow Communications of Everest, Kansas, provides fiber connectivity to Highland Community College, the oldest college in the state. The network enables the college to offer numerous courses at various sites. The college also supports the agricultural industry through courses that include precision agriculture and diesel mechanics; both are necessary as farms rely increasingly on precision agriculture that blends traditional mechanical equipment with analytical tech and GPS guided systems.[24] Meanwhile, in Alaska, the arrival of a submarine cable line allowed for one family to move back to its hometown while allowing the parents to retain their current jobs that required access to high-speed internet. This increased connectivity also provided their children with the ability to participate in classes and coursework that were not offered at the local school.

Of course, while substantial distances in rural areas make broadband access a necessity for many aspects of life, there may be no more uniquely rural application for high-performing broadband than precision agriculture. Precision agriculture has revolutionized farming practices and enhanced the overall agricultural landscape. By leveraging advanced technologies such as GPS, drones, sensors, and data analytics, precision agriculture enables farmers to make informed decisions based on real-time information, leading to increased productivity, resource efficiency, and sustainability. In rural areas where farming is a vital economic activity, precision agriculture offers immense benefits. The value of precision agriculture is conveyed effectively when agriculture is viewed as a business of logistics. Row and specialty crops are particularly suited to tech-enabled efficiency during planting and cultivation that enable farmers to harvest and deliver product to market at peak

[24] "Rural Broadband and the Next Generation of American Jobs." NTCA—The Rural Broadband Association: *https://www.ntca.org/sites/default/files/documents/202103/SRC_whitepaper_the_next_generation_of_american_jobs.pdf.*

times. Precision agriculture also facilitates better future planning. Visual inspection of crop development (either by surface imaging or drones) combined with sensors that assess soil conditions can help farmers create a forward-looking plan of action. Or, in one instance, an NTCA member's customer in South Dakota uses a live-video feed in a calving barn to monitor newborn calves and mothers from the comfort of home.[25] As the President of the Missouri Farm Bureau aptly observed during a hearing hosted by this Committee last September, "Truly the farm of the future has to be connected . . . with at least 100 [symmetrical]. It's what we need to be shooting for. My rural hospital says the same thing, they need a hundred up, a hundred down in order to do telemedicine in a way that is truly a good experience for the provider as well as the patient."[26] These broadband-enabled benefits combine to serve greater economic efficiencies and opportunities for the agriculture industry as a whole.

Building Future-Proof Networks

With billions of dollars and millions of unserved Americans at stake, it is prudent and responsible for the Federal Government to invest taxpayer resources based upon more than speculation as to potential performance, marketing hype, and overstated claims of capability not borne out of real-world applications throughout rural America. The minimum speed and other performance criteria for receiving Federal funding must be determined by the needs of rural consumers and not set by the maximum capabilities some in the industry feel they can offer. With so much on the line in terms of dollars and unserved customers, this is not the time to award participation trophies. Setting standards is not a matter of technological neutrality— it is a matter of public interest and fiscal responsibility.

To keep pace with consumer demand, the minimum speed for eligible projects administered by USDA to receive funds should be set at 100/100 Mbps—just as was the case in Rounds 3 and 4 of the ReConnect Loan and Grant Program. It has been argued that the 100/100 Mbps minimum speed threshold is too high and that it may prevent certain providers from applying

---

[25] "From Fiber to Field: The Role of Rural Broadband in Emerging Agricultural Technology." NTCA—The Rural Broadband Association: *https://www.ntca.org/sites/default/files/documents/2021-07/06.14.21%20SRC%20Ag%20Tech%20Final.pdf*.

[26] *See, https://agriculture.house.gov/calendar/eventsingle.aspx?EventID=7426* at minute 2:48:00.

for the program. However, during Rounds 3 and 4, the program was oversubscribed by four to five times, proving that more than enough providers are willing and able to build the kinds of networks that consumers need today and well into the future.

While some will argue that such an approach is not "technology neutral" and that this would favor fiber, we have seen providers and manufacturers of technologies of all kinds proclaim the ability to deliver services at these speeds or even higher, and providers that prevailed in the FCC's USF auctions similarly pledged that they could use technologies of all kinds to deliver even Gigabit speeds—so it is unclear why some feel as if demanding this minimum level of performance would now somehow shut them out.[27] Moreover, it is not a violation of technological neutrality merely to set high standards and expectations—the public interest and fiscally responsible use of government funds demands nothing less. It is true that not all technologies are equally capable in all cases, and it does not violate a principle of "technological neutrality" to take stock of and account for the relative attributes and limitation of different technologies as demonstrated in the marketplace.

For example, while many NTCA members have experience leveraging fixed wireless technology to serve end-users in hard-to-reach areas, the consensus with respect to such services among these members is that even as they may offer a means of initiating service, they are less desirable as long-term solutions to overcome the digital divide (which, as the title of this hearing suggests, is what programs like ReConnect should aim to achieve). In addition to interference and other reliability issues that can affect unlicensed spectrum specifically, fixed wireless networks require relatively clear lines of sight and other optimal conditions to realize their potential. Technologies that rely upon high-band spectrum in particular can be difficult to implement in rural areas given limited propagation over great distances. Finally, spectrum capacity can present a substantial issue, as the more users that place demands on a cell site or antenna can degrade the experience of the other users sharing that capacity. Put another way, just because certain technologies can perhaps be used to serve *anyone* does not mean they necessarily can serve *everyone* at a sustained level of performance—which is the essential long-term objective of sound universal service policy.

---

[27] *See, e.g., https://www.prnewswire.com/news-releases/gigabit-6-ghz-fixed-wireless-is-a-reality-301553129.html* and *https://www.fiercewireless.com/tech/tarana-provides-1-gig-speeds-its-fixed-wireless-access.*

To be clear, wired and wireless facilities are necessary to support the full complement of ag tech solutions. Therefore, the collective interest of the ag and tech industries, alongside policymaker interest in supporting U.S. farm markets and expanded broadband deployment, should drive actions to develop and maintain robust future-proof scalable broadband networks that can enable wired and wireless solutions alike.

Some will also claim that consumers do not need 100 Mbps symmetrical services, and we should therefore build lesser networks leveraging government dollars. But the marketplace indicates that consumers—your constituents and our members' customers—already believe and expect otherwise. Ookla, the global speed test provider, reported average U.S. fixed broadband speeds of 179/65 Mbps in January 2021— which means the "build-to" speeds that some in the industry are advocating for now (100/20 Mbps) were outdated more than 2 years ago. It is predicted that the average U.S. fixed broadband speeds will be 1,500/599 Mbps by 2030.[28] In other words, anything less than 100/100 Mbps is outdated and even this speed threshold may soon be surpassed, which is why treating it as a minimum standard that can evolve over time as new awards are made is a sensible and pragmatic approach.

A letter addressed to this Committee on March 14, 2023, underscores the robust support by rural stakeholders of all kinds—county governments, educational institutions, electric utilities, rural broadband providers, health care providers, economic development organizations, and banking institutions—for robust symmetrical broadband. In addition to NTCA, the following organizations signed onto that letter:

National Rural Electric Cooperative Association
Rural Community College Alliance
Fiber Broadband Association
National Rural Telecommunications Cooperative
National Association of Counties
Farm Credit Council
National Association of Development Organizations
CoBank
National Rural Health Association
National Cooperative Business Association
National Rural Economic Developers Association

[28] "Eliminate the Digital Divide in Rural North America with Fiber." The Fiber Broadband Association.

National Utility Contractors Association
The Power and Communication Contractors Association
Rural Telephone Finance Cooperative
National Rural Education Association

These stakeholders represent a broad cross-section of entities with a vested interest in the vitality and long-term viability of rural America, and their constituencies are at the heart of the communities that are intended to be benefit from the farm bill.[29]

I would again encourage this Committee to make sure program requirements are driven ultimately by the long-term needs of rural communities. I would also encourage this Committee to avoid the mistakes of too many broadband programs past, where 4/1 Mbps or 10/1 Mbps sounded like terrific ideas to build—only to find a few years later that we needed to start over because we had aimed too low. Indeed, if anything, Congress should view the 100 Mbps symmetrical threshold as a *baseline,* and give USDA the flexibility to increase this standard over time as needs and use cases for broadband evolve.

NTCA's Farm Bill Priorities

Meeting the Needs of Consumers Today and Tomorrow

Federal broadband investments should support technology that can be readily upgraded to deliver the fastest speeds over the long-term life of the assets being built, rather than supporting technologies that may appear cheaper to deploy now but will be unable to provide meaningful internet access over time that keeps pace with consumer demand without the need to be substantially rebuilt (perhaps again at the expense of Federal dollars). To this end, the farm bill should support high-speed symmetrical broadband networks that offer a minimum of 100/100 Mbps speeds. As discussed above, this is a reasonable threshold that will ensure consumers realize the benefits of these investments backed by Federal dollars for years to come, while also promoting meaningful competition among providers of all kinds to seek to win such awards and serve these customers.

---

29 "100 Symmetrical ReConnect Coalition Letter." March 13, 2023. Letter. *https://www.ntca.org/sites/default/files/documents/2023-06/100SymmetricalReConnectCoalitionLetter.pdf.*

Identifying Eligible Areas

Close coordination among Federal and state agencies is essential to avoid deploying duplicative government-funded broadband networks in a rural area that cannot support even a single network without such funding. The farm bill should specify the ways in which ReConnect funds will interact with funds already awarded under other programs; specifically, ReConnect funds should not be awarded to any provider in an area where a different provider is already the recipient of: (a) an RUS telecom program loan or grant (so that the agency does not put at risk its own prior committed awards); (b) support from Federal universal service programs that is being used to deploy 100/20 Mbps or better service (so that RUS does not undermine the FCC's important sustainability initiatives); and/or (c) an award under any other Federal or state broadband grant program where the recipient is obligated to deliver 100/20 Mbps or better service and is meeting those obligations.

Relatedly, to ensure that broadband deployment funds are targeted to where they are most needed, an area should not be deemed eligible for ReConnect funding unless 90% of locations in that area lack at least 100/20 Mbps service. To be clear, networks built in eligible areas should be required to meet a minimum threshold of 100/100 Mbps speeds as noted above—in other words, 100/100 Mbps should be considered the minimum of ***what** to build.* But using 100/20 Mbps as the criterion for determining ***where** to build*—what areas will be considered unserved—will help in making the most of government broadband funding and bringing as many Americans as possible up to better standards of service.

Project Delays after Notice of Awards

The 2023 Farm Bill should address historical preservation requirements and environmental reviews that often result in significant delays between notice of awards and receipt of the funds necessary to commence construction. While RUS can take certain steps on its own to mitigate such delays to some degree by, among other things, allowing providers to work toward seeking approval of environmental and historical reviews prior to an award, Congress should consider other means of streamlining network deployment while still providing reasonable protections for important historical and environmental concerns that apply in certain contexts. We appreciated the opportunity to testify before, and the recent work by, the House Energy and Commerce Committee regarding bills to address broadband-related permitting delays, and NTCA is supportive of that legislation. We encourage this Committee, however, to consider additional means of providing relief specific to deployments pursuant to USDA and RUS programs, including promoting programmatic agreements and evaluating other measures that the agency could implement to streamline preservation reviews and environmental clearances.

Matching Funds

The farm bill should make clear that providers receiving grants need not spend matching funds in full prior to drawing down grant funds. The obligation to expend all matching funds prior to receipt of any grant resources is onerous and unnecessary to ensure providers have "skin in the game" with respect to grant-funded deployment. Consideration should also be given, as it has been in the Broadband Equity, Access, & Deployment program, to reducing the need for matching funds in deeply rural areas that often present the most significant economic challenges to serve.

No Provider Preference Based upon Corporate Structure

The farm bill should codify that providers seeking grants or other funding will not be favored based merely upon their form of organization or commercial status. Providers of all kinds should be allowed to apply to programs on a level playing field where they can meet the substantive standards for doing so.

Conclusion

In an era of transformative technological developments, regulatory challenges, and marketplace competition, NTCA members are advancing efforts to close the digital divide by delivering robust and high-quality services over networks that are built to last. Their commitment to building sustainable networks makes rural communities fertile ground for innovation in economic development, e-commerce, health care, agriculture and education, and it contributes billions of dollars to the U.S. economy each year. The rural broadband industry and our nation as a whole can tell a great story of success to date in delivering service, but we still clearly have much work to do both in deploying networks where they remain lacking and operating networks where they have already been built—and this is where public policy plays an important role in helping to build and sustain broadband in rural markets that would not otherwise justify such investments and ongoing operations.

I thank the Committee for its leadership on and interest in these issues, and I look forward to working with you on behalf of NTCA members and the millions they serve to realize a shared vision of a rural America that gets and stays connected.

The CHAIRMAN. Thank you, Mrs. Bloomfield, for your testimony, and thank you all for your important testimony today. At this time Members will be recognized for questions in order of seniority, alternating between Majority and Minority Members, and in order of arrival for those who joined us after the hearing convened. You are going to be recognized for 5 minutes each in order to allow us to get to as many questions as possible. And I now recognize myself for 5 minutes.

Mr. Matheson, as you know, USDA is the prime agency to help address the needs of rural America, including access to high quality, broadband connectivity. Since the early 2000s USDA has received billions of dollars to accomplish this goal, with thousands of projects receiving Federal funding. Do you believe that USDA is best suited to address the rural connectivity issues?

Mr. MATHESON. Well, clearly the other agencies are involved, like the FCC and NTIA, as has been mentioned, but I do think USDA is uniquely positioned to be an important voice in this circumstance because USDA, number one, understands rural America, and the Rural Utilities Service specifically understands what it takes to provide utility services in these very expensive, hard to serve parts of our country. I think that makes the program work better. I think USDA's participation in broadband deployment has had an effect where it has moved other Federal agencies to be more aggressive than they might otherwise have been. I think USDA has been a leader in pushing for better speeds, better requirements, and so I wholly endorse RUS being active in rural broadband development, and I think that perspective is very valuable to rural America.

The CHAIRMAN. Very good. Thank you for that. Mrs. Bloomfield, Mr. Zumwalt, do you share similar views?

Mrs. BLOOMFIELD. My members have long used RUS as their primary banker, actually. So, when I think about an agency that has really taken on the mantle of broadband, RUS was actually an early leader in funding a lot of the network and infrastructure that we see across the country. And, just playing upon Mr. Matheson's remarks, the other thing is the agency has general field reps that are out in the field. So, when we talk about what are the speeds, what are the demands, what the community's needs are, they actually have folks in the field who are verifying where is the infrastructure, where is the infrastructure not yet to be built? So I also think they have made the wise use of some of the investments.

We certainly have other Federal programs that are in place, we have state programs that are in place, but I think RUS has been very diligent, and has probably been the early leader in ensuring that rural America has connectivity.

The CHAIRMAN. Very good, thank you. Mr. Zumwalt, thoughts?

Mr. ZUMWALT. Most of our members have had success in other programs besides the RUS programs, although some are participating. I would agree that USDA is the proper place for this activity because of a longstanding history that USDA has representing the interests of farmers and our agricultural community. But as precision ag, in particular, comes into the forefront, our members are wanting to participate more. Historically, RUS has tended towards established players in the cooperative industries, for example, so what we would be looking for is to certainly encourage USDA to continue to work closely in collaborating with the other agencies. For example, the FCC National Broadband Map is important in making sure that we don't have overlapping funding programs at a Federal level trying to serve the same need from different directions.

But I have experience with RUS as well, and my feedback would be anything that we can do to broaden the inclusion of any solution, any provider that can close the digital divide, I think USDA can do that, and so absolutely support efforts to do that.

The CHAIRMAN. Thank you. Mr. Assey, according to a December 2022 GAO report, some stakeholders have expressed concern regarding the ability of the broadband infrastructure deployment industry to attract enough workers needed to deploy broadband infrastructure, and I have also heard this concern as rural America continues to face a lack of skilled workers in key sectors, including telecommunications. Given the influx of Federal funding for broadband infrastructure, what can we do to strengthen private workforce development opportunities and grow labor opportunities for those in this sector?

Mr. ASSEY. Yes, I think that you have put your finger on an issue that affects anybody who is in the communications network building arena, and it really goes to where we stand today, at the precipice of a major initiative to extend networks. It is one of the things that many of the companies that I represent are in the business of doing this on a day in, day out basis. Whether or not they are applying for government support or not, it is important for them to have a skilled workforce to be able to extend, upgrade networks on a regular basis. So, we work with private industry groups to make sure there is workforce certification and development.

But there is no question that we are going to need more people if we want to advance rapidly in building networks, and we are going to be competing in a labor pool for workers that are going to not just be building communications networks, they are going to be building roads, bridges, other sorts of things too. So it is certainly something that we welcome working with this Committee, and others in Congress, to try and improve.

The CHAIRMAN. Thank you so much. My time has expired. I am now pleased to recognize the gentleman from Georgia, the Ranking Member, for 5 minutes of questions.

Mr. DAVID SCOTT of Georgia. Thank you, Mr. Chairman. Lady and gentlemen, as I mentioned in my opening statement, since the Rural Electrification Act (Pub. L. 74–605) in 1936, the U.S. Department of Agriculture has been the only Federal department with the primary mission to serve rural America. And with their presence in rural communities across our country, they are, in my opinion, the best equipped to meet the needs of rural communities. However, out of the $65 billion that we provided through bipartisan infrastructure investment, only $2 billion was provided for USDA's Rural Development broadband. And also, in the bipartisan legislation that Chairman Thompson and I passed through the Committee last Congress, we will invest $43.2 billion in the Rural Development broadband programs to reach the most underserved rural areas.

And so, to each of you, I got this important question. Could you tell us the importance of giving the U.S. Department of Agriculture the leadership role in deploying broadband to rural America, and also what, in your opinion, level of financial resources will be necessary for rural communities to access Federal funding, and to meet our collective goal of expanding broadband service to 100 percent of rural America? Each of you, please. Mr. Matheson, we will start with you and go down.

Mr. MATHESON. Okay.

Mr. DAVID SCOTT of Georgia. And after you, the lady, so we can get—

Mr. MATHESON. Okay. Look, to expand on what I previously said about the value of the Department of Agriculture perspective, they know rural America, they prioritize issues that matter to rural America in their broadband funding, in terms of rurality or low population density. That is one of their criteria they look at. Look, this is important for these rural areas. Let us put this out there. Internet service matters, affordability matters. America's electric cooperatives serve 92 percent of the persistent poverty counties in America, so investments in broadband for these counties that have persistent poverty, it is an opportunity for economic development to mean something, in terms of looking forward in the future. I think the Department of Agriculture has the right perspective to do this.

Look, there is a lot of other money you mentioned, Mr. Scott, in terms of programs.

Mr. DAVID SCOTT of Georgia. Yes.

Mr. MATHESON. I get that, and we are going to pursue all those opportunities, but we are glad RUS has an important role.

Mr. DAVID SCOTT of Georgia. Mrs. Bloomfield?

Mrs. BLOOMFIELD. Thank you very much. I think that USDA understands rural America like nobody else. No other Federal agency understands the needs on the ground, and how important connectivity is for rural Americans, who, frankly, suffer from the handicap of distance, whether it is to education, medical services, whether it is tools for precision ag. So, there is no other agency that is more in tune to what rural America actually needs. But that is one of the reasons why I think they have taken a leadership role, and, frankly, set a higher standard for service than other agencies, and any of these other programs have, in part because they know that rural Americans really do need these services.

We saw during the pandemic how people used internet and broadband for all of the different reasons that they did, but I still see—I look at companies like Pineland Telephone Cooperative down in Georgia, that, frankly, today all of their customers have symmetrical speeds because they know that that is the way people can utilize getting to market, doing the services they need, and, frankly, make sure that we continue economic development. So, USDA has been primarily focused on really how to best serve rural America, so I think they are a very critical player.

Mr. DAVID SCOTT of Georgia. And, Mr. Stroup?

Mr. STROUP. Thank you. Thank you. Unlike most of the other representatives here, our infrastructure is deployed in space, and so there is no further cost associated with covering rural America. The service that you get is comparable between cities, between rural America. So, really, the additional funding would be made available for access to Earth stations, to consumer equipment. But, I definitely feel that USDA has an important role to play. I would also like to emphasize the point that Mr. Zumwalt made previously, which is the need for coordination between the other funding organizations. Thank you.

Mr. DAVID SCOTT of Georgia. So, the entire panel, my time has passed, but it is important that each of you do agree that the United States Department of Agriculture is the one best suited to lead and coordinate the effort. Is that correct?

Mr. ZUMWALT. Yes.

Mr. DAVID SCOTT of Georgia. Thank you.

Mr. ROUZER [presiding.] The gentleman's time has expired.

Mr. DAVID SCOTT of Georgia. Yes. Thank you.

Mr. ROUZER. I recognize Mr. Crawford for 5 minutes.

Mr. CRAWFORD. Thank you, Mr. Chairman. Mrs. Bloomfield, talking about long-term, we know what it looks like now, we know what broadband looks like currently, and USDA's role in that. How do you think Congress should help to ensure that we are looking long-term, meeting the needs of consumers, specifically with regard to broadband deployment loan and grant programs?

Mrs. BLOOMFIELD. So, I think the Committee has really taken a forward look, so I really appreciate your asking that question. I think we get really wrapped up in capital expenses, so what does it cost to actually build the infrastructure? And I think one of the other reasons we are very bullish about different technologies—it is going to take every tool in the toolkit, but definitely focused on fiber deployment where possible. Because of the fact that in a rural area, for example, at the end of the day your op-ex (operation-expenses) becomes lower it means—we have a thing in rural America, when we provide service, that is called windshield time. Our techs have to drive 3, 4, 5 hours to get out to a home that has a troubleshoot. Using technology that will reduce those op-exes actually just makes these operations more efficient.

The other thing is I think we are just on the cusp, in these rural areas, of actually seeing some of the services that really can transform lives, like telemedicine. And I think having that future-proof network, thinking forward, not just what we need today, but what we need tomorrow in those networks also makes a great deal of sense. The other thing I will say, when I look at how Americans are consuming broadband, the idea if you build something, that you have to go back in 3 years to upgrade, I think it will force all of us to look back and say we missed an opportunity to do it right the first time.

Mr. CRAWFORD. Thank you. From your perspective, what do you think is the best way to streamline coordination to avoid a duplicative process among the agencies? Things like overbuilding, bureaucratic holdups with other agencies. One of the things that I have heard—recurring theme from all of you all is that USDA is best positioned as the Executive agency, so I think that we can agree. But how do you harmonize that effort? Give me your thoughts on how we can reduce that.

Mrs. BLOOMFIELD. That is going to be the literally billion dollar challenge coming up. But that is where—and I know you have heard reference today to the maps that are coming out that the FCC produced. Congress appropriated $7 million to produce these maps. We are going to see the results in just a matter of days. I think making sure that every agency, as they are rolling out funds, as USDA is making an award in an area, that those areas get taken off those maps, that they show as served, so that we continue to make sure that we are really focused on the unserved.

That really needs to be a priority, that those who are waiting for connectivity get it, then those who are underserved, and then those who, filling in some of those other gaps. So, I would say the mapping is going to be key. I know that there are ongoing discussions. I know that USDA and the Secretary have been very engaged in coordinating, but that coordination is going to become even more necessary in 2024, when the BEAD money starts to flow out the door from NTIA.

Mr. CRAWFORD. I know you represent a lot of rural telecoms across the country, so could you give me some insights into how your member organizations have worked with USDA to sort of advocate for resource allocation for those projects?

Mrs. BLOOMFIELD. So, they have been traditional borrowers since the telephone program was created decades ago. So, they traditionally had telephone loans, and obviously morphed very quickly into broadband because the need was so great in rural America. So, I think there are a couple of things that—one of the things that has really struck us is we think, through getting USDA to really take on that leadership mantle, has been some of the streamlining. Getting some of the reviews, and things like—when you have had previously disturbed areas, that you don't have to go through the regulatory process again, because USDA, just like every one of us, is looking for workforce. So they really don't have a lot of the staff that they need to actually process a lot of the funding.

But I think, again, the leadership mantle that they have taken really comes through, and I think their long history in making business cases for putting money in low density parts of the country really speaks to their ability to kind of manage through where we go next on infrastructure.

Mr. CRAWFORD. Thank you. And real quick, Mr. Hurley, I want to talk about precision ag. I think that is relevant here in how broadband affects precision ag applications. What kind of policy changes do you think Congress should consider to help ag equipment manufacturers, for example, better meet the needs of rural America without leaving rural farming communities behind?

Mr. HURLEY. Yes. I think, in regards to a policy that needs to be implemented, programs, bills that need to be approved, we have really got three primary bipartisan pieces that we feel are critical to the further implementation of precision technologies across all of rural America, and that is the PAL Act (H.R. 1495), the PRECISE Act, and the Promoting Precision Agriculture Act of 2023 (H.R. 1697) as well.

Mr. CRAWFORD. Thank you, I appreciate it. Thank you all for being here today.

Mr. ROUZER. Mr. McGovern?

Mr. MCGOVERN. Well, thank you, and thank you all for being here today. This is an important topic. Access to high-speed internet is crucial for people to effectively do their jobs, participate in school, and access healthcare. And, unfortunately, far too many Americans still lack access, including 16 percent of Massachusetts residents, with a disproportionate number living in rural parts of my district. And I will say I am proud of the steps that we have taken over the last few years to close the digital divide, and we are only beginning to see the impact.

For example, the bipartisan infrastructure law included the largest Federal broadband investment in our nation's history and will bring over $100 million to Massachusetts. The Commonwealth also received $145 million in the American Rescue Plan Capital Project funds to expand rural broadband, which will connect nearly 1/3 of the homes and businesses currently lacking broadband. I am just glad that these funds were obligated in time and weren't part of the $27 billion clawed back during the debt ceiling debacle, but that is a whole other hearing.

But, we have seen the most significant broadband investments in our nation's history over the past few years, and it is imperative that we approach the broadband provisions in the farm bill with great care. And, quite frankly, I have concerns about what I have heard from some who want to lower the standards for those receiving Federal funding to build-out our rural networks. Mr. Assey, I know that one of your members, Charter, has a large presence in rural parts of my district, so I will direct this question to you. There has been a lot of talk about future-proofing networks. Can you tell the Committee what you think that means, and if your members' networks are future-proof?

Mr. ASSEY. Thank you for the question. I think it is an important point, because when I think of future-proofing, I really think of— can networks grow with the society to meet their needs? Are they *scalable?* I think Mr. Matheson used the same word. So, the question is, are we going to be able to build networks that, without significant new capital investment, are going to be able to grow in the capabilities that they offer? And, without a doubt, the cable networks are.

As I mentioned, 99 percent of the homes passed in rural America by cable networks already have 100 megabit per second speed capabilities, and we are fast moving on to the next iteration of cable technology, so-called 10G technology, that is going to offer the capability of multi-gigabit connections in both directions. So we are always trying to skate to where the puck is going to be, and we feel very confident that cable networks are future-proof.

Mr. MCGOVERN. So do you have any recommendations for how we can make sure that we are future-proofing broadband networks to make sure the internet speeds are fast enough for future speeds and uses?

Mr. ASSEY. There is always going to be this balance between trying to pick a minimum level of performance that is forward-leaning, and that will meet both the immediate and near-term needs, and there is always going to be a desire to ensure that the technologies and the platforms we pick can scale up to meet future capabilities. I think what we would worry about, are we picking standards in order to manage specific types of platforms that will discourage other types of solutions that may be better suited to particular environments or particular areas? So it is really a balance.

Mr. MCGOVERN. Yes, no, and look, I believe it is crucial to make sure that we take advantage of the historic levels of funding and ensure that it means connectivity that meets the needs of the future. It is clear that rural America has diverse needs, and we can't take a one-size-fits-all approach. Could you, or anyone expand on how we can connect unserved areas, while also increasing access for underserved communities?

Mr. ASSEY. Yes. I think, when you are talking about unserved *versus* underserved, you are talking about the difference between communities that have no connectivity, or connectivity that is below 25 megabits per second, *versus* some that are above that. I think our concern is that the laws of economics always make the people most in need the last in line, and we need to orient our solutions so that we actually try to prioritize getting service to those who have been waiting for it for so long.

Mr. MCGOVERN. I just closed them out of time—I wanted to tell you—but I just want to add that we must not overlook the importance of affordability when expanding access. I mean, ensuring that people can afford broadband only services, once they become available. I think it is crucial if we are going to truly close the digital divide, but I am out of time. Thank you very much.

Mr. ROUZER. The gentleman yields back. I now recognize myself, in order of arrival. So a couple broad points here. Obviously, I am very grateful to have each of you before us today, and I appreciate your testimony very much. This is a very important issue. Connectivity is everything, whether it is healthcare, business, education. You can't do without it, and if you are doing without it, you are severely behind the curve, in terms of whatever the question may be.

According to the National Telecommunications and Information Administration Database, there are 80 broadband programs currently at the Federal level, including, dependent on how you want to count them, nine housed at the Department of Agriculture. We have had a lot of money flowing through a lot of different programs in recent years, multiple agencies, not to mention what individual states are doing as well. I think it is crucial we keep track of the areas where service is being implemented and where it is not, and why it is not.

In North Carolina, for example, the North Carolina Broadband Infrastructure Office uses NC One Map, an open source, interactive, GIS mapping tool to visualize data collected by the state, as well as other resources, related to broadband availability and adoption, and other matters as well. So the question is—just gave you an example in North Carolina—how are Federal and state leaders overall keeping track of projects, both deployed and in the pipeline for deployment, to ensure underserved areas are addressed, and overbuilding doesn't occur? And I open that up for anybody.

Mrs. BLOOMFIELD. So—thank you very much. We actually have a number of NTCA members in the State of North Carolina who participate both in the state program, but have also been big recipients of RUS. So your point on the coordination is really key, and I think that is going to be critical, as each state not only notes where some of the deployment is supposed to be, but also that we are coming back afterwards to ensure that any provider who is the recipient of Federal or state funding actually is able to show that they have actually lived through their commitment, because, if we don't have some type of oversight, if we don't have some type of verification on that, what we are going to see is those constituents, those consumers who were in those areas, are actually—that don't get service are going to be at the bottom of the line.

So I think making sure that that coordination between state and Federal is going to be important, and I think that will be a focus of what NTIA is going to be doing with BEAD as well.

Mr. ROUZER. Any other comment there?

Mr. ZUMWALT. Yes. Thank you. I think it is really important to keep in mind that the intent of these programs is to serve the unserved, and, so far, we are not getting there fast enough. This has to be a whole of nation effort, and it has to be one that incorporates every available technology to meet the need, instead of setting up a standard where existing networks can be overbuilt because we changed the standard by which we are going to measure whether they are served, or underserved, or what.

And I think this is important because, as someone who has had experience actually running a wireless ISP, we delivered fiber and broad—and wireless services to roughly 10,000 customers, and less than five percent of those ever asked for or required symmetric speeds from us. And this included government agencies, enterprises, academic institutions, residential customers, small businesses, and—I think I already covered enterprise.

So when you actually look at download and upload speeds, if you are going to adopt that as the standards, you have to be careful because, generally speaking, the way that that is consumed is it is consumed much greater on the download than on the upload, and that is true across all of the WISPA membership as well. Thank you.

Mr. ROUZER. I only have about 48 seconds left. To follow up on that, my experience with government is you have a lot of stove-piping. When I read there are 80 different programs, I am certain that one agency is not necessarily talking to the other agency. We will get into that later. Here is my final question, though. Technology changes rapidly. You could lose your shirt in broadband. Elon Musk says he will have the whole world covered in 3 years. I think I read that somewhere. Maybe a little bravado in that, but hey, technology changes. How do you balance the equation of financing technology, where the ball is going to be in the future? That is a big question for all of you.

Mr. ZUMWALT. Well, what we are seeing is that the total cost of ownership of a network is going to define what a carrier is actually willing to be doing. Now, if you are willing to subsidize operations and say we are going to give you a bunch of money to buy something for 30 years, perhaps they would buy something differently. But the market actually is a very effective source for determining what the best technology is to use in a time. And if you look at what the broadband carriers are doing, they all upgrade as demands change over time.

Mr. ROUZER. Yes. My time has expired. I now recognize the gentlelady from North Carolina, and my friend, Ms. Alma.

Ms. ADAMS. Thank you very much, Mr. Chairman, the gentleman from North Carolina, and Ranking Member, for hosting this hearing on the digital divide, and for your opening remarks. I do want to thank the witnesses as well for offering your insights on this important topic. The digital divide and broadband equity are important to me because the constituents that I represent disproportionately shoulder the effects of this divide. The picture in Mecklenburg County in North Carolina's 12th District, where I represent, is a stark one.

A recent estimate from the Center for Digital Equity found that 21 percent of Mecklenburg County households had, at best, dial-up speeds for their home internet, and 14 percent of households, almost 55,000 in number, had no internet at all. So, looking at the entire state, more than one million Carolinians are, in the words of our governor, "On the wrong side of the digital divide."

It was especially revealing how disproportionately communities of color, especially African Americans, are suffering, especially at our HBCUs, our predominantly African American institutions, 1890s. There are 19 across the country, and we have one in North Carolina. The pandemic showed our communities how crucial dependable internet access is for education, for medicine, and for finding employment, so this hearing has been edifying in thinking about coordinated approaches to bring access to all.

I have several questions for the panel, and any of you can answer this. As broadband continues to be deployed to unserved and underserved communities, how can we ensure that those within each community are actually able to afford high-speed, high quality services post deployment?

Mrs. BLOOMFIELD. I will just take the first crack.

Ms. ADAMS. Yes, ma'am.

Mrs. BLOOMFIELD. There is——

Ms. ADAMS. Yes, you.

Mrs. BLOOMFIELD.—very important program called ACP (Affordable Connectivity Program), which is part of the Infrastructure Act that really ensures that those who are low-income have access to connectivity. So one of the things that my carriers, and I am sure carriers across this table, are doing is working with their communities to basically get the word out to say, if you can't afford internet access, there is a Federal program that is available. Now, I will say I worry that this program is going to run out of funding in a year or 2, but I think it has been really important, in terms of digital equity, and inclusion, and getting folks online. So there is a piece in place, it is already underway, and I think that most of the carriers probably represented here today are actively looking to get subscribers that you mentioned online.

Ms. ADAMS. Thank you. So could any of the others of you speak about how your associations, and the internet service providers within your associations, are focusing on addressing these disparities?

Mr. ASSEY. We would echo what Ms. Bloomfield said. Our companies are committed to trying to make sure that all their customers can get access through ACP. We are working with many trusted digital navigators, civic organizations, to get the word out about this program, show people the full benefits of broadband, and we are committed to this cause.

Ms. ADAMS. Okay. Does anybody else want to comment? Yes, sir?

Mr. ZUMWALT. I would just like to add that, in addition to hoping for the continuation of ACP, which may or may not happen, if you look at the individual service provider performance, they are looking for a way to keep their costs low so that they can pass those savings on to their customers regardless of what level of assistance they have. And I think that that is really important, because for internet service providers who are active in their community, they understand their communities, they understand what the community can afford, and they want to be able to deliver broadband that is going to meet the needs of their communities by making sure that they have their own cost structures in line.

Ms. ADAMS. Okay.

Let me—thank you very much. And let me ask anyone else, if you have—what, if anything, have you learned from the pandemic that Congress should focus on in this farm bill? If you give me just one thing, each of you? I have 40 seconds.

Mr. ZUMWALT. Serve the unserved first.

Ms. ADAMS. Thank you.

Mr. ASSEY. Agreed. Agree.

Ms. ADAMS. All right. Yes, sir?

Mr. MATHESON. I think we make—we have learned the—it is—broadband is so important to day to day life, we want to make sure we all have access, but it has got to be at the right speed, it has got to be scalable to the future it has got to be affordable.

Ms. ADAMS. Okay.

Great. Yes, sir? Got two more people down there.

Mrs. BLOOMFIELD. Agree.

Ms. ADAMS. Agree.

Mr. HURLEY. Yes.

Ms. ADAMS. Okay. So everybody is in agreement? Okay. I just certainly hope that we will take all these things into consideration, because these underserved communities are still not being served, and there is a lot we can do about it. Thank you very much. Mr. Chairman, I yield back.

Mr. ROUZER. The gentlelady yields back. Mr. Lucas?

Mr. LUCAS. Thank you, Mr. Chairman. And I would note to our participants on the panel today—and, of course, Mr. Matheson has been through this process many times on both sides of the room— many times the discussions we have seem to be reinforcing constantly certain points of view, so let us go down that trail.

As all of you know, the ReConnect Program was established through the Fiscal Year 2018 omnibus, and the legislation provided USDA with authority to make grants, as well as loans, for construction of retail broadband networks in rural America. Since then the ReConnect Program has become the most funded broadband program in USDA, receiving almost $2½ billion. But because ReConnect was established with minimum program parameters, USDA has had broad discretion over how the rules should apply during each funding round. And this has caused each round of funding to consist of, sometimes, dramatically different standards and rules. So, as a sitting Member of the Committee, I note bringing this program under the 5 year farm bill gives this Committee to thoughtfully reform, and improve, and authorize this key broadband program.

So, with that, I turn to the Committee to discuss—to the panel, I should say, to discuss what you would consider to be important program parameters that need to be put in place to ensure a more effective and consistent ReConnect Program. And in addition, what flexibilities need to be maintained or included to ensure rural consumer and business needs are met?

And just before we start this, I punched the little test button, and I examined the access to broadband that I have at the teeny tiny efficient apartment I have here in D.C., 339 upload speed and 306 download speed, but I noted that, on the test of my program at the farm in Roger Mills County, it was 5 up and 5 down. It was a son of a gun trying to do Zoom calls during COVID on 5. Matter of fact, it didn't always work. So with that, I turn to the panel. You are getting the defined program coming in this farm bill. What should the parameters be, and what flexibility should be maintained? We are going to help you.

Mr. MATHESON. I will jump in. First of all, it ought to be in the farm bill. This was created through the appropriations process. It has created a lack of certainty and consistency in the program. I think bringing it into the farm bill——

Mr. LUCAS. And we are going to clean it up.

Mr. MATHESON. Yes. It—I think it'll be helpful for everyone involved to have more certainty and clarity going forward. You want to make sure that you are prioritizing minimum speeds and scalability for the future. You have heard *future-proof* used a lot in this discussion. Let us not forget, the last farm bill was only 5 years ago, 2018. Back then we were talking 25/3. So let us not continue to make a mistake of underestimating where the future is going, and that—it is hard to define it specifically, but scalability matters as well.

Let us make sure that we also invest in middle-mile, I mentioned that in my opening statement. Backbone middle-mile matters a lot, in terms of the—participation for anyone else for that last mile to the end-user. And electric cooperatives invest a lot in middle-mile technology in terms of their electric utility operations, so it can be a great access to leverage for rural broadband to the end-user.

Mr. ASSEY. I would say, first of all, with your experience with 5 down and 5 up, you are the paradigmatic case for the unserved, and one of the reasons why——

Mr. LUCAS. And, ironically, I am 1 mile from fiber, but it is a 1965 copper line between me and fiber.

Mr. ASSEY. Yes. Well, you should be high up on the list for the next round of provider subsidies. I do think, as we do this, there are a couple things that we ought to focus on as well. One is to really try to change and modernize some of the eligibility rules at RUS. I think there is a historic—whether it is a historic artifact or not, a lot of the rules and processes in place that RUS uses are just not suited to the multiplicity of types of companies, including large established companies that offer service. And we ought to make it easier for people who want to participate in this program than harder.

And, second, I think Congress really needs to give some guidance as far as what is a proper priority when we are scoring and evaluating projects. Things like experience of a provider, the performance of the network, the need of the area, that seems to be totally fine. But some of these priorities that have been adopted seem to be completely artificial, and designed more to steer a particular result rather than get performance to the areas of need.

Mr. LUCAS. I think the Chairman will probably tolerate one more answer on my behalf, if anyone else wishes to touch that.

Mr. ZUMWALT. I was just going to add that I think that it—that the program needs to be technology-neutral, in the spirit of what the infrastructure Act called for. I think it needs to focus on serving the unserved, rather than adopting a technology. Most of our members are deploying fiber, so even though we represent wireless ISPs, we are very familiar with fiber. And the measurements that we take of customers all around the country suggest that most residential subscribers are not even using more than 50 megabits per second of download, even if they have gigabit delivery. So the speed tests that you run are not indicative of what you are actually using. So when you put in place a requirement for something, recognize that the requirement may not be what you are using now, or even need to use in the future.

Mr. LUCAS. My time is——

Mr. STROUP. And if I may, very quickly, I can give you the names of at least three companies that can provide much faster service than you are receiving on your farm.

Mr. LUCAS. Thank you. I yield back, Mr. Chairman.

Mr. ROUZER. I was going to say, Mr. Lucas, maybe you should call your Congressman.

Mr. LUCAS. Well, actually, the guy that owns the company was a year ahead of me in high school.

Mr. ROUZER. Or better yet, call your two Senators. Ms. Spanberger?

Ms. SPANBERGER. Thank you, Mr. Chairman. Thank you to our witnesses for being here today. I love the topic of broadband. I have been passionate about this issue since I first arrived in Congress in 2019, because I represent communities that have really experienced the divide. Just a few years ago the idea of universal broadband accessibility in Virginia seemed really far off, but now I am really proud to say that our Commonwealth, because of investments from the Bipartisan Infrastructure Law, the American Rescue Plan, Virginia is really within reach of this goal.

And the district that I represent, it spans localities where we have suburban communities with easy access, and many rural communities that, over the years, have really known the hardships. It has been discussed, of course, that during COVID we saw what this divide was like, and even across superintendents, county to county, some were able to have Zoom classes for the students, and some were putting up mobile hotspots at the Food Lion parking lots because that is the way the kids were learning, and they were giving packets out, and that just shouldn't exist.

But I know that we are on this, like, trajectory towards making the strides that need to be made. And we, in Virginia, have expanded access to millions of Virginians. In fact, and I will say this again, as a proud Virginian, we have been heralded as really a nationwide example for broadband internet expansion through what we have done correctly, Federal, state, local coordination, often through building partnerships, many times with rural electric coops, with wireless providers, and in the localities, really driven by the localities. So I am proud of the progress that we have made. There is more to do, but we are on our way to connecting 100 percent of Virginia's families, small businesses, farms, and students. And so, with that general frame—and you do not have to mention Virginia just to flatter me since I asked the question—are there examples of states that have done things right, from your vantage point, that while we are here looking at how to make sure that our Federal dollars are well utilized for the states and localities, are there examples that you would point us to as we are looking at how these programs are really, actually operationalized on the ground?

Mrs. BLOOMFIELD. I will jump in, because I think Dr. Holmes, who runs the Virginia Broadband Office, is exemplary. But I think that is a key component, right, and we are entering a new era, because for the first time—there used to be a few states that had a broadband office.

Ms. SPANBERGER. Yes.

Mrs. BLOOMFIELD. Virginia was early because you had some of the tobacco funding, and it has gotten very active.

Ms. SPANBERGER. That is right.

Mrs. BLOOMFIELD. And you had Minnesota, you had Wisconsin, you had some of those out there. Now that we are entering this world of BEAD with NTIA, every state has to establish a State Broadband Office. That is part of the deal. They have to submit a plan. They have to show a plan by—I think in the next month or so—of how they are actually going to take all that Federal funding from BEAD and utilizing it. They then coordinate with NTIA. So you have a state person on the ground, you have NTIA here, and an NTIA person in each state.

So I think utilizing the State Broadband Offices to help coordinate on the Federal front is going to be really important, because they are almost going to be the gatekeeper, as Federal funding comes from these different programs, and they are going to be looking at the Federal amounts that are released, in addition to their our state amounts, and really trying to very strategically fill in— where do you have those gaps, and where do you have those underserved gaps?

So not just flattery, but Dr. Holmes is key, but I think each state now has the opportunity to meet that level. Some are just going to be a little bit more challenged, some are going to get mired down in politics, and that is most unfortunate. But I think we have a real opportunity with the fact that there will be a State Broadband Office in every state.

Ms. SPANBERGER. Fantastic. Anyone else want to add to that?

Mr. Assey?

Mr. ASSEY. I agree, and I think it really points to the value of coordination.

Ms. SPANBERGER. Yes.

Mr. ASSEY. What you have experienced in Virginia, really needs to be replicated at a much larger scale. It is going to be incredibly difficult; but, if we are looking at this as solving a problem, we need to all have a common understanding of what the problem is if we want to devote the resources to actually spending it. So I would say that coordination needs to happen at a much stronger level, not just at the Federal level, but also down into the state and the local level, and back up to the Federal level, so that we all are working to take whatever that number of unserved and underserved is and drive it down to zero.

Ms. SPANBERGER. And certainly one of the things that we have seen on the ground is that flexibility in how those Federal dollars can be spent is incredibly important in allowing our state—again, our state offices to do good things. I am running out of time, but I just want to say thank you all for being here. Thank you for bringing your voices to this discussion, because it is so vitally important that we get this right, and that, in this farm bill, we ensure the investments we are making really help our communities across the board and add to what we have already done with prior legislation. So thank you so much. Mr. Chairman, I yield back.

Mr. ROUZER. The gentlelady yields back. Ms. Miller, you are recognized for 5 minutes.

Mrs. MILLER of Illinois. Last Congress, I voted for bipartisan legislation to support rural broadband because it is a critical issue to our farmers and rural communities across the country. So several of my constituents had brought up that state mapping is better than Federal mapping, which is a little bit what you were talking about, but I just walked in here, so I don't know if I missed something. What suggestions, then, do you have to increase coordination among the Federal and state? Did you just answer that? Okay. Then——

Mrs. BLOOMFIELD. I would be more than happy to.

Mrs. MILLER of Illinois. Thank you.

Mrs. BLOOMFIELD. I think the challenge process is going to be really important, because some states have gone ahead—and states are closer to the ground. They know—they are working—one of the things each of these State Broadband Offices has to do is they have to do stakeholder meetings across the state, so they get a sense of what is going on there. But that is where I think challenges are going to be important. Whether it is a provider who says I have already got service here, and here is my speed, whether it is a consumer who says, this map shows I have broadband, and I actually don't. So I think there is going to be further refinement.

The problem with the map is it is an evolving thing. You are— it is never static. So as soon as you finish it, it is actually out of date already. So I think staying on top of it is going to be very critical.

Mrs. MILLER of Illinois. Yes. Does anybody have any other ideas on how to coordinate this between Federal and state and make it more efficient?

Mr. MATHESON. I think that is happening.

Mrs. MILLER of Illinois. Good.

Mr. MATHESON. Look, the FCC maps are not perfect, but they are better than they used to be through this first round.

Mrs. MILLER of Illinois. Yes.

Mr. MATHESON. The challenge process is going to continue to— it is— as Ms. Bloomfield said, this is an evolving process. You are never going to get perfection. But having state engagement on that process is going to be key to making the national maps better.

Mrs. MILLER of Illinois. Also, I have heard from several of my constituents that broadband providers in their area are having trouble signing up for the USDA broadband programs. We were talking about how complicated it is. And have any of your members faced the same issue, and how do you think we can improve on the application process?

Mr. ASSEY. We have experienced problems like that in the past. I mean, we have had issues where one company was organized as a partnership, and it wasn't eligible under the application rules that RUS was interpreting.

Mrs. MILLER of Illinois. Yes.

Mr. ASSEY. I think that got worked out, but there are a lot of— kind of these informal roadblocks that we face with a program that has traditionally been oriented to a very different profile of company than a large cable operator.

Mrs. MILLER of Illinois. Yes.

Mr. ASSEY. It is one of the reasons that—one of the things that we like in the—Representative Cammack's bill is really an opportunity to use the notice and comment process to really try to come up with alternative ways of demonstrating financial viability as companies, and to provide security interests that are different from what may have traditionally been used. Because it—this is all about getting qualified companies to want to come participate and that is what we ought to be aiming towards.

Mrs. MILLER of Illinois. Right.

Ms. Bloomfield, do you have—and then—sorry.

Mrs. BLOOMFIELD. I think the programs are very competitive, which is great. The fact that you get four to five times the number of applications than you have funding for I think shows to the benefit of the program. I would say, USDA, and RUS in particular, have staffing needs. I think some of the biggest challenges are actually getting some of the permitting through, getting the process through USDA's pretty antiquated portal. So I think some of those things that can make the process more efficient would definitely help get the funding out there faster.

Mrs. MILLER of Illinois. That is great. Mr. Stroup, did you have a——

Mr. STROUP. And my members would encourage that Congress specify that satellite and other service providers are eligible, and, despite the intention of legislation being technology-neutral, very often in the implementation phase, that is not how it plays out.

Mrs. MILLER of Illinois. Okay. Mr. Matheson, we have heard from several stakeholders about the concerns regarding permitting on Federal lands within existing rights of way, which can take up to 3 years to get an approval. Can you talk about the experiences of your members with these agencies, and what can Congress do to help expedite this process, and ensure our eligible rural communities are getting connected?

Mr. MATHESON. Yes, this is clearly an issue. We have a specific member in Colorado that was experiencing—where they got funding through RUS, but then they had to cross BLM land, Bureau of Land Management land, and ran into a significant permitting delay, and the——

Mrs. MILLER of Illinois. Yes.

Mr. MATHESON. This is not new, that any committee in Congress has heard this, that when you have multiple Federal agencies that don't talk to each other, and you are the person trying to get the permit to get something done, it can be really frustrating.

Mrs. MILLER of Illinois. Yes.

Mr. MATHESON. And so some of the steps that we are taking— most recently, in the permitting reform for the debt ceiling Act (Pub. L. 118–5, Fiscal Responsibility Act of 2023), are a step in the right direction. We need to keep that momentum going, however, in terms of creating appropriate time limits on the permitting process, but also the coordination across Federal agencies has got to be better than it is. It is just a question where the left hand and the right hand aren't talking to each other. And we have felt that specifically on Federal lands in the West.

Mrs. MILLER of Illinois. Okay. Did anybody else have a comment? Oops, I am out of time. Thank you, and I yield back.

Mr. ROUZER. The gentlelady yields back. Ms. Brown?

Ms. BROWN. Thank you, Mr. Chairman and Ranking Member Scott. Access to high-speed affordable internet is no longer a privilege. It is a necessity for everyday work and life in a modern 21st century society. The COVID–19 pandemic exposed how deep the digital divide cuts when everything from school, to business meetings, and doctor's appointments were moved online. This hit hard in communities like Cleveland, where almost 1⁄3 of households lacked internet access. In fact, during the first weeks of the pandemic, Cleveland Metropolitan School District was unable to transition to remote leaning since almost 1⁄2 of its students didn't have internet service at home.

I know this is the same story that so many of our constituencies face, including those in rural districts. This is why accurate and detailed mapping of fixed and mobile broadband service is so important. If we are truly going to connect every American to the internet, we need to be able to target areas that have been left behind. So, Mrs. Bloomfield, to start, what should the Committee consider a minimum acceptable speed when evaluating if a household is serviced?

Mrs. BLOOMFIELD. So I am going to go back to—I think that USDA has done it right with 100 symmetrical speed because, again, I think—I—it—I may have a different experience, but my members actually track what their customers use, and how they utilize it, and I will say that we see a huge demand from consumers. I have companies that I asked prior to this hearing who are telling me that 100 symmetrical is entry-level service. When you have five or six devices at one time working in a household, you need that bandwidth. So, again, as I think about this moment in time historically that we are at, to not utilize and look for that type of speed, we are missing an opportunity.

I also think it is technology-neutral. For example, during the FCC's Rural Digital Opportunity Fund auction, there were a number of fixed wireless providers that also said they had the ability to do 100 symmetrical, so we are not talking just about prioritizing fiber. We are saying that is the right speed, and that is what we should be building to ensure that, again, the capacity is met not just today, which we are seeing that demand for right now, but for 3, 5, 10 years from now.

Ms. BROWN. So that is the speed you would recommend we should aim for it to be future—ready in the future as well?

Mrs. BLOOMFIELD. I would say 100 symmetrical is important right now, yes.

Ms. BROWN. Okay. And what additional improvements and investments can we make on the Committee to ensure accurate and reliable maps? I know this is a—maybe a redundant question, but if you could speak to that, Mrs. Bloomfield?

Mrs. BLOOMFIELD. Mapping is going to be really—that is going to be our—literally our roadmap, in terms of what we know about served and unserved. I actually have a map here that shows where 25/3 exists across the country. You see a lot of white spaces, particularly out West, and dotted throughout the country. But I think that the ability to make sure that we have a process in place—the FCC built the map. We are going to need to make sure that we continue to invest in that map, that we are constantly updating it, that every program that touches building broadband allows us to track not just where there is connectivity, but what is the speed? What is the technology?

Ms. BROWN. Yes.

Mrs. BLOOMFIELD. Where are the providers? So I do think that is going to be an ongoing investment to ensure that future dollars go in the right places.

Mr. MATHESON. And if I could?

Ms. BROWN. Thank you.

Mr. MATHESON. We want the maps to be consistent over time. We have heard stories where people game it. Well, they may— when the test is happening the speed looks good in that area, but that speed isn't consistent over time for people in that service territory. So the integrity of the map has got to be one where that speed exists all the time, not just in certain moments.

Ms. BROWN. Thank you. The bipartisan infrastructure law established the Affordable Connectivity Program to provide targeted discounts for low-income households and Tribal communities. The most recent round of USDA ReConnect grants requires applicants to participate in the Affordable Connectivity Program to ensure that households are not only able to access internet but afford it as well. Now, for anyone on the panel, what additional measures can we take in this farm bill to improve the affordability and the reliability of high quality broadband?

Mr. ASSEY. I think whether it is in this farm bill or separate and apart, I think continuing to strengthen and extend ACP support is important. And I would say it is important not just to help low-income families purchase affordable broadband, but it is really going to be important for infrastructure as well. When companies are deciding how much private capital they are willing to marry up with public funds in order to build to unserved areas, they have to make assumptions about, well, how many people are going to take to this service, how quickly?

And being able to ensure that continuity of support I think is not only going to be important for people in downtown Cleveland, but it is going to be important for people in unserved areas as well.

Ms. BROWN. Anyone else?

Mrs. BLOOMFIELD. I would also jump in and say, ensuring that we have the resources to advertise about the program, and thinking about doing it in an unconventional way, as you can't, obviously, put it on the internet, because people don't have internet access.

Ms. BROWN. Right.

Mrs. BLOOMFIELD. But, what are you doing with local libraries, and local leadership, and municipalities to get the word out? I have a cooperative up in Minnesota that literally goes to their Tribal communities with a traveling van with applications, and they sit down, and they share with the Tribal residents how do you get online, what is the value of being online, and actually literally do the signups. Because our community-based providers have every incentive to have every member of that community online. It really speaks to the economic health of the community in the long run. So I think we have to think about how do you educate those who don't even know this program exists, and then we have to ensure there is funding for it going down the road.

Ms. BROWN. Thank you so much. Thank you for the courtesy, Mr. Chairman. I yield back.

The CHAIRMAN [presiding.] You are welcome. It is a pleasure to recognize the gentleman from South Dakota, Mr. Johnson, for 5 minutes.

Mr. JOHNSON. Well, it won't surprise anybody that when I was outside in the rain talking to some South Dakota 4–H kids right now, we were talking about rural broadband, because listen, it matters to this whole country. We all know that a network gains in value the larger the network is. You wouldn't want an internet that only lets Manhattan access Manhattan websites, right? So this is not just about helping rural America, this is really about helping us be one connected nation in the same way that rural electrification did that, in the same way the Interstate Highway System did that, in the same way Universal Service did that so long ago.

And so I have a great friend on the panel today, Shirley Bloomfield, and so I thought we would just have a little bit of a colloquy here to tease out some of these issues surrounding speed. So, in your written testimony, Mrs. Bloomfield, you noted that Ookla— their study said that in 2021 the average broadband speeds in this country were 179/65. Am I remembering that right? And so your good friend and mine, Larry Thompson, a few years ago, when I was co-owner of a telecom engineering firm, had taught me about Nielsen's

Law, which I think indicates that the user's broadband speed increases by 50 percent a year, all other things being held equal. My understanding of that is roughly right, right?

Mrs. BLOOMFIELD. That is correct.

Mr. JOHNSON. And then I think in your testimony you talked about—you didn't mention Nielsen's Law because you are not as dorky as I am, but you did——

Mrs. BLOOMFIELD. That is correct.

Mr. JOHNSON. That is right, exactly. You noted information that, consistent with Nielsen's Law, said that by 2030 broadband speeds in this country will be 1,500/599. That is right, isn't it?

Mrs. BLOOMFIELD. That is correct.

Mr. JOHNSON. The 1996 Telecom Act (Pub. L. 104–104, Telecommunications Act of 1996) had a provision we haven't talked about today, but to me it is fundamental to this whole conversation. And the provision in the Telecom Act, if I am remembering it right, Mrs. Bloomfield, is that service in rural areas, rates and service, must be "reasonably comparable to those found in urban America." I am not wrong about that, am I?

Mrs. BLOOMFIELD. You are correct again.

Mr. JOHNSON. And so in your testimony, in your close, I thought you really hit the nail on the head about making sure that we don't invest in networks delivering speeds that are not only antiquated today, but will be woefully antiquated in the years to come. And so—I mean, I have a couple more questions, but just—any finer points you want to put on that?

Mrs. BLOOMFIELD. I think we haven't even touched the applications that we can be providing in rural America. One of the things NTCA does is we actually also provide healthcare to tens of thousands of rural Americans through a group health trust. What we are seeing in terms of telehealth, that—you can't do some of this diagnostic work. You can't—we have created virtual living rooms across the country for veteran care connecting VA, local, state to vets who live in rural America, which is a very high population of veteran community. You can't do the work that you need to do with telemedicine without utilizing some of those speeds, and we haven't even begun to see where the American demand will go.

Mr. JOHNSON. And I have tremendous respect for the members of each of these organizations, and I do think that there is a role for everybody to play in getting American—America connected. So I understand the value of us talking about technology and neutrality, and I believe in that, but I don't want us to use the guise of being technologically-neutral to water down the standards that we need to build to.

Now, the good thing is that doesn't need to cut anyone out, and I thought y'all's testimony did a good job of that. Mr. Matheson, you talked about the need for us to be building to at least 100 megabits per second. Of course, your members in this business are doing way more than that. Mr. Assey mentioned that—your members are routinely delivering over a gigabit per second. That is pretty robust. Mr. Stroup, you mentioned satellite can easily do 200 megabits per second. Mr. Zumwalt, with WISPS, you mentioned download speeds in excess of 1 gigabit per second are possible. And so, by all means, let us make sure that we are technology-neutral, because there is a role for everybody to play. This is a real big country. We have a lot of people who need help.

But Mr. Chairman, as we look toward this next farm bill, let us not water down the standards. If we are going to spend this nation's taxpayer dollars in continuing this unbelievable story of one America, connected, let us make sure that we are not investing in something that'll keep us connected for a year, or 2, or 5. These networks can be built to last a lot longer than that. Let us heed the words of Mrs. Bloomfield. Let us make sure we do it right. With that, I would yield back.

The CHAIRMAN. Well, I thank the gentleman for yielding back, and now I am pleased to recognized the gentlelady from Kansas, Congresswoman Davids, for 5 minutes.

Ms. DAVIDS of Kansas. Thank you, Mr. Chairman, and thank you to you and the Ranking Member for holding this hearing today. I mean, we have heard a lot about the need for high-speed broadband networks to bridge the digital divide, to allow families and communities to access the—particularly rural communities to access those unique broadband needs. Telemedicine, of course, is in there, education. Technologies to support small businesses, and that includes our agriculture community. A bunch of the family farms that I know are not just in my district in the Kansas Third, but in the State of Kansas. And we are definitely seeing the need for that accessible, reliable, and affordable broadband access.

And, I have a district with a good mixture of types of counties. I have three rural counties in the Kansas Third, and, similar to what we heard from Rep. Brown, in terms of metrics, up to 32 percent of the farms in those counties didn't have internet access, according to the 2017 Census of Agriculture that took place, and that doesn't touch the upload/download speeds. That is just baseline access. I think that we have already heard quite a bit about the problems that can cause for our farmers and producers, much less for folks who are trying to utilize the vibrant ag technologies that are being developed.

I think that, as we continue to try to figure out the best practices for working in coordination with rural communities, whether it is state, local, Federal, communities trying to stay connected, I think that what we see and have heard a lot about already is the—that idea of unserved, and what that looks at, and making sure that programs like ReConnect, or BEAD, or other Federal funding mechanisms aren't overlapping in a way that might impede our goal of internet access for everybody with maybe some overly restrictive definitions?

I would love to hear from, like, the whole panel about whether you see there being a mechanism, or maybe a happy medium, I will call it, between this 50 percent or 90 percent definitions of *unserved*. How do we get to a place where that overbuilding, maybe, doesn't happen, but also that we aren't impeding our ability to stay on track to connect every community?

Mr. ZUMWALT. May I start with that?

Ms. DAVIDS of Kansas. Yes.

Mr. ZUMWALT. I think the first and most important thing is to make serving the unserved the number one priority. Every other definition of *underserved* is going to be based on some understanding of speed, and so, if the speed standard changes, then you are going to find a lot of existing networks are going to be subject of rebuilding with Federal funds. And many of those networks were already built with Federal funds, or certainly with private capital, and so you have taxpayer money chasing taxpayer money not serving the unserved.

Mr. MATHESON. I think we need to be real careful on this discussion, though. This overbuilding is a lot more nuanced than I think some people describe it. And——

Ms. DAVIDS of Kansas. Yes.

Mr. MATHESON. And let—let us be careful—if people have substandard technology and service, then that is substandard. And you are saying, too bad, you are stuck with what you got. I also think we have to be very careful about saying we only want to serve unserved, but underserved don't matter anymore. That is where I hear this it is good enough for rural America, and my members don't buy that. They expect to have the same service that people in urban areas have. So I understand there is a difference between unserved and underserved, but let us be careful about creating a false choice where we can only do the unserved, and all those folks with underserved are stuck with what they have, which are legacy investments that aren't meeting today's broadband needs in many cases, not in all cases.

Of course we don't want to duplicate Federal funding where it is not providing an increase in service, but I think we have to be really careful, though, when we talk about overbuilding and underserved and unserved. I think it becomes too much of a simplistic description, and I encourage the Committee to take a more nuanced approach.

Mr. ASSEY. I think we are just, though—I mean, I don't know that we are necessarily disagreeing. I think it is a matter of priority, as far as those that literally have broadband below 25/3 or nothing at all as being the people who have waited the longest for this technology to reach them. I think the problem that you touch on, which is when you are getting down to 50 percent of the homes have to be either unserved or unserved and underserved, is you are really saying that 50 percent of the homes could have 1 gigabit. And then you are starting to subsidize areas where private capital has already built out capabilities to this area.

So you are not only interfering with the private investment that is trying to reach out into rural America, but you are also using scarce resources that ought to be going to the place that have nothing, or not good enough, and spending it to overbuild.

Ms. DAVIDS of Kansas. Thank you. And I can see that I asked a question that warrants quite a bit of feedback. Please, I would encourage you to submit written answers if you didn't get a chance to speak. Thank you, Mr. Chairman, I yield back.

The CHAIRMAN. Very good. Thank you so much. I now recognize Mr. Baird for 5 minutes of questions.

Mr. BAIRD. Thank you, Mr. Chairman. And I want to thank all of our witnesses for being here. This is a very important concept for our farm community, as all of you well know. When we have machinery that utilizes precision ag techniques and technology in order to improve the efficiencies on the farm, as well as fertilizer placement and pesticide placement and so and so, it is increasingly important that we have access to high-speed internet, as you have talked—and I didn't hear all the discussion, but I am sure you went into that.

So my question starts with—Mr. Matheson, in your testimony you talk about FCC's National Broadband Map, and that continues to show discrepancies between what the map displays and the realities on the ground as it relates to broadband connectivity. As you know, USDA entered to a memorandum of understanding, an MOU, with the FCC and the NTIA to share data on how each agency implements its broadband program, which includes mapping information.

Mr. MATHESON. Yes.

Mr. BAIRD. So what can Congress do to strengthen this coordination so we can ensure our broadband maps protect rural communities, and prevent them from being further left behind?

Mr. MATHESON. Yes, that is a great question. Congress has already taken the steps to encourage improvement of these maps, and it is an evolving process. But, to the extent the FCC put out its first updated map last year, and the challenge process has continued, where people around the country say, whatever the map says, here in my place, that is not true, and they challenge the map, that is an effective process to finally have more of a bottomup grassroots effort to get accurate information for these maps, coupled with the role of the states.

And I think that is really important, that—the FCC maps are important, and they are always going to be an important asset or vehicle for us to assess where we have unserved and underserved areas, but states are also an important part of how we look at those maps. States are involved in that challenge process as well. So I think we are going down the right path, quite candidly. We are not where we want to be yet, but I think it is going in the right direction.

Mr. BAIRD. Thank you. Then my next question goes to Mr. Stroup. In your testimony you talk about how the precision GPS, which I just mentioned, technologies allow farmers to increase yield by utilizing use of fertilizer, pesticides, herbicides, and apply the site specific treatments to fields. You also mentioned how Earth imaging satellites provide farmers high resolution imagery to determine when to plant, water, or monitor their crops. So how do you feel satellite technology services fill in the gaps in remote areas, where other technologies may not be suitable?

Mr. STROUP. Thank you for the question. And, in addition to the satellite services that you noted, the ability to be able to provide broadband and IoT services, and one of the great advantages to the satellite systems is the ubiquitous coverage. And, as I had mentioned previously, the service that you receive in rural North Dakota, where I grew up, is comparable to the service that you would receive in Washington, D.C. So the ability to fill in the gaps because we provide coverage to all rural areas across the country is the key to our ability to be able to provide broadband connectivity.

Mr. BAIRD. Very good. Anyone else have any comments on either of those questions, about the maps or about the satellite technology?

Mr. ZUMWALT. I would just state, and concur with my colleagues, I think that the FCC is taking the right steps. It is going to take a while before they can achieve perfection on this, but I like what I see so far. We are in for another probably year or 2 of some pretty gnarly work ahead of us, but I think the FCC is going to get there.

Mr. BAIRD. Anyone else?

Mrs. BLOOMFIELD. I would just offer to the Committee that— those of you who are going back home to your rural districts in August, to take the time to connect with one of your community-based providers, whoever they may be on this Committee, and go out and see some of the ag applications. I think being able to watch some of the livestock monitoring, watching some of the ability to do remote work with your livestock, and monitor the health of your animals, and what they are doing in the field, in terms of tractor technology, is really exciting to see.

Congressmen Feenstra from Iowa, his local provider has a new saying, which is—we call fiber-to-the-home, FTTH, and they call it fiber to the hog, because of the ability to connect these farms. So I would just say there is an open invitation to go out and do a tour.

Mr. BAIRD. Thank you for that comment, and especially bringing in the livestock. Got a livestock background. And, Mr. Feenstra, we have cattle and hogs in Indiana too, you know that?

Mr. FEENSTRA. I knew that.

Mr. BAIRD. Good to see you. I yield back, Mr. Chairman.

The CHAIRMAN. The gentleman yields back. I am now pleased to recognize the gentlelady from Colorado, Ms. Caraveo, for 5 minutes.

Ms. CARAVEO. Thank you, Chairman Thompson. Thank you to you, and Ranking Member Scott, for hosting today's hearing, and to the panel for being here this morning to share your testimony. As a doctor, accessible health care remains one of my highest priorities. Unfortunately, over the past several decades, Colorado has seen more and more rural hospitals, excuse me, close, and care options remain extremely limited, or sometimes non-existent, unless you are able to travel very long distances to receive health care. As a result, residents of rural areas experience significant health care disparities.

We have several opportunities to improve health outcomes through USDA broadband programs, not only to provide the funding to build-out or improve the broadband infrastructure, but also to provide the equipment necessary to support telemedicine. So, to anyone on the panel, do any of you have insights into the specific speeds or other network characteristics necessary to support telemedicine specifically?

Mr. ZUMWALT. If I can start with that, I have some experience working with an urgent care center in a previous—a role that I had with a wireless ISP. They were generally using gigabit speeds for their urgent care facility, which included imaging, but I would want to emphasize that that was for that facility. That was not for interacting with people in their homes using telemedicine services, which tended to be more of a residential broadband service.

So, to the extent that you want to differentiate between those services, just make sure that you recognize that no matter who is providing that area, that they have the capacity to provide the unique support that is going to be required by facilities that have a need for greater broadband.

Mrs. BLOOMFIELD. And I would jump in and say that we work very closely with the National Rural Hospital Association, who also endorses 100 symmetrical speeds for that very reason, the ability to be able to do the work that they need to do to transfer the medical files. And I think that the applications out there really kind of demand a lot of bandwidth, the ability to—I have a telephone cooperative that actually put fiber into the ground because of the fact that the general manager's workman fell off the roof, broke his leg, and it was going to take 2 days to get all the files transmitted over to the Vanderbilt Hospital.

So it was kind of that real need on the ground to be like, "Hey, you know what, we can do this, and we can actually ensure that our people don't have to drive 2 hours over to Vanderbilt." They can actually do some of the care with cardiac care, here back in the rural community, before it becomes urgent to relocate some of these patients, which, as you know, can be very traumatic.

Ms. CARAVEO. Well, thank you very much for those answers. Switching gears, I have been meeting with farmers in my district over the past few months who have shown me some of the technologies, Mrs. Bloomfield, that have improved the way that they farm. I would like to touch on the promise of precision agriculture what we have talked about kind of more broadly, and how we build-out broadband networks that will support further adoption of these technologies.

We have focused on delivering internet service to the home, but supporting agriculture—precision agriculture means we also have to expand to the fields. So once we deliver broadband to the home, what equipment or technologies, more specifically, are necessary to expand that coverage to the field, and what are some of the common barriers that farmers are facing to incorporate precision agriculture into their operations? And we can start with Mr. Hurley, and then if anybody else has thoughts.

Mr. HURLEY. Yes, thank you for bringing that up, and it is absolutely one of the most essential pieces of our being able to further the adoption and reap the benefits of precision agriculture, whether that is through an increase in yield, or a reduction in the inputs, and the impact that that has on the environment. And, as we stated, and I stated in my testimony, we need to be neutral in regards to the technologies that we invest our dollars in as we go forward, because we look at the various different aspects of—whether it is satellite, whether it is wireless, or whether it is fiber, we need coverage across the fields, and into the barn, into the—whether it is the chicken house, the hog house. But we have also got to be able to follow, and interact, and communicate with the tractor, and the combine, and the sprayer as they move through the field.

Mr. ASSEY. I would just say that it—this may not be the correct analogy, but if you think about it, precision agriculture is just another type of business application. It is very similar to, if you were to bring broadband to a school, you wouldn't want to just bring it to the principal's office. You would want to make sure that it is campus-wide. And, essentially, the campus in a precision agriculture environment are the fields, and the barn, and the hogs.

I think what we are going to see is, as the power of technology extends to rural America, we are going to see those solutions develop. They are already being developed, and we just need to encourage their development through kind of hybrid solutions that rely on cable or fiber technology to a particular area, and then extending out into the fields using either unlicensed technology or 5G CBRS (Citizens Broadband Radio Service) technology to basically provide that campus-wide or field-wide connectivity. But it is a very exciting part of getting connectivity to rural America to help people not just in their home, but in their day to day business as well.

Ms. CARAVEO. Thank you all. I yield back, Mr. Chairman. Thank you for the courtesy of extra time.

The CHAIRMAN. I thank the gentlelady, and now recognize the gentleman from Iowa, Mr. Feenstra, for 5 minutes.

Mr. FEENSTRA. Thank you, Chairman Thompson and Ranking Member Scott, and I want to thank each of our witnesses for testifying. It has been very impressive. Mr. Hurley, you spoke at length in your written testimony about the benefits of precision technology. I am from Iowa, one of the largest farm districts in the country, and at a time when our farmers are feeling the real pinch on inflation in inputs, and all these other costs going up, it is advantageous for us to create precision farming. You mentioned that innovations that could be adopted at a 90 percent rate would reduce herbicide costs by 15 percent, fertilizer would be reduced by 14 percent, water would decrease by 21 percent, and our crop production would increase by six percent. Okay, this is very significant, but our problem here is the cost.

I was at the Farm Progress Show last year, and we saw all these incredible technologies. My larger farmers and my larger producers can probably afford some of these, but my smaller producers cannot. And you noted this, and I appreciate you highlighting my bill, Precision Ag Loan Act, which gives loans through the USDA. Can you talk, Mr. Hurley, about why this is so important, and what we can do as an Agriculture Committee to try to get this new technology in the hands of our smaller producers?

Mr. HURLEY. Yes, I would be glad to do that. And, as you so note, the technologies continue to advance, and the innovation continues to be developed as we go forward, and there are costs associated with that. Representative, I would more approach that as investment, and think there are some key aspects of that. One, if someone was to come in and try to convert 100 percent of an operation that had no previous investment in precision technologies, it would be a very steep cliff to climb.

But the great thing about precision technologies, number one, is it is scalable. And so, from that perspective, I think that it is prudent for each and every individual farmer, producer, rancher, whether they are in the poultry business—to really sit down and understand what is most important to their business, and prioritize where they want to invest, based on the return. But I think critically, and you mentioned your bill, as did I, the Precision Ag Lending Act is one of those, along with PRECISE, that, for us to expand beyond the 25 percent or so of farmers that actually utilizes technology today, we have to have supportive programs—loans with flexible terms that allow these other growers to be able to go, and be able to invest, and borrow the money—the capital to put these technologies in place.

Mr. FEENSTRA. Yes. Thank you, Mr. Hurley. And I fully agree with that, and you can see what it does. I mean, the cutting down of the input—inputs that are going into the crop, or whatever it might be, into milking and so forth. And I just think this farm bill that we have coming up has this great opportunity to do that, and I look forward to working with that.

I want to pivot just a little bit. Mrs. Bloomfield, thank you for your comments about Iowa. Obviously you probably know we have 120 locally-owned, community-based broadband providers, and they are all fighting like ever to get to every subscriber, to get to every community, and every rural producer. My big issue is that the Rural Broadband Modernization Act, which I am on, the ReConnect *underserved* definition is that 90 percent—and it notes that we need 100 percent megabit downstream, 120 percent—or 120 percent upstream, and recently that definition got lowered to 50 percent. Can you talk about why that is so concerning, and why we need to be at 90 percent? I mean, to me, especially in Iowa, this is a huge issue.

Mrs. BLOOMFIELD. Thank you for the question, and thank you for your leadership in the introduction of the Rural Broadband Modernization Act (H.R. 3964). It is a very important piece of legislation which also does kind of go to the 100 symmetrical speed. When you talk about 50 percent, and you set that standard, most of the Federal programs, ReConnect, BEAD, all of these programs, Treasury look at that 80 to 90 percent coverage as kind of the basis.

Problem with 50 percent is you are really encouraging overbuilding. And we have talked about when you have scarce resources, the ability, because we are all so focused on unserved Americans, to make sure that any money goes as far as possible, the ability to overbuild in using government resources, to overbuild government resources, really becomes duplicative efforts that are just wasteful. So that 50 percent is way too low, and I think leads to a lot of issues.

Mr. FEENSTRA. Yes. I agree 100 percent, Mrs. Bloomfield, and thank you for noting that. I mean, we have to be at 90 percent, and I agree 100 percent. Thank you so much for your comments. And I yield back.

The CHAIRMAN. I thank the gentleman for yielding back. I now recognize Congresswoman Salinas from Oregon for 5 minutes.

Ms. SALINAS. Thank you, Mr. Chairman, and thank you to the— you and the Ranking Member for holding this important hearing, and thank you to all the witnesses for staying with us for this long. So, as we have talked about, Congress has essentially allocated billions of dollars to build-out broadband capacity for our unserved and underserved areas across the country, including mine in Oregon. Where my concern lies is about the ability of our state and local governments and small providers to successfully navigate this huge rollout while keeping track of any ongoing opportunities that USDA might have.

And so one of my top priorities for the farm bill, especially as I am talking to my communities, is really ensuring that we are providing that robust technical assistance to ensure that our rural communities can easily access Federal programs. And I will start with Congressman Matheson. Does the existing Broadband Technical Assistance Program provide that adequate assistance to help our rural utilities, co-ops, and small businesses access that Federal funding?

Mr. MATHESON. Yes. Yes, I think you have raised a fair question. I do think the program's adequate, actually. I think that people have access to enough information to make these decisions. These are capital-intensive decisions people make to go into this business. They should not take it lightly. Many of my members, through electric cooperatives, are actually hiring some third party entities to help them do their feasibility analysis on the front-end to try to make the good decisions that go into this. I don't see where there is a huge gap right now, in terms of what you are asking.

Ms. SALINAS. Thank you. And then for—the follow-up, for anyone who might want to answer, how should we be thinking about removing any barriers to access for these smaller providers that don't necessarily have the same resources as some of the bigger players?

Mr. ASSEY. Well, I will take a shot. I think one of the things— and we represent large and small companies, but one of the things really goes to what we talked about earlier, and the fact that Agriculture has tremendous expertise in rural America. They have a very capable Administrator in Administrator Burke. But this really requires a whole of government type of approach to the problem, and we have to figure out a way to promote greater consistency and greater coordination in how we apply for these programs where we can. It makes little sense to me to have—to be able to have to fill out a form one way for a grant in one agency and have to do it—completely different way in another agency.

Ms. SALINAS. Yes.

Mr. ASSEY. We ought to be trying to make it easy to get more providers into the system that are experienced and that can do the job.

Ms. SALINAS. Thank you. Does anybody else wish to comment?

Mrs. BLOOMFIELD. I will just say, one of the things that I think there can be a role somewhere in here is thinking about—when you think about those local municipalities, or those anchor institutions that really have that need, I think creating the opportunity for collaboration, and thinking about—and can USDA play that central point of—if you have an area that is really tough to serve, what can you do about bringing providers together? What can you do about connecting a municipality with a broadband provider who knows how to do the service. How about NTCA rural broadband provider along with an electric cooperative?

How do you think about, in some of those really tough to serve areas, where you just can't make a market case for doing so, what is the role of some of these agencies, like USDA, to actually support some collaboration?

Ms. SALINAS. Thank you. And my time has almost expired, but I really do want to get to this. Do we have the tools, through other USDA/NTIA programs to support—and we see a lot of wildfires in Oregon—to support resilient middle-mile infrastructure? And to anyone on the panel who wants to answer.

Mr. MATHESON. Look, I have advocated in my opening statement that I want to make sure that when you—the Committee considers—you look at the next farm bill about—important investment in middle-mile. I think that that is a key factor in creating a platform for last mile broadband service, and I think it is something that USDA has looked at and funded in the past. I think it should be continued in the next farm bill.

Ms. SALINAS. Thank you. I yield back.

The CHAIRMAN. I thank the gentlelady. I now recognize the gentlelady from Texas, Congresswoman De La Cruz, for 5 minutes.

Ms. DE LA CRUZ. Thank you so much, Mr. Chairman, and thank you to all of the witnesses for joining us today and sharing your valuable insight. As we all know, access to high-speed internet is no longer a luxury, but a necessity for economic growth, education, health care, and social connectivity. Unfortunately, many rural communities across our country still lack access to reliable broadband services. This digital divide has created significant disparities in economic opportunities, educational outcome, and healthcare access between urban and rural communities. It is important that Americans, regardless of where they live, have access to reliable and affordable broadband services.

My question is, first, for Mr. James Assey, Executive Vice President here for The Internet and Television Association, what improvements should we consider to USDA broadband programs to make broadband infrastructure grant programs more accessible, flexible, and locally-led?

Mr. ASSEY. Thank you for the question. As I stated in my testimony, I think one of the things that it is most important is for there to be kind of a review of the processes by which we attract eligible providers to make sure that we are taking stock of the different corporate profile and organizations that we have in attracting applicants. I also think it is important that we review and put limits on the types of scoring priorities that our U.S. gives, and when those aren't related to an entity's experience, or the performance of the network, or the need of the particular area, we should get rid of those, because what we really want to do is find who can provide the best solution at the cheapest price for the area of need. So I think those are two important places to start.

The last thing I think is very important is that we get back, as has been stated earlier, to really focusing the distribution of dollars to the areas that are unserved so that we make sure we are getting the most bang for the buck that we can.

Ms. DE LA CRUZ. Thank you. And, Mrs. Bloomfield, we continue to hear from stakeholders about struggles with USDA's lengthy approval process for broadband loan applicants. In your testimony you highlight the delay of Federal funding to entities due to historical preservation requirements and environmental reviews. What specific improvements should Congress consider to streamline the application process?

Mrs. BLOOMFIELD. It is a wonderful question, because I think it is kind of the secret obstacle that nobody really knows about. So when I think of some of my companies who were actually awarded funding as far back as 2019 who have yet to see the money flowing into the field, I think that obstacle of not getting that process moving through quickly enough is really holding up a lot of infrastructure deployment.

So I would say there are a couple of things. I think some recent legislation, hopefully, is looking to streamline it. But I also think that if you have gone through a process where an area has been deemed previously disturbed, where you have already gone through the historicals, and now you are going back to deploy additional infrastructure, you have already gone through those steps. So doing it a second time I think really further holds it back. But it is a very important point, and something we need to ensure that, as you do the farm bill, that there is more streamlining available.

Ms. DE LA CRUZ. So what I am hearing is that if they have already done the research, or the analysis, for a prior application, perhaps?

Mrs. BLOOMFIELD. Exactly, and previous construction, but they still have to go back through it additionally for a new construction, whether you are building further out, you are upgrading existing infrastructure. So once you have already approved it, let us move on.

Ms. DE LA CRUZ. Right. Sounds like a waste of time, materials, and money, is what it sounds like.

Mrs. BLOOMFIELD. And it becomes expensive, because with inflation, honestly, the longer the delays go, you may have gotten a grant 3 years ago, but the cost, between labor supply and the supply of the actual infrastructure, has gone up significantly. So suddenly you are in a position where you actually got that award in 2019, and now your cost to build what you committed to build to has gone up exponentially.

Ms. DE LA CRUZ. Absolutely. That can pose a big problem. Thank you so much. Mr. Chairman, I yield back.

The CHAIRMAN. The gentlelady yields back. I am now pleased to recognize another gentlelady from Texas, Congresswoman Crockett, for 5 minutes.

Ms. CROCKETT. Thank you so much, Mr. Chairman, and to all the witnesses for your time. I am glad to hear that so many Members are talking about what we all know, which is that reliable access to the internet is a non-negotiable these days. Yet, sadly enough, there is a fringe group that believes we have done everything that we needed to do and should go no further. But tell me, how can we have accomplished our goal when over ten million Americans still don't have access to broadband?

For decades we let rural Americans fall farther and farther behind. Without reliable internet access, it is harder to find a job, harder to share special moments with your family, and ultimately people are robbed of opportunities. Finally we are lending folk a helping hand. But just as broadband is starting to be deployed, our colleagues on the Agriculture Appropriation Subcommittee want to cut broadband funding by almost $100 million. It seems some of my colleagues believe we have done enough, and, after an initial investment, we need to just pack up and go home. So let me set the record straight.

Mrs. Bloomfield, you make a excellent point about healthcare in your testimony. Could you expand upon the importance of telehealth access in communities, and maybe talk a little bit more about other important use cases?

Mrs. BLOOMFIELD. I would be more than happy to. It is something near and dear to my heart because I think it is an application that we have only just scratched the surface of. And to your point about USDA, and all of these other programs, I will say, as we look at all this Federal funding coming down, I encourage my members to look at ReConnect, the USDA program, first because I do think it is that immediate opportunity with a very well run program.

So we partner a lot with the National Rural Health Association, and we have been working in collaboration to talk about what it takes to build smart rural communities. Healthcare is really a foundation. If you don't have access to healthcare in these communities, you find that people don't move there. It is one of those things people look for. So really thinking through what we could do more aggressively to not just build the right networks to ensure that you can do healthcare, but how do you get the devices in people's hands? How do you actually do digital literacy so you are educating techs and healthcare clinicians on how to actually manage some of this?

And the thing I will share, that—what we see from our own experience, running a teledoc and other programs as an association, mental health care in rural America is really critical. And there is also a stigma in rural America. People don't want to see their truck outside of a local mental health care clinic. The ability to do mental health care using telemedicine at home, in the comfort of your living room, is powerful. So I think as we look at some of these applications, and what we can do in terms of digital literacy to educate more Americans, and get more Americans online to utilize these resources, I think we are going to have a healthier rural America.

Ms. CROCKETT. I think I will actually skip around on my questions, since you touched on something, which was the ReConnect Program. But I do want to highlight what you are saying. As it was mentioned, I am out of Texas, I am out of urban Texas, but we went through redistricting last cycle, when I was in the Texas House. And when we went through redistricting, what we saw is that rural Texas was bleeding population. And when we talked to people, and they talked about the next generation, they talked about the fact that there just weren't opportunities, and so their children were leaving rural Texas. So we have plenty of land in Texas, and we want to make sure that everyone feels like they have all the opportunities that they need, no matter where they want to live in the State of Texas, so thank you for that.

So I am going to skip to a different question now. As we are considering how to bring the ReConnect Program into the farm bill, I would like to know, specifically from Mr. Matheson, good to see you again, about—I know that you are big on the co-ops, but talk to me about the things—and anyone can feel free to kind of jump in— about opportunities that we see to improve the ReConnect Program.

Mr. MATHESON. Well, I am big on the co-ops, I appreciate you noticing. Look, I think that this program that has had success, but there are opportunities for improvement, and that—it is not a program that has been around too long, so it is good to assess where we can go. Number one, let's get it in the farm bill. It is subject to the annual appropriations process. It ought to be authorized by this Committee and by the Congress. So that would be an important step to create consistency and clarity for the program.

The program should include minimum speeds, 100 up, 100 down, symmetrical, we think, as a criteria. We think that the middle-mile investment matters a lot. It is not the top of mind issue for a lot of folks, but if you don't have robust middle-mile, it is difficult to provide broadband service to rural

America in an adequate, so that ought to be important, probably look at. Look, I think that this Committee's got great opportunity with this farm bill to really make some important steps to establish, ReConnect, and build on the success it has already had.

Ms. CROCKETT. Thank you so much. With that, I will yield back.

The CHAIRMAN. I thank the gentlelady. I now recognize the gentleman from Tennessee, Mr. Rose, for 5 minutes.

Mr. ROSE. Thank you, Chairman Thompson, and thanks to Ranking Member Scott for holding this hearing, and thank you to all of our witnesses for your time and thoughtful attention to today's hearing. I want to talk a bit about the future of telemedicine, and how important it is that we ensure that USDA broadband programs keep up with new technologies. In an article in FORBES entitled, *An Exciting, Surprisingly Imaginative, Techy Vision Of Telemedicine's Future,** author Michelle Greenwald, who is the CEO of Catalyzing Innovation, described some potentially game-changing advances in telemedicine.

Ms. Greenwald describes the possibility of remote monitoring devices for use at home, such as a stethoscope, or a device for looking in the ear, nose, and throat. These readings could be digitally transmitted to the doctor to interpret. Additionally, Ms. Greenwald's article brings up the possibility of using artificial intelligence, machine learning, and pattern recognition to potentially flag serious illnesses, all from an image of a patient.

In the not too distant future we could be living in a world where AI flags a potentially serious illness during a telemedicine visit that otherwise may not have been diagnosed. What really scares me is the possibility that many Americans will not be able to utilize these life-saving technologies because they don't have access to broadband that is strong enough, fast enough, to support these emerging telehealth technologies. Mrs. Bloomfield, as the CEO of NTCA—The Rural Broadband Association, can you talk about the ways in which USDA rural broadband programs help to support access to telehealth technologies?

Mrs. BLOOMFIELD. Absolutely, and thank you for the question. So, as we look at the statistics about the number of rural hospitals that are closing on a regular basis, I think the ability to look at the evolution of telemedicine is going to be really important. So you hit on a few of them. We also see in rural America the ability to monitor your diabetes, your cardiac care, some of those

* Editor's note: the article referred to is located on p. 89.

things that are really pretty prevalent in rural populations is going to be important.

And I think another application to be thinking about, and that will need some of this capacity and bandwidth, are things like how do we allow seniors to age in place in their homes? The ability to monitor has our mother taken her pills, because you have the sensor that actually reads some of these things. I don't even think we have scratched the surface on the different things that we can do. So USDA, with their program, has some additional support on the telehealth side. I think it is getting folks comfortable with some of the technology, but you absolutely need the bandwidth. And the other thing that we find with rural communities, where I think the bandwidth, and the ability to transport whatever type of medical technology you are transporting, is the expert care that you get in some more urban hospitals. If you have something that's complex that you can't deal with in a rural clinic, that you actually need to go into Mayo, or you need to have that access.

The other thing that I will say is we think a lot about privacy when we think about healthcare. And it is another reason why, again, remaining technology-neutral, I think fiber optics is a really important technology to look at because, when you think about cybersecurity, the pulses of light that move through fiber are actually harder to intercept. So when we think about security of networks, and, again, when I think about healthcare, and all of that private data, that's another thing that I think is really important, and I think that's where USDA has a role as they fund some of these programs like ReConnect.

Mr. ROSE. Thank you. And, I am going to use the remaining time to prompt each of you on this question. We are here today talking about the farm bill USDA programs as it relates to rural broadband, but I have been of the opinion for a long time, living in a rural area, that we simply have to think about this in an ongoing, holistic manner, and that the money that we are sending through USDA, and even the COVID-era money, doesn't really address the fundamental challenge that we face as a country of building-out broadband infrastructure that reaches all Americans, and then maintaining it over time so that we know we are always going to be on the cutting edge.

And my own view is that we found a solution to that decades ago, but we haven't made the changes to keep it up to date, and that is the Universal Service Fund. And I am curious—probably not time for it—all of you to respond, but would anyone like to dive onto that question and tell me, am I wrong or am I right that we need to address the Universal Service Fund to make sure that it is providing the resources to keep America wired with broadband access?

Mrs. BLOOMFIELD. I hate to be a microphone hog, but I will tell you, hit on a really important—it is not just building these networks, it is making them sustainable and affordable, and Universal Service is key. Yes, we need to reform contribution reform.

Mr. ROSE. And, I know my time has expired, but I would appreciate for the record comments from the rest of you about that question. Thank you.**

Mr. MATHESON. I agree with Ms. Bloomfield as well.

Mr. ROSE. I——

Mr. BAIRD [presiding.] Next we have Mr. Gluesenkamp Perez from Washington.

Ms. PEREZ. Thank you, Mr. Chairman. We know that access to high-speed internet is essential to participating in the economy, including telehealth and telework. That's why it is so important that the bipartisan infrastructure law provided almost $2 billion for the ReConnect Program. In fact, last week—in one of my counties, Lewis County, was awarded—$24.2 million ReConnect grant. And this money will be used to deploy a fiber network and make high-speed internet available to 2,863 people, 119 businesses, 487 farms, and four educational facilities. And this will serve an area in which 91 percent of residents do not currently have access to adequate broadband. And right—this all hit really close to home during the pandemic. You can't attend online school if you don't have internet. So I am thrilled that these dollars are getting to where they need to be.

Mrs. Bloomfield, you state in your testimony that what matters most to rural America is not the mere deployment of network, but the quality of the service they receive. And I am agreeing with you, but I also wonder, how do we balance that pursuit of quality, pursuing quality, when we still have so many places that don't have access at all?

Mrs. BLOOMFIELD. Well, first, congratulations to Whidbey, who received that USDA grant, which I think is going to go really far. I think some of these Federal programs can also be looked at as complimentary, right? Because we have BEAD coming out in 2024, and they are really focusing primarily on getting the unserved done first. So I think that all of these programs kind of fit together, and I think about—it is one of the reasons why I am pretty adamant about, like, let's not dumb down what we have with ReConnect at the 100/100, because I think complimentarily we are going to

---

** Editor's note: the responses to the information referred to are located: for Mr. Assey, on p. 93; Mr. Zumwalt, on p. 93; Mr. Stroup, on p. 94; and Mr. Hurley, on p. 95.

have NTIA's program coming in—really filling in those unserved pockets as well. I think the two programs should work very well together.

Ms. PEREZ. And following up on that, in many rural communities like mine there will only be one internet provider. So what are we going to ensure that these resources remain affordable, and we haven't created an untenable situation?

Mrs. BLOOMFIELD. Trying to spur competition in markets where you can't even have one provider without getting Federal support really makes it tough to actually subsidize competition in these areas, so I think that there are going to be a lot of checks and balances along the way. Washington State, for example, has a pretty robust State Broadband Office. In thinking through the affordability programs, thinking through the digital education programs, I think all of those things packaged together are really going to be an important part of ensuring that you get unserved served, but then you are also able to kind of ensure that you are utilizing the networks to the best capability.

Ms. PEREZ. Yes. Thank you. Mr. Assey, in your testimony you talk about some of the potential fixes that could be made to better ensure that the ReConnect Program is able to serve the most rural and unserved or underserved areas. I am wondering if you could elaborate on some of the current challenges, on some of the potential changes you would like to see made?

Mr. ASSEY. Sure, and thank you for your leadership on the Rural Internet Improvement Act as well. I think chief among them is to ensure that the funding goes to the projects just like the one you mentioned, where we have 90 percent of the households that are going to be reached are those that actually are the most in need of being reached. So making sure that the dollars are used efficiently is probably chief among them. I do think we need to modernize the eligibility screens, and the way in which the agencies attract eligible and experienced participants so that we get qualified applicants who are willing to provide service.

I think we need to, again, refocus the way in which a lot of these applications are scored to make sure that we are not giving priority just to companies based on who they are, but we are actually focused on what they can perform and execute on in building these networks. And last, we just need to really promote coordination with the FCC, with NTIA, with state governments, because this really is going to be a case in which the holistic approach and working together is going to be better than the sum of the parts.

Ms. PEREZ. Thank you all so much. And—yes?

Mr. STROUP. I would like to respond to the question that you raised about competition.

Ms. PEREZ. Yes?

Mr. STROUP. There are at least three companies in the satellite industry providing direct to consumer broadband services in competition with all of the other industries that are represented here. Another one will be launching within the next couple years, and others that are providing partnership with rural telco companies. So there are a variety of means of providing that competition.

Ms. PEREZ. Thank you so much for that additional point. And, Mr. Chairman, I yield back. Thank you.

Mr. BAIRD. Yes. Mr. Nunn, from Iowa, please.

Mr. NUNN. Thank you, Mr. Chairman, and thank you very much for the panel being here today, specifically for the help that we need in rural Iowa. I was just in Des Moines, Iowa yesterday, at Mercy One Hospital talking with a nurse as she was talking to me—or—conversation with a patient who was getting their update as they went. We can see, even during that quick conversation, from a metropolitan area to a very rural area, how challenging it was based on latency *versus* the amount of times we dropped and were interrupted, *versus* trying to keep that patient engaged.

Now, if that patient had a critical issue, it had been one of our veterans who needed assistance, if it had been somebody who had a life-saving recommendation coming from their physician unable to have that communication, think we—put us all in a very dangerous spot. The alternative was that patient could have driven 21⁄2 hours to Des Moines to try and get the assistance they needed. A single mother, leaving their job, coming to Des Moines, when at the same time somebody in a community right next door had unparalleled access to it.

Which gets me to my concern that my home state right now is 45th in the nation for broadband access and is the second lowest speeds. So at a topical level, yes, are we covered? But is it an effective use of the internet? Absolutely not. To fix this, I have introduced a bipartisan ReConnecting Rural America Act of 2023 (H.R. 4227), alongside many of my colleagues in this room. We think it is very important to become part of the farm bill conversation. Our bill would make permanent the ReConnect Program and expand broadband access to increase speeds in rural America.

Now, Mr. Assey, I know that you feel differently than I do on this, and I think that we can get to a point where we can help a lot of these folks. But my concern here is that if you have ever tried to plant precision agriculture with a delayed speed, you are losing crop. If you are a person in immediate medical need, and you have a delayed speed, it is almost like having no internet at all. Or if you are just an individual who's trying to improve their education and you have latency here, whether it is an urban area or a rural area, you are being left behind. And I think we all agree that's unacceptable.

So I would like to speak specifically here to Mrs. Bloomfield on your comments, as well as Mr. Matheson, the 100 up, 100 down and the robust middle-mile. Now, how would you respond to the difference between no access, or delayed access, or diminished access? Because, in my mind, they are all not enough access for what's necessary. Mrs. Bloomfield, I will start with you.

Mrs. BLOOMFIELD. So you—first of all, thank you for your leadership, and thank you for the legislation that you have introduced. It is very important, I think sets the future stage on the right course. So when you reference latency, I will just share that when you talk about the livestock, we have a lot of folks who actually run livestock sales. You have just lost the ability to either purchase or sell something if you are not being able to do it in real time.

I think all of that—and when you look at the symmetrical speeds that you set in your legislation, it is really to ensure that rural Americans aren't second class citizens, that they are able to receive the same robust services that those in urban areas of the country receive, and I think that is a critical reset for this country.

Mr. NUNN. I would like to turn further—thank you. Mr. Matheson, on the ReConnect side, for our broadband networks, *versus* just keeping what I would call low grade infrastructure, everything in the future, from our combines, to our refrigerator, to our medical devices are going to be connected to this. Talk to me about the long-term needs of rural communities and how broadband highspeed is going to be essential for this.

Mr. MATHESON. Yes. Appreciate—again, I will echo—I appreciate your leadership on this legislation that you have introduced. Look, we all know that the internet and use of broadband is only increasing, in terms of—it affects every aspect of our lives in rural America. There have been challenges. The pandemic helped highlight some of those challenges when it came to work at home, when it came to school at home, when it came to access to healthcare. And so I don't think we need to make that case. I think that is settled, that we all agree there is value in having access to real broadband.

And I appreciate your comment about the difference between the fully served or underserved or not served. And I made some comments earlier about the fact that—let's be careful about simplistic description of unserved *versus* underserved.

Mr. NUNN. Right.

Mr. MATHESON. It is not that simple.

Mr. NUNN. Right.

Mr. MATHESON. And that—while unserved clearly deserve service, the underserved do too, if it is not adequate.

Mr. NUNN. And let's not leave them behind on that. I appreciate that.

Mr. MATHESON. Absolutely.

Mr. NUNN. I know that's where we all want to get to ultimately.

Mr. MATHESON. Yes.

Mr. NUNN. Mr. Hurley, I am going to change topics, very quickly ask you, as a guy who served in cybersecurity for quite a while, as we roll out this new infrastructure, talk to us specifically about the vital equipment that's essential so that we can maintain good hygiene throughout the network.

Mr. HURLEY. Yes. I think, as you look at the technology that's coming on, and the connectedness of it, I would encourage this Committee, when you think about cybersecurity, think about food security and ag security, because—and I would equate that to national security. Because today, and all these gentlemen and ladies do their job, we become more connected. We have—it is not just a single tractor, it is not a planter, it is a sprayer, or a hog house, or a poultry farm. They are all connected, and can all be vulnerable, and we need to give that the focus that it deserves.

Mr. NUNN. Thank you, Mr. Chairman. My time has expired. I yield back, and I appreciate all the ag references in today's hearing as well. Thank you.

Mr. BAIRD. Thank you. The gentleman yields back. And now we go to Illinois with Representative Budzinski.

Ms. BUDZINSKI. Thank you, Mr. Chairman, and thank you Ranking Member, and thank you to the panelists. I appreciated your testimony and the discussion that's happened so far. I am really building on that. I wanted to make a note, I am the former Chairwoman of the Illinois Broadband Advisory Council. This is a topic that is very near and dear to my heart, as it is, I know, to many of us on this Committee. And very important—more importantly to my constituents that I represent in central and southern Illinois.

I really believe we are on the precipice of true generational change in this space, where we can finally capture underserved areas, and rural communities will no longer have to settle, which I think we all want to see. This is why it is important to set our sights high, and ensure that all residents have access to quality, affordable, high performance internet and cell phone access at home.

The 2018 Farm Bill amended the Rural Broadband Program to require 90 percent of residents in proposed service areas be without—in a proposed service area be without sufficient access to broadband or unserved to be eligible for grant funding, and a 50 percent unserved requirement to be eligible for loans. Prior to the 2018 Farm Bill, the Rural Broadband Program required just 15 percent of households in a proposed service area be unserved. I agree that our first priority should be to deliver services to areas most in need, but I also strongly believe that the introduction of unnecessary and unprecedented program rigidity does not serve rural Americans, or our goal of closing the digital divide.

Furthermore, as we get closer to 100 percent nationwide connectivity, it is critical, I believe, that USDA have the necessary flexibility to reach those final communities. So my first question, actually, is for Mr. Matheson. With the historic broadband infrastructure investments made over these last several years, wouldn't it make more sense to add more program flexibility in order to reach every part of rural America? What are your thoughts on the flexibilities that will be necessary for the USDA's broadband programs to address as we get closer to 100 percent nationwide connectivity? And maybe you could connect this to under—the underserved donut hole issue as well.

Mr. MATHESON. Yes. Look, one thing that is often said in the electric co-op world is when you met one electric co-op, you met one electric co-op.

Ms. BUDZINSKI. Thanks.

Mr. MATHESON. They pride themselves on—they are in a unique circumstance. Everyone is different.

Ms. BUDZINSKI. Yes.

Mr. MATHESON. And so adding that flexibility you mentioned to accommodate specific areas——

Ms. BUDZINSKI. Right.

Mr. MATHESON.—in terms of what the needs are and the circumstances, of course that makes sense, particularly as we are trying to fill in these gaps, which are the hardest ones to fill.

Ms. BUDZINSKI. Yes.

Mr. MATHESON. That's why they are still unserved today.

Ms. BUDZINSKI. Yes.

Mr. MATHESON. And so I think that flexibility is all the more important now than perhaps it was previously, because of the nature of the task at hand. That being said, I also think it is important that we—that the flexibility—to not allow specific parameters to shut people out. If you are in an area where

50 percent have access to broadband and 50 percent don't, you say, well, too bad for that 50 who don't we are defining that as one block of area.

Ms. BUDZINSKI. Right.

Mr. MATHESON. When what happens is the economics go—the 50 percent who have it are probably in the high population density areas, where there is money to be made and the folks out in the low population density areas are left out. And if they are coupled into one category, and we just looked at it through that frame, they are never going to get service, right?

Ms. BUDZINSKI. Right.

Mr. MATHESON. So that's the argument—that's an example where that flexibility matters.

Ms. BUDZINSKI. Okay. Thank you very much. And just to add onto that—so building out broadband infrastructure in rural America must account for the needs of every facet of rural areas. I believe households, farms, businesses, and anchor institutions— though adequate for many households, a recent GAO report found that 25/3 is likely just to be too slow to meet the speed needs of many small businesses. Many small businesses and farms reported wanting download speeds of up to at least 100, and as—as did the Connect Illinois—excuse me, the Connect Illinois Broadband Grant Program that we helped to launch.

So one quick question in my last less than 60 seconds, Mrs. Bloomfield, do you think that 25/3 is sufficient broadband access? What factors should we take into consideration when determining the speed minimum?

Mrs. BLOOMFIELD. I would just note, for example, this hearing room itself is 126/113, I believe. So, if you look at 25/3, you are saying you are willing to give rural Americans a standard that is lower than you have in this hearing room to transmit this hearing. So I think we have just grown beyond. I think, as—everybody on this Committee has been talking about applications with healthcare, and, having served on the Illinois Advisory Board, you know all of the different applications, whether it is agriculture, economic development, I think that speed is something that—it—we are beyond that.

And, again, when I think about the fact that I have companies, Country Fiber in South Carolina just shared that 1⁄3 of their customers take their gig service. We are there. We are not just looking at it, we are there. So——

Ms. BUDZINSKI. Thank you very much, and I yield back the rest of my time.

Mr. BAIRD. Thank you. The gentlelady yields back. And next we have Representative Molinaro from New York.

Mr. MOLINARO. Thank you, Mr. Chairman. I appreciate the witnesses, and I come from a part of New York where this continues to be a significant challenge. And, despite the influx of significant Federal, and even state funding, we continue to experience not only deep challenges, but a shortage in workforce and the challenge of expanding job opportunities. So workforce availability is one of the items that we have been focusing on.

Last year the GAO published a report indicating that over 30,000 additional telecom workers are needed to deploy high-speed internet infrastructure on a scale that matches the recent funding levels. And, Mr. Matheson, although—do we call you Congressman still?

Mr. MATHESON. Call me whatever you want.

Mr. MOLINARO. Jim, I know that you and your organization have had a long history of trained skill workers out into rural communities.

Mr. MATHESON. Yes.

Mr. MOLINARO. Could you speak to what you observe are the causes of the workforce shortage, and what tools maybe we might consider to open up those job opportunities?

Mr. MATHESON. Yes. It is a timely question. And while it is not unique to the telecom fiber space, or even the electric utility space, I think we have seen workforce shortages hitting a lot of segments of the economy. But in this place, where we are talking about the significant infusion of Federal money to make these investments, this is one of the potential trip hazards, if you will for being effective, and we are feeling that.

Mr. MOLINARO. Yes.

Mr. MATHESON. We are feeling that in terms of finding qualified technicians, qualified people to do the construction, the operations. Again, not unique to the telecom sector, but it is important. I know, for our local electric cooperatives, they are trying to partner with local community colleges, trying to find other partnerships to develop and train people, and create the workforce of the future. But I can tell you, we haven't found the secret sauce that fixes this yet, and I do think that it is an issue that merits some consideration at the Federal level about what we can do to encourage folks to go into these fields to meet these workforce needs.

Mr. MOLINARO. Yes. I think we have undervalued this kind of work. We certainly have diminished its presence in public education, and, frankly, have encouraged people to only learn in a particular way when we should be expanding those opportunities.

Mr. MATHESON. Right.

Mr. MOLINARO. Mrs. Bloomfield, I just wanted to turn to some of the obstacles we—I know that we are facing in New York in particular. We held a roundtable recently with some of our service providers. We are not even—in New York, in my part of the state, it is not the last mile, it is not the donut hole. I mean, it is truly, like, 50′. I mean, we are talking about making the last connection in very small numbers.

The challenges that many of them face, the providers in particular, are costs related to redundancy and bureaucracy, both state and Federal, but also, then, the make-ready costs for pole access, working with public utilities. These are real challenges that I don't think we look at with great detail because they are fine—they are sort of granular, but I hear more and more that that's the last challenge. Can you speak to how those impediments have kept access—or expanding access, and then what have others done to overcome them? And what might we do to streamline that process?

Mrs. BLOOMFIELD. They are very real. When I think about pole attachments, I think about railroad crossings, I think about local barriers, local permitting, everybody kind of—you kind of go through your different pounds of flesh, you go through the process. So I do think there is something to be said for—from a Federal perspective, looking at some streamlining. I also think that a lot of things that can be done when you think about, like there is, going through Forest Service land, and working with municipalities in these State Broadband Offices to say what can they do? How do you trickle down from the Federal Government to minimize some of those barriers that folks are seeing on the local ground?

And if I could just jump in one last point, because I do think it ties to broadband, we think a lot about workforce development, particularly in rural communities, because, again, you have fewer folks to actually choose from. We have actually been working with our companies on—we produced a guide for—K through 12 guides to careers in broadband, getting kids to understand this is a great career, this is a great path forward.

And, frankly, if you look at your gamers—we may talk about different applications here today, your gamers—my companies that sponsor their e-sport teams, that is their future—those are their future technicians. Those are their future IT folks.

Mr. MOLINARO. Yes.

Mrs. BLOOMFIELD. So watching that evolution, using broadband networks to do something kids love to actually groom that workforce is something we are really very focused on.

Mr. MOLINARO. I thank you for saying that. And I will say perhaps establishing timelines, and sort of specific expectations for states to move or remove some of those access obstacles, if you will, tied to Federal dollars might incentivize them. I have 10 seconds. I just would say you bring up one point, there is a labor force, those with disabilities, who rarely have access to jobs. Eighty percent are unemployed. The gaming space is a space that creates a level playing field for those individuals to learn and access your workforce, and it would be something that we should pay attention to. Thank you, Mr. Chairman.

Mr. BAIRD. And the gentleman yields back, and next we go to Mr. Sorensen from Illinois.

Mr. SORENSEN. I would like to begin by thanking the Chairman and Ranking Member for convening this important hearing, and our witnesses for your testimony. I know it is getting into the afternoon. I really appreciate you sticking through this. I am proud to represent northwestern and central Illinois, where we have farming, urban, and rural constituents. Many of our constituents face the challenge of per—poor quality broadband. They have service that meets the definition of *broadband* set by the FCC, but the service is not sufficient to meet their needs.

Yesterday, I introduced the bipartisan ReConnecting Rural America Act, along with my colleagues in this Committee, Representative Nunn from Iowa, Representative Craig from Minnesota, along with Representative LaHood. This bill sets standards to target broadband investment to unserved and underserved communities. The approach my bill takes will ensure that underserved constituents can benefit from ReConnect grants and loans, just like unserved constituents.

Currently broadband providers can access ReConnect funds to service areas that are 50 percent unserved. Now, my bill increases the standard to 75 percent, with minimum service speeds of 100 up—or 100 down and 20 up, with a preference for service areas with 90 percent unserved. And, finally, the bill sets mandatory build-out speeds, what we have been talking about here today, 100 by 100 symmetrical. I am thankful, Mrs. Bloomfield, you mentioned that in your opening statement today, so I will begin with you. Could you speak to why this standard needs to be met?

Mrs. BLOOMFIELD. There are so many reasons the standard needs to be met, but I would also—I think I would start off with the fact that, again, it is looking at current usage, current network capacity, and really thinking about—making sure that we build for what we need right now, but also what we need in a few years from now. And so I think the ability to say, we are not going to get this type of funding again, so let's make sure that what we are not doing is turning around in 3 years, and digging back up, and looking to upload the speeds, and increase the speeds. Let's go ahead and ensure that we are putting what is probably the most logical target in place as a start. So, again, we commend you for your leadership, and think that there are so many things in your piece of legislation that are actually very commendable.

Mr. SORENSEN. Thank you for that. I plan to introduce the House version of the Access to Capital Creates Economic Strength and Supports Rural America Act, or the ACCESS Rural America Act (H.R. 4360), alongside Representative Tiffany, and Senators Baldwin and Ernst. The bicameral and bipartisan bill will provide regulatory relief to small rural broadband providers, allowing them to focus on delivering broadband to the most remote areas of our country.

So, if I could continue, Mrs. Bloomfield, could you share with the Committee some of the potential impact of this, and also maybe some of the stresses that we see in the rollout of rural broadband?

Mrs. BLOOMFIELD. So this is an area where your leadership is really important, because I will say that when we think about Sarbanes-Oxley, it was put in place because of large corporate interests, large publicly traded companies.

Mr. SORENSEN. Right.

Mrs. BLOOMFIELD. My members are community-based providers, but if you have a commercial company that is locally held, they maybe have 490 shareholders, and somebody in the family decides to gift to somebody else in the family some of their shares, suddenly you hit 500, and all of these requirements from the SEC kick in. That is hundreds of thousands of dollars a year annually in terms of things that you need to file that are compliance oriented. Then you need to get auditors, and then you need to get lawyers.

And, again, what is—the regs are understandable, but they are really meant for publicly traded companies, and what they are doing in some of these small towns is they are really having people focus spending money and dealing with these regulations, rather— and reporting, and reporting, and reporting, rather than actually being able to build the broadband.

Mr. SORENSEN. Yes.

Mrs. BLOOMFIELD. So, we greatly appreciate your introduction of the legislation.

Mr. SORENSEN. Thank you for that. Mr. Stroup, you mentioned in your testimony the need to incentivize satellite internet providers. In the past there have been concerns for providing Federal funds for satellite internet, given the limitations to the technology. With technological advancements, and the introduction of low-Earth orbit satellite networks, have those concerns for satellite network capacity changed?

Mr. STROUP. Thank you for the question, and I think that they certainly have. Given the advances in satellite technology, the everincreasing speeds, the ever-increasing capacity—as I had mentioned in my testimony, companies are providing speeds up to 200 megabits per second. They continue to launch additional satellites just to—and in—10 years ago there were 1,000 satellites. Today there are approximately 8,000 satellites, just to give you a sense of the expansion in the numbers of satellites in the same capability. Ten years ago the speeds were much different than they are today. So I think that that's an argument—a relic of the past, quite frankly.

Mr. SORENSEN. As the Ranking Member on the Space Subcommittee, I appreciate you here, and there, and I yield back the balance of my time.

Mr. BAIRD. Thank you. And then we go to the very patient Representative Van Orden from Wisconsin.

Mr. VAN ORDEN. Thank you, Mr. Chairman. I would like to acknowledge some of my constituents in the back from Grant County. I appreciate you showing up, very much. Mr. Zumwalt, are you related to Admiral Zumwalt?

Mr. ZUMWALT. Yes, I am, distantly.

Mr. VAN ORDEN. All right. He is a good dude. Politicians have been running on providing rural broadband since Al Gore invented the internet, and I want to share with you how broken this system is. And it is not on your side, it is on this side. I want to give you an example here. We have spent, over the last 5 years, $166.6 billion. The private-sector has spent $185 billion. That's $351 billion. This is a penny. See the penny? Look at it sideways. If you were to stack up 351 billion pennies, it would reach almost 11⁄2 times to the Moon, and 13.3 times around the Earth.

Speaking of the Moon, in 1961 John F. Kennedy said, "We are going to go to the Moon." Eight years later, a man stepped on the Moon, Neil Armstrong. I met him. Another good dude. That cost $257 billion. So for two—that's inflation adjusted dollars. It cost $257 billion to put a man on the Moon, 8 years after John F. Kennedy said we are going to do it. We have spent $351 billion in the last 5 years, and I can't do precision agriculture, going from Crawford to Grant County, where those people are from. This is a stent—a systemic failure of this system. I work with all my rural co-ops. I am good with all you cats. I want to ask you one question. When is the last time you all sat together in a room? When?

Mr. MATHESON. Well, some of us sit——

Mr. VAN ORDEN. No.

Mr. MATHESON. All of——

Mr. VAN ORDEN. When's the last time all of you sat in a room?

Mr. MATHESON. Well, all six of us have never done that.

Mr. VAN ORDEN. Yes.

Okay. Guess what? I am planting a flag this morning. I am appointing myself in charge of this. I am formally inviting all of you to sit in my office and talk about things, regardless of how you provide services. So right now you can Netflix and chill, and smoke check a Russian check in Bakhmut, Ukraine, right? And my combine, it can't do precision agriculture in Grant County. That's wrong, okay? So I am formally inviting all of you to my office. Leave your jerseys at the door, and let's fix this problem. Because it ain't about you, it ain't about me, it is about those people in the back of the room. With that, I yield back.

Mr. BAIRD. Thank you. The gentleman yields back. Next we go to Mr. Langworthy. You have 5 minutes.

Mr. LANGWORTHY. Thank you, Mr. Chairman, Mr. Ranking Member. Whether it is managing a vineyard, operating a dairy, broadband access plays a crucial role in supporting our farming operations and initiatives. The nature of running a farm, much like operating a small-to medium-size business, requires reliable and fast internet connectivity to ensure efficient and effective management.

Now, everything from ordering supplies, to monitoring farm data, to managing pesticide use, it is all done using the internet. We can't imagine a local convenience store or a gas station operating without full broadband. Yet, today our farming operations are really no different. Like too many parts of our country, only 75 percent of my district is considered to be *served* by fast, reliable broadband. So while billions of dollars has been made available through new and existing programs to deploy broadband infrastructure, I share the goal of many of my colleagues here today to focus these abundant resources first and foremost on the areas that are unserved. And, with that, Mr. Assey, last month I sent a letter, with several of my colleagues here today, to Secretary Vilsack regarding the Rural eConnectivity Pilot Program. We expressed to the Secretary that he prioritizes the pressing issue of connecting unserved rural Americans in bridging the digital divide by keeping the ReConnect Program of the Rural Utilities Service focused on this objective. Unserved households are unserved for a reason. They are often not economically viable for private entities to provide networks there, so those unserved areas require the help of Federal dollars.

And for this reason, we need to ensure that the mission of ReConnect is to serve unserved areas first. This makes certain that the government is overbuilding, and developing competing networks where networks already exist. Like the cafeteria line, we need to make sure everyone is served first, and then, if there is still food left, others can get back in line for seconds, to build their networks to even higher speeds and higher capacities.

I am a little concerned with how new or additional funding for ReConnect and other programs will be adequately and appropriately targeted towards areas that are genuinely unserved. So can you talk a little bit about the importance of prioritizing unserved *versus* underserved areas?

Mr. ASSEY. Sure. And thank you for the question and for the letter. I think what it expresses is consistent with what was the original intent of the program, to really focus on our hardest problems first, because if we don't, things have a way of always trying to get places that may have a larger economic return. And what we have seen in the past is the people that don't have even standard broadband at 25/3 are continually left behind. So I think it is a good reminder, it is a good way to kind of refresh people's focus on the areas that we need to focus on first that are the hardest problems to solve. But, with resources and resolve, I believe they can be solved.

Mr. LANGWORTHY. Well, we certainly have enough resources. Mr. Assey, for the past 2 decades we have seen significant Federal investment in broadband development. And given the influx of all of these funds to build-out internet connectivity, how can we prevent overbuilding and duplication of Federal efforts in funding for the broadband systems?

Mr. ASSEY. I think we have to have consistent standards for the areas that we are trying to serve with Federal dollars. We have to recognize that, no matter how much money that we put into the system to provide support, and I would say necessary support in areas where it is otherwise uneconomic to serve, there is a substantial capital investment that's being made by private companies, and we need to harvest the benefits of competition in order to solve the problem.

Mr. LANGWORTHY. Mr. Matheson, is there anything you would like to add on that topic?

Mr. MATHESON. I am sorry, can you—I couldn't—the door—what did you say again?

Mr. LANGWORTHY. Okay. Is there anything you would like to add on that topic of overbuilding?

Mr. MATHESON. I think that comment I made—it is easy to oversimplify the term *overbuilding,* and *unserved* and *underserved.* I think there is a more nuanced approach we ought to be talking about here. I am concerned about folks that are underserved that are going to be left behind, and it is good enough for them. And in—for rural—it is good enough for rural. I don't buy that. So I understand that unserved are an important priority. I don't think I would summarily reject all unserved as being secondary to that. There is a more nuanced approach that I think this Committee needs to think about as they write the next farm bill.

Mr. LANGWORTHY. Very good. Thank you very much, and I yield back, Mr. Chairman.

Mr. DAVID SCOTT of Georgia [presiding.] Thank you. And now the gentleman from North Carolina, Mr. Davis.

Mr. DAVIS of North Carolina. Thank you so much——

Mr. DAVID SCOTT of Georgia. You are recognized for 5 minutes.

Mr. DAVIS of North Carolina. Thank you so much, Mr. Ranking Member, and to all the witnesses who are here today. In eastern North Carolina, which I represent in the First Congressional District, broadband accessibility is one of the largest roadblocks people face to advance: 42 percent of people in the First Congressional District do not have broadband access. Whether it be in their education, small business, or applying for grants and loans, USDA often tells people in my district that they can go online and apply for the grant. But how can they do that when there is not internet connectivity? That's a big hurdle. That's a comment. I would like to move into a more technical question here and would love to hear from any of the witnesses.

There are a lot of different ways, then, to bring broadband connectivity to rural households. Fiber may work best in one place, but then—increasingly noticed fixed wireless in certain locations. How should USDA consider place-based policies when constructing broadband networks? And I would love to hear from any of the witnesses on this.

Mrs. BLOOMFIELD. I will just jump in and say that I think that you can be technology-neutral, because I do think it is going to take every—you may be serving—you may have a mountain that is tougher to lay fiber to. You may have an area that has line of sight obstruction, which makes fixed wireless a little bit more challenging. But that is where I think there is a real value to USDA setting that speed of 100 symmetrical, because what you are saying is it is about this capacity, it is not about how you actually—what technology you are using to actually bring the technology to the consumer.

Mr. ZUMWALT. I think we can stipulate that Shirley likes 100/ 100, because we have heard this a lot today, and I am certainly not trying to argue against the best that we can do for every American. But when you look at actual streams of data, a Zoom call or a Teams call is about 5 megabits per second. A 4K stream from a streaming service like Netflix is about 5 megabits per second. Gaming is about 5 megabits per second each way. It takes a lot of those to get up to 100/100 in every single location. And if we insist on 100/100 service everywhere, we will have people who are unserved because we will overbuild existing networks that do have service today.

And I think that when we talk about future-proofing, we need to be talking about future-proofing the people of the United States of America, including the people who are unserved today. And that's why we are passionate about making sure that the unserved get served first, and then we can solve for how we get connectivity enhancements along the way.

Mr. STROUP. And, Representative Davis, from the equipment manufacturer's perspective, specifically focused on how do we continue to deploy, and utilize, and reap the benefits of precision ag, our position is strongly that we have to be neutral on the technology because it is going to take all of the different types of technology for us truly to be able to utilize and reap the benefits, whether that is from increasing yields, whether that is reducing fuel usage, all of the advantages that precision technology brings, because it has to be in the middle of the field, it has to be in the barn, and it has to be at—wherever the analytics are being done.

Mr. DAVIS of North Carolina. Yes. Well, let me just ask this question, then. Do we believe we have been neutral so far in the technology?

Mr. ASSEY. Have we been neutral?

Mr. DAVIS of North Carolina. Yes.

Mr. ASSEY. I look to a program like the FCC RDOF Program, where we set a baseline. We obviously don't want to invest in yesterday's technology, but we want to incent the best technology platform we have. Cable is a connectivity company. We offer hybrid fiber/coax solutions, we build fiber networks, we offer wireless solutions. We want to provide whatever the connectivity is that the consumer's going to need in the future.

And what's important is that the technology platforms we build can meet not only the needs of today and tomorrow, but that they are scalable. And we believe that, in the very near future, cable technology is going to make this entire debate moot because we are going to be able to provide multi-gigabit speeds in both directions.

Mr. DAVIS of North Carolina. Well, I greatly appreciate the responses today, and, Mr. Chairman, I do yield back.

Mr. LANGWORTHY [presiding.] Thank you very much. And before we adjourn today, I invite—thank you. And before we adjourn today, I invite Ranking Member Scott to share any closing comments he may have.

Mr. DAVID SCOTT of Georgia. Thank you very much. Lady and gentlemen, this has been an extraordinary hearing at an extraordinary and historic time. We are recognized around the world as having the best, foremost, number one agriculture system in the world. But a lot of that is at stake if we don't connect with ourselves and the rest of the world where we produce our food supply. And that is making what we have to do now a national security issue. No more pussyfooting around. It has got to end. Your testimony here today has opened our eyes up on this Committee to much of what we were only dimly aware.

And thank you for this, but don't stop here. We have just 12 weeks to complete this task of making sure that we don't cut any corners in connecting rural America full speed ahead on the same basis that we have connected urban America. That's where our food supply is. It is—and our food supply is becoming more and more an issue. Precision agriculture, all of the technological benefits that we need to make sure is in our communities where we produce our food. There are worlds and nations who are envious of us. We look at the European Union, who looks at us, and says that they are more interconnected with the internet than the United States. We have to put that to an end.

And so I want to thank Mrs. Shirley Bloomfield, Chief Executive Officer of NTCA—The Rural Broadband Association. Your testimony was most helpful. Thank you. Mr. James Assey, Executive Vice President of NCTA—The Internet and Television Association, you did a masterful job. David Zumwalt, President and CEO of WISPA—The Wireless Internet Service Providers Association. Mr. Tom Stroup, President of the Satellite Industry Association, thank you. Jim Matheson, Chief Executive Officer of National Rural Electric Cooperatives Association, and my friend, and former Member of Congress. We have traveled together, we have worked together. Keep up the good work. And Mr. Bill Hurley, Chair of the Agriculture Sector Board, Association of Equipment Manufacturers, AEM.

You all did a fantastic job, and you saw and heard, from the participation of our Members on both sides of the aisle. We are Republicans and Democrats working in a bipartisan way to make sure we finally cross the Rubicon and establish rural broadband in rural America. God bless you, and thank you for your wisdom, your advice, and please continue to work with us over next 12 weeks. We must get this farm bill done by the end of September, and that's just 3 months away. So our work is ahead for us, and we want you to continue to be involved. And, most importantly, make sure we got the right amount of money so that we don't short circuit our rural communities from having the financial resources to do this job the right way. Thank you.

Mr. LANGWORTHY. Thank you, Ranking Member Scott, and thank you to all our witnesses for their expert testimony here today, and all of your cooperation and time. Under the Rules of this Committee, the record of today's hearing will remain open for 10 calendar days to receive additional material and supplementary written responses from the witnesses to any of the questions posed by a Member. This hearing of the Committee on Agriculture is adjourned.

[Whereupon, at 1:19 p.m., the Committee was adjourned.]

[Material submitted for inclusion in the record follows:]

Submitted Article by Hon. John W. Rose, a Representative in Congress from Tennessee

[*https://www.forbes.com/sites/michellegreenwald/2021/04/06/an-exciting-surpris-ingly-imaginative-techy-vision-of-telemedicines-future/?sh=6fbb57647a03*]

An Exciting, Surprisingly Imaginative, Techy Vision Of Telemedicine's Future

MICHELLE GREENWALD,[30] Contributor, *Corporate Innovation Expert, Systematic, Creative, Product Development*

Apr. 6, 2021, 08:51 a.m. EDT

[30] *https://www.forbes.com/sites/michellegreenwald/.*

Avatar of Dr. Yaa Kumah-Crystal at Vanderbilt University Medical Center to potentially use in future patient interactions. Dr. Yaa Kumah-Crys-al.

Avatars, virtual waiting rooms, virtual scribes, in-home testing devices, "syndromatic" facial analysis using AI and machine learning, screen-sharing, and sentiment analysis . . . There are many exciting innovation possibilities on the horizon that will make telemedicine even more productive, informative, helpful and dare I say fun and personable, than current, in-person doctor visits. Several weeks ago I heard Dr. Yaa Kumah-Crystal, MD MPH, Assistant Professor of Biomedical Informatics at Vanderbilt University Medical Center, speak at the Disruption Lab's excellent series on the Future of Health Care. Dr. Kumah-Crystal defined telehealth as "care unbound by distance, physical location or setting."

While many of the ideas Dr. Kumah-Crystal shared have a long way to go, they paint a picture that's exciting to imagine, and can be instructive and inspiring to a range of industries outside of healthcare. The guiding objective for these ideas is how to make telemedicine even better than current in-person care, in certain instances. While telemedicine visits have been reimbursed by most insurance companies at the same rate as in-person visits since the onset of [COVID] due to restrictions and the need to encourage care, going forward telemedicine may have to prove its comparable worth for insurers to maintain parity payments. What follows are some of the more exciting, creative, effective possibilities Dr. Kumah-Crystal shared.

Screen-Sharing

It can be hard for patients to understand verbal explanations by physicians of their conditions, or through wall-charts or plastic models of body parts in their offices. With screen-sharing, it's easier for doctors to show more still visuals that can be easier for patients to understand, or even short, explanatory videos.

Chart Photos

It can be difficult for physicians to match patient names with what they look like between or before visits. While not a common occurrence, there can be errors in writing prescriptions for the wrong person. What if each person's photo always appeared in their telehealth chart?

Syndromatic Facial Detection Using AI, Machine Learning & Pattern Recognition

One way physicians diagnose is looking at the patient's eyes, face and tongue. AI and Machine Learning benefit from millions of observations, correlations with diseases, and pattern recognition. Using image recognition of the patient, computers have more data points to draw upon than any one physician, and therefore the conclusions can be even more accurate.

Virtual Waiting Rooms

Waiting rooms can be boring and not a great use of a patient's time. What if once a patient was logged in for their appointment, while they were waiting for the doctor online, there was content tailored either to their interests, or even better, relating to the issue they came to see the doctor about.

Remote Monitoring Devices & Virtual House Calls

What if patients had in their homes, simplified yet effective versions of routine monitoring devices normally found in a doctor's office, such as a stethoscope or a device for looking in the ear, nose and throat. These readings could be digitally transmitted to the doctor to interpret.

Sentiment Analysis Based on Facial Expression

The patient experience, while historically not given enough attention, can become easier to assess by analyzing facial expressions in response to each step of their care journey, from filling out forms (even digital ones), to speaking with the doctor, to understanding new terminology, to understanding a bill. Anonymized facial expression analysis could help interested doctors' offices realize what areas of the end-to-end patience experience they most need to improve.

Better Understanding How Patients' Everyday Life Affects Their Health

Imagine how effective it would be for a patient to show their doctor how they organize their medications, the foods they eat, or how they exercise, right from their home. The patient could take the doctor or physical therapist for a virtual tour of their medicine cabinet, their refrigerator or pantry, or their exercise routine.

Avatars

It's been shown that people can feel more comfortable sharing personal things with through avatars of themselves and people they're interacting with. Avatars of doctors can seem more approachable and easier to talk to about difficult subjects. Advances in avatar creation has enabled them to be even more realistic, with movements like raising eyebrows, smiling, and other facial expressions.

Virtual Scribes

Since the advent of electronic medical records, physicians have found themselves spending more and more time, both during and after patient visits, typing notes about the patients' symptoms and condition. It's hard to make eye contact with the patient while doing it. Virtual scribes that use voice recognition to hear and transcribe/diarize the entire conversation, free doctors to make eye contact with patients so they feel they're being paid better attention and getting better care. Patients can then receive a copy of the notes with a patient dictionary or glossary of terms, so they can more easily understand unfamiliar terminology used by the doctor.

Improved Accessibility and Speech Captions

Due to [COVID] concerns and patients and physicians wearing masks in-person or online, the sound can be muffled and patients can't read lips to help decipher the speech. With virtual visits, there could be captions to what was being said to be sure nothing was missed. For hearing impaired patients this is even more essential.

Text Check-Ins between Visits

While there will always be circumstances that require in-person visits, some can be replaced by text check-ins, including photos. Telemedicine is envisioned as only a partial replacement for in-person care. For seniors, the disabled, and individuals without good transportation options, the ability to not have to physically come into an office is not only easier, it can increase medical provider/patient communication, and therefore improve outcomes. This could correlate with a different compensation mechanism that rewards how well the patient does, rather than basing compensation solely on office visit and procedure fees.

Doctor/Patient Portals

With digitized remote monitoring devices like glucose monitors, heart monitors, and scales, doctors can check-in periodically to monitor the data for aberrations that might warrant attention. The software can be programmed to alert the doctor when aberrations occur and is therefore a 24/7 kind of monitoring that's more effective than waiting for a scheduled visit to discover an issue.

Conclusion

We live in a very exciting time for medicine because of the combination of advances in science, technology, creativity, and increased focus on customer experience, speed and efficiency. What's key is bringing together individuals with different expertise to jointly problem solve and imagine more effective processes, independent of legacy procedures and systems.

I've heard Scott Friedman, another speaker at the Disruption Lab series on the Future of Health Care, who is a Professor and Chief of the Division of Liver Diseases at Mount Sinai Hospital in New York (considered by many to be the most innovative medical center in New York), speak about Mount Sinai's new BioMedical Engineering and Imaging Institute. Launched in September 2019, its goal is to develop novel medical inventions in the fields of imaging, nanomedicine, artificial intelligence, robotics, sensors, medical devices, and computer vision technologies that include virtual, augmented, and extended reality. Mount Sinai's pioneering FlexMed medical school program allows applicants to apply who don't have traditional science majors and they're not required to take the MCAT for admission. It encourages a student body with broader set of interests and skills such as engineering, computer science, software engineering, or robotics, that will help graduates create the healthcare of the future.

There's much to be learned by other industries in the way healthcare, due to necessity, is adapting to a post-[COVID], more contactless, more visual, virtual, and data driven world. [COVID] was the accelerant for changes that were long needed, causing us to think sooner, more intensely, broadly, and imaginatively about what the future can hold.

Follow me on Twitter[31] *or* LinkedIn.[32] *Check out my* website[33] *or some of my other work* here.[34]

---

[31] *https://www.twitter.com/CatalyzingInnov.*

[32] *https://www.linkedin.com/in/catalyzinginnovation.*

[33] *http://www.catalyzinginnovation.com/.*

[34] *https://books.apple.com/us/book/catalyzing-innovation/id794016507.*

Submitted Letter by Hon. Nicholas A. Langworthy, a Representative in Congress from New York

May 18, 2023
Hon. THOMAS J. "TOM" VILSACK,
Secretary,
U.S. Department of Agriculture Washington, D.C.

Dear Secretary Vilsack,

We write to you today to request that you prioritize the pressing issue of connecting unserved rural Americans and bridging the digital divide by keeping the Rural eConnectivity (ReConnect) Pilot Program of the Rural Utilities Service (RUS) focused on this objective.

For years, rural communities have long been neglected due to their remote location and lack of economic viability, making it difficult to provide them with broadband service without the aid of targeted subsidies.

The Rural eConnectivity (ReConnect) Pilot Program has provided funding for broadband deployment in rural communities without access to broadband service since its establishment in 2018 and has two main strategies to effectively distribute its funding.

First, it prioritizes rural areas where at least 90 percent of households lack access to broadband, ensuring that the most unserved regions receive support. Second, it avoids duplicative efforts by not providing funding to areas that are already receiving broadband service through other programs, thus making the most efficient use of its resources. These measures, in addition to other improvements like refining broadband coverage data and expanding program access to more qualified providers, are meant to allow ReConnect to accurately allocate funding and provide services to the most unserved rural areas.

However, as RUS begins to award a fourth round of funding, we are deeply concerned that the program may not be focused on this objective, and that these funds for the next round of ReConnect could go to places that already have strong broadband service. In the Infrastructure Investment and Jobs Act (IIJA), Congress directed RUS to focus funding on rural areas "without sufficient access to broadband defined . . . as having speeds of not less than 25 megabits per second downloads and 3 megabits per second uploads." In addition, Congress directed RUS to set aside a portion of the appropriated funding specifically to prioritize areas where at least 90 percent of households to be served lack 25/3 megabits per second (Mbps). And yet, in its most recent funding opportunity announcement, RUS increased the threshold for "sufficient access to broadband" to 100/20 Mbps. Coupled with IIJA's lowering the percentage of households within a project that are unserved, RUS could be allocating a significant portion of its resources to subsidize additional broadband deployment in areas where more than half of households can already subscribe to 100/20 Mbps or better from an existing provider, diverting funding away from rural areas that require broadband the most.

The concerns regarding the duplication of Federal resources are amplified due to the significant amount of broadband funding that has been allocated to NTIA through the IIJA. As you know, to ensure the maximum impact of Federal and state broadband programs, it is crucial for ReConnect to collaborate with other initiatives such as the FCC's Rural Digital Opportunity Fund (RDOF) program, NTIA, Treasury, and state broadband programs. This collaboration will prevent any duplication of services in project areas that are already funded by other government agencies. Duplicating services will not only hinder the efforts to bridge the digital divide but also deprive numerous rural communities of reliable, affordable, and high-speed internet services.

Therefore, through the next farm bill, Congress should have proper oversight and authority for ReConnect and other programs that directly impact rural Americans, as the lack of checks and balances in the ReConnect funding program have been a cause for concern. In addition, we strongly urge the agency to make every effort to give priority to communities with the highest percentage of unserved households and those not being served by other broadband funding programs, as meeting our shared goal of connecting all Americans is dependent on these crucial actions.

Sincerely,

Hon. NICHOLAS A. LANGWORTHY,
Member of Congress

Hon. DON BACON,
Member of Congress

Hon. TRENT KELLY,
Member of Congress

Hon. LORI CHAVEZ-DEREMER,

Member of Congress
Hon. ZACHARY NUNN,
Member of Congress

Hon. JOHN S. DUARTE,
Member of Congress

Hon. MARCUS J. MOLINARO,
Member of Congress

Supplementary Material Submitted by James M. Assey, Jr., J.D., Executive Vice President, NCTA—The Internet and Television Association

Insert

Mr. ROSE. Thank you. And, I am going to use the remaining time to prompt each of you on this question. We are here today talking about the farm bill USDA programs as it relates to rural broadband, but I have been of the opinion for a long time, living in a rural area, that we simply have to think about this in an ongoing, holistic manner, and that the money that we are sending through USDA, and even the COVID-era money, doesn't really address the fundamental challenge that we face as a country of building-out broadband infrastructure that reaches all Americans, and then maintaining it over time so that we know we are always going to be on the cutting edge.

And my own view is that we found a solution to that decades ago, but we haven't made the changes to keep it up to date, and that is the Universal Service Fund. And I am curious—probably not time for it—all of you to respond, but would anyone like to dive onto that question and tell me, am I wrong or am I right that we need to address the Universal Service Fund to make sure that it is providing the resources to keep America wired with broadband access?

* * *

Mr. ROSE. And, I know my time has expired, but I would appreciate for the record comments from the rest of you about that question. Thank you.

With the passage of the Infrastructure Investment and Jobs Act, there is a rare opportunity for policymakers to reassess the scope and scale of the Universal Service Fund's (USF) programs to ensure optimal use of USF's resources in achieving the goal of universal service. The Infrastructure Act's programs, such as the $42.5 billion Broadband Equity, Access, and Deployment (BEAD) program, will fund new broadband infrastructure in many of the same unserved and underserved areas that are supported by USF's high-cost program.

NCTA recognizes that broadband providers that deploy broadband networks with government funding will continue to incur operational and maintenance costs in high-cost areas; however, there is no basis for a blanket assumption that providers will be unable to cover these costs in the future because modern, fiber-rich networks tend to have lower operating costs than the legacy copper networks they are supplanting. In the event a provider does seek USF support for operational and maintenance expenses in an extremely rural, high-cost area, NCTA believes the provider should be required to demonstrate such support is necessary and not duplicative of other government support. All stakeholders will soon have the opportunity to address these issues in response to the Notice of Inquiry that recently was commenced by the FCC.

The extensive and overlapping funding provided by the new programs recently created by Congress should reduce the fiscal demands on USF. NCTA believes this is an opportune time to focus on stabilizing USF through increased efficiency and better targeted spending.

Supplementary Material Submitted by David M. Zumwalt, President and Chief Executive Officer, Wireless Internet Service Providers Association

Insert

Mr. ROSE. Thank you. And, I am going to use the remaining time to prompt each of you on this question. We are here today talking about the farm bill USDA programs as it relates to rural broadband, but I have been of the opinion for a long time, living in a rural area, that we simply have to think about this in an ongoing, holistic manner, and that the money that we are sending through USDA, and even the COVID-era money, doesn't really address the fundamental challenge that we face as a country of building-out broadband infrastructure that reaches all Americans, and then maintaining it over time so that we know we are always going to be on the cutting edge.

And my own view is that we found a solution to that decades ago, but we haven't made the changes to keep it up to date, and that is the Universal Service Fund. And I am curious—probably not time for it—all of you to respond, but would anyone like to dive onto that question and tell me, am I wrong or am I right that we need to address the Universal Service Fund to make sure that it is providing the resources to keep America wired with broadband access?

* * *

Mr. ROSE. And, I know my time has expired, but I would appreciate for the record comments from the rest of you about that question. Thank you.

Thank you for this important question. Many rural communities across America do not have the same access to broadband as their urban and suburban counterparts. This disparity has long-term adverse economic and social consequences for those left behind. These challenges are particularly acute for our nation's farmers. Connectivity, real-time data, and opportunities to sell their commodities in an expedient and efficient manner are more critical than ever. And many applications used by farmers, such as precision agriculture, require wireless broadband to blanket vast acres of farmland. WISPA is committed to addressing this disparity.

The Universal Service Fund (USF) has played a major role in connecting communities and remains important today. However, for it to be most effective in today's technological environment, USF should be updated to better accommodate small, broadband-only providers who deliver needed internet access to millions of Americans in high-cost areas that are on the wrong side of the digital divide.

More specifically, WISPA recommends the following:

- Congress should update the FCC's USF programs from Title II telecommunications programs to allow support for broadband programs; an important step will be to decouple or eliminate the hurdle that requires recipients of high-cost support to first be designated as Eligible Telecommunications Carriers ("ETCs").

- Federal and state broadband funding programs should be carefully crafted and implemented to avoid duplicating government support to providers in the same area.
- USF programs should focus on functionality, consumer demand, deployment costs and speed of deployment to encourage timely and efficient distribution of ratepayer and taxpayer contributions.
- The E-rate program should fund support of off-campus use of broadband services for library patrons/students who would otherwise lack access; and allow schools/libraries to use funds for broadband access for K–12 students within the footprint of a school or school district, with such support available for all technologies, including fixed wireless networks using unlicensed spectrum.
- The FCC should permit high-cost support recipients that are not the only Lifeline provider in their Census block to fulfill their obligations by either offering Lifeline discounts or participating in the Affordable Connectivity Program.
- And, if the Commission requires entities that do not provide voice services to contribute to USF, it should raise the *de minimis* contribution threshold to prevent unfair burdens on small providers.

Every American—regardless of where they live—should have access to the very best internet and reliability that they need. Americans in rural areas have no less a need for broadband than those in urban and suburban centers. Modernizing USF is an important step to ensuring that all communities benefit from connectivity.

Supplementary Material Submitted by Thomas A. "Tom" Stroup, J.D., President, Satellite Industry Association

Insert

Mr. ROSE. Thank you. And, I am going to use the remaining time to prompt each of you on this question. We are here today talking about the farm bill USDA programs as it relates to rural broadband, but I have been of the opinion for a long time, living in a rural area, that we simply have to think about this in an ongoing, holistic manner, and that the money that we are sending through USDA, and even the COVID-era money, doesn't really address the fundamental challenge that we face as a country of building-out broadband infrastructure that reaches all Americans, and then maintaining it over time so that we know we are always going to be on the cutting edge.

And my own view is that we found a solution to that decades ago, but we haven't made the changes to keep it up to date, and that is the Universal Service Fund. And I am curious—probably not time for it—all of you to respond, but would anyone like to dive onto that question and tell me, am I wrong or am I right that we need to address the Universal Service Fund to make sure that it is providing the resources to keep America wired with broadband access?

* * *

Mr. ROSE. And, I know my time has expired, but I would appreciate for the record comments from the rest of you about that question. Thank you.

The Satellite Industry Association (SIA) submits this in response to the request for formal reply to the question raised during the House Agriculture Committee Hearing on June 21, 2023, concerning whether "we need to address the Universal Service Fund to make sure that it is providing the resources to keep America wired with broadband access?"

The USF is one of many current Federal funding programs seeking to support the deployment of broadband in rural and other unserved areas of the United States. For example, the FCC, NTIA, Department of Agriculture, Department of Health and Human Services, Department of Housing and Urban Development, Department of the Treasury, and the Institute of Museum and Library Services all provide funding to build-out rural broadband infrastructure.[35],[*]

SIA believes these programs should be technology inclusive and that satellite operators should be eligible for funding through them. As noted in SIA's written testimony, no single broadband technology holds all the advantages. With finite resources and widely varying topography, we need a flexible combination of all available access technologies to bridge the digital divide and satellites are a key part of that ecosystem. Fortunately, multiple satellite providers currently provide broadband access to consumers

---

[35] U.S. Congressional Research Service, *Overview of the Universal Service Fund and Selected Federal Broadband Programs* (updated June 25, 2021), at *https://crsreports.congress.gov/product/pdf/R/R46780*.

[*] Editor's note: the referenced report is retained in Committee file.

nationwide, including in rural and remote areas. They provide connection to all 50 states with speeds of up to 200 megabits per second (Mbps) without the need for additional build-out.[36] Satellite companies continue to launch new capacity and plan to deploy tens of thousands of new satellites adding to the approximately 8,000 satellites on orbit today. The satellite industry is currently increasing production of satellites capable of providing connections to rural America while reducing costs. For example, the cost of manufacturing satellites as measured by cost per throughput has decreased approximately 90% resulting in lower costs to consumers, including those in rural areas.[37]

Supplementary Material Submitted by Bill T. Hurley, Vice President, Distribution, Americas, AGCO Corporation; Chair, AG Sector Board, Association of Equipment Manufacturers

Insert

Mr. ROSE. Thank you. And, I am going to use the remaining time to prompt each of you on this question. We are here today talking about the farm bill USDA programs as it relates to rural broadband, but I have been of the opinion for a long time, living in a rural area, that we simply have to think about this in an ongoing, holistic manner, and that the money that we are sending through USDA, and even the COVID-era money, doesn't really address the fundamental challenge that we face as a country of building-out broadband infrastructure that reaches all Americans, and then maintaining it over time so that we know we are always going to be on the cutting edge.

And my own view is that we found a solution to that decades ago, but we haven't made the changes to keep it up to date, and that is the Universal Service Fund. And I am curious—probably not time for it—all of you to respond, but would anyone like to dive onto that question and tell me, am I wrong or am I right that we need to address the Universal Service Fund to make sure that it is providing the resources to keep America wired with broadband access?

---

36 *https://docs.house.gov/meetings/AG/AG00/20230621/116129/HHRG-118-AG00-Wstate StroupT-20230621.pdf.*

37 BryceTech, *Satellite Industry Association: State of the Satellite Industry Report 2023,* at 10, 16 (2023).

* * *

Mr. ROSE. And, I know my time has expired, but I would appreciate for the record comments from the rest of you about that question. Thank you.

The Association of Equipment Manufacturers (AEM) supports updates to the Universal Service Fund that take into consideration advancements in precision agriculture and the connectivity needs that they require. We believe that the spirit of the Communications Act of 1934 called for universal services to be administered as an evolving level of service. Precision agriculture wasn't initially theorized until the 1980s and policymakers then could not possibly have foreseen what innovations would be developed 50 years into the future.

As such, as policymakers approach updating any Federal broadband deployment program, AEM would encourage a multifaceted strategy that includes fiber optic, low earth orbit (LEO) satellites, and 5G. It is imperative that the system supports connectivity between all aspects of rural America, from the hospital to the school and from the farmhouse to the field.

Index

N

O

P

Q

R

S

T

U

V

W

Y